MISS DAISY CELEBRATES

TENNESSEE

HILLSBORO PRESS

FRANKLIN, TENNESSEE

MISS DAISY CELEBRATES

TENNESSEE

DAISY KING

RESEARCHED AND WRITTEN WITH
JAMES A. CRUTCHFIELD AND WINETTE SPARKMAN

 TENNESSEE HERITAGE LIBRARY
Bicentennial Collection

This publication has been recognized by Tennessee 200, Inc.

Copyright 1995 by Daisy King, James A. Crutchfield, and Winette Sparkman

Printed in the United States of America

00 99 98 97 96 95   10 9 8 7 6 5 4 3 2

Library of Congress Catalog Card Number: 95-79050

ISBN: 1-881576-54-X

Credits appear in the acknowledgments (*see p. 260*) for contributions, illustrations, and previously published material other than the following: quotations at the beginning of each section reprinted from *Since Eve Ate Apples* © 1994 by March Egerton with permission; recipes on pages 95 and 152 reprinted from *McCord Family Reunion Cookbook* © 1994 by Mary V. Golding with permission of Providence House Publishers, Franklin, Tennessee; recipes on pages 57, 82, and 142 reprinted from the *Animaland Cookbook* © 1989 by Dixie Hall with permission; recipe on page 107 reprinted from *Southern Food* © 1987 by John Egerton with permission; recipes on pages 133, 136, and 137 reprinted from *The Original Tennessee Homecoming Cookbook* © 1985 edited by Daisy King with permission of Rutledge Hill Press, Nashville, Tennessee; recipes on pages 41, 56, and 251 reprinted from *Miss Daisy Entertains* © 1980 by Daisy King with permission of Rutledge Hill Press, Nashville, Tennessee; recipes on pages 57, 72, 100, 188, and 253 reprinted from *Recipes from Miss Daisy's* © 1978 by Daisy King with permission of Rutledge Hill Press, Nashville, Tennessee; and artist's rendering of the Tennessee State Capitol cupola used throughout is from *Official History of the Tennessee Centennial Exposition: Nashville 1897*.

Cover design: Schwalb Creative Communications Inc. Cover illustrations/photography: Andrew Jackson, used by permission of The Hermitage, Home of President Andrew Jackson; Elvis Presley, used by permission of Elvis Presley Enterprises, Incorporated; Loveless Cafe, used by permission of Shepard Bentley, Loveless Cafe; all other cover photography by Schwalb Creative Communications Inc. including the photograph of Daisy King in the dining room of The Hermitage (*see also* p. 195), used by permission of The Hermitage, Home of President Andrew Jackson, and photographs used as design elements in the front matter and as chapter opening pages.

Published by
HILLSBORO PRESS
an imprint of
PROVIDENCE HOUSE PUBLISHERS
238 Seaboard Lane
Franklin, Tennessee 37067
615-771-2020 • 800-321-5692

EDICATED TO

all Tennesseans throughout time who have appreciated our heritage as citizens of this nation's sixteenth state and who have cherished this land and the bounty it yields.

May the loyalty, pride, and vision Tennesseans share with each other and with the world continue always.

CONT

ENTS

Governor Don and Martha Sundquist
Tania and David Williamson
Deke Sundquist
Andrea and Art Jeannet

FOREWORD

When we think of special moments or people in our lives, we are inextricably bound to memories of special foods. For me, it is Christmas Eve with Swedish potato sausage (potates korv) and rye bread (limpa) followed by rice pudding and lingonberries. It is also memories of Sunday dinner and Nonie, my grandmother, walking down the hill carrying her beautiful porcelain bowl of coleslaw laid in a bed of cabbage leaves. I can still envision my grandmother rolling the yeast dough between her hands to form the braids for Swedish cardamom coffee bread, a recipe I have shared with Daisy King for this Bicentennial Collection.

Miss Daisy is known throughout the nation as *Tennessee's First Lady of Southern Cooking.* It is no wonder then that she was chosen to bring us this exceptional collection in honor of the state's birthday. Believe me, we are in for a treat because the recipes are combined with interesting sidebar features about Tennessee people, places, products, and each of our ninety-five counties.

Celebrating two hundred years of Tennessee history in 1996 will cause each of us to think back to those special times and people who have made our state the place we call home. As we try some of these heritage recipes, rich aromas will fill our kitchens, and we will experience fond memories of past generations. Just as significantly, we will be creating new memories for family members and guests who will enjoy these foods today.

My hope for this book is that it will help each of you share with me a feeling for what it means to be a Tennessean.

Martha Sundquist
First Lady of Tennessee

PREFACE

MISS DAISY CELEBRATES TENNESSEE is more than just a cookbook or a compilation of Tennesseana. This Bicentennial Collection is the story of how Tennesseans came to "set a fine table" for our former statesmen, our Presidents, foreign diplomats, literary geniuses, talented musicians, proud athletes—a celebration of people, places, and products that extends beyond two centuries of statehood recognizing the warmth and tradition of serving food and the most important ones we serve—our families.

Award-winning author John Egerton writes in his book *Southern Food*, "Whatever else they may have to offer, many southerners can still set a fine table and surround it with conversation and laughter and love. On such occasions, special things can happen, and nothing—not even the fewness of the vittles—can keep those present from receiving and enjoying an elegant sufficiency. It's an old southern skill, a habit, a custom, a tradition, and it deserves to last as long as the corn grows tall." Many folks can set a fine table, but the folks from Tennessee make Tennessee cooking the very special thing that it is to those of us who love it and live here.

The land that we now embrace as *Tennessee* has been known by many names:

the Hunting Grounds; Land Beyond the Alleghenies; Territory of the United States of America, South of the River Ohio; Tanasi; Western North Carolina; the MERO District; and State of Franklin among other titles.

Whatever the land has been called it has always been called *home* by someone—ancient mound builders, native North Americans, European explorers, French fur traders, longhunters from the East, settlers with prophetic vision, Revolutionary War veterans, and slaves from across the Atlantic—all have descendants who are now Tennesseans.

The early settlers of Tennessee came over the mountains from the Carolinas with names such as William Bean, Daniel Boone, Kasper Mansker, Uriah Stone, John Rains, John Holliday, and many others who were known simply as *longhunters*.

Which meats did Thomas Sharpe Spencer hang on pegs inside his hollow sycamore tree the year it was his home? Did Davy Crockett know his beef jerky recipe would one day be a part of this region's folklore? The Cherokees taught the settlers to make Johnny Cake variations that are still being prepared today. Middle Tennessee's Shawnee Indians were known for their broiled venison steak. Fort Watauga and the Nolichucky settlements had meat preparations that were shared with migrating families in the 1700s. When the first settlers of Fort Nashborough crossed the frozen Cumberland River on Christmas Day 1779, "Roasted Bear Meat" was the main course served by James Robertson's party. John Donelson's flotilla endured many dangers such as overcoming hunger before meeting the Robertson party to join families together again in 1780.

Yes, food has played a major role in Tennessee memories. As familiar names come to mind, look for them in this Bicentennial Collection. You will find recipes and stories from: the now-famous Sam Houston Schoolhouse in Maryville, Tennessee, where Tennessee's great statesman began teaching around 1812; Travellers Rest, the home of Judge John Overton renowned for its country hams and beaten biscuits; The Hermitage, President Andrew Jackson's beloved plantation, where Hickory Nut Cake became part of the menu that Jackson and his lovely bride Rachel enjoyed sharing with others; and Belle Meade Plantation, owned by Colonel William Giles Harding, where Savannah, the cook became known for her Syllabub.

Look for James K. Polk and his wife Sarah who enjoyed extravagant entertaining while at the White House during his term as our eleventh president; another Tennessee president Greeneville's Andrew Johnson and his wife Eliza who were the first to host White House holiday functions for young people; and James Winchester and John Overton, founding fathers of the city of Memphis—because of ties to the Mississippi River, this port town's hostesses prided themselves on oysters from New Orleans, meats and vegetables in season, and again rich desserts inspired from Louisiana.

Tennessee mothers, during the War Between the States, prepared foods for their loved ones to take along to battle. Many a soldier went to sleep hungry in those days, whether wearing blue or gray, and at times, a compassionate Tennessee family provided someone's last taste of food.

In later years, hotels in Tennessee played an enormous role in establishing fine dining in this state. The Maxwell House Hotel in Nashville, for over one hundred years, was famous for its Spiced Round and its glorious desserts.

The Peabody Hotel in Memphis, which stands today, opened in 1925. Many families and cotton planters from the Delta dined regularly on Tennessee ham, corn pudding, assorted vegetables, and desserts.

Some of Tennessee's most elegant dining took place in private homes. The Woodruff-Fontaine House in Memphis is still open for private parties. Belmont, the Italian villa built for Adelicia Hayes Acklen is home today to Belmont University in Nashville. Cheekwood, Nashville's fine art center, is open for private tours and is home to the famous Swan Ball. Blount Mansion in Knoxville, home of William Blount, was a center of cultural activity including meals with Tennessee River fish. The Blounts also entertained at historic Rocky Mount while he was Governor of the Southwest Territory. The Ramsey House, east of Knoxville, was home to many lavish parties.

James A. Crutchfield and Winette Sparkman join me in this celebration of Tennessee's birthday. Crutchfield has written anecdotal material about each of our ninety-five counties and even the one that no longer exists; Sparkman shares significant information about the origins of Tennessee brand-name food products, distributors and grocers, as well as material from historic sites and legendary Tennesseans; lastly, I have shared with you many heritage dishes. (It should be noted that some of these recipes are directly from pioneer Tennessee kitchens and do not necessarily adapt themselves to modern cooking. Other early recipes are still usable by today's standards. Some have been edited to fit modern preparation methods. We felt they were each important to this Bicentennial Collection.) These favorite recipes from past to present reflect a downhome people who take great pride in setting a fine Tennessee table.

Happy Birthday, Tennessee!

—Daisy King
Summer 1995

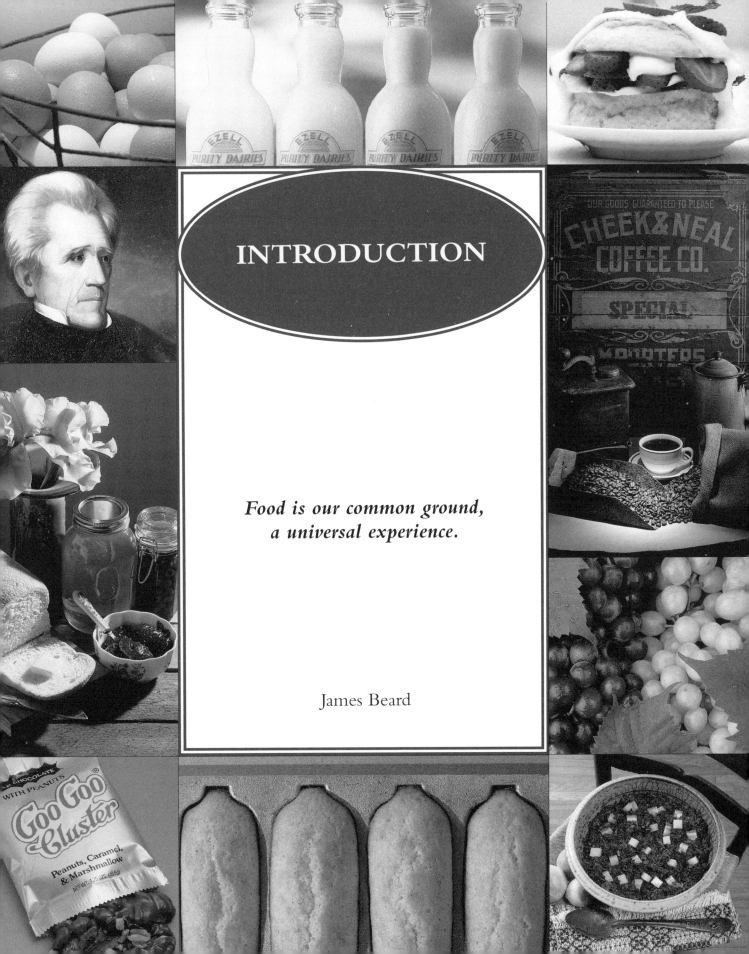

INTRODUCTION

*Food is our common ground,
a universal experience.*

James Beard

INTRODUCTION

TENNESSEE GROCERS— YESTERDAY AND TODAY

Tennessee's grocers began family by family across the state through individuals with insight and ability to recognize community needs. The grocery industry has adapted as the market has changed. A major part of American  lifestyle is American food. Food distribution and products have changed with the country. Tennesseans in the Memphis area were fortunate to be customers of Arthur Seessel. In 1912, Arthur decided that the city was ready for a store he opened at 15 South Second Street. He provided his customers with meats, poultry, and fresh vegetables. Arthur's father, Arthur Seessel, Sr., followed suit by changing his renowned butcher shop into a second *Seessel's* at 18 North Second Street two years later.

Across town, Clarence Saunders began the first *Piggly Wiggly* in 1916.

Saunders was the man who developed a way for shoppers to serve themselves. His methods astounded the industry. His store was at 79 Jefferson Street in Memphis. As shoppers entered, they went through a turnstile and were furnished baskets to carry. Price-tagged merchandise was displayed on shelves. For the first time, shoppers could shop at their own pace, without waiting for store clerks to assist. National advertising soon began to address the individual self-shopper. Thus, *Piggly Wiggly* was the first to franchise independent self-service food merchandising.

In 1908 over in Chattanooga, Frank McDonald recognized the need for food

from their store on Lischey Avenue, known as *Crook Brothers. Bill Crook's Food Town* followed in 1960. Steven Crook, a third-generation family member, opened *Steven's Fun Fresh Food Stores* in 1985—a sensory food experience reflecting today's lifestyle. The Crook family was the first grocer to use technology in scanning, offering credit cards and "double coupons."

Over in Knoxville, Frank McDonald found himself bidding on a chain of stores called *L.O. Rogers and Sons.*

Frank won the bid, and after previously calling his Chattanooga line of stores *Red*, he proceeded to call his new stores *White.* Thus, Knoxville's *White Foods* began in 1922.

Further east into the mountains, *Humphreys Store* in Greeneville began in 1918. It was the forerunner of *Quality Foods.* Sam Humphreys was destined to begin an empire from his first store on Depot Street. His remarkable nephew, Lionel N. Humphreys, had visions that enabled him to pursue with stores called *Super Dollar.* Today, that same family business is known as *Food City.*

Other families have contributed to Tennessee's needs with grocery markets such as *E. W. James* in Union City, *Pruitt's* in Chattanooga, and *Cas Walker's* in Knoxville.

As Steven Crook of Nashville indicates "Tennessee grocers have kept evolving with the reality of the times."

stores which were readily accessible to the residential areas of the city. Chattanooga was rapidly growing as he opened a group of stores located at terminating points of the streetcar line. The *Rolling Red Wagon Mobile Food Stores* began to "roll" in 1920. A fleet of twenty-five "grocery stores on wheels" greeted Chattanoogans then. Thus began *Red Foods.*

Up in Nashville, twenty-two-year-old Horace Greely Hill had opened his first store at 18th Avenue and State Street in 1895. By 1929, that small store had multiplied to 600 *H.G. Hill's* stores, with 100 in Davidson County alone—some even as far as New Orleans. Hill pioneered the "cash and carry" policy in 1917. *H.G. Hill's* continues today.

Another Nashville family entered the grocery arena in 1917. Hatton and Tom Crook served customers with classic "horse and buggy" delivery

Grocery Distributors

Around the turn of the century a significant part of this evolution included distributors such as *C. T. Cheek and Sons* in Nashville. Also typical of

the many wholesale grocers across the state were *Malone & Hyde* of Memphis and *Robert Orr* in Nashville.

In Memphis by 1907 rural commissaries were found at various plantations in and around Shelby County. The trade was mainly in dry goods. The road systems did not encourage effective delivery times for grocery wholesaling, yet Taylor Malone and Joseph R. Hyde, Sr. found a way to succeed. They made it out to the commissaries and began building warehouse after warehouse for storing the products they offered. Fourteen warehouses were full within a 125-mile radius of Memphis by the 1920s. Malone & Hyde finally gathered its operation to one main site in 1938. Joe Hyde, Sr. now would attempt to convey to the new supermarket chains in the area that Malone & Hyde offered a source of opportunity. As a grocery wholesaler, it could provide low-price foods and comprehensive support services.

In 1945, the company's Voluntary Plan provided retailers with goods on a cost-plus basis. The company also expanded into meat, dairy, produce, drugs, and housewares. The system now serves more than 2,500 independently owned supermarkets! In 1985, the *Fleming Companies* bought Malone & Hyde. It is now the nation's number one grocery wholesaler.

As Tennessee celebrates the beginning of a third century, it's a comfort to know long-standing institutions such as these still remain. Another such institution is *Robert Orr-SYSCO*. In 1859, a young

Irish immigrant named Robert Orr started a dry goods trading post on the banks of Nashville's Cumberland River. Soon after, he and his four brothers opened *Orr Brothers,* a full-fledged wholesale grocery on the corner of Broad and Market Streets (now the bustling Second Avenue). They played an important role in the city's growth during the latter part of that century. (They once gave a young upstart named H.G. Hill $300 credit to start a small retail grocery.)

Changing its name to *Robert Orr & Co.*, the store experienced continued success through the twentieth century. The company merged with the world's largest wholesale food service distributor to become *Robert Orr-SYSCO* in 1972. Named the sixth-oldest business in Nashville by *Nashville Magazine,* the company can still be found near the Cumberland River in the Cockrill Bend area of Nashville.

Grocery Superstores

Foods and other products are now available from what we call the "superstore." In Tennessee, examples of giant chains and warehouse-style grocers are Kroger, FoodMax, Food Town, and Megamarket.

From the small neighborhood grocer with a delivery wagon to the modern warehouse superstore with sack-it-yourself austerity, Tennessee's grocery trade has served the needs of the residents of this great state.

Tennessee Celebration Menus

SUMMERTIME BRIDGE LUNCHEON

Chicken and Fruit Salad
Corn Fritters
Pecan Cheese Wafers
Lemon Sherbet with
Sugar Cookies

BRIDAL TEA

Herbed Nuts
One-Hundred-Year Cheese Straws
Cucumber Tea Sandwiches
Chicken Salad in Pastry Shells
Pecan Tassies
Tea Cakes
Whole Strawberries with Whipped Cream
and Brown Sugar for Dipping
Hot Spiced Tea

WEDDING BRUNCH

Ambrosia with Mint Leaves
Eggs Poached in Cream
Broiled Linked Sausage
Toasted Buttered English Muffin
with Lemon Curd
Champagne with Strawberries

HUNTER'S DINNER

Stuffed Mushrooms
Duck Breasts over Herbed Rice
Hot Curried Fruit
Spinach Soufflé
Spoon Bread
Pumpkin Cheesecake

BARNYARD BARBEQUE

Pork Barbecue with Pit Barbecue Sauce
Brunswick Stew
Baked Beans
Hot Potato Puffs
Coleslaw
Corn Light Bread
Lemon Chess and Fudge Tarts

TAILGATE PICNIC

Southern Fried Chicken
Ham and Rolls or
Baked Ham Biscuit
Corn Salad
Three Bean Salad
Bulla's Fudge Cake
Lemon Squares

$\mathcal{T}$ENNESSEE $\mathcal{C}$ELEBRATION $\mathcal{M}$ENUS

THANKSGIVING DAY

Shrimp Bisque
Holiday Turkey and Giblet Gravy
Southern Corn Bread Dressing
Festive Cranberry Salad
Candied Yams and Apples
Broccoli Casserole
Hot Rolls
Holiday Mincemeat Pie
Southern Pecan Pie

CHRISTMAS EVE DINNER

Smoked Oyster Paté with Crackers
Wilted Spinach and Orange Salad
Standing Rib Roast
with Yorkshire Pudding
Green Bean Casserole
Sweet Potatoes in Orange Cups
Angel Biscuits
Eggnog and Fruit Cake

NEW YEARS DAY BUFFET

Good Luck Dip with Corn Muffins
Marinated Pork Roast
with Raisin Sauce
Hoppin' John • Southern Greens
Corn Relish • Cole Slaw
Spoon Bread
Buttermilk Pie

EASTER SUNDAY

Roast Leg of Lamb with Rosemary
Peach Chutney
Hot Pepper Jelly
Fresh Asparagus with Hollandaise Sauce
Herbed Rice
Ratatouille
Dinner rolls
Coconut Cake

ST. PATRICK'S DAY

Spinach Dip with Fresh Veggies
Spiced Corn Beef
Lima Bean Casserole
Old Fashioned Potato Puffs
Quick Spoon Rolls
Chilled Lime Soufflé

LABOR DAY DINNER

Cold Sliced Tenderloin and Baked Ham
with Dinner Rolls
Green Pea Salad
Corn Salad
Baked Egg Plant Slices
Bread Pudding with Whiskey Sauce

MEASUREMENTS AND EQUIVALENTS

Ingredient	Amount Before Preparation	Amount After Preparation
Apples	3 medium	3 cups sliced
Bacon	8 slices cooked	1/2 cup crumbled
Bananas	3 medium	2 1/2 cups sliced or about 2 cups mashed
Beans, dried: Limas	1 pound (3 cups uncooked)	7 cups cooked
Navy	1 pound (2 cups uncooked)	6 cups cooked
Red Kidney	1 pound (2 2/3 cups uncooked)	6 1/2 cups cooked
Biscuit mix	1 cup	6 biscuits
Bread	1 pound loaf	12 to 16 slices
Bread crumbs	1 1/2 slices	1 cup soft crumbs
Cabbage	1 pound head	4 1/2 cups shredded
Carrots	1 pound	3 cups shredded
Cheese, American/Cheddar	1 pound	4 to 5 cups shredded
Coffee	1 pound	about 40 cups perked
Corn	2 medium ears	1 cup kernels
Crackers/Wafers: Chocolate	19 wafers	1 cup crumbs
Graham	14 squares	1 cup fine crumbs
Saltine	28 crackers	1 cup finely crushed
Vanilla	22 wafers	1 cup crushed
Cream, whipping	1 cup (1/2 pint)	2 cups whipped
Dates, pitted	1 pound	2 to 3 cups chopped
Eggs	5 large	1 cup
Whites	8 to 11	1 cup
Yolks	12 to 14	1 cup
Green pepper	1 large	1 cup diced
Lettuce	1 pound head	6 1/4 cups torn
Lemon	1 medium	2 to 3 tablespoons juice & 2 teaspoons rind
Lime	1 medium	1 1/2 to 2 tablespoons juice
Macaroni	1 cup (uncooked)	2 1/4 cups cooked
Mushrooms	3 cups raw (8 ounces)	1 cup sliced cooked
Noodles	2 1/2 cups (8 ounces)	5 cups cooked
Nuts, shelled: Almonds	1 pound	3 1/3 cups chopped
Peanuts	1 pound	2 to 3 cups nutmeats
Pecans	1 pound	4 1/2 to 5 cups halves
Walnuts	1 pound	4 cups chopped
Oats, quick cooking	1 cup	1 3/4 cups cooked
Onion	1 medium	1/2 cup chopped
Orange	1 medium	1/3 cup juice & 2 tablespoons grated rind
Peaches	4 medium	2 cups sliced
Pears	4 medium	2 cups sliced
Potatoes, white	3 medium	2 cups cubed cooked or 1 3/4 cups mashed
Sweet	3 medium	3 cups sliced
Rice, long grain	1 cup	3 to 4 cups cooked
Pre-cooked	1 cup	2 cups cooked
Spaghetti	2 1/2 cups (8 ounces)	5 cups cooked
Strawberries	1 quart	4 cups sliced

Low-fat Recipe Modifications

Ingredient	Substitution
1. American, Cheddar, Colby, Edam, Monterey Jack, Mozzarella, and Swiss cheese	Cheese with 5 grams of fat or less per ounce
2. Jarlsberg	Jarlsberg Lite
Boursin	Boursin Lite
3. Cottage cheese	Nonfat or lowfat cottage cheese
4. Cream cheese	Nonfat or light process cream cheese, Neufchatel cheese
5. Sour cream	Nonfat sour cream, light sour cream, lowfat or nonfat yogurt
6. Whipping cream/heavy cream	Chilled evaporated skim milk, non-dairy whipped topping
7. Whole or 2% milk	Skim Milk, nonfat dry milk mixed with water
8. Ice cream	Ice Milk, nonfat or lowfat frozen yogurt
9. Milk shakes	Frozen yogurt shakes
10. Whole egg	2 egg whites or 1/4 cup egg substitute
11. Margarine/Butter	Reduced calorie margarine, fat-free mayonnaise, unsweetened applesauce with fat-free mayonnaise
12. Vegetable oil	Polyunsaturated or non-unsaturated oil
13. Condensed cream soups	Broth or lowfat, low sodium soups
14. Salad dressings	Nonfat or oil-free salad dressing
15. Sugar	Sugar substitute or 1/2 cup frozen fruit juice concentrate for each cup
16. Unsweetened chocolate	3 tablespoons unsweetened cocoa plus 1 tablespoon polyunsaturated oil or margarine
17. Coconut	Coconut extract
18. Potato chips	Fat-free potato chips
19. Tortilla chips	Fat-free tortilla chips
20. Bacon	Turkey Bacon or Canadian Bacon
21. Poultry	Skinless poultry
22. Ground beef	Extra lean ground beef, ground turkey
23. Beef, veal, lamb, pork, high-fat cuts	Chicken, turkey or lean cuts of meat trimmed of all visible fat
24. Tuna packed in oil	Tuna packed in spring water
25. Luncheon meats	Fat free Deli meats—ham, turkey, roast beef, chicken

Nutritional Analysis

As we celebrate the history of food in Tennessee, it's interesting to learn that the first printed cookbook was published in 1480. Not only did it contain recipes, but also dietary advice. As the science of nutrition advanced, a new profession was born. In 1899 the title of "dietitian" was coined. The definition established was "a person who specializes in the knowledge of food and can meet the demands of the medical profession for diet therapy." At the turn of the century with the discovery of the calorie the era of calculating diets had begun.

Today we continue to calculate diets but with up-to-date technology like the computerized nutrient analysis program used to analyze the recipes in MISS DAISY CELEBRATES TENNESSEE.

Just like the first dietitians, we at Baptist Hospital use our knowledge of food and nutrition to help speed recovery for our patients and lay the groundwork for long-term health.

—Lisa Sheehan-Smith

Thanks to the following people at Baptist Hospital, Nashville, Tennessee, for their contributions to this book:

Lisa Sheehan-Smith, M.Ed., R.D., L.D.N.
Sharolyn Balsley, R.D., L.D.N.
Debby Boutwell
Teri Briley, R.D., L.D.N.
DeeAnna Carney, R.D., L.D.N.
Sonya Douglas
Marj Moore, R.D., L.D.N.
Patty Waller, R.D.
Pam York

Baptist Hospital is a not-for-profit, 759-bed facility that has served the health care needs of the Middle Tennessee region since 1919.

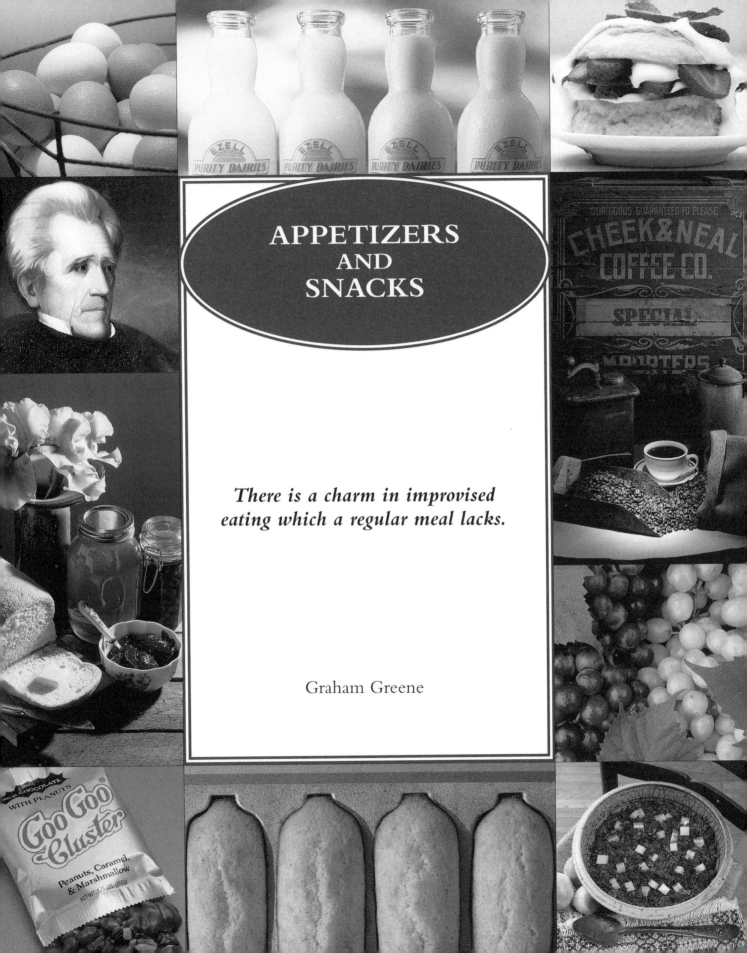

APPETIZERS AND SNACKS

*There is a charm in improvised
eating which a regular meal lacks.*

Graham Greene

Appetizers and Snacks

Miss Daisy's Party Sausage Balls 3
Frankie Mayo's Sausage Pinwheels 4
Drunken Meatballs 4
Black-Eyed Susans 4
One-Hundred-Year Cheese Straws 5
Pecan Cheese Wafers 5
Pineapple Cheeseball 5
Hot Artichoke Dip 6
Dill Dip 6
Good Luck Dip 7
Dried Beef Dip 7
Clifty Farms Hot Country Ham Dip 8
Baked Seafood Dip 9
Spinach Dip 9
Tamale Dip 10
Stuffed Mushrooms 10
Herbed Nuts 11
Nuts and Bolts 11
Chutney Cheese Paté 12
Smoked Oyster Paté 12
Salmon Log 13
Davy Crockett's Beef or Venison Jerky 14

Miss Daisy's
Party Sausage Balls

3	CUPS BISQUICK OR BISCUIT MIX
1	POUND HOT SAUSAGE
1	10-OUNCE PACKAGE CHEDDAR CHEESE, GRATED
2	TABLESPOONS DRIED PARSLEY FLAKES
1	TABLESPOON WORCESTERSHIRE SAUCE
1	TEASPOON MINCED ONION
1	TEASPOON BLACK PEPPER
1	TEASPOON OREGANO
1	TEASPOON GARLIC POWDER

Assemble all ingredients and utensils. In a bowl, combine all ingredients and mix well. Roll into small balls. Place on ungreased baking sheet and bake in a 375 degree oven for 15 to 20 minutes or until brown. Serve warm. Yield: about 100 balls.

Serve these with warm Apple Butter to dip in (*see* p. 157).

Per serving: 44 calories; 3 g fat; 7 mg cholesterol; 125 mg sodium.

A "BURR" UNDER THE SADDLE

Some politicians never change. And, as a group, they are no different today than they were two hundred years ago. There are good ones and bad ones and mediocre ones. Some are extremely popular for a while, only to quickly fall from grace with a fickle voting public. Witness, for example, Richard Nixon. It is far too soon for history to determine the extent that his Watergate indiscretions will have on his once-good name and reputation two centuries from now. When Anderson County was created in 1801, Aaron Burr was quite possibly the second most popular man in America. Only recently elected to the vice-presidency of the United

States, Burr was handsome and charming, and although he was not on the most friendly terms with the new president, Thomas Jefferson, the two tolerated each other and appeared to make a good team. It was during that era of good feeling that Anderson County residents named their new seat of government "Burrville" after the likeable vice-president. As time passed, however, Burr became involved in a western land scheme that sought to separate parts of the newly acquired South and to align them with Spain. He was now a wanted man. And, to make bad matters worse, he had recently killed Alexander Hamilton in a duel. Accordingly, in 1809, residents requested and were awarded permission by legislative decree to change Burrville's name to Clinton in honor of DeWitt Clinton, mayor of New York City at the time.

Mayo's Smoked Sausage

Mayo Sausage began in 1932 with Lawrence H. Mayo's intuition that there would be a market for quality hickory smoked sausage. He had his sausage packed in cloth bags and took it home to smoke in his mother's smokehouse. His wife Lillie would hand-sew the cloth bags that delivered the Mayo quality to local grocers. H.G. Hill was the first retail grocery outlet to feature Mayo's

Hickory Smoked Sausage. Today, the product is still produced using time-honored recipes and procedures. Mayo Sausage is primarily known in Middle Tennessee and Southern Kentucky. The company is now a division of Wampler's of Lenoir City, Tennessee.

Frankie Mayo's Sausage Pinwheels

2 1/3	CUPS BISQUICK
1 1/2	POUNDS MAYO SMOKED SAUSAGE
2/3	CUP WATER

Mix dough and roll out to 1/8 inch thick. Spread thin with crumbled sausage. Roll as for jelly roll. Freeze or refrigerate. Slice thin and bake in 450-degree preheated oven for 12-15 minutes.

Drunken Meatballs

3	POUNDS GROUND BEEF
1	LARGE ONION, GRATED
2	TEASPOONS SALT
1	TEASPOON BLACK PEPPER
1/8	TEASPOON GARLIC POWDER
1/4	CUP WATER
1	14-OUNCE BOTTLE CATSUP
1	12-OUNCE CAN BEER

Assemble all ingredients and utensils. In a bowl, combine meat and seasonings. Form into bite-sized balls. Heat water, catsup and beer in saucepan. Carefully drop balls into liquid. Boil slowly for 60 minutes. When ready to serve, transfer meatballs and sauce to a chafing dish. Yield: 50 to 60 meatballs.

Per serving: 57 calories; 3 g fat; 14 mg cholesterol; 164 mg sodium.

Black-Eyed Susans

2	8-OUNCE PACKAGE PITTED DATES
1	CUP BUTTER, SOFTENED
1	POUND SHARP CHEDDAR CHEESE, GRATED
	PECAN HALVES
3	CUPS ALL-PURPOSE FLOUR
1/4	TEASPOON SALT
1/4	TEASPOON BLACK PEPPER

Assemble all ingredients and utensils. In large bowl of mixer, cream butter and grated cheese until smooth. Sift flour with salt and pepper. Add to cheese mix to make dough. Stuff each date with a pecan half and cover with a tablespoon of dough. Place on an ungreased baking sheet and bake in a 350-degree oven about 20 to 25 minutes or until browned. Yield: 12 servings (45 to 55 pastries).

Per serving: 130 calories; 7 g fat; 18 mg cholesterol; 95 mg sodium.

One-Hundred-Year Cheese Straws

6   CUPS SHARP CHEDDAR CHEESE, SOFTENED
1 1/2   CUPS BUTTER, SOFTENED
3 1/2   CUPS SELF-RISING FLOUR
1/4   TEASPOON RED PEPPER

Assemble all ingredients and utensils. Grate cheese, mix with butter in a bowl. Add flour and red pepper. Mix well. Press out with a cookie press. Bake in a 350 degree oven on an ungreased cookie sheet on bottom rack until bottom begins to brown; then move to top rack. Bake approximately 20 minutes. Yield: 100 cookies.

Per serving: 66 calories; 5 g fat; 15 mg cholesterol; 114 mg sodium.

Pecan Cheese Wafers

8   OUNCES SHARP CHEDDAR CHEESE
1   CUP BUTTER, SOFTENED
1 1/2   CUPS SELF-RISING FLOUR
1   CUP FINELY CHOPPED PECANS
1/8   TEASPOON CAYENNE PEPPER

Assemble all ingredients and utensils. Grate cheese. Let it soften with butter in a bowl. Mix in remaining ingredients. Roll dough into rolls about 1 1/2 inches in diameter. Place on waxed paper. Chill for several hours. Slice in thin wafers about 1/8 inch thick. Bake in a 350 degree oven about 8 minutes or until browned. Yield: about 75 wafers.

Per serving: 52 calories; 4 g fat; 10 mg cholesterol; 78 mg sodium.

Pineapple Cheeseball

2   8-OUNCE PACKAGES CREAM CHEESE, SOFTENED
1   4-OUNCE CAN CRUSHED PINEAPPLE, DRAINED WELL
1/4   CUP FINELY CHOPPED GREEN PEPPER
2   TABLESPOONS GRATED ONION
1   TABLESPOON SEASONED SALT
1   CUP CHOPPED PECANS

Assemble all ingredients and utensils. In a bowl, mix all ingredients except pecans. Form into two balls. Chill. Roll in pecans. Refrigerate until ready to serve. Serve with water wafers or your favorite crackers. Yield: 20 servings.

Per serving: 119 calories; 12 g fat; 25 mg cholesterol; 261 mg sodium.

TENNESSEE'S LITTLE PRINCETON

William R. ("Sawney") Webb couldn't have known when he moved his small boys' school from Culleoka to Bell Buckle in 1886, that the institution would achieve an international reputation for excellence. Old Sawney, a Civil War veteran who was handicapped with a lame right arm, and his brother, John M. ("Old Jack") Webb, ran the school together, and the rural folk throughout Bedford County treated the pair with a great deal of respect. The Webb brothers' educational mission was to prepare young men for

BEDFORD COUNTY

college, and this was accomplished by teaching rigorous curricula in Latin, Greek, and math. Discipline was at the top of the list of traits instilled to teenaged boys at Webb, and before long, the school had such a reputation that local mothers warned their small children that if they weren't good, "Old Sawney" would come after them. When Woodrow Wilson was president of Princeton University, he learned that many of his college's students were Webb graduates. As he heard more about the unique preparatory school nestled in the Middle Tennessee hills, he came to believe that Webb was about the finest such school in the country. Later, as president of the United States, Wilson employed several Webb graduates in his administration. Webb graduates designed Princeton's honor code which later became known as the "Princeton System," and at one time Webb sent more Rhodes scholars to England than any other secondary school in the United States.

Sassafras Herbs

The Sassafras Shop was founded in 1976 by four Nashville women interested in herbs and gardening. The name came about because sassafras was

one of the first products (before tobacco) exported profitably by the American Colonists. The sassafras leaf has a very distinctive pattern and was chosen as a wonderful logo for the new business.

The hallmark of the shop's early popularity was the dip and seasoning mixes which were specially formulated by the founders. Today, a vast array of herb products and gifts are available as well. The Sassafras Shop is extremely proud of its long tradition of providing quality products. The shop moved from the Barn at Belle Meade Mansion to Travellers' Rest to its present location in a Belle Meade shopping area.

Hot Artichoke Dip

1	14-OUNCE CAN ARTICHOKE HEARTS, DRAINED
1/2	CUP MAYONNAISE OR MORE TO TASTE
1/2	CUP PARMESAN CHEESE
1/8	TEASPOON GARLIC POWDER
1/8	TEASPOON PAPRIKA FOR GARNISH

Assemble all ingredients and utensils. In a bowl, mash artichokes well. Mix in mayonnaise, Parmesan cheese, and paprika. Pour into a 1-quart ovenware glass dish and bake in a 350-degree oven for 20 minutes or until bubbly. Yield: 8 servings.

Serve with melba toast rounds or your favorite tortilla chips.

Per serving: 133 calories; 12 g fat; 12 mg cholesterol; 261 mg sodium.

Dill Dip

2	CUPS MAYONNAISE
2	CUPS SOUR CREAM
3	TABLESPOONS MINCED FRESH PARSLEY
3	TABLESPOONS DILL WEED
2	TABLESPOONS GRATED ONION
1	TABLESPOON SEASONED SALT

Assemble all ingredients and utensils. In large bowl of mixer, blend together all ingredients. Chill several hours. Dip may be prepared several days in advance. Yield: 4 cups.

Serve with crisp raw vegetables: broccoli flowerets, cherry tomatoes, cauliflower pieces, carrot and celery strips.

Per serving: 262 calories; 28 g fat; 29 mg cholesterol; 417 mg sodium.

Good Luck Dip

4	CUPS COOKED BLACK-EYED PEAS, DRAINED
5	JALAPEÑO PEPPERS
1	TABLESPOON JALAPEÑO JUICE
1/4	CUP CHOPPED ONION
1	4-OUNCE CAN GREEN CHILIES
1	CLOVE GARLIC, CRUSHED
1/2	POUND OLD ENGLISH SHARP CHEESE
1/4	CUP BUTTER

Assemble all ingredients and utensils. Combine peas, peppers and juice, onion, chilies and garlic in blender. Work with 1/4 mixture at a time until well blended.

In a double boiler, heat cheese and butter until melted. Stir in pea mixture. Yield: 25 to 30 servings.

Renowned Black-Eyed Pea recipe for New Years Day. Serve in chafing dish with tortilla or corn chips.

Per serving: 63 calories; 4 g fat; 10 mg cholesterol; 201 mg sodium.

Dried Beef Dip

3	8-OUNCE PACKAGES CREAM CHEESE
2	JARS CHOPPED DRIED BEEF
4-5	CHOPPED GREEN ONIONS
2	TABLESPOONS WORCHESTERSHIRE SAUCE
1	TABLESPOON ACCENT

Mix all ingredients and serve with crackers.

Co-author Jim Crutchfield and wife Regena shared this recipe which they especially enjoy with the Bicentennial Collection. Jim is a descendant of John and Sally Buchanan of Nashborough days.

A WARTIME GOVERNOR

Thomas Clark Rye was probably Benton County's most illustrious citizen. Born in the county seat of Camden in 1863, Rye was educated locally, studied to become a lawyer, and was admitted to the Camden bar in 1884. Newspaper work attracted him as a young man, and he served as the editor of the *Benton County Enterprise* for several months before being elected to the office of clerk and master of his

BENTON COUNTY

home county's chancery court. In 1893, he moved to Washington, D. C., where he accepted a position as department head in the U. S. Pension Bureau. Tom Rye and his family returned to Camden in 1897, and in 1900, he was elected mayor of the small town near the Tennessee River. He eventually left Benton County, moved to Paris, Tennessee, and became the attorney general for the state. In 1914, he defeated incumbent Governor Ben Hooper and began serving in 1915. During Rye's four-year administration, he was responsible for the implementation of a strict budget system for each of the state's departments; the creation of a highway commission; the establishment of a board of control to supervise the several schools and institutions across the state that accommodated the deaf, blind, and insane; and the reorganization of the state board of education. Since he was governor of Tennessee during the great war in Europe, Rye is sometimes called Tennessee's "wartime" governor. When he died in 1953, he was eulogized as "a dignified and respected representative of the old school of public servants."

Clifty Farms
Real Tennessee
Country Ham

There was a day when every farmer cured his own hams. The flavor of a man's hams was his trademark and a source of family pride. In the late forties and early fifties, J. D. Murphree and Truman Murphey gained great reputation with their country hams in Paris, Tennessee. They found out they could supplement their incomes by selling their hams to passers-by and even some of their neighbors! The men teamed together selling hams on the open market in the spring of 1955.

Today, J. D.'s and Truman's sons, Terry Murphree and Dan Murphey, still follow the old country curing from beginning to end.

Clifty Farms
Hot Country Ham Dip

2	8-OUNCE PACKAGES CREAM CHEESE, SOFTENED
1	CUP SOUR CREAM
1/2-1	CUP CHOPPED CLIFTY FARM COOKED COUNTRY HAM
1/4	CUP FINELY MINCED ONION
1/2	TEASPOON GARLIC POWDER
1	TABLESPOON BUTTER
1	CUP CHOPPED PECANS
1/2	TEASPOON WORCESTERSHIRE SAUCE

Preheat oven to 350 degrees. Combine cream cheese, sour cream, country ham, onion and garlic powder in a small bowl and place in a baking dish. Then sauté butter, pecans, and Worcestershire sauce and sprinkle over baking dish. Refrigerate until serving time. Bake for 20 minutes. Serve hot with crackers or raw vegetables (also good served cold). Yield: 6 to 8 servings.

AMERICA'S MOST WANTED— TENNESSEE-STYLE

To many of Pikeville's residents, he was just a recent arrival who operated one of the town's two blacksmith shops, pounding away every day at the anvil, turning out horseshoes, iron spikes, nails, and other necessities for the farm folk in this tiny community of one hundred and fifty souls nestled on the Sequatchie River. Rumor had it that the man, who called himself John Murrell, actually had served in prison in Nashville, but that didn't matter to Bledsoe Countians. He was a good smithy, and that was the important thing. Actually, Murrell had served time—ten years in fact—and had Pikeville's townspeople known the real reason for

BLEDSOE COUNTY

his imprisonment, they might have been a little more cautious in their acceptance of him. Murrell, a convicted horse thief, was the "brains" behind an abortive slave rebellion that was to occur all over the South on Christmas Day, 1835. He formed an organization called the "Mystic Clan" which maintained several levels of authority and adopted a code system, an identification sign, and other bizarre rituals. To finance his grandiose scheme, Murrell and his associates stole slaves from southern plantations, carried them off on the pretense of liberating them, then sold the poor victims again. By the time the revolt was to begin, Murrell had again crossed the law and was serving time in Nashville. After his release from prison, he moved to Pikeville, where he died soon afterward. He is buried in Smyrna Cemetery.

Baked Seafood Dip

1	CUP CHOPPED GREEN PEPPER
1	CUP CHOPPED ONION
1/2	CUP CHOPPED CELERY
2	TABLESPOONS BUTTER
1/2	10 3/4-OUNCE CAN CREAM OF SHRIMP SOUP OR LOBSTER SOUP
1	CUP MAYONNAISE
8	OUNCES PARMESAN CHEESE, GRATED
1	6-OUNCE CAN CRAB MEAT, DRAINED
1	6-OUNCE CAN SHRIMP, DRAINED
1/2	TEASPOON WHITE PEPPER

Assemble all ingredients and utensils. In a skillet, sauté green pepper, onion and celery in butter. Combine shrimp soup, mayonnaise, Parmesan cheese, crabmeat, shrimp and pepper in a bowl. Stir in vegetables. Pour mixture into a 2-quart casserole dish and bake in a 325 degree oven for 30 minutes. Serve with crackers or toast points. Yield: 12 servings.

Tasty as an entrée over cooked Herbed Rice (*see* p. 148).

Per serving: 281 calories; 23 g fat; 70 mg cholesterol; 646 mg sodium.

Spinach Dip

1	CUP PLAIN YOGURT
1	CUP MAYONNAISE
1	1 5/8-OUNCE VEGETABLE SOUP MIX
1	10-OUNCE PACKAGE FROZEN, CHOPPED SPINACH, THAWED AND DRAINED
1	8-OUNCE CAN SLICED WATER CHESTNUTS, DRAINED

Assemble all ingredients and utensils. In a food processor or blender, mix yogurt, mayonnaise, spinach and water chestnuts. Chill at least 8 hours, so flavors will combine. If using a mixer, water chestnuts will retain crunch. Yield: 3 cups.

To serve:

1. Red cabbage hollowed out and filled with dip. Serve raw vegetables or crackers for dipping.

2. Round loaf of pumpernickel bread, hollowed out. Fill with the dip. Serve with the hollowed bread pieces.

Per serving: 40 calories; 2 g fat; 4 mg cholesterol; 184 mg sodium.

"PROFESSOR" SAM HOUSTON

There can be no doubt about it, Sam Houston was a poor student. One of his early teachers once remarked that, "Sam . . . seldom or never recited a good lesson in his life; he did not take to books, and of course, learned little from them. But he was a boy and man of most remarkably keen close observation." And, Sam later became quite a reader, preferring classics like the *Iliad*. Ironically, despite his aversion to learning as a boy, Sam became a teacher, and, in later life, he was a leading advocate for young people obtaining a good education. Sam's

BLOUNT COUNTY

stint at teaching took place in Blount County, near Maryville, where he had lived as a boy since 1807, when his widowed mother moved to East Tennessee from Virginia. The schoolhouse was a log, one-room affair where students of all ages and grades were taught together. Sam's career didn't last but a year or two, when he decided to join the army. Making the short journey to the Blount County Courthouse in 1813, he "took a dollar from the drum," signifying that he had enlisted in the service. He served in the Creek Wars and was later elected U. S. congressman from Tennessee, then governor of Tennessee. Houston resigned the governorship, went west, eventually migrated to Texas, and became commander-in-chief of the Texas army. After his decisive defeat of Santa Anna at San Jacinto, Houston rose to new heights of glory, first as president of the Texas Republic, then as governor of the State of Texas, and later as a U. S. senator from Texas.

FAREWELL THE HILLS

There is little argument today that one of the saddest episodes in American history occurred in the late 1830s when thousands of Cherokee Indians were forcibly driven from their native lands in East Tennessee and northern Georgia far across the Mississippi River to the unfamiliar prairies of Indian Territory (today's eastern Oklahoma). The eminent poet, Ralph Waldo Emerson, once described the process of Cherokee removal as "a dereliction of all faith and virtue," and added that "such a denial of justice, and such deafness to screams for mercy

were never heard of in times of peace and in the dealing of a nation with its own allies and wards, since the earth was made." Bradley County, when it was organized in 1836, was home to hundreds of Cherokee families who lived much like the white man of the times, complete with farms, a constitution, a syllabary, a newspaper, and other amenities of so-called "civilization." However, at New Echota, in Georgia in late 1835, under constant pressure from officials in Washington, a minority element of the Cherokee nation signed a treaty which ceded all Cherokee lands east of the Mississippi to the U. S. government. Earlier in the summer, at Red Clay in Bradley County, the Cherokees had overwhelmingly rejected similar terms. Government authorities recognized the New Echota treaty, however, and accordingly, in 1838, thirteen thousand Cherokee men, women, and children left nearby Rattlesnake Springs on their long "Trail of Tears" to Oklahoma.

Tamale Dip

2   TABLESPOONS BUTTER
1   MEDIUM ONION, CHOPPED
1   POUND VELVEETA CHEESE
1   15-OUNCE CAN CHILI WITHOUT BEANS
1   13 1/2 OUNCE JAR TAMALES, CHOPPED

Assemble all ingredients and utensils. In a skillet, sauté onion in butter. Drain off butter. Add cheese, chili and chopped tamales. Heat thoroughly. Serve warm in a chafing dish with corn chips. Yield: 6 servings.

A taste of Mexico!

Per serving: 420 calories; 30 g fat; 83 mg cholesterol; 1869 mg sodium.

Stuffed Mushrooms

36   SMALL FRESH MUSHROOMS
1/2   CUP BUTTER, MELTED
1/8   TEASPOON GARLIC POWDER
3/4   CUP MONTEREY JACK CHEESE
1   1.4 OUNCE TOASTED ONION DIP MIX
2   TABLESPOONS DRY RED WINE
1   TABLESPOON SOY SAUCE
1   2 3/4-OUNCE PACKAGE CORN CHIPS, FINELY CRUSHED

Assemble all ingredients and utensils. Remove stems from mushrooms. Wash, pat dry and brush caps with part of melted butter. Combine rest of butter with garlic powder. Add cheese and onion dip mix. Mix well. Add soy sauce, wine and corn chips. Fill mushroom caps with paste. Place on a baking sheet and broil in oven for 3 minutes. Yield: 9 to 12 servings.

Delightful served on a silver tray at an elegant cocktail party.

Per serving: 159 calories; 12 g fat; 27 mg cholesterol; 664 mg sodium.

Herbed Nuts

3	TABLESPOONS MELTED BUTTER
3	TABLESPOON WORCESTERSHIRE SAUCE
1	TEASPOON SALT
1/2	TEASPOON CINNAMON
1/4	TEASPOON GARLIC POWDER
1/4	TEASPOON CAYENNE PEPPER
1/8	TEASPOON TABASCO SAUCE
1 1/2	POUNDS PECAN HALVES

Assemble all ingredients and utensils. In a large pan mix all ingredients and add pecans. Toss until well coated. Place in a deep baking pan and bake in a 300 degree oven for 20 to 25 minutes, stirring often. Yield: about 4 cups.

Fun to snack while watching your favorite football game.

Per serving: 303 calories; 31 g fat; 6 mg cholesterol; 200 mg sodium.

Nuts and Bolts

1	CUP BUTTER
1/2	CUP BACON DRIPPINGS
2	TABLESPOONS WORCESTERSHIRE SAUCE
1	TEASPOON CELERY SALT
1	TEASPOON SEASONED SALT
1	TEASPOON GARLIC SALT
1	TEASPOON CAYENNE PEPPER
1/2	12-OUNCE BOX WHEAT CHEX
1/2	12-OUNCE BOX RICE CHEX
1/2	12-OUNCE BOX CHEERIOS
1	10-OUNCE BOX PRETZELS, BROKEN
1	7-OUNCE CAN PEANUTS
2	CUPS PECAN HALVES

Assemble all ingredients and utensils. In a saucepan, melt butter and bacon drippings. Add seasonings and simmer. Mix cereal and nuts together in large roaster pan. Pour butter mixture over cereal mixture and mix gently. Bake in a 250 degree oven for 60 minutes. Stir every 20 minutes. Yield: 8 to 10 cups of mix.

Per serving: 822 calories; 56 g fat; 59 mg cholesterol; 1660 mg sodium.

GREAT FOOD GIFT. MY IN-LAWS, THE KINGS, MAKE THIS SNACK FOR MY HUSBAND WAYNE AND OUR COLLEGE SON KEVIN. IT HAS BEEN ENJOYED BY OUR FAMILY FOR THE PAST TWENTY YEARS.

Miss Daisy

Chutney Cheese Paté

1   8-OUNCE PACKAGE CREAM CHEESE, SOFTENED
1   CUP GRATED MILD CHEDDAR CHEESE, SOFTENED
1/2 TEASPOON CURRY POWDER
1/4 TEASPOON SALT
4   TEASPOONS SHERRY

Topping

MAJOR GREY'S CHUTNEY
GREEN ONIONS, CHOPPED

Assemble all ingredients and utensils. In mixer, combine first 5 ingredients. Shape into a ring mold or mound with hands. Refrigerate until serving. Top with chutney and green onions. Place on top of lettuce and encircle with combination of crisp crackers. Yield: 8 to 10 servings.

Per serving: 145 calories; 12 g fat; 36 mg cholesterol; 258 mg sodium.

A PATÉ I REALLY ENJOY SERVING. PLEASE NOTE THAT UNLESS YOU PREPARE YOUR OWN CHUTNEY RECIPE, MAJOR GREY'S IS A FAVORITE.

Miss Daisy

Smoked Oyster Paté

1   3 3/4-OUNCE CAN SMOKED OYSTERS
1   8-OUNCE PACKAGE CREAM CHEESE
2   TABLESPOONS DRY RED WINE
1   TEASPOON DIJON MUSTARD
1/2 TEASPOON SAGE
1/2 CUP CHOPPED WALNUTS
2   TABLESPOONS FINELY CHOPPED FRESH PARSLEY

Assemble all ingredients and utensils. Drain oysters and purée in food processor. Add cream cheese and process until smooth. Mix in red wine, mustard, and sage. Form into a ball. Refrigerate until firm. On a platter or flat plate, combine walnuts and parsley; coat oyster ball. Yield: 12 servings.

Delicious with French bread or crackers.

Per serving: 110 calories; 10 g fat; 23 mg cholesterol; 84 mg sodium.

NOT MANY PEOPLE CAN RESIST THE TASTE AND TEXTURE OF THIS PATÉ. BELIEVE ME, YOU WILL ALWAYS HAVE REQUESTS FOR THIS RECIPE.

Miss Daisy

Salmon Log

1	15 1/2-OUNCE CAN PINK SALMON
1	8-OUNCE PACKAGE CREAM CHEESE, SOFTENED
1	TABLESPOON LEMON JUICE
2	TEASPOONS GRATED ONION
1 1/2	TEASPOONS HORSERADISH
1/8	TEASPOON SALT
3	TABLESPOONS MINCED FRESH PARSLEY
1/2	CUP CHOPPED PECANS

Assemble all ingredients and utensils. Drain and flake salmon, removing all bones and skin. Place in a bowl and combine remaining ingredients except parsley and pecans. Chill several hours and shape salmon mixture into a log. Roll in combined parsley and pecans. Yield: 8 to 10 servings.

Serve with your favorite crackers. May be made ahead.

Per serving: 177 calories; 14 g fat; 42 mg cholesterol; 307 mg sodium.

King Brothers Old Fashioned Coffee

King Brothers Old Fashioned Coffee was established in 1978 in Dandridge, Tennessee. Paul King, president and CEO, searched extensively for an excellent blend of coffee. The company only uses gourmet, washed beans and takes pride in its consistent roast which maintains its high standards. King Brothers is a full service coffee roaster, packager and distributor concentrating on the office coffee industry.

A WILDERNESS PARADISE

Today, it is difficult to realize just how wild and primitive Tennessee once was. Wildlife literally teemed in the forests of the state, and dozens of species of birds and mammals that have been extinct for years roamed the wilderness. Witness what a man by the name of Emmanuel Hatfield, who was born in 1805 in Campbell County, had to say in 1890 of the Cumberland River region in which he grew up as a boy. "That territory was marked by lofty mountains, covered with tall, heavy timber, beneath which there was a thick, and in some places, almost impenetrable growth of laurel brush whose leaves are green throughout the year. . . . Along up the mountain slopes were

to be found numerous caverns and holes entering the ground; there were also many cliffs and pinnacles of great and rugged heights. . . . The timber which covered the country was mostly oak, chestnut, hickory, pine, and poplar. . . . The creeks and brooks were replete with fishes of all species. . . . The game most abundant was deer, bear, turkey, ducks, and geese. Deer generally roamed in herds of from five to ten, and were as plentiful, and more so perhaps, my reader, than rabbits where you now live. . . . Also the fierce panther, the treacherous wolf, the prowling wild cat and catamount went sneaking through the woods and among the hills. The fox and raccoon were anywhere to be found. . . . [T]here were beavers in large numbers to be found along the Little Cumberland River, and along the small creeks. . . ."

Crockett Creek
Beef Jerky

The Bob W. Hitch family began a tradition in Maryville, Tennessee, because so many friends "kept after them" to do so. Crockett Creek Beef Jerky Company exists because Bob's son made an exceptional beef jerky product that friends and co-workers loved. They complained if he didn't have enough available, so the family bought a commercial dehydrator, qualified for USDA inspection, and went into business. The traditional longhunter and raccoon logo represents Crockett Creek products.

Davy Crockett's
Beef or Venison Jerky

LEAN MEAT
SOY SAUCE
BLACK PEPPER
RED PEPPER
GARLIC POWDER

First, cut all fat away from meat, then cut into strips. Put strips of meat in bowl; cover with soy sauce and marinate in refrigerator overnight.

After marinating, sprinkle with pepper and garlic powder to taste.

For drying in oven, set temperature to lowest setting. If the temperature is too high, the meat will cook, not dry. Stick toothpicks in one end of the strips and hang on oven rack. Leave 6 to 8 hours or until dry. For drying in a dehydrator, just lay strips flat on trays.

Note: Thickness of strips will determine drying time. Be sure to cover bottom of oven or dehydrator with foil for easy clean up.

This recipe came from Lowell McAuley, a fourth great-grandson of Davy Crockett.

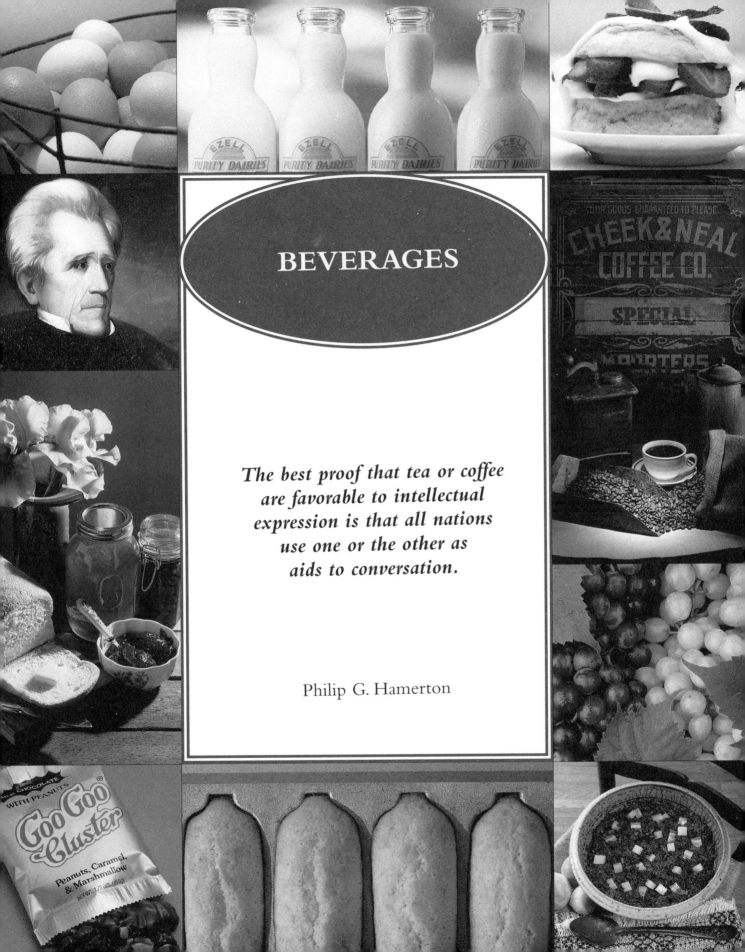

BEVERAGES

The best proof that tea or coffee
are favorable to intellectual
expression is that all nations
use one or the other as
aids to conversation.

Philip G. Hamerton

Beverages

Celebration Wassail 17
Homestead Hills Fall Harvest Favorite 18
Homemade Tomato Juice 18
Hot Spiced Cider 18
Instant Hot Chocolate 19
Coffee Punch 19
Teenie Hooker Buchtel's
Blount Family Blackberry Wine 20
John Overton's Southern Egg Nog 20
Oliver's Smoke House Apple Frost 21
Assembly Grounds Summer Lemonade 21
Orange Julius 21
Reception Punch for Darrell Waltrip 22
Choices' Restaurant Tea Punch 22
Hot Spiced Tea Mix 23
Jack Daniel's Mint Juleps for Twenty 23
Belle Meade Plantation Syllabub 24
Mint Tea 24

Celebration Wassail

5   ORANGES
    WHOLE CLOVES
5   CUPS PINEAPPLE JUICE
3   QUARTS APPLE CIDER
2   STICKS CINNAMON
1/2 CUP HONEY
1/2 TEASPOON NUTMEG
1/3 CUP LEMON JUICE
2   TEASPOONS LEMON RIND
2   CUPS RUM

Assemble all ingredients and utensils. Stud 5 oranges with whole cloves, about 1/2 inch part. Place in baking pan with 2 cups water. Bake in a 350-degree oven for 20 minutes. Meanwhile, heat cider and cinnamon sticks and honey in a large pot. Bring to boil over medium heat; simmer covered for 5 minutes. Add remaining ingredients. Pour over spiced oranges that have been transferred from oven to punch bowl. Yield: about 40, 4-ounce cups.

Per serving: 77 calories; 0 g fat; 0 mg cholesterol; 3 mg sodium.

THE MAN EVERYONE LOVED

Of all the men and women who have served Tennessee in the state legislature, one name surfaces above all the others as an example of an honest, caring, dedicated representative of the people: "Mr. Jim" Cummings. James H. Cummings was born near Woodbury in Cannon County in November 1890. Educated locally, Cummings went on to study law at the YMCA Law School in Nashville and at Cumberland University in Lebanon. In 1922, he began his long practice of law in his hometown. In 1929, Cummings decided to give a try at being elected to the Tennessee Legislature. He was successful in his bid, and for the next forty-three years (except for four during which time

CANNON COUNTY

he was Tennessee's secretary of state), he served his constituency in Nashville. A strong advocate of education for Tennessee's youth, Cummings was in large measure responsible for bailing out present-day Middle Tennessee State University at Murfreesboro when it was suffering serious financial woes during the Depression. For his dedication to the people and institutions of Tennessee over the years, Mr. Jim was honored with a highway, a wing of the legislative office building, and a building at MTSU, all named after him. When he retired from state service in 1972, well-wishers from all over the state and from both political parties descended upon Woodbury to wish him well. Mr. Jim Cummings, one of the last of his breed in today's fast-paced political arena, died on November 1, 1979, and is buried near Woodbury.

Homestead Hills Herbs

Dean and Judi Gardner have Clarksville's Homestead Hills Herbs available for Tennesseans interested in various herbal products. They not only provide fresh and hand-processed herbal foods, they bring specialists in to conduct many workshops for the community.

The use of several herbs is observed in the Herbal Jellies workshop. Delightful flavors are available for enhancing poultry and meats, biscuits, toast and pancakes.

The Herbal Breads and Spreads workshop highlights the importance of using whole wheat in one's diet. The making of freshly flavored butters and spreads is demonstrated.

Dean and Judi offer vinegars, teas, breads and bread mixes, dried cooking herbs, and plants for personal herb gardens. They feel the Middle Tennessee soil is perfect for herbs.

It may be a surprise to learn that the recipe on this page is a constant hit especially for parties in the months when the weather has started turning cooler. Many folk heat cider but not many know how delicioius this combination can be.

Homestead Hills Fall Harvest Favorite

Mix equal amounts of Tennessee cider with V-8 Juice, toss in a handful of fresh basil or a healthy pinch or two of dried. Heat in a crockpot until simmers.

Homemade Tomato Juice

5-8	TOMATOES, HOME GROWN AND RIPE
1/2	TEASPOON SALT
1/4	TEASPOON ONION SALT
1/4	TEASPOON BLACK PEPPER
	JUICE OF 1 LEMON

Assemble all ingredients and utensils. Wash very ripe tomatoes, cut out stem and quarter them. Heat over low temperature until mushy. Strain through a sieve. To 5 cups of juice add remaining ingredients. Reheat to boiling. Refrigerate until ready to serve. Yield: 6 to 8, 8-ounce glasses.

Per serving: 24 calories; 0 g fat; 0 mg cholesterol; 184 mg sodium.

Hot Spiced Cider

1	GALLON APPLE CIDER
2	3-OUNCE PACKAGES RED HOTS
1/2	TEASPOON NUTMEG
1/2	TEASPOON ALLSPICE
3	CINNAMON STICKS

Assemble all ingredients and utensils. In a large pot, heat cider. Add red hots and stir until dissolved. Add remaining ingredients and keep warm until ready to serve. Yield: 20 to 25 servings.

Per serving: 105 calories; 0 g fat; 0 mg cholesterol; 5 mg sodium.

Instant Hot Chocolate

1   2-POUND BOX NESTLES QUICK
1   1-POUND BOX CONFECTIONERS SUGAR
1   11-OUNCE JAR COFFEEMATE
1   8-QUART BOX POWDERED MILK

Assemble all ingredients and utensils. In a deep bowl combine all ingredients and mix well. Store in air-tight container. To serve, use 2 rounded teaspoons of mix per 1 cup of hot water. Yield: about 75-80 cups.

A fun recipe for children to help prepare for teachers' gifts.

Per serving: 181 calories; 2 g fat; 5 mg cholesterol; 171 mg sodium.

Coffee Punch

2   QUARTS STRONG BREWED COFFEE (8 CUPS)
1   PINT COLD MILK (2 CUPS)
2   TEASPOONS VANILLA EXTRACT
1/2 CUP SUGAR
2   QUARTS VANILLA ICE CREAM
1/2 PINT HEAVY CREAM
1/2 TABLESPOON GROUND NUTMEG

Assemble all ingredients and utensils. In a deep bowl, combine coffee, milk, vanilla, and sugar. Chill. Break ice cream into chunks in punch bowl just before serving; pour chilled coffee mixture over ice cream. Whip cream, spoon into mounds on top of punch. Sprinkle with nutmeg. Yield: 18 servings.

Per serving: 206 calories; 12 g fat; 48 mg cholesterol; 72 mg sodium.

American Tea & Coffee

I f you don't get American Ace Coffee, go back to bed" is a phrase that has echoed through televisions and radios for years since the campaign for new American Ace customers began in the 1970s. Minnie Pearl and Roy Acuff were the company's early radio spokespeople on the Grand Ole Opry.

The American Tea & Coffee Co. began in the early years of this century. A peddler named David Bubis began selling coffee door-to-door from a backpack. Prior to 1919, he was operating out of a horse drawn wagon under the name of Economy Tea & Coffee Co. In 1919, the business was incorporated as American Tea & Coffee Co., Inc.

Four years later, the American Ace name appeared to replace an earlier brand called Bluebird. It honored the Aviator or Flying Ace of World War I fame.

Over the years, innovations in the coffee industry were reflected by American Tea & Coffee Co. American Ace was the first in the mid-South to put coffee in pop-top vacuum cans. The company also introduced instant and freeze-dried coffee to the area.

Today, American Tea & Coffee Co. continues as a supplier to wholesale and retail grocers.

Teenie Hooker Buchtel's
Blount Family Blackberry Wine

1 GALLON FRESH BLACKBERRIES, MASHED
1 QUART HOT WATER

Combine in a pot and let sit for two days. Strain through cheese-cloth. Then add 1 1/2 pounds white sugar and 1/2 glass of your favorite whiskey. Pour into bottles, seal and let sit in a dark place for a year.

Sugar cookies were often served with this wine.

*T*HIS VERY OLD RECIPE CAME FROM TEENIE'S MOTHER, DORTHULA WILLIAMSON, WHO WAS NAMED FOR GOVERNOR WILLIAM BLOUNT'S WIFE DORTHULA. A RECIPE FROM BLOUNT MANSION IS ON PAGE 109.

Miss Daisy

John Overton's
Southern Egg Nog

12 EGGS
 1 QUART HEAVY CREAM, WHIPPED
12 TABLESPOONS SUGAR
24 TABLESPOONS WHISKEY

Beat egg yolks well then beat in sugar a spoonful at a time. Add whiskey, beat. Beat in half of whipped cream. Fold in other half so that the egg nog will be light and fluffy.

The secret of egg nog is in the beating of the eggs and in the sugar. This can be made several hours ahead and allowed to stand but do not add whipped cream until about ready to serve. Will serve 20.

*T*HIS RECIPE IS FROM MRS. JESSE OVERTON (MISS SAIDEE), 1872-1964. MR. OVERTON WAS GRANDSON OF JUDGE JOHN OVERTON. AROUND 1900 THEY BUILT OVERTON HALL (NOW CREIVE HALL SUBDIVISION) ON OVERTON LAND NEXT TO TRAVELLERS REST IN NASHVILLE (*SEE ALSO P. 77 FOR THE OVERTON RECIPE FOR SUGAR CURING HAM*).

Miss Daisy

Oliver's Smoke House Apple Frost

1	PINT LIME SHERBET
1 1/2	CUPS CHILLED APPLE JUICE
	APPLE SLICES

Assemble all ingredients and utensils. Beat lime sherbet until soft. Gradually blend in the apple juice. Garnish with apple slices.

Assembly Grounds Summer Lemonade

1 1/4	CUPS SUGAR
1/2	CUP BOILING WATER
1 1/2	CUPS FRESH LEMON JUICE
4 1/2	CUPS COLD WATER
10	LEMON SLICES

Assemble all ingredients and utensils. In a saucepan bring water to boiling. In a heat-proof pitcher combine sugar and boiling water. Stir until sugar dissolves. Add lemon juice and cold water. Stir well. Chill until serving time. Pour into ice-filled glasses. Garnish with lemon slices. Yield: 10 servings.

This beverage is served during the Front Porch Parties at the Assembly Grounds, Monteagle, Tennessee.

Per serving: 105 calories; 0 g fat; 0 mg cholesterol; 1 mg sodium.

Orange Julius

1	6-OUNCE CAN FROZEN ORANGE JUICE
1	CUP MILK
1	CUP WATER
1/2	CUP SUGAR
1	TEASPOON VANILLA
12	ICE CUBES

Assemble all ingredients and utensils. Combine all ingredients in blender. Cover and blend until smooth, about 30 seconds. Favorite of "Big Orange Fans."

Per serving: 146 calories; 1 g fat; 6 mg cholesterol; 21 mg sodium.

Jim Oliver's Smoke House

It's been over a decade since a country boy named Jim Oliver opened the Smoke House restaurant in Monteagle and set about trying to preserve the good old Southern traditions of country cooking. He used his momma's know-how in the kitchen and his daddy's secrets of dry-curing and hickory smoking. But the family tradition doesn't stop there. They make visitors feel at home and son James David even handles sales and marketing.

Jim's reputation may have been built on southern home cookin', but folks are discovering that with the addition of private cabins and honeymoon suites, the Smoke House is a great get away for a few days. Today, Jim Oliver's Smoke

House restaurant packs in an estimated 400,000 visitors annually.

Reception Punch for Darrell Waltrip

2 GALLONS SWEETENED TEA
3 46-OUNCE CANS PINEAPPLE JUICE
3 46-OUNCE CANS ORANGE JUICE
1 6-OUNCE CAN FROZEN LEMONADE CONCENTRATE, THAWED
3 QUARTS GATORADE, CHILLED
1 GALLON PINEAPPLE SHERBET

Assemble all ingredients and utensils. Combine tea and juices and and put in gallon containers and cool. Add Gatorade just before serving. Pour all over sherbet in your favorite punch bowl.
Yield: 75 servings.

*D*ARRELL WALTRIP WAS HONORED AT A RECEPTION IN 1977 AT MISS DAISY'S TEA ROOM IN FRANKLIN, TENNESSEE. HIS RACE CAR SPONSOR AT THE TIME WAS GATORADE. THE OFFICIALS ASKED ME TO CREATE A RECIPE USING GATORADE. DARRELL WALTRIP, HIS WIFE, STEVIE, AND FAMILY MEMBERS ALONG WITH NASCAR OFFICIALS AND THE HONORABLE SENATOR HOWARD BAKER WERE AMONG THE HUNDREDS OF V.I.P.s WHO ATTENDED.

Miss Daisy

Choices Restaurant Tea Punch

2 GALLONS BREWED TEA
2 12-OUNCE CANS FROZEN ORANGE JUICE CONCENTRATE, THAWED
2 12-OUNCE CANS OF FROZEN LEMONADE CONCENTRATE, THAWED
4 6-OUNCE CANS PINEAPPLE JUICE, THAWED
2 CUPS (OR MORE) SUGAR

Assemble all ingredients and utensils. Combine tea, orange juice concentrate, lemonade concentrate, pineapple juice and sugar in punch bowl. Mix well. Ladle into glasses filled with cracked ice.
Yield: 30 servings.

Per serving: 192 calories; 0 g fat; 0 mg cholesterol; 11 mg sodium.

*I*N 1974 CALVIN LEHEW WAS LOOKING FOR A TENANT IN HIS NEWLY DEVELOPED CARTERS COURT SHOPPING VILLAGE IN FRANKLIN, TENNESSEE, AND I WAS SPIRITED ENOUGH AT THE AGE OF TWENTY-SEVEN TO THINK I COULD OWN AND OPERATE A TEA ROOM. MISS DAISY'S TEA ROOM OPENED AUGUST 12, 1974, WITH CALVIN AND MARILYN AS MY PARTNERS. THEY HAVE CONTINUED TO HELP RESTORE AND BUILD HISTORIC DOWNTOWN FRANKLIN. STOP IN CHOICES RESTAURANT ON MAIN STREET IN FRANKLIN, HAVE A GLASS OF TEA PUNCH AND ENJOY THE LEHEW'S ECLECTIC SOUTHERN MENU AND WARM HOSPITALITY.

Miss Daisy

Hot Spiced Tea Mix

2   CUPS INSTANT ORANGE DRINK MIX
10   OUNCES LEMONADE MIX
4   OUNCES INSTANT TEA
2   TEASPOONS GROUND CINNAMON
1   TEASPOON CLOVES
1 1/2 CUPS SUGAR

Assemble all ingredients and utensils. In a bowl combine ingredients. Store in tightly covered jars. For each cup of tea use 2 teaspoons mix dissolved in 1 cup of boiling water. Yield: about 16 to 18 cups of tea.

This is another recipe which one can make easily for gifts.

Per serving: 233 calories; 0 g fat; 0 mg cholesterol; 15 mg sodium.

Jack Daniel's
Mint Juleps for Twenty

1   CUP SUGAR
6   OUNCES ICE WATER
30   OR MORE TENDER MINT LEAVES, DIVIDED
36   OUNCES JACK DANIEL'S TENNESSEE SIPPIN' WHISKEY
     CRUSHED ICE
     SMALL PUNCH BOWL OR
     1/2 GALLON PITCHER

Assemble all ingredients and utensils. Pour sugar and water combination in bottom of punch bowl or pitcher. Add 10 of the mint leaves. Carefully bruise the leaves but do not crush the leaves because this releases the bitter, inner juices. Pack the punch bowl or pitcher with crushed ice and pour whiskey to cover. Stir with a long spoon and move contents up and down for a few minutes. Add more whiskey if necessary. Pour mixture into individual silver julep cups or hi-ball glasses and place in refrigerator for 10 minutes to frost the glass. When ready to serve garnish with 20 additional mint leaves.

This recipe was served at a state event in 1984, when the National Governors' Conference was held in Nashville, Tennessee.

Per serving: 164 calories; 0 g fat; 0 mg cholesterol; 1 mg sodium.

Jack Daniel's Distillery

Eighteen-year-old Jack Daniel couldn't have known way back in 1866 when he bought out his partner's half of a distillery located on Louse Creek in present-day Moore County that his name would go in the history books as the organizer of the oldest registered distillery in the United States. Before Mr. Jack died in 1911, his fine Tennessee sippin' whiskey was known all over the world and was the recipient of countless national and international awards beginning with a gold medal at the Louisiana Purchase Exposition in 1904. Later, when Mr. Jack was joined in the business by his nephew, Lem Motlow, young Lem's business mind took the company to even higher levels of success. Today, the Jack Daniel's Distillery is owned by the Brown-Forman Distilling Corporation. But every drop of Mr. Jack's Tennessee whiskey is still made in Lynchburg, using the same special charcoal mellowing process it always has.

Belle Meade Plantation

The Belle Meade Plantation, in Nashville, Tennessee, one of the first nurseries for thoroughbred horses in America, is noted for its traditional hospitality and decadent southern food.

Over the years, Belle Meade received many famous guests. President Grover Cleveland and his bride spent their honeymoon there in 1887. Presidents Jackson, Polk, Harrison, and Teddy Roosevelt also enjoyed the hospitality of William Giles Harding and his wife, Elizabeth.

Food had to be grown and produced in large quantities, and 350 to 400 hogs were killed each season to keep the smokehouse filled. But the plantation's speciality was Syllabub, a beverage similar to eggnog. Syllabub is made with cream and Madeira wine.

Belle Meade Plantation Syllabub

3	CUPS APPLE CIDER
1/4	CUP LEMON JUICE OR MADEIRA WINE
1	TEASPOON LIGHT CORN SYRUP
3	TABLESPOONS GRATED LEMON RIND
1	CUP SUGAR
2	EGG WHITES
1/4	CUP SUGAR
2	CUPS WHOLE MILK
1	CUP LIGHT CREAM

Mix all ingredients in a large bowl. Stir until sugar dissolves. Then refrigerate until cold. Just before serving, beat 2 egg whites until frothy; add 1/4 cup sugar, a small amount at a time until meringue stands in peaks. Then beat 2 cups milk and 1 cup of light cream into cider mixture. Pour into punch bowl and spoon meringue on top. Garnish with nutmeg.

Mint Tea

4	INDIVIDUAL TEA BAGS
14	LARGE MINT LEAVES
3	CUPS BOILING WATER
1	CUP SUGAR
1/4	CUP FRESH LEMON JUICE
1	CUP ORANGE JUICE
6	CUPS COLD WATER

Garnish

8	SPRIGS MINT
1	ORANGE, SLICED
1	LEMON, SLICED

Assemble all ingredients and utensils. Place tea bags and mint leaves in a large pitcher. Add boiling water and allow to steep for 10 minutes. Add sugar and stir very gently. Cool completely; stir and strain mixture. Discard tea bags and mint. Pour mixture back in pitcher; add remaining ingredients. Serve over ice in tea glasses. Garnish with mint and slices of fruit. Yield: 8 to 10 servings.

Per serving: 90 calories; 0 g fat; 0 mg cholesterol; 1 mg sodium.

SALADS
AND THEIR
DRESSINGS

*You can put everything, and the
more things the better,
into salad, as into a conversation;
but everything depends
upon the mixing.*

Charles Dudley Warner

Salads and their Dressings

FRUIT
Apricot Salad With Custard 27
Frozen Strawberry Salad 28
Grandmother's Frozen Fruit Salad 28
Pink Arctic Freeze 29
Lucille Clement's Fruit Salad Compote 29
Ambrosia 29
Bing Cherry Salad 30
Orange-Mallow Salad 30
Spiced Peach Salad 31
Grapefruit Mold 31
Festive Cranberry Salad 32
Pineapple-Olive Salad 32
Brenda Lee's Pretzel Salad 33

VEGETABLE
Three Bean Salad 33
Amy Grant's Easy Chopped Salad 34
Corn Salad 34
Green Pea Salad 35
Picnic Potato Salad 35
Wilted Spinach and Orange Salad 36
Tomato Aspic 36
Sweet and Sour Slaw 37
Creamy Slaw 37

POULTRY AND SEAFOOD
Yarrow Acres' Hot Tarragon and Basil
Chicken Salad in Puff Pastry 38
Hot Chicken Salad 38
Chicken and Fruit Salad 39
Turkey Salad 40
Festive Shrimp Mold 40
Party Shrimp Salad 41
Tea Room Tuna Salad 41

DRESSINGS
Buttermilk Salad Dressing 42
Cucumber Dressing 42
Milky Way Farm House Dressing 43
Oil and Vinegar Dressing 43
Poppy Seed Dressing 44
Tomato Dressing 44
Saddle Restaurant Salad and Dressing 45
Walking Horse Hotel's Special
Thousand Island Dressing 45
Miss Daisy's Cooked Dressing for
Chicken Salad 46
Yogurt Salad Dressing 46

Apricot Salad With Custard

1   6-OUNCE PACKAGE APRICOT GELATIN
4   CUPS HOT WATER
1   CUP MINIATURE MARSHMALLOWS
1   14-OUNCE CAN CRUSHED PINEAPPLE, DRAINED,
      RESERVING JUICE
2   LARGE BANANAS, MASHED

Assemble all ingredients and utensils. In a saucepan, heat water to boiling; add gelatin and marshmallows and stir until dissolved. Let cool. Add crushed pineapple and bananas. Pour mixture into a 13x9-inch glass casserole dish and refrigerate until salad congeals.

      RESERVED PINEAPPLE JUICE
1/2   CUP SUGAR
2   TABLESPOONS ALL-PURPOSE FLOUR
1   TABLESPOON BUTTER
1   8-OUNCE PACKAGE CREAM CHEESE, SOFTENED
1   4-OUNCE CARTON WHIPPED TOPPING

In a saucepan combine pineapple juice, sugar, flour and butter. Cook until thick, add cream cheese and let cool. Fold in whipped topping and spread over top of congealed gelatin. Yield: 12 servings.

Per serving: 240 calories; 10 g fat; 23 mg cholesterol; 113 mg sodium.

GORDON BROWNING

During Tennessee's two hundred year history, seven governors of the state—including John Sevier, the first governor—have served in their office, sat out a term or more, and then were elected later to serve again. One of the more recent of these men was Gordon Browning. Browning was born in Carroll County in 1895, but as a child moved to neighboring Gibson County where he finished high school. He later attended Valparaiso University in Indiana. Completing his higher education with a law degree from Cumberland University, Browning returned to his native county and started a law practice in Huntingdon. After serving in World War I as a captain, he resumed his law

practice, married, and ran for U. S. congressman, but was defeated by the Republican nominee, Lon Scott. Two years later, Browning was elected to the House of Representatives and served in Washington for six consecutive terms. Browning's friendship with Memphis ward-healer Ed "Boss" Crump helped him win the governor's chair in 1937, but a later falling out with Crump cost Browning the 1939 election. Browning made a political comeback in 1949, was elected to two more successive terms, and then was defeated by Frank G. Clement in 1952. Among Governor Browning's achievements while in office the second time was the removal of the payment of a poll tax before one could vote. Browning died in 1976, at the age of eighty-six, and is buried in Oak Cemetery in Huntingdon.

Despite the large number of career personnel that have always been present in the different branches of the Nation's military, most people are satisfied to obey their call to one or the other of the services and to quickly and quietly revert to civilian life. Not so with Samuel Powatan Carter of Carter County. Born in Elizabethton in 1819, Carter went to college in Virginia and New Jersey before being appointed a midshipman in the United States Navy in 1840. He served at different ports around the world until 1845, when he was sent

**CARTER
COUNTY**

to the U. S. Naval Academy. Upon graduation the following year, Carter saw service in the Mexican War and later as a teacher back at the Academy. When the War Between the States broke out in 1861, Carter, still an active member of the U. S. Navy, was placed on special assignment to organize Tennessee volunteers for the Union army. Operating primarily in heavily Union-sympathetic East Tennessee, he had no problem quickly filling a regiment, then a full brigade, the command of which he was given with the rank of brigadier-general. General Carter saw action throughout the remainder of the War and upon his discharge from the army as a brevet major-general, he returned to his first love, the U. S. Navy. Before he retired in 1882, Carter was advanced to rear admiral, thus becoming the only man in the Nation's history to receive the commissions for both a general in the army and an admiral in the navy.

Frozen Strawberry Salad

1	8-OUNCE PACKAGE CREAM CHEESE, SOFTENED
3/4	CUP SUGAR
3	LARGE BANANAS, SLICED
1/2	CUP CHOPPED PECANS
1	14-OUNCE CAN PINEAPPLE CHUNKS, DRAINED
1	16-OUNCE PACKAGE FROZEN STRAWBERRIES, THAWED
1	8-OUNCE CARTON WHIPPED TOPPING, THAWED

Assemble all ingredients and utensils. In large bowl of mixer, cream together cream cheese and sugar. Add bananas, pecans, pineapple, strawberries and whipped topping. Mix well. Pour mixture into a 13x9-inch dish. Freeze. Yield: 12 to 15 servings.

Another fruit salad recipe: grapefruit, orange, and avocado slices, garnished with green pepper with a sweet and sour dressing.

Per serving: 211 calories; 11 g fat; 16 mg cholesterol; 45 mg sodium.

Grandmother's Frozen Fruit Salad

1	8-OUNCE PACKAGE SOFTENED CREAM CHEESE
1/2	CUP SUGAR
1/4	CUP LEMON JUICE
1/4	TEASPOON SALT
2	CUPS SOUR CREAM
1	CUP SEEDLESS GRAPES
1	PINT BLUEBERRIES, FRESH
2	CUPS CHOPPED PEACHES
1	CUP CHOPPED STRAWBERRIES

Assemble all ingredients and utensils. Wash and drain all fruit. Place paper liners in muffin tins. In large bowl of mixer beat cream cheese, sugar, lemon juice, salt and sour cream. Stir in grapes, blueberries, peaches and strawberries. Pour mixture into 16 muffin tins or a large casserole dish, 13x9x2. Freeze. To serve, unmold on a piece of leafy or romaine lettuce. Garnish with a teaspoon of mayonnaise and a whole fresh strawberry. Yield: 16 servings.

Serve banana or strawberry bread slices filled with cream cheese as an accompaniment to this refreshing salad.

Per serving: 165 calories; 11 g fat; 28 mg cholesterol; 92 mg sodium.

Pink Arctic Freeze

1	16-OUNCE CAN WHOLE BERRY CRANBERRY SAUCE
1	8-OUNCE CAN CRUSHED PINEAPPLE, DRAINED
1	TEASPOON LEMON JUICE
1	CUP SOUR CREAM
1/2	CUP MAYONNAISE

Assemble all ingredients and utensils. In a bowl, combine all ingredients. Pour mixture into a glass 3-quart casserole dish. Freeze until firm. Yield: 12 to 15 servings.

Delicious served with ham and rolls for a luncheon.

Per serving: 151 calories; 9 g fat; 11 mg cholesterol; 61 mg sodium.

Lucille Clement's Fruit Salad Compote

1 1/2	CANS OF PINEAPPLE CHUNKS, DRAINED
1	CAN SLICED PEARS, DRAINED
2	SMALL JARS MARASCHINO CHERRIES WITH JUICE
1	SMALL PACKAGE OF CHOPPED PECANS
1	BAG OF MINIATURE MARSHMALLOWS
3	SLICED BANANAS

Assemble all ingredients and utensils. Mix all of the above in a large mixing bowl. When ready to serve top with whipped cream or Cool Whip. Yield: 6 servings.

*L*UCILLE CLEMENT WAS IN FLORIDA WHEN I FIRST CALLED, SO HER SON'S OFFICE (CONGRESSMAN BOB CLEMENT) GRACIOUSLY SENT A RECIPE FOR HER. LATER SHE SENT HER OWN FAVORITE RECIPE FOR THIS BICENTENNIAL COOKBOOK. MRS. CLEMENT WAS FIRST LADY DURING HER HUSBAND'S (GOVERNOR FRANK CLEMENT) TWO TERMS OF OFFICE, 1953-1959 AND 1963-1967.

Miss Daisy

Ambrosia

1	QUART ORANGE SECTIONS
1	CUP SLICED BANANAS
1/2	CUP PINEAPPLE BITS
1/2	CUP COCONUT, FRESH IF POSSIBLE
1/2	CUP MARASCHINO CHERRIES
1/2	CUP CHOPPED PECANS
1	CUP SUGAR

Assemble all ingredients and utensils. In a glass bowl, mix all ingredients thoroughly. Chill. Yield: 6 to 8 servings.

A holiday tradition in Tennessee.

Bing Cherry Salad

1   8 1/4-OUNCE CAN CRUSHED PINEAPPLE, DRAINED, RESERVING LIQUID
1   16-OUNCE CAN DARK PITTED CHERRIES, DRAINED, RESERVING LIQUID
1   6-OUNCE PACKAGE CHERRY-FLAVORED GELATIN
    JUICE FROM DRAINED LIQUID, PLUS ENOUGH WATER TO EQUAL 2 CUPS
8   OUNCES COCA-COLA
1/2 CUP CHOPPED PECANS

Assemble all ingredients and utensils. Drain juice from pineapple and cherries and reserve. Heat in a saucepan juice-water mixture to boiling and add gelatin to dissolve. Add drained pineapple, cherries, Coca-Cola and pecans. Pour mixture into a 9x9-inch square pan. Refrigerate until firm. Yield: 8 to 10 servings.

Another fruit salad: fresh peach halves filled with cottage cheese on lettuce, garnish with watercress.

Per serving: 167 calories; 4 g fat; 0 mg cholesterol; 57 mg sodium.

Orange-Mallow Salad

1   6-OUNCE PACKAGE ORANGE GELATIN
1   8-OUNCE CARTON SOUR CREAM
1   12-OUNCE CARTON WHIPPED TOPPING
1   11-OUNCE CAN MANDARIN ORANGE SECTIONS, DRAINED
1   CUP MINIATURE MARSHMALLOWS

Assemble all ingredients and utensils. In a bowl, combine orange gelatin and sour cream. Mix until dissolved. Fold in whipped topping. Lightly stir in Mandarin oranges and marshmallows. Chill at least 60 minutes. Yield: 8 servings.

For a fruit salad recipe that is quick and easy, try sliced oranges, red delicious apples, pears and mayonnaise dressing served over baby lettuce.

Per serving: 314 calories; 16 g fat; 13 mg cholesterol; 88 mg sodium.

Spiced Peach Salad

1   29-OUNCE JAR SPICED PEACHES, RESERVE JUICE
1   3-OUNCE PACKAGE LEMON GELATIN
1   ENVELOPE UNFLAVORED GELATIN, DISSOLVED IN 2
     TABLESPOONS WATER
1/2 CUP ORANGE JUICE
1   8 1/4-OUNCE CAN CRUSHED PINEAPPLE, DRAINED
3   TABLESPOONS ORANGE MARMALADE

Assemble all ingredients and utensils. In a saucepan, heat 1 cup peach juice and dissolve both gelatins in hot juice. Add orange juice. Cool slightly. Slice peaches; add to gelatin with pineapple and marmalade. Pour into a 1-quart mold or 8x8-inch square pan. Refrigerate until set. Yield: 8 servings.

Per serving: 136 calories; 0 g fat; 0 mg cholesterol; 40 mg sodium.

Grapefruit Mold

3   LARGE PINK GRAPEFRUIT, RESERVE JUICE
1 1/2 TABLESPOONS GELATIN
1   CUP COLD GRAPEFRUIT JUICE
1   CUP BOILING GRAPEFRUIT JUICE
3   TABLESPOONS LEMON JUICE
3/4 CUP SUGAR
3/4 CUP CHOPPED CELERY
1/2 CUP SLIVERED ALMONDS

Assemble all ingredients and utensils. Peel grapefruit and remove membrane. In a bowl, let gelatin soften in cold grapefruit juice; add boiling grapefruit juice, lemon juice and sugar. Allow gelatin to partially set before adding grapefruit, celery and almonds. Pour into a greased 1 1/2-quart mold or 8x8-inch square pan. Refrigerate until set and ready to use. Yield: 8 servings.

Hint: Use a small amount of mayonnaise to grease gelatin molds to help unmold the salad.

Per serving: 184 calories; 5 g fat; 0 mg cholesterol; 13 mg sodium.

THE LAST OF THE IRON MASTERS

When Montgomery Bell left his native Pennsylvania as a youngster, he was determined that he would someday become a wealthy man. He migrated to Tennessee, apprenticed himself to James Robertson, one of Nashville's co-founders, at Robertson's iron forges in present-day Dickson County, and commenced to learn the iron-master's trade. By 1804, the industrious Bell had bought Robertson out, and over the next few years, he established a number of iron mills throughout the western fringes of Middle Tennessee. Bell's favorite fur-

nace and iron works were located at the "Narrows" of the Harpeth River, in today's Cheatham County. Called Pattison Forge, the works were built to take advantage of a dramatic fall in elevation of the river from one side of a sheer cliff to the other. The river flows into a long bend at this spot, and although the water distance between the two points is several miles, the straight-line distance, through the solid rock of the cliff, is only a couple of hundred feet. With slave labor, Bell and his workmen dug and blasted a tunnel through the rock, taking a full year to complete the task. When the tunnel was completed the water from the upstream side, some fifteen feet higher, rushed through the giant hole to the low side at a speed of more than 2,500 cubic feet per minute. The fast-moving water developed enough energy to turn a giant wheel, which in turn, operated the forge equipment. In 1865, Bell bequeathed the money to establish Montgomery Bell Academy in Nashville.

COUNTRY MUSIC'S FIRST CROSSOVER

Today, when one style of melody is oftentimes confused with another, some older people can still remember when music was classified into rather straight-forward categories, such as country, popular, classical, jazz, rock, etc. But recent years have also experienced many so-called "crossovers" in the music industry wherein an artist of one genre switches to another style, Ray Charles singing country, for example.

One of the first crossovers in the history of country music was Eddie Arnold. Arnold, whose mellow-sounding, smooth voice captured

CHESTER COUNTY

the hearts of millions in the 1940s and 1950s, was born in Henderson, Tennessee, in 1918, to a sharecropper family. After teaching himself to play music on a Sears-Roebuck mail-order guitar, young Arnold joined Pee Wee King's Golden West Cowboys band as a singer. In 1944, with quite a following of his own, Arnold, now dubbed the "Tennessee Plowboy," began to sing on Nashville's WSM radio station and soon started making records for RCA Victor. By 1947, the Chester County native had sold nearly three million records, a staggering number during those days. With the assistance of Colonel Tom Parker, who later became Elvis Presley's manager, Arnold made a successful crossover from a purely country image to one that appealed to a more urbane audience, one interested primarily in popular music. For a while, he appeared on his own national TV show. In 1966, Eddie Arnold was elected to the Country Music Hall of Fame.

Festive Cranberry Salad

3	CUPS COARSELY GROUND CRANBERRIES
1/2	CUP CHOPPED PECANS
1	CUP SUGAR
1	8 1/4-OUNCE CAN CRUSHED PINEAPPLE, DRAINED
1	CUP FINELY CHOPPED CELERY
2/3	CUP DICED RED DELICIOUS APPLE, UNPEELED
1	3-OUNCE PACKAGE RASPBERRY GELATIN
1	CUP BOILING WATER

Assemble all ingredients and utensils. In a bowl, combine cranberries, pecans, sugar, pineapple, celery and apples. Dissolve gelatin in the 1 cup boiling water in a saucepan. Add the dissolved gelatin mixture to the bowl of cranberry and nut mixture. Pour into a 9-cup mold or an 8x8-inch pan. Refrigerate until ready to serve. Yield: 9 to 12 servings.

For a festive fruit salad recipe: wedges of honeydew melon wrapped with thinly sliced to shaved prosciutto ham. Enjoy!

Per serving: 152 calories; 3 g fat; 0 mg cholesterol; 32 mg sodium.

Pineapple-Olive Salad

1	16-OUNCE CAN PINEAPPLE CHUNKS, DRAINED, RESERVING JUICE
	WATER TO MAKE 2 CUPS LIQUID
1	6-OUNCE PACKAGE LEMON GELATIN
1	2-OUNCE JAR SPANISH OLIVES, SLICED
1/4	CUP CHOPPED GREEN PEPPER
2	TEASPOONS WORCESTERSHIRE SAUCE
3	TABLESPOONS LEMON JUICE
1	TABLESPOON GRATED ONION

Assemble all ingredients and utensils. Drain pineapple and reserve juice. Add enough water to reserve juice to fill 2 cups. In a saucepan, put liquid and add gelatin. Bring to a boil. Chill until partially set. Stir in remaining ingredients. Pour into a 1-quart mold or an 8x8-inch pan. Refrigerate until ready to serve. Yield: 8 servings.

Per serving: 170 calories; 1 g fat; 0 mg cholesterol; 325 mg sodium.

Brenda Lee's Pretzel Salad

1 1/2	CUPS CRUSHED PRETZELS
1/2	CUP GRANULATED SUGAR
1/2	CUP MELTED MARGARINE
1	8-OUNCE PACKAGE SOFTENED CREAM CHEESE
1	9-OUNCE CONTAINER COOL WHIP
1/2	CUP POWDERED SUGAR
2	SMALL PACKAGES STRAWBERRY GELATIN
1	CUP CRUSHED PINEAPPLE
1	16-OUNCE PACKAGE (1 POUND) FROZEN STRAWBERRIES (1 QUART)

Assemble all ingredients and utensils. Combine crushed pretzels, sugar, and margarine and spread in a 9x13-pan. Bake for 10 minutes in a 325-degree oven. Set aside to cool. Blend cream cheese, Cool Whip, powdered sugar and spread on pretzel layer. Dissolve gelatin in 2 cups hot water. Drain pineapple. Stir pineapple and frozen strawberries into gelatin. When thickened slightly, pour over mixture. Keep refrigerated. Can be made a day ahead. Yield: 9 to 12 servings.

*B*RENDA SUGGESTED I CALL HER SISTER-IN-LAW, PAT SHACKLETT, FOR THIS RECIPE SO IT WOULD BE EXACT. I SPENT DAYS CALLING PAT'S HOME PHONE, CODE-A-PHONE, AND CAR PHONE. AT LAST, HERE IS THE RECIPE, AND IT IS DELICIOUS. SOME FOLKS SERVE THIS SALAD AS A DESSERT.

Miss Daisy

Three Bean Salad

1	16-OUNCE CAN CUT GREEN BEANS, DRAINED
1	16-OUNCE CAN KIDNEY BEANS, DRAINED
1	16-OUNCE CAN CUT YELLOW WAX BEANS, DRAINED
1	MEDIUM ONION, THINLY SLICED
1/2	CUP CHOPPED GREEN PEPPERS

Dressing

1/2	CUP SUGAR
1/2	CUP APPLE CIDER VINEGAR
1/3	CUP VEGETABLE OIL
1	TEASPOON SALT
1	TEASPOON BLACK PEPPER

Assemble all ingredients and utensils. Rinse beans well, drain. In a large bowl combine beans, onion and green pepper. Combine remaining ingredients and add to bean mixture. Mix well and refrigerate several hours. Yield: 8 to 10 servings.

Many different combinations of beans will work in this recipe. Keeps well refrigerated for several days.

Per serving: 163 calories; 7 g fat; 0 mg cholesterol; 430 mg sodium.

Amy Grant's Easy Chopped Salad

Amy wrote me a little note on her recipe card that said "This sounds too simple to try when you're looking for something new—but trust me— its a hit!"

Miss Daisy

Chop and toss:

1	HEAD ICEBERG LETTUCE
10	LEAVES FRESH BASIL
2	TOMATOES

Sprinkle generously with Parmesan cheese and fresh ground pepper. Toss salad generously with dressing: Good Seasons Italian Mix Packet, made with olive oil and balsamic vinegar.

Corn Salad

Of the many food products indigenous to Tennessee, corn is the winner because of its versatility. This salad helps prove my point.

Miss Daisy

2	12-OUNCE CANS WHITE OR YELLOW WHOLE KERNEL CORN, DRAINED, OR FRESH COOKED CORN
4	GREEN ONIONS, CHOPPED
1	LARGE TOMATO, CHOPPED
2	TABLESPOONS MAYONNAISE
1/2	TEASPOON SALT
1/2	TEASPOON GROUND BLACK PEPPER

Assemble all ingredients and utensils. Drain corn. Chop onion and tomato. Combine corn, onion and tomato in a bowl. Stir in mayonnaise and salt and pepper. Yield: 8 servings.

Per serving: 97 calories; 3 g fat; 2 mg cholesterol; 386 mg sodium.

GATEWAY TO THE WEST

Mountains have always been a hindrance to colonization. When Virginia and North Carolina settlers cast their eyes toward the sunset, ready to act upon the tales of fine land and abundant game that could be found hundreds of miles to the west, their dreams were immediately dampened by the presence of the towering Appalachian Mountains. Sure, the lone explorers and long hunters could negotiate the forest wilderness and heights of the mountains, but how could families— women, children, livestock, and wagons—get through to the paradise that lay beyond? These settlers were lucky, for at a spot in Claiborne County, near the meeting of the

CLAIBORNE COUNTY

present-day states of Tennessee, Kentucky, and Virginia, there occurred a natural passageway through the mountains. Discovered in 1750 by Dr. Thomas Walker, the opening was called Cave Gap, and Dr. Walker wrote in his journal that it "may be seen at a considerable distance, and there is no other, that I know of, except one about two miles to the North of it. . . . " This was the famous Cumberland Gap, which eventually provided the entranceway for pioneer families moving into Kentucky and Tennessee. After Richard Henderson purchased several million acres of land lying between the Kentucky and Cumberland Rivers from the Cherokees in 1775, he sent Daniel Boone and a company of axmen to blaze a trail across the mountains through Cumberland Gap. It was this thoroughfare, the Wilderness Road, that carried thousands of emigrants to the promised land of the West.

Green Pea Salad

2	10-OUNCE PACKAGES FROZEN GREEN PEAS, THAWED
1/2	SMALL ONION, CHOPPED
1/2	CUP CHOPPED CELERY
3/4	CUP SOUR CREAM
1/4	CUP CUBED CHEDDAR CHEESE
1	2-OUNCE JAR PIMENTO, DRAINED AND SLICED

Assemble all ingredients and utensils. Thaw green peas. In a bowl, combine all ingredients and refrigerate several hours before serving. Yield: 8 servings.

Quick and easy salad or side dish.

Per serving: 116 calories; 6 g fat; 13 mg cholesterol; 97 mg sodium.

Picnic Potato Salad

1	POUND POTATOES, BAKING OR NEW, 3 CUPS COOKED
1	CUP CHOPPED GREEN PEPPER
1	CUP CHOPPED CELERY
1	CUP CHOPPED PIMENTOS
1/2	CUP DICED SWEET PICKLES OR DRAINED SWEET PICKLE RELISH
2	HARD COOKED EGGS, CHOPPED
1	TEASPOON SALT
1	TEASPOON BLACK PEPPER
1/2	CUP MAYONNAISE
1/4	CUP SOUR CREAM

Assemble all ingredients and utensils. Peel and cube potatoes. In a large pot, cook potatoes until tender. Cool. In a bowl combine remaining ingredients except mayonnaise and sour cream. Combine with cooled potatoes then fold in mayonnaise and sour cream gently. Chill before serving. Yield: 6 to 8 servings.

For a low-fat version use low-fat mayonnaise and non-fat sour cream; just as delicious.

Per serving: 213 calories; 14 g fat; 80 mg cholesterol; 499 mg sodium.

Mrs. Grissom's Salads

Grace Grissom was born in Meigs County, Tennessee. After working briefly in Oak Ridge with Southern Railway Company, she married. Herbert and Grace Grissom moved to Nashville in 1952. The Grissoms

kept in contact with a couple in Knoxville that was developing a small company of salad spreads called "Mrs. Weaver's." Grace and Herbert bought half interest in that company and eventually moved the operation to Nashville. Later, as sole owners of the company, the Grissoms changed the name to "Mrs. Grissom's."

Grace took care of all the business from a small converted eaterie on South Second Street in East Nashville. She and her crew prepared chicken salad, coleslaw and potato salad. They filled the containers and marketed the products themselves.

By the mid 1950s, people began to "eat on the go" more. TV dinners and "instant" foods became popular. Grocery chains began to order Mrs. Grissom's salads regularly. By 1959, larger facilities were needed and the company moved to its present site on Bransford Avenue.

AN EARLY MEDICAL JOURNAL

As the year 1890 began, Clay County physician James Talley-rand McColgan was putting the finishing touches on a new periodical to be distributed among Tennessee's medical community. Entitled *The Country Doctor,* the weekly journal was published at the now-forgotten town of Arcot, nestled in the forested hill country of Clay County. Dr. McColgan proudly proclaimed in the first issue of the journal, which appeared on January 29, 1890, that "We call it *The Country Doctor* because we have very high appreci-

CLAY COUNTY

ation and regard for the hard worked and poorly paid country and village practitioner. And though he is the equal of his city brothers, and in most subjects their interests are identical; still, there are subjects of interest to him, owing to his surroundings, in which the city physician has little or no interest." The magazine sold for one dollar per year. After four years of continuous publication, it became a monthly. Finally, in 1899, it went out of business altogether. At its inception, *The Country Doctor* was one of only seven weekly medical journals published in the entire United States. In some cases, the material that Dr. McColgan provided his readers was far ahead of its time. In an early issue, for example, his prophecies were eerie. He wrote, "The great sanitary problem of the future is the disposal of the sewerage of our large cities in some other or better manner than furnish it to our next neighbor below [downriver] to drink."

Wilted Spinach and Orange Salad

1	POUND FRESH SPINACH, WASHED AND DRIED
8	GREEN ONIONS, CHOPPED
3	ORANGES, PEELED, CUT INTO BITE-SIZE PIECES
8	SLICES BACON
3	TABLESPOONS BACON DRIPPINGS
3	TABLESPOONS VEGETABLE OIL
3	TABLESPOONS LEMON JUICE
1	TABLESPOON SUGAR
1/2	TEASPOON SALT

Assemble all ingredients and utensils. Stem spinach and tear leaves into bite-sized pieces. Toss with green onions in a salad bowl. Fry bacon in a skillet, reserve drippings. Crumble and set aside. Mix 3 tablespoons drippings, lemon juice, oil, sugar and salt in a saucepan. Bring to a boil and pour over spinach and green onions. Add orange pieces and bacon. Toss again and serve immediately. Yield: 6 to 8 servings.

Serve this salad with Brunswick Stew (*see* p. 57) and Sally Lunn Bread (*see* p. 248).

Per serving: 176 calories; 13 g fat; 11 mg cholesterol; 301 mg sodium.

Tomato Aspic

4	ENVELOPES UNFLAVORED GELATIN
1/2	CUP WATER
4	CUPS TOMATO JUICE
3	TABLESPOONS LEMON JUICE
2	TEASPOONS SALT
1	TEASPOON ONION JUICE
1/8	TEASPOON CAYENNE PEPPER
1/4	CUP SLICED STUFFED OLIVES
4	STALKS CELERY, CHOPPED FINELY

Assemble all ingredients and utensils. Let gelatin stand in 1/2 cup water for 10 minutes. In a double boiler, add tomato juice, lemon juice, salt, onion juice, and cayenne pepper; bring to a boil. Add olives and celery. Pour into a 1 1/2-quart mold or an 8x8-inch pan. Refrigerate until congealed. Yield: 8 servings.

Per serving: 47 calories; 1 g fat; 0 mg cholesterol; 1189 mg sodium.

Sweet and Sour Slaw

1	MEDIUM CABBAGE, SHREDDED
1	LARGE GREEN PEPPER, CHOPPED
1	MEDIUM ONION, CHOPPED
1	CUP SUGAR
1	CUP APPLE CIDER VINEGAR
2/3	CUP VEGETABLE OIL
1	TEASPOON SALT
2	TABLESPOONS SUGAR
1	TEASPOON DRY MUSTARD

Assemble all ingredients and utensils. In a bowl, combine shredded cabbage, green pepper, and onion; pour sugar over mixture. In a saucepan, combine remaining ingredients and bring to a full boil. Pour over cabbage mixture. Cover and refrigerate at once. Chill for several hours, before serving. Yield: 10 to 12 servings.

Excellent slaw for your favorite picnic or tailgate party.

Per serving: 207 calories; 12 g fat; 0 mg cholesterol; 192 mg sodium.

Creamy Slaw

1	MEDIUM CABBAGE
1/2	MEDIUM WHITE ONION
1	TEASPOON SALT
1/2	TEASPOON BLACK PEPPER
1/4	TEASPOON DILL SEED
1	CUP MAYONNAISE
1/4	CUP WHITE VINEGAR

Assemble all ingredients and utensils. Shred cabbage very fine. Slice onion very fine and separate rings. In a bowl, toss together; add salt, pepper and dill. Sprinkle sugar over mixture. Combine mayonnaise and vinegar; pour over cabbage mixture. Toss. Chill until ready to serve. Yield: 8 to 10 servings.

Enjoy this recipe with catfish or barbecue and hush puppies.

Per serving: 183 calories; 18 g fat; 13 mg cholesterol; 355 mg sodium.

AMERICA'S NIGHTINGALE

It is a long way from the forested slopes of Cocke County's Appalachian Mountains to the Metropolitan Opera, but one native made it and became one of America's most popular singers along the way. Grace Moore was born in a small cabin near the village of Del Rio in 1901. She later moved to Jellico, then Nashville, where she attended Ward-Belmont College. Later, Grace studied music in Washington, D. C. and New York City, before she was "discovered" by the great playwright and songwriter, George M. Cohan. Cohan per-

COCKE COUNTY

suaded the talented young Tennessean to enter musical comedy. She did and quickly landed a role in Hitchcock's review *Hitchy-Koo.* In 1926, Grace left musical comedy and traveled to Europe where she studied with Richard Barthélemy in Paris for two years. After performing in France with the American-German Opera Company, she returned to the United States in 1928 and debuted as Mimi in the Metropolitan Opera's production of *La Bohéme.* Following a four-year stay at the Met, Miss Moore tried her hand in Hollywood, and appeared in several motion pictures, including *New Moon, Love Me Forever,* and *One Night of Love.* She then toured England before returning to the Metropolitan in 1934. Credited with doing much to popularize opera in the United States, the forty-five-year-old soprano was at the height of her career when she was killed in an airplane crash near Copenhagen, Denmark, in January 1947.

Yarrow Acres' Hot Tarragon and Basil Chicken Salad in Puff Pastry

1	10 3/4-OUNCE CAN CREAM OF CHICKEN SOUP (UNDILUTED)
1/2	CUP MARGARINE
1/4	CUP MILK
1	TABLESPOON LEMON JUICE
1/2	TEASPOON SALT
1	TABLESPOON CHOPPED FRESH BASIL
1/2	TABLESPOON CHOPPED FRESH TARRAGON
3	HARD COOKED EGGS, CHOPPED
3	CUPS CHOPPED COOKED CHICKEN
1	CUP COOKED RICE
1	8-OUNCE CAN SLICED WATER CHESTNUTS, DRAINED
1	2-OUNCE JAR DICED PIMENTO, DRAINED
1/2	CUP CHOPPED CELERY
1/4	CUP CHOPPED GREEN ONIONS
1/4	CUP SLIVERED ALMONDS

Mix first 7 ingredients, stir until blended then add next 8 ingredients, stir well, heat until bubbly and then simmer slowly for about 10 minutes. Bake puff pastry shell according to package instructions. Fill shell just before serving. Yield: Filling for 8 to 10 pastry shells.

Hot Chicken Salad

2	CUPS COOKED, DICED CHICKEN BREAST
2	CUPS DICED CELERY
3/4	CUP MAYONNAISE
1/2	CUP TOASTED ALMONDS
2	TABLESPOONS FINELY CHOPPED ONION
2	TABLESPOONS LEMON JUICE
1/2	TEASPOON SALT
1	CUP GRATED MILD CHEDDAR CHEESE
1	CUP CRUSHED POTATO CHIPS

Assemble ingredients and utensils. In a large bowl mix first seven ingredients. Place in a 2-quart casserole dish. Top with cheese and potato chips. Bake in a 350-degree oven for 20 to 25 minutes. Yield: 6 servings.

Per serving: 500 calories; 41 g fat; 76 mg cholesterol; 586 mg sodium.

Chicken and Fruit Salad

2 1/2 TO 3 CUPS COOKED DICED CHICKEN BREASTS
1   CUP CHOPPED CELERY
2   TABLESPOONS CHOPPED GREEN ONION
1   TEASPOON SALT
2   TABLESPOONS LEMON JUICE
1   11-OUNCE CAN MANDARIN ORANGES, DRAINED
1   8-OUNCE CAN PINEAPPLE CHUNKS, DRAINED
1/2 CUP TOASTED CHOPPED PECANS
1/2 CUP MAYONNAISE
     FRESH MINT FOR GARNISH

Assemble all ingredients and utensils. In a bowl, combine chicken, celery and green onion. Mix in salt and lemon juice; cover and chill for 2 hours. When ready to serve add the oranges, pineapple and pecans. Mix in mayonnaise gently. Yield: 6 servings.

Chicken Salad is especially delicious with Miss Daisy's Cooked Dressing for Chicken Salad (*see* p. 46).

Per serving: 368 calories; 24 g fat; 70 mg cholesterol; 534 mg sodium.

JFG Coffee Company

The JFG Coffee Company originated in Morristown, Tennessee, as a wholesale grocery in 1882. The company began selling green coffee to stores in Knoxville. Around the late 1890s, Jefferson Franklin Goodson, the company's founder, began purchasing roasted whole bean coffee from an old coffee company in New York for his personal use. This blend was to become the basis for what is known today as JFG's Special Blend. In 1924, JFG moved operations to Knoxville and began using the slogan: "JFG—The Best Part of the Meal." By 1926, the company began

producing peanut butter, and in 1927, it introduced mayonnaise as well.

Dubbed "the first truly modern instant coffee plant in the South," JFG opened its instant coffee plant in 1959 on Mynatt Avenue in Knoxville. This paved the way for expansion with tea production in 1965. That same year, the company was sold to William B. Reily and Company, Inc.

Through the years, JFG has had extensive growth and continues today with distribution into eleven states. The company employees know many consumers still consider JFG as "The Best Part of the Meal."

THEORIES ABOUT OLD STONE FORT

Ever since the first Anglo-American settlers arrived in Coffee County almost two hundred years ago, the question, "Who built the Old Stone Fort?" has been asked. Theories for its origins range from twelfth-century Welshmen to the Ten Lost Tribes of Israel, to the predecessors of the American Indians. Despite the fact that the prevalent scientific view suggests that the large, enclosed fortifications were built in the early years of the Christian era by Woodland Indians, old beliefs die hard and, on occasion, one still hears serious talk

COFFEE COUNTY

about other sources being responsible for its construction. The most popular theory has always been that the followers of a Welsh nobleman named Madoc, while wandering through Middle Tennessee after a shipwreck in the Gulf of Mexico around 1170, built the fort as protection from marauding Indians. But, in mid-1966, University of Tennessee archaeologists performed the most comprehensive dig to date at the fort, and their findings prove beyond a shadow of a doubt that prehistoric American Indians did indeed build the massive fortifications, possibly for use as a ceremonial center. The State of Tennessee now owns the site and several hundred surrounding acres and has developed it into a state historical park. Today, a well-groomed pathway wanders among the extensive ramparts, and although the real builders have been identified, one can almost see a lurking Welshman peering from behind the ancient walls.

Turkey Salad

3	CUPS DICED COLD TURKEY
1	CUP DICED CELERY
1/3	CUP MAYONNAISE
1	TABLESPOON FRESH LEMON JUICE
1	TEASPOON SALT
1/2	TEASPOON GROUND THYME
1/8	TEASPOON GROUND BLACK PEPPER
1/8	TEASPOON GARLIC POWDER

Assemble all ingredients and utensils. In a bowl, combine all ingredients and keep refrigerated until ready to serve. Yield: 6 to 8 servings.

Toasted slivered almonds make a tasty garnish for this salad.

Per serving: 151 calories; 9 g fat; 42 mg cholesterol; 365 mg sodium.

Festive Shrimp Mold

1	10 3/4-OUNCE CAN TOMATO SOUP
1	8-OUNCE PACKAGE CREAM CHEESE, SOFTENED
2	ENVELOPES PLAIN GELATIN
1/2	CUP COLD WATER
1	CUP MAYONNAISE
1	POUND COOKED SHRIMP, CHOPPED
1	CUP DICED (VERY FINE) CELERY
1/2	CUP DICED (VERY FINE) GREEN PEPPERS
1/4	CUP GRATED ONION

Assemble all ingredients and utensils. In a saucepan, heat tomato soup. Add cream cheese and stir until well blended. Soften gelatin in cold water. Add to soup mixture. Cool. Combine mayonnaise, shrimp, celery, green peppers and onion. Add to soup mixture. Pour into a lightly greased 1 1/2-quart mold. Refrigerate. Keep covered while refrigerated. Yield: 8 servings.

For a seafood mold: use a combination of cooked shrimp, lobster and scallops.

Per serving: 388 calories; 33 g fat; 157 mg cholesterol; 646 mg sodium.

Party Shrimp Salad

2	CUPS COOKED SHRIMP, FRESH OR FROZEN
1/2	CUP CHOPPED CELERY
2	TABLESPOONS GREEN ONIONS, CHOPPED FINELY
1	TABLESPOON DRAINED CAPERS
3/4	CUP MAYONNAISE
1	TEASPOON PREPARED HORSERADISH
1/2	TEASPOON SALT
1/2	TEASPOON BLACK PEPPER
	LEMON WEDGES
	TOMATOES, ARTICHOKES

Assemble all ingredients and utensils. In a large bowl combine all ingredients except lemon wedges and mix well. Refrigerate until ready to serve. Garnish with lemon wedges. Stuff in a cooked artichoke or fresh tomato. Yield: 6 servings.

Various additions for Shrimp Salad may be: cucumber, chives, parsley, water chestnuts or grated egg.

Per serving: 299 calories; 23 g fat; 164 mg cholesterol; 593 mg sodium.

Tea Room Tuna Salad

1	7-OUNCE CAN ALBACORE WATER-PACKED TUNA, DRAINED
1/2	CUP CHOPPED CELERY
1/2	CUP MAYONNAISE
1/3	CUP SWEET PICKLE RELISH, DRAINED
2	TABLESPOONS LEMON JUICE
2	HARD BOILED EGGS, CHOPPED

Assemble all ingredients and utensils. In a bowl, combine all ingredients and mix gently. Refrigerate until ready to serve. Yield: 6 servings.

Delicious served in a fresh tomato, an avocado wedge or your favorite pastry shell.

Per serving: 218 calories; 17 g fat; 114 mg cholesterol; 370 mg sodium.

A VALLEY FORGE VETERAN

Thomas Conyers, Sr. was eighty-eight years old in 1845, when he moved from Middle Tennessee to a farm located between present-day Alamo and Hales Point in Crockett County. What a tiring trip it must have been for the Revolutionary War veteran to make during those early days when travel conditions in backwoods Tennessee were less than ideal. When he arrived at his new home, Conyers was more than likely the only surviving ex-soldier of the Revolution in those parts. He had joined the Continental Army in 1776, and he had spent the horrible

CROCKETT COUNTY

winter of 1777 with the rest of General George Washington's ragtag army at Valley Forge, Pennsylvania. During the months ahead, while Washington and his commanders plotted the following spring's campaign, the men of the army, including Conyers, suffered from hunger and severe frostbite. Supplies were practically non-existent, and Washington wrote, "To see men without clothes to cover their nakedness, without blankets to lie on, without shoes for want of which their marches might be traced by the blood from their feet, is proof of patience and obedience which in my opinion can scarce be paralleled." Three thousand of Conyers' companions died from lack of food and medical supplies, and from exposure before the spring thaw. No doubt, old Tom Conyers thought about that horrible winter many times and told the story over and over to his new neighbors, before he died just two years after arriving at his new home.

Buttermilk Salad Dressing

1	CUP MAYONNAISE
1	CUP SOUR CREAM
1	TABLESPOON MINCED ONION
2	TABLESPOONS CHOPPED FRESH PARSLEY
1	TABLESPOON CHOPPED FRESH CHIVES
1/2	TEASPOON SALT
1/2	TEASPOON GROUND BLACK PEPPER
1/2	TEASPOON CELERY SALT
1/4	TEASPOON GARLIC POWDER
1	CUP BUTTERMILK

Assemble all ingredients and utensils. In large bowl of mixer combine all ingredients except buttermilk. Slowly stir in buttermilk. Chill before serving. Yield: 3 cups.

For a lower fat version, try low-fat mayonnaise and non-fat sour cream.

Per serving: 188 calories; 19 g fat; 20 mg cholesterol; 279 mg sodium.

Cucumber Dressing

2	CUPS MAYONNAISE
1	CUP CHOPPED ONION
1	CUP SLICED CUCUMBER, PEELED AND SEEDED
1/8	TEASPOON GARLIC POWDER
2	TABLESPOONS LEMON JUICE
1/4	TEASPOON SALT
1/8	TEASPOON WORCESTERSHIRE SAUCE

Assemble all ingredients and utensils. Combine all ingredients in a blender and blend. Refrigerate until ready to use. Yield: 4 cups.

A variation of this recipe: Increase mayonnaise to 2 1/2 cups and add 1/2 cup champagne for Champagne Cucumber Dressing.

Per serving: 202 calories; 22 g fat; 16 mg cholesterol; 191 mg sodium.

Milky Way Farm House Dressing

1/4	CUP VINEGAR
1	SMALL ONION FINELY CHOPPED
1	CUP OIL
3/4	CUP SUGAR
1	TABLESPOON WORCESTERSHIRE SAUCE
1/2	CUP CATSUP

Assemble all ingredients and utensils. Blend well.

Salad ingredient suggestions: instead of iceberg lettuce use 1/2 spinach and 1/2 Romaine lettuce; toppings may include shredded Swiss cheese, shredded carrots; chopped eggs; crumbled bacon.

Oil and Vinegar Dressing

2	CUPS SALAD OIL
2/3	CUP APPLE CIDER VINEGAR
2/3	CUP SUGAR
1	TEASPOON DRY MINCED ONION
1	TEASPOON DRY MUSTARD
1	TEASPOON PAPRIKA

Assemble all ingredients and utensils. Combine all ingredients in blender. Blend for 5 to 7 minutes. Refrigerate until ready to use. Yield: about 4 cups dressing.

Per serving: 138 calories; 14 g fat; 0 mg cholesterol; 0 mg sodium.

Milky Way Farm

In Pulaski, Tennessee, there is a historic mansion with twenty-one bedrooms and twelve baths situated among the largest privately owned stand of magnolias in the nation!

The beautiful Milky Way Farm mansion was built in 1932 by Frank C. Mars, the founder of Mars Candy Company. "The Candy King" chose Giles county as the spot for his estate that was to be recognized as one of the top five farms in the nation. In its heyday, Milky Way Farm consisted of 2,700 acres and thirty-eight barns. It produced prize-winning cattle and horses of the highest quality—even a Kentucky Derby winner!

This Tudor mansion is now open to the public for tours and delicious luncheons served in old-world style at the twenty-eight-foot-long by twelve-foot-wide dining table. The table is the largest privately owned dining table in Tennessee and one of the largest in the nation!

Milky Way Farm is prepared to host a variety of special events, overnight stays, receptions, weddings, reunions and celebrations.

The "Forever Yours" shoppe is also available for collectibles and gifts. The farm that kept jobs viable in the area during "Depression days" still shines near Pulaski.

Poppy Seed Dressing

2/3	CUP SUGAR
1	TEASPOON DRY MUSTARD
1	TEASPOON PAPRIKA
1/2	TEASPOON SALT
1/4	CUP HONEY
3	TABLESPOONS LEMON JUICE
3	TABLESPOONS APPLE CIDER VINEGAR
2	TEASPOONS GRATED ONION
1	CUP SALAD OIL
2	TABLESPOONS POPPY SEEDS

Assemble all ingredients and utensils. Combine first 4 ingredients in a bowl. Add honey, lemon juice, vinegar and onion. Stir well. Pour into a blender container. Cover and blend on high speed 1 minute. While blender is running, slowly pour in oil through opening in cover. Blend. Remove cover and stir in poppy seeds. Pour into a container and refrigerate until ready to use. Yield: 1 pint.

Per serving: 358 calories; 28 g fat; 0 mg cholesterol; 135 mg sodium.

A must dressing for any kitchen! Helen Corbitt, the proprietress of The Zodiac Room Restaurants of the Neiman-Marcus Stores, shared this recipe with me in 1979.

Miss Daisy

Tomato Dressing

1	10 3/4-OUNCE CREAM OF TOMATO SOUP
3/4	CUP VINEGAR
3	TABLESPOONS LEMON JUICE
1	TABLESPOON SUGAR
2	TEASPOONS SALT
1/4	CUP FINELY CHOPPED ONION
1/8	TEASPOON GARLIC POWDER
	SALAD OIL, ABOUT 1 1/2 CUPS

Assemble all ingredients and utensils. Combine first 7 ingredients in a quart jar and fill with oil. Shake well. Yield: 1 quart.

Per serving: 200 calories; 21 g fat; 0 mg cholesterol; 399 mg sodium.

*T*omato Dressing will keep indefinitely in the refrigerator. For Marinated Carrots: add cooked sliced carrots and chopped green pepper to the dressing recipe.

Miss Daisy

Saddle Restaurant
Salad and Dressing

Tear up lettuce and add slices of hard boiled eggs, Swiss cheese, and small green onions. For the dressing: mix the following ingredients in blender or with rotary beater. Add olive oil last.

1/3	CUP WINE VINEGAR
2/3	CUP OLIVE OIL (POMPEII IN CAN)
1	TABLESPOON PREPARED MUSTARD
	SALT TO TASTE
1	TEASPOON ACCENT
	PAPRIKA TO COLOR

Shelbyville's Saddle Restaurant was always a favorite with Walking Horse Celebration folk.

Walking Horse Hotel's
Special Thousand Island Dressing

1	8-OUNCE PACKAGE CREAM CHEESE
1	PINT SOUR CREAM
3/4	CUP CATSUP
1/4	CUP CIDER VINEGAR
1/4	CUP SALAD OIL
1	TABLESPOON WORCESTERSHIRE SAUCE
1	TABLESPOON HORSERADISH
2	DASHES TABASCO SAUCE
1	CUP HELLMAN'S MAYONNAISE
1/2	CUP SWEET RELISH
1	TEASPOON PAPRIKA
	SALT AND PEPPER TO TASTE

Cream the cheese in a large mixing bowl; add sour cream, mixing well. Add remaining ingredients; mix well. Serve on lettuce or boiled shrimp salad. Yield: 1 quart.

Walking Horse Hotel

Wartrace, Tennessee, founded in 1851, rapidly grew into a thriving railroad community in the beautiful rolling hills of Middle Tennessee. The powerful steam locomotives would chug and whistle their way into town picking up and leaving passengers from all across the nation.

The hotel was built in 1917 by Jessie and Noral Overall. The "Hotel Overall" became known as the ultimate southern railroad inn. Floyd and Olive Carothers purchased the hotel in 1933. Floyd, one of Tennessee's finest equestrians, came upon a Tennessee Walking Horse named "Strolling Jim." Within months, Floyd and Strolling Jim were competing on the show circuit. In September 1939, the team won the World Grand Championship Honors at the first Walking Horse National Celebration. After winning the celebration, Floyd and Olive named their hotel "The Walking Horse Hotel."

In 1980, George Wright became the proprietor of the hotel. The hotel was sold in 1993 and closed shortly thereafter. The memory of this gracious place is still vivid in the memory of generations of Tennesseans.

For years the Cumberland Plateau has drawn immigrants from afar who were interested in making new beginnings in Tennessee. Part of the region's appeal has been its lush agricultural conditions. An editorial that appeared in the September 6, 1894, issue of the local Crossville newspaper gives additional information about the qualities of Cumberland County. "The August crop report of the Bureau of Agriculture shows that notwithstanding the protracted drouth, the main crop of corn, cotton, millet, and sorghum are very nearly up to

CUMBERLAND COUNTY

the average condition. . . . With good crops, cheap fuel, and ideal climate, and the coming revival of our manufacturing industries, the South is today better prepared to welcome the coming industrious immigrants from the drouth stricken fields of the west and northwest than ever before. No portion of the South can present greater inducements than the Cumberland Plateau. Here in Cumberland County we have a soil especially addapted [sic] to fruits and vegetables, and a county which will be rapidly developed by the new railroads which will place our farmers within reach of the best northern markets. We have cheap lands, good schools, low taxes, a moral, law-abiding population, a climate unsurpassed for healthfulness, and a county rich in natural resources. New settlers find a warm and hospitable welcome, and will be aided in every way in making their new homes. Cumberland County cordially invites you to come and share her coming prosperity."

Miss Daisy's Cooked Dressing for Chicken Salad

2	TABLESPOONS BUTTER
2	EGGS, SEPARATED
2	TABLESPOONS SUGAR
2	TABLESPOONS VINEGAR
1/2	TEASPOON SALT
1/2	PINT HEAVY CREAM, WHIPPED

Assemble all ingredients and utensils. Melt butter, add beaten egg yolks, salt, and sugar. Add vinegar, a drop at a time to butter mixture, stirring constantly. Place in double boiler, stir and cook until thickened. Cool, add beaten egg whites. Before using, fold in whipped cream.

Yogurt Salad Dressing

1	CUP PLAIN YOGURT
1/2	CUP MAYONNAISE
1	TABLESPOON FINELY CHOPPED PARSLEY
2	TEASPOONS MINCED FRESH CHIVES
1	TEASPOON LEMON JUICE

Assemble all ingredients and utensils. Combine all ingredients in a deep bowl and mix well. Refrigerate several hours before serving. Yield: 1 1/2 cups.

Per serving: 156 calories; 15 g fat; 13 mg cholesterol; 131 mg sodium.

You'll be amazed how good this dressing is on green salad or tomatoes. Also delicious as a raw vegetable dip.

SOUPS
AND
SANDWICHES

*Over the years since I left home,
I have kept thinking
about the people I grew up with
and about our way of life.
I realize how much the
bond that held us had to do
with food.*

Edna Lewis

Soups and Sandwiches

SOUPS

Black Bean Soup 49
Chicken Soup 50
Chicken Vegetable Soup 50
Corn Chowder 51
Garden Gazpacho 51
Dottie West's Peanut Soup 52
Cream of Potato Soup 52
Quick Okra Gumbo 53
Shrimp Bisque 53
Elvis Presley's Homemade Vegetable Soup 54
Tomato Basil Soup 54
Vichyssoise 55
Favorite Chili 55
Beef Stew 56
Brunswick Stew 57

SANDWICHES

Naomi & Wynona Judd's Corn Dogs 57
Crab Sandwiches 58
Egg Salad Party Sandwiches 58
Baked Ham Biscuit with Dressing 59
Cheddar Pecan Surprises 59
Cucumber Tea Sandwiches 60
Club Tomato Sandwiches 60

Black Bean Soup

1	POUND DRIED BLACK BEANS
1	POUND SPICY STUFFED SAUSAGE
3	LARGE ONIONS, CHOPPED
3	CLOVES GARLIC, CHOPPED
3	MEDIUM GREEN PEPPERS, CHOPPED
1/2	CUP OLIVE OIL
3	BAY LEAVES
1/4	TEASPOON BASIL
1	TABLESPOON RED WINE VINEGAR
1	TEASPOON SALT OR TO TASTE
1	TEASPOON GROUND BLACK PEPPER
1/8	TEASPOON CAYENNE PEPPER
	COOKED RICE, APPROXIMATELY 2 CUPS

Assemble all ingredients and utensils. Clean and wash beans. Place in large pot and cover with cold water. Add sausage cut into 1-inch slices and bring to a boil. Reduce heat to a simmer. Sauté vegetables in olive oil. Add to beans. Add bay leaves and basil. Cook until beans are tender, about 2 hours or longer. Remove 1 1/2 cups drained beans and combine with vinegar in blender or food processor. Blend until mixture forms a paste. Add paste back to soup pot along with salt, black pepper and cayenne pepper. Stir until well mixed. Serve warm over 1/4 cup of rice per serving. Yield: 8 to 10 servings.

Per serving: 312 calories; 12 g fat; 0 mg cholesterol; 217 mg sodium.

"SLAP LEATHER, YOU DIRTY COWARD"

Today, when the word gunfight is mentioned, we usually think of some primitive Western town, its dusty streets lined with saloons, and four or five Wyatt Earp-looking characters facing each other down over drawn six-shooters. But, even before there was a "Wild West," gunfights were being fought, and one of the most interesting ones ever recorded in American history occurred on Nashville's Public Square in September, 1813.

Andrew Jackson had liked Tom Benton ever since he became acquainted with the younger man shortly after his arrival in the Nashville area in 1801. When war broke out with Great Britain in

DAVIDSON COUNTY

1812, Jackson, by now a general in the U. S. Army, chose Benton to command a regiment of Tennessee infantry, and, as time passed, the two became even closer friends. During the summer of 1813, however, Benton learned that Jackson had recently taken sides against his

brother, Jesse Benton, in a duel. Jackson and Tom Benton exchanged angry words, and the fiery Jackson vowed that the next time he saw Tom, he would publicly horsewhip him. "Old Hickory" got his chance on September 4, 1813, when he and two nephews ran into the Benton boys on the Public Square in Nashville. Several shots were exchanged, Jackson was seriously wounded, and Tom Benton was ostracized to Missouri, where he eventually became a noted U. S. senator. Fortunately for history, Jackson and Benton later patched up their differences and often worked together on matters of national concern.

Mr. Kelly Williamson began Kelly Foods in a small building in his backyard. In 1938, he made potato salad and potato chips and delivered them "store to store" in the Jackson, Tennessee, area. Later, he sold pickles the same way.

Kelly Foods was incorporated in 1948. New products were canned vegetables and Brunswick Stew. Later, the "Kelly Man" also appeared on cans of chili and pork barbecue. The "Kelly Man" is a Leprechaun serving food from a kettle. This trademark is now known throughout the area within a 250-mile radius of Jackson—quite a way from Mr. Williamson's backyard!

Chicken Soup

1	2-OUNCE CAN OF SLICED MUSHROOMS
1	4-OUNCE JAR OF PIMENTOS, CHOPPED
1	#2 CAN OF GREEN PEAS
2	CANS OF MUSHROOM SOUP
1/2	CUP PARSLEY FLAKES
1	QUART OR MORE OF CHICKEN STOCK
6	POUNDS OF CHICKEN, COOKED AND CHOPPED
1	CUP LONG GRAIN RICE, COOKED AS DIRECTED USING BOUILLON CUBE (CHICKEN BOUILLON)
1	CUP CHOPPED ONION, SAUTÉED
1	CUP CHOPPED BELL PEPPER, SAUTÉED
1	CUP CHOPPED CELERY, SAUTÉED

Put all ingredients in pot using liquid from vegetables and chicken. Simmer 30 minutes. Makes 5 or 6 quarts. Freezes well.

Betty Elrod from Murfreesboro, Tennessee, submitted this recipe from her congressman's (Bart Gordon) mother.

Per serving: 101 calories; 3 g fat; 14 mg cholesterol; 603 mg sodium.

Chicken Vegetable Soup

1	MEDIUM CARROT
2	STALKS CELERY
1	MEDIUM GREEN PEPPER
1	MEDIUM YELLOW ONION
3/4	CUP CHOPPED COOKED CHICKEN BREAST
1/2	CUP PEELED CHOPPED APPLE
4	TABLESPOONS BUTTER
1/3	CUP ALL-PURPOSE FLOUR
2	WHOLE CLOVES
3	CUPS CHICKEN BROTH
1	CUP CHOPPED FRESH TOMATOES
2	CUPS WHOLE MILK
	FRESH PARSLEY FOR GARNISH

Assemble all ingredients and utensils. Chop carrot, celery, green pepper and onion. In a saucepan sauté in butter, stirring often. Add chicken and all ingredients, except milk. Simmer for 60 minutes. Add milk; bring to a boil; turn off burner and simmer for 10 minutes. Yield: 6 to 8 servings.

Per serving: 168 calories; 9 g fat; 35 mg cholesterol; 404 mg sodium.

Corn Chowder

1/4	CUP BUTTER
1	SMALL ONION, CHOPPED
1/2	CUP CHOPPED GREEN PEPPER
1	TABLESPOON ALL-PURPOSE FLOUR
1/2	CUP BEEF BROTH
1	16-OUNCE CAN CREAM STYLE CORN
1	14-OUNCE CAN DICED TOMATOES, DRAINED
1	TEASPOON SALT
1	TEASPOON SOY SAUCE
1	BEEF BOUILLON CUBE
1	16-OUNCE CAN WHOLE KERNEL CORN
1/2	CUP WHOLE MILK
1	GREEN ONION, CHOPPED

Assemble all ingredients and utensils. In a large saucepan or Dutch oven, sauté onion and peppers in butter until clear. Add flour and cook for 1 minute. Add next 7 ingredients. Bring to a boil and then simmer for about 20 minutes. Remove from heat and purée in blender or food processor. Return to heat and add corn, milk and green onion. Yield: 8 to 10 servings.

Per serving: 135 calories; 6 g fat; 14 mg cholesterol; 798 mg sodium.

Garden Gazpacho

1/4	CUP OLIVE OIL
2	TABLESPOONS LEMON JUICE
3	CUPS TOMATO JUICE
1	CUP BEEF BROTH
1/4	CUP FINELY CHOPPED ONION
1	LARGE FRESH TOMATO, CHOPPED
1	CUP CHOPPED CELERY
1/2	CUP CHOPPED, PEELED AND SEEDED CUCUMBER
1/2	CUP CHOPPED GREEN PEPPER
1	TEASPOON SALT
1	TEASPOON CHOPPED FRESH BASIL
1/2	TEASPOON FRESHLY GROUND BLACK PEPPER
1/8	TEASPOON TABASCO SAUCE

Assemble all ingredients and utensils. In a pot or bowl, combine oil and lemon juice. Slowly, mix in the remaining ingredients. Chill several hours before serving. Lasts for weeks in the refrigerator. Garnish with sour cream when serving. Yield: 4 to 6 servings.

Per serving: 120 calories; 9 g fat; 0 mg cholesterol; 947 mg sodium.

WHAT'S IN A NAME?

As one reviews a map of Tennessee, it is interesting to note all of the strange names that have been bestowed on villages, creeks, and towns. In many cases, names of now-extinct wildlife have been utilized, bearing testimony to the presence of these animals in bygone days. Buffalo River, Swan Creek, and Elkmont are just a few examples. Other features, especially counties, have been named after famous people such as Franklin, Sevier, and Decatur. Why the people of Decatur County, located in landlocked Tennessee, would name their entity after U. S. naval hero, Stephen

DECATUR COUNTY

Decatur, has been lost to history. Decatur, who rose to national prominence during the war with Tripoli in 1804, had died a quarter of a century before the establishment of Decatur County was even considered. Perhaps the name was chosen because the new county's location on the banks of the Tennessee River reminded some folks of the nation's water heritage. Two small communities in Decatur County are also strangely named. One of them, called Tie Whop, supposedly received its moniker when a resident fisherman drank to excess, became rowdy with crew members from passing steamboats, fought with them, and "whopped them over the head." The origin of the name of another village, Lick Skillet, goes back to the days when a starving hunter made his way into camp, only to find all of the food gone. He "licked the skillet," and the community that sprang up around the spot has been called Lick Skillet ever since.

Dottie West's Peanut Soup

1	CUP PEANUT BUTTER (SMOOTH)
6	CANS CHICKEN STOCK (CAMPBELL'S LIGHT ONES)
1/2	CUP DICED ONION
1/2	CUP DICED CELERY
1/2	PINT HEAVY CREAM
1	TABLESPOON CORNSTARCH
	BUTTER

*M*CMINNVILLE'S OWN
DOTTIE WEST ENJOYED COOKING.
SHE HAD AN ENORMOUS LIBRARY OF
COOKBOOKS. SHELLY, HER DAUGHTER,
SHARED THIS RECIPE OF DOTTIE'S.
Miss Daisy

In a large soup kettle, sauté onions and celery in butter until soft, not brown. Add cornstarch and stir for a couple of minutes. Add peanut butter and stir and then add chicken stock. Stir and bring to a boil. Pour through a sieve to strain celery and onions. Pour soup back into pot and add cream. Heat thoroughly, but do not boil. Serve immediately. Garnish with chopped, dry-roasted, unsalted peanuts.

Cream of Potato Soup

6	CUPS POTATOES, 5 LARGE
1/2	CUP SLICED CARROTS
6	SLICES BACON
1	CUP CHOPPED ONION
1/4	CUP CHOPPED CELERY
1 1/2	TEASPOONS SALT
1/2	TEASPOON GROUND BLACK PEPPER
2	CUPS WHOLE MILK
2	CUPS LIGHT CREAM
1	CUP SHREDDED, MEDIUM CHEDDAR CHEESE OR MORE
	FRESH PARSLEY, CHOPPED, ABOUT 2 TO 3 TABLESPOONS

*T*HIS SOUP IS A MEMBER OF
THE "COMFORT FOOD" CATEGORY.
IT SPIRITS THE SOUL AS WELL AS THE
STOMACH.
Miss Daisy

Assemble ingredients and utensils. In a pot, cook potatoes and carrots in boiling water until tender, drain. In a skillet, sauté bacon until crisp, drain and crumble, set aside. Sauté onion and celery in 2 tablespoons of the bacon fat. Add sautéed vegetables, salt, pepper, milk, cream and crumbled bacon. Cover and simmer for 30 minutes, but do not boil. Garnish with 2 or more teaspoons of cheddar cheese and fresh parsley. Yield: 8 servings.

Per serving: 339 calories; 21 g fat; 67 mg cholesterol; 630 mg sodium.

Quick Okra Gumbo

1	10 3/4-OUNCE CAN CHICKEN WITH RICE SOUP
1	CUP CHICKEN BROTH
1	16-OUNCE CAN WHOLE TOMATOES WITH JUICE
1	SMALL CAN TOMATO BITS WITH PEPPERS AND/OR ONIONS WITH JUICE
1	LARGE PACKAGE FROZEN OKRA, WHOLE OR SLICED
1/2	CUP CHOPPED ONION
1	TABLESPOON CHOPPED GREEN PEPPERS
1	TEASPOON SALT OR LESS TO TASTE
1	CUP UNCOOKED RICE

Assemble all ingredients and utensils. In a large pot, combine all ingredients and simmer over low heat for 1 1/2 hours. Yield: 8 to 10 servings.

Add cooked black-eyed peas or gumbo filé for an added accompaniment to this Gumbo.

Per serving: 86 calories; 1 g fat; 2 mg cholesterol; 635 mg sodium.

Shrimp Bisque

2	TABLESPOONS BUTTER
2	GREEN ONIONS, CHOPPED
2	TABLESPOONS ALL-PURPOSE FLOUR
2	CUPS WHOLE MILK
1	3 1/2-OUNCE CAN CREAMED CORN
1	4 1/2-OUNCE CAN SHRIMP, RINSED FOR ABOUT 5 MINUTES
1/4	TEASPOON WORCESTERSHIRE SAUCE
1/8	TEASPOON CAYENNE PEPPER

Assemble all ingredients and utensils. In a saucepan, melt butter and sauté onions. Add flour and mix. Add milk, stirring over heat until thickened. Add corn, shrimp, Worcestershire sauce and pepper. Heat to boiling point and then simmer for about 15 minutes. Yield: 4 to 6 servings.

Per serving: 131 calories; 7 g fat; 58 mg cholesterol; 165 mg sodium.

Graceland

Graceland, Elvis Presley's fourteen-acre walled estate, was a major Memphis attraction even in his lifetime. "The King of Rock and Roll" bought the twenty-three room mansion in March of 1957 for $100,000. It had been built in 1939 by Dr. Thomas Moore. Mrs. Moore's great aunt had been named Grace.

Elvis' remarkable career left him little time to spend at home. He left a twenty-year legacy of more than 650 recordings and 33 motion pictures. When home at Graceland, he considered it his definite refuge.

Perhaps one of the most startling exhibits at Graceland today is the Trophy Room which houses dozens of stage costumes, plaques, awards, photos and personal items. Several foreign record awards are also seen even though Elvis never did a live performance outside of the United States and Canada. Tourists today find the dining room across from the entry hall. Wedding china and silverware are carefully arranged on a huge mirrored table. Elvis used to have ten to twelve guests for dinner. He would usually eat around 9 or 10 P.M. One may imagine this talented man surrounded by family and friends in his Tennessee home, Graceland. Memphis proudly welcomes visitors to the site.

Elvis Presley's
Homemade Vegetable Soup

1	CAN WHOLE TOMATOES (OR TWO FRESH ONES)
2	POUNDS FRESH STEW MEAT
1	CUP CHOPPED BELL PEPPER
1	CUP CHOPPED CELERY
1	CUP CHOPPED ONION
5	PIECES OF GARLIC, FINELY CHOPPED
2	BOXES FROZEN MIXED VEGETABLES
2	CUPS DICED WHITE POTATOES
1	CAN CREAM STYLE CORN
1/2	CUP OKRA
1/2	CUP CATSUP
2	TABLESPOONS SALT
2	TABLESPOONS BLACK PEPPER

Cook together meat, onion, celery, bell pepper, garlic, and tomatoes for 1 1/2 hours. Add mixed vegetables for 1/2 hour. Then mix in corn, potatoes, okra, salt, and pepper. Cook for 30 minutes longer. Yield: 10 to 12 servings.

This recipe was prepared for Elvis by Mary Jenkins, one of his favorite cooks!

Tomato Basil Soup

8	BEEF BOUILLON CUBES
2	CUPS BOILING WATER
4	TABLESPOONS BUTTER, MELTED
4	LARGE FRESH TOMATOES, PEELED
6	STALKS CELERY, LEAVES REMOVED
2	TEASPOONS SALT
2	TEASPOONS BLACK PEPPER
1/2	TEASPOON CAYENNE PEPPER
	BASIL TO TASTE, OR 1 TABLESPOON

Assemble all ingredients and utensils. In a pot, combine bouillon cubes with the boiling water. Slowly mix in the remaining ingredients. Cover and simmer about 30 to 45 minutes. Remove celery stalks before serving. Yield: 4 servings.

Cheese sandwiches or cheese straws complement this soup.

Per serving: 43 calories; 3 g fat; 8 mg cholesterol; 820 mg sodium.

Vichyssoise

2   MEDIUM ONIONS, THINLY SLICED
1   CUP CHOPPED CELERY
3   TABLESPOONS BUTTER
4   MEDIUM-SIZED POTATOES, PEELED AND DICED
4   CUPS CHICKEN BROTH
2   CUPS LIGHT CREAM
1   TEASPOON SALT
1   TEASPOON BLACK PEPPER
2   TABLESPOONS FRESH CHIVES FOR GARNISH

Assemble all ingredients and utensils. In a large pot, sauté onions and celery with butter until tender, but not brown. Add potatoes and broth. Continue cooking until potatoes are tender. Purée in blender or food processor with salt and pepper added. Chill until ready to serve. Garnish with 1 teaspoon fresh chives per bowl of soup. Delicious served hot, also. Yield: 6 servings.

Per serving: 293 calories; 22 g fat; 68 mg cholesterol; 1457 mg sodium.

Favorite Chili

2 1/2   POUNDS LEAN GROUND BEEF
2   16-OUNCE CANS DICED TOMATOES, UNDRAINED
1   CUP CHOPPED ONION
1   CUP CHOPPED GREEN PEPPER
3   BLACK PEPPERCORNS
4   TABLESPOONS CHILI POWDER
2   BAY LEAVES
1/4   TEASPOON PAPRIKA
2   CUPS WATER
1   16-OUNCE CAN KIDNEY BEANS
1   16-OUNCE CAN PINTO BEANS
1/4   TEASPOON CAYENNE PEPPER
1/8   TEASPOON TABASCO SAUCE

Assemble all ingredients and utensils. In a very large skillet or saucepan, brown ground beef and drain very well. Add next 8 ingredients and simmer covered for 2 hours. Add beans and seasonings and simmer uncovered for another 50 to 60 minutes. Yield: 8 to 10 servings.

Per serving: 317 calories; 14 g fat; 68 mg cholesterol; 624 mg sodium.

HANGED BY THE NECK

Back in the old days, justice was harshly dispensed to criminals. There was no such thing as a convicted murderer spending eight or ten or more years on "death row," hoping that appeal after appeal might get him off the hook. Usually, within several days after judgement was passed on a felon, the sentence was carried out. Punishment in the case of murder or other serious crimes was hanging, while for lesser offenses, one might receive a public lashing and, perhaps, a branding on the cheek or hand. DeKalb County has on record only two public executions. One, involv-

DEKALB COUNTY

ing a slave named Jim, occurred on January 14, 1843. Jim had killed another slave named Isaac, and for the murder, he was hanged before a curious crowd in Smithville. The other hanging, which drew an unbelievable eight thousand spectators from far and wide, took place in May 1872. Seventeen-year-old John Presswood had visited the home of a neighbor, Jim Billings. When it appeared that Jim was not on the premises, Presswood attempted to take advantage of Mrs. Billings. Mrs. Billings, while trying to fight off her attacker, was brutally beaten, but remained healthy long enough to identify Presswood as the culprit. A week before he was sentenced to hang, Presswood found religion and was baptized. On May 24, his funeral was preached, he publicly confessed his crime, and he was hoisted from the gallows. Before the curious stares of thousands of onlookers on Smithville's public square he was hanged by the neck until he was dead.

Beef Stew

3	POUNDS ROUND STEAK OR STEW BEEF, CUT IN SMALL PIECES
1	CUP OR MORE ALL-PURPOSE FLOUR
2	TABLESPOONS VEGETABLE OIL
12	SMALL ONIONS, HALVED
1	CLOVE GARLIC
4	CUPS WATER
1	CUP TOMATO JUICE
6	MEDIUM CARROTS, CHOPPED
8	SMALL POTATOES, QUARTERED
1	CUP CHOPPED CELERY
2	TEASPOONS SALT
2	TEASPOONS GROUND BLACK PEPPER

Assemble all ingredients and utensils. Lightly flour beef. In a deep saucepan, brown beef in oil; add onions and garlic. Cook carefully about 10 minutes. Add water and tomato juice. Cover and simmer for 2 hours. Add vegetables and seasonings; cook an additional hour. Strain 1 cup juice from stew and thicken with 3 tablespoons flour. Stir back into the stew. Simmer about 15 to 20 minutes and serve. A great recipe for your crockpot. Yield: 8 to 10 servings.

Per serving: 506 calories; 25 g fat; 89 mg cholesterol; 537 mg sodium.

Arlington Brunswick Stew

According to Arlington's late town historian, Rachel H.K. Burrow, Brunswick Stew events were begun in 1930 by Jasper Brockwell and a group of Boy Scouts. Gardens around town were picked clean of vegetables, and canned items from previous crops were pulled from home shelves. Originally, rabbit was a key ingredient, but eventually the townspeople changed over to chicken. Annually, residents and former residents returned to the center of town near the old depot, dipped a ladle into big black pots, and enjoyed a heaping helping of stew. Though not done annually anymore, the event is held occasionally, always to the delight of present and former residents. Any opportunity to gather around a warm pot, chat with neighbors, and rekindle memories is a welcome time in small towns. Arlington is starting to change from small town to mini-city, but chances are the aroma of Brunswick Stew will continue to linger as a reminder of a simpler time in small-town Tennessee.

BRUNSWICK STEW

Cook chicken and beef, cubed, about three pounds each for a crowd; reserve broth. Remove chicken from bones and return to broth with beef. Add one large onion, sliced, three pints of tomatoes, one pint of lima beans, one pint of corn, and four large white potatoes, diced. Add salt and pepper to taste and one small red pepper pod, if you like. Cover, simmer, and stir frequently for as long as you like, but for at least one hour. Add a stick of butter and melt it into broth just before serving.

Brunswick Stew

1	6-POUND BAKING HEN
2	POUNDS CHICKEN BREASTS
3	QUARTS WATER
2	BAY LEAVES
4	SMALL ONIONS
1	TABLESPOON SALT
1	TEASPOON BLACK PEPPER
1	TEASPOON CAYENNE PEPPER
2	TABLESPOONS SUGAR
1	TABLESPOON WORCESTERSHIRE SAUCE
1	TEASPOON HOT SAUCE
2	10-OUNCE PACKAGES FROZEN SLICED OKRA
4	CUPS FRESH OR 2 (16-OUNCE CANS) TOMATOES
2	10-OUNCE PACKAGES FROZEN LIMA BEANS
2	16-OUNCE CANS CREAM STYLE OR CORN NIBLETS
1/2	CUP SHREDDED CABBAGE
3	MEDIUM POTATOES, PEELED AND DICED

Assemble all ingredients and utensils. Cut chicken into pieces and simmer in 3 quarts of water seasoned with bay leaves, onions, salt, black and red pepper, until meat can easily be removed from bones-about 2 1/2 hours. Remove chicken from broth; dice and set aside. Add vegetables, except potatoes, and seasonings to broth and cook slowly for 6 hours. Add diced chicken and cook another hour. Thirty minutes before serving add potatoes and cook until potatoes are tender. This stew benefits from slow cooking. The flavor improves as it sets overnight and is reheated. Yield: 12 to 16 servings.

Per serving: 243 calories; 3 g fat; 57 mg cholesterol; 450 mg sodium.

Naomi & Wynona Judd's Corn Dogs

1	EGG
1/2	CUP MILK
1	CUP BUTTERMILK BAKING MIX
2	TABLESPOONS CORNMEAL
1/4	TEASPOON PAPRIKA
1/2	TEASPOON DRIED MUSTARD
1/8	TEASPOON PEPPER
8 TO 10	FRANKFURTERS
	OIL FOR DEEP FRYING

Combine first 7 ingredients in bowl; mix well. Coat frankfurters with batter. Fry in hot oil in skillet until brown; drain. Yield: 4 servings.

AN EARLY ATTEMPT AT SOCIALISM

As the nineteenth century rushed to a close, several groups across the United States experimented with socialism as a way of life among their democratic neighbors. The teachings of the English social theorist, John Ruskin, were in vogue at the time. Although socialism was far from being a new discipline throughout the world, Julius A. Wayland, a resident of Indiana who published a socialist newspaper called *The Coming Nation,* decided to try to organize a successful following in Tennessee. The spot selected by Wayland and his twenty-

DICKSON COUNTY

five colonists was a thousand acres of Dickson County land near today's town of Tennessee City. They arrived in July 1894, and promptly established the Ruskin Co-operative Association, each member purchasing one share of the organization for $500. After nearly two years of attempting to farm the rocky hillsides in the area, the group moved to another plot of land on Yellow Creek, located about five miles north of the old farm. There, the Ruskin colony flourished, and before long, its members boasted a sawmill, bookstore, schoolhouse, library, barbershop, and printing office for their newspaper. Another attraction on the new site was a large cave (today's Ruskin Cave) where women stored fruits, vegetables, and dairy products. By 1899, when it disbanded due to internal dissention among its members, the Ruskin colony had grown to three hundred followers and was one of the more successful socialist experiments in the United States.

EDD WINFIELD PARKS
A CRITIC'S CRITIC

Over the years, many "literary" types—men and women—have hailed from Tennessee. Andrew Lytle, Donald Davidson, Mary Noilles Murfree, and T. S. Stribling are just a few. All of these writers have left a rich heritage upon which future authors must continuously build. One of the state's most distinguished writers was Edd Winfield Parks. Parks, born in 1906 in the small town of Newbern in Dyer County, not only excelled in his own writing achievements, but he was recognized as a leading literary critic as well. Parks attended school

DYER COUNTY

at Occidental College, Harvard University, and Vanderbilt. He taught English at Vanderbilt while he worked on his Ph.D., and later, from 1935 until his death in 1968, he served at the University of Georgia, where he ultimately became Distinguished Professor of English. He was a Fulbright lecturer in Brazil and Denmark and saw duty as a U. S. State Department lecturer in several South American countries. Called by some of his peers the "dean of Southern literary scholarship," Parks was also a writer, some of his works being *Sidney Lanier: The Man, The Poet, The Critic,* and *Edgar Allan Poe as Literary Critic.* One of Dr. Parks's lesser-known books, published when he was thirty-one years old, was a novel entitled *Long Hunter: The Story of Big-Foot Spencer.* The book was a realistic depiction, although fictionized, of the long hunter's life and times during his early exploration of Middle Tennessee.

Crab Sandwiches

12	SLICES THIN SLICED, CRUSTS REMOVED, BUTTERED BREAD, USING 4 TABLESPOONS SOFTENED BUTTER
1	7 1/2-OUNCE CAN CRABMEAT, FLAKED AND DRAINED
1/2	POUND CHEDDAR CHEESE, GRATED
4	EGGS, BEATEN
3	CUPS WHOLE MILK
1/2	TEASPOON SALT
1/2	TEASPOON CURRY POWDER

Assemble all ingredients and utensils. Place 6 slices bread, buttered side up, in a buttered 13x9x2-inch baking dish. Spread crabmeat and cover with remaining 6 slices. Place cheese on top. Combine eggs, milk and seasonings and pour over sandwiches. Bake in a 325-degree oven for 50 to 60 minutes or until puffy and brown. Yield: 6 servings.

Try the Pineapple-Olive salad recipe (*see* p. 32) with this sandwich.

Per serving: 489 calories; 30 g fat; 292 mg cholesterol; 914 mg sodium.

Egg Salad Party Sandwiches

1	CUP FINELY CHOPPED PECANS
2	HARD-COOKED EGGS, FINELY CHOPPED
1	2-OUNCE BOTTLE SPANISH OLIVES, DRAINED AND FINELY CHOPPED
1	TABLESPOON MINCED ONION
1	CUP MAYONNAISE
16	SLICES SANDWICH BREAD, CRUSTS REMOVED, HALF WHITE-HALF WHOLE WHEAT

Assemble all ingredients and utensils. In a bowl, combine pecans, egg, olives, onion and mayonnaise; mix well. Chill. Spread filling on 8 slices of bread; top with remaining slices. Cut into thirds. Yield: 24 finger sandwiches.

Egg Salad may also be used as a stuffing for cherry tomatoes.

Per serving: 144 calories; 12 g fat; 17 mg cholesterol; 191 mg sodium.

Baked Ham Biscuit With Dressing

1/4	CUP BUTTER, MELTED
6	TABLESPOONS MAYONNAISE
3	TABLESPOONS PREPARED MUSTARD
1	TEASPOON SUGAR
1/2	TEASPOON WORCESTERSHIRE
	POPPY SEEDS, OPTIONAL
	BAKED HAM, ABOUT 1/4 POUND
	BISCUITS, ABOUT 10 OR 12
	CHEESE, GRATED, ABOUT 1/4 POUND

Assemble all ingredients and utensils. In a saucepan, melt butter and remaining ingredients except ham and biscuits and your favorite cheese. Slice or chip enough baked ham to fill a biscuit (great way to use leftover ham). Grate or slice enough of your favorite cheese. Spread dressing over bottom of biscuit; add ham and cheese. Cover with top of biscuit. Place in a baking pan. Cover with foil and bake in a 350 degree oven for 5 to 10 minutes or until heated. Serve hot! Yield: about 10 to 12 biscuits.

Original recipe was written in a narrative form from one of my Grandmother's cookbooks. I have given it modern language for easier preparation.

Per serving: 245 calories; 18 g fat; 29 mg cholesterol; 481 mg sodium.

Cheddar Pecan Surprises

1	CUP SHREDDED SHARP CHEDDAR CHEESE
1/2	CUP MAYONNAISE
1/3	CUP CHOPPED PECANS
1	TABLESPOON FINELY CHOPPED ONION
3	STRIPS WELL-COOKED BACON, CRUMBLED
8	ENGLISH MUFFINS OR 16 BREAD SLICES

Assemble ingredients and utensils. In large bowl of mixer, combine and mix all ingredients except bread. Refrigerate for an hour before spreading. Yield: about 2 cups.

Great served as hot toasted sandwiches or appetizers (makes 16).

Per serving: 170 calories; 10 g fat; 13 mg cholesterol; 291 mg sodium.

IN THE NATION'S SPOTLIGHT

In many parts of the United States, the decade of the 1960s was one of violence, misunderstanding, and hatred. Civil rights was the political issue in the forefront of the news, and an entirely new generation of Americans dedicated themselves to correcting all of the wrongs that had been perpetrated upon black people in the South for the past several hundred years. But just as determined were factions on the other side who preferred the status quo and were ready to resort to any measure to keep it. During the 1960s, integration

FAYETTE COUNTY

was the law, but in many places, it was still not being practiced. Because Fayette County's population during the 1960s was about evenly divided between blacks and whites, the federally imposed edict of integration of all public schools was particularly difficult to implement. A federal court suit filed in 1959 charged that many blacks, although registered at the polls, were still not allowed to vote. College students from New York, calling themselves "freedom riders," descended upon Fayette County and mounted a campaign to force local officials to register black citizens. Even the FBI was called in to look into charges that black tenant farmers had been thrown out of their homes by white landowners. National attention focused on the county, and its residents soon found themselves under the glaring scrutiny of the news media. Peace and tolerance gradually returned to Fayette County, and today, it is difficult to visualize that the troubles of the 1960s were ever present.

A TENNESSEE FARM BOY IN FRANCE

Young Alvin York was always known around his hometown of Pall Mall to be an expert shot with a rifle. When he was growing up in Fentress County during the late 1890s, he often trudged through the woods hunting deer or wild turkey. Nearly every time, he returned home with his prize. Although he was too young to serve his country during the Spanish-American War, he was one of the first to volunteer when the United States went to war with Germany in April, 1917. York served in the 328th Infantry Regiment of the 82d Division,

FENTRESS COUNTY

sometimes called the "All American" division. He had attained the rank of corporal when he was sent to France with his unit. There, during heavy fighting with the Germans in the Argonne Forest in early October, 1918, the thirty-one-year-old York found himself in command of his platoon, when three other non-commissioned officers were disabled. Surrounded by the enemy, York and seven other men charged and knocked out a German machine gun nest. During the blistering battle, twenty-five German soldiers were killed. Four German officers and 128 enlisted men were captured by York and returned to the American lines as prisoners of war. For his daring feat, York was presented the Congressional Medal of Honor, the nation's highest award, as well as France's most prestigious military award, the Croix De Guerre. After the war, York returned to Pall Mall and, several years later, he was immortalized in a movie starring Gary Cooper.

Cucumber Tea Sandwiches

1/2	SMALL ONION, COARSELY CHOPPED
2	8-OUNCE PACKAGES CREAM CHEESE, SOFTENED
1	LARGE CUCUMBER, PEELED, SEEDED AND COARSELY CHOPPED
1/2	TEASPOON SALT
1/4	TEASPOON GROUND WHITE PEPPER
1/2	TEASPOON MINCED FRESH DILLWEED
80	SLICES BREAD (40 WHOLE WHEAT AND 40 WHITE) CRUSTS REMOVED AND THIN SLICED

Assemble ingredients and utensils. In food processor combine onion, cream cheese and cucumber. Process until smooth. Add seasonings and mix. Make sandwiches with filling: whole wheat bread on bottom and white on top. Cut sandwiches into thirds. Yield: 120 rectangular sandwiches.

Per serving: 46 calories; 2 g fat; 5 mg cholesterol; 85 mg sodium.

Club Tomato Sandwiches

2	MEDIUM-SIZED FRESH TOMATOES
12	SLICES WHITE BREAD
1/2-3/4	CUP MAYONNAISE
2	TEASPOONS OR TO TASTE GRATED ONION
3/4	TEASPOON SALT
1/8	TEASPOON WHITE PEPPER, OPTIONAL FRESH CHOPPED PARSLEY FOR GARNISH (ABOUT 2 TABLESPOONS)

Assemble all ingredients and utensils. Slice tomatoes crosswise into 12 pieces. Pat dry and set aside. With a biscuit cutter, cut 12 rounds from slices of bread; spread each one with combined mayonnaise, onion, salt and pepper. Place a tomato slice on each bread round. Garnish with fresh chopped parsley. Yield: 12 servings.

A tradition for weddings in Tennessee.

Per serving: 170 calories; 12 g fat; 9 mg cholesterol; 340 mg sodium.

ENTRÉES

*It is not the quantity of the meat,
but the cheerfulness of the guests,
which makes the feast . . .
where there is no peace,
there can be no feast.*

Earl of Clarendon

ENTRÉES

BEEF AND VEAL/LAMB

Family Spaghetti Sauce With Meat 63
Miss Daisy's Favorite Lasagna 64
Dinah Shore's Tennessee Lasagna 65
Pot Roast Meat Loaf 66
Barbecued Meat Loaf 67
Miss Daisy's Favorite Roast With Gravy 68
Beef Stroganoff 69
Spiced Corned Beef 69
Spiced Round 70
Standing Rib Roast 71
Music City Beef Casserole 71
Miss Daisy's Beef Casserole 72
Stuffed Peppers 72
Sam Davis Home
1871 Beefsteak With Onions 73
Cabbage Rolls 73
Oven Steak With Potatoes 74
Lemon Veal 74
Miss Daisy's Veal With Pecan Sauce 75
Red Grooms' Family Kusa 76
Miss Daisy's Mint Stuffed Leg of Lamb 76

PORK AND SAUSAGE

Overton Recipe for Sugar Curing Ham 77
Apple Cider Pork Chops 78
Oven Barbecued Pork Chops 79
Fettuccini Carbonara (Bacon or Ham) 79
Country Sausage 80
Sausage and Rice Casserole 81
Ralph and Joy Emery's Lasagna 82
Scrapple 82
Andrew Jackson's Favorite Pigs' Feet Pickled 83
Sweet and Sour Pork 83
Roast Pork With Currant Mustard Sauce 84
Pit Barbeque Sauce 85
Glazed Ribs 85

POULTRY AND GAME

Barbecued Chicken 86
Easy Fried Chicken 86
Chicken Enchiladas 87
Baked Chicken Breasts With Wild Rice 87
Chicken Almond Casserole 88
Hot Chicken Salad Casserole 88

Alex Haley's "Chicken George"
Chicken and Dumplings 89
Miss Daisy's Make-Your-Own Chicken Stock 89
Grandmother's Chicken and Dumplings 90
Macaroni With Chicken,
Tennessee Ham and Truffles 91
Carnton Chicken Croquettes 92
Chicken Livers Over Toast Points 92
Miss Daisy's Creamed Chicken 93
Animaland's Big John Chicken 94
Chicken Pot Pie 95
McCord Family Orange Chicken 95
Hope Family Fondue of Chicken 96
Hot Chicken Soufflé 97
Tipper Gore's Spiced Roast Chicken 98
Minnie Pearl's Chicken Tetrazzini 99
Miss Daisy's Turkey Divan 100
Turkey Tetrazzini 101
Baked Cornish Hens 101
John Sevier's Braised Doves 102
Duck Breasts Over Wild Rice 102
Betty Blanton's Smothered Quail 103
Baked Squirrel Pot Pie 103
Shawnee Broiled Venison Steak 104
Ames Plantation Venison Stew 104

FISH AND SHELLFISH

Baked Fish With Shrimp Sauce 105
Carl's Catfish 106
John Egerton's Pan Fried Catfish 107
Bucksnort Trout 108
Sour Cream Tuna Casserole 108
Blount Mansion "Made" Dish of Crabmeat 109
Company Crab Cakes 109
Honey Alexander's Crab Victoria 110
Fried Oysters 110
Parson's Table Salmon Cashew 111
Deep Fried Salmon Puffs 112
Party Salmon Steaks 112
Broiled Scallops 113
Seafood Casserole 113
Seafood Gumbo 114
Grilled Marinated Shrimp 115
Creole Shrimp 115
Storytelling Shrimp Gumbo 116

Family Spaghetti Sauce With Meat

2	TABLESPOONS OLIVE OIL
3	CLOVES GARLIC, MINCED
1	LARGE GREEN PEPPER, CHOPPED
1	WHITE ONION, CHOPPED
1	POUND FRESH MUSHROOMS, SLICED
1	POUND GROUND ROUND STEAK
1	POUND SAUSAGE WITH SAGE
2	16-OUNCE CANS ITALIAN PLUM TOMATOES
2	6-OUNCE CANS TOMATO PASTE
2	TABLESPOONS MINCED FRESH PARSLEY
1	TABLESPOON SALT
1	TEASPOON BLACK PEPPER
3/4	CUP RED WINE
	COOKED SPAGHETTI
	GRATED FRESH PARMESAN

Assemble all ingredients and utensils. In a heavy skillet or Dutch oven heat olive oil and sauté garlic, green pepper, onion and mushrooms until tender. In another, brown ground round and sausage; drain thoroughly. Add beef and sausage back to vegetable mixture. Add next 5 ingredients and simmer for 2 hours. Stir wine in during the 2 hours. Serve over cooked spaghetti; sprinkle with Parmesan. Yield: 10 to 12 servings.

Per serving: 492 calories; 18.8 g fat; 53 mg cholesterol; 1072 mg sodium.

A KNIGHT IN SHINING ARMOR

Today, when one thinks of knights in shining armor, images of King Arthur and his knights of the Round Table are conjured up, or maybe, Richard the Lion-hearted, doggedly returning home from the Holy Land. But, once upon a time, Tennessee had its own knight. He was a quiet, humble man who was born in Franklin County in 1832. His name was Francis Joseph Campbell. When he was a mere lad, Francis was blinded, but had to wait until he was ten or twelve years old, when the Tennessee Legislature established a school for blind students in Nashville, to pursue his education. It is said that after arriving at the new

FRANKLIN COUNTY

facility, young Campbell learned the entire Braille alphabet within forty-five minutes. Several years later, when he graduated, he was at the top of his class. From Tennessee, Campbell traveled to Boston, where he taught music for a while, then on to England, where he co-founded and headed the Royal Normal College for the Blind. It was there, in 1909, that King Edward VII knighted Joseph, who at the time, was the only native-born Tennessean to ever be so honored. During his long career, Campbell is said to have been so successful in teaching music to blind students, that more than ninety per cent of them went on to become music instructors, musicians, and tuners of musical instruments. An advocate of rigorous outdoors activity, Sir Francis became the first—and as far as is known, the only—blind man to ascend Mont Blanc, the highest peak in the Alps.

THE KINGDOM OF "SKULLBONIA"

Most Tennesseans don't realize that a "kingdom" exists within the borders of our state. It's true, and it's called the "Kingdom of Skullbonia." Located in Gibson County, the kingdom has been around for a very long time, but it was not until 1953, that it was given "official" status by Governor Gordon Browning. In a proclamation, Browning declared that "in order to dispel any doubt about the wholesomeness and justified pride of a great region do hereby 'recognize' and proclaim the 'existence' of the Territory of Skullbonia down in

GIBSON COUNTY

West Tennessee—as a place of tradition and song and happiness, as a delightful place to live and a worthy successor to the rugged frontiersmen who built its early tradition." Skullbonia had its origins in the early part of the nineteenth century as the site where bareknuckles boxers from all over the region came to test their bloody skills on others of the same bent. However, special rules applied to the boxing here, specifically the one that outlawed all punches not made to the head. In time, the vicinity became known as "Skullbonia," due to this brutal custom. For some reason, residents of Skullbone, the "capital" of Skullbonia, have always been politically conservative. For example, locals cast their votes, two to one, against Franklin D. Roosevelt every time he ran for president, although the state at large usually reversed that vote and gave FDR a two-to-one margin.

Miss Daisy's Favorite Lasagna

1	CLOVE GARLIC, MINCED
1	MEDIUM ONION, CHOPPED
1/2	CUP CHOPPED CELERY
1/2	CUP CHOPPED GREEN PEPPER
1 1/2	POUNDS GROUND ROUND
1	TABLESPOON OLIVE OIL
1	6-OUNCE CAN TOMATO PASTE
1	8-OUNCE CAN TOMATO SAUCE
1	16-OUNCE CAN TOMATOES
1	TABLESPOON OREGANO
2	TEASPOONS BASIL
1/2	TEASPOON SALT
1/2	TEASPOON BLACK PEPPER
1/2	TEASPOON SUGAR
1	12-OUNCE PACKAGE LASAGNA NOODLES, COOKED AND DRAINED
1	8-OUNCE CARTON SOUR CREAM
1	16-OUNCE CARTON COTTAGE CHEESE
8	OUNCES MOZZARELLA CHEESE, GRATED GRATED PARMESAN CHEESE

Assemble all ingredients and utensils. In a big saucepan or Dutch oven, sauté garlic, onion, celery, green pepper and beef in olive oil. Add tomato paste, tomato sauce, tomatoes and seasonings and sugar. Simmer for 2 hours. Layer in a large 3-quart baking dish: noodles, sour cream, cottage cheese, meat sauce, and mozzarella. Repeat to make two layers. End with Lasagna noodles and top with Parmesan cheese. Bake in a 350-degree oven for 45 minutes. Yield: 10 to 12 servings.

This is a great recipe to double. You may serve half now and freeze the other half for later.

Per serving: 413 calories; 20 g fat; 91 mg cholesterol; 760 mg sodium.

Dinah Shore's
Tennessee Lasagna

Cook one, 1-pound package of elbow macaroni in salted water until just done.

1	POUND OF SHARP CHEDDAR CHEESE, CUT IN CUBES
	PARMESAN OR CHEDDAR CHEESE, GRATED

Sauce

2	POUNDS GROUND MEAT (GROUND CHUCK OR
	1 POUND GROUND CHUCK AND 1 POUND HOT
	ITALIAN SAUSAGE, IF YOU LIKE)
1	SMALL BUNCH OF CELERY, COARSELY CUT
2	CLOVES OF GARLIC, CHOPPED FINE
1	MEDIUM ONION, CHOPPED COARSELY
1	GREEN PEPPER, CUT IN BROAD STRIPS
6-8	WHOLE MUSHROOMS, SLICED THIN
4	CUPS TOMATOES (2 16-OUNCE CANS)
1	8-OUNCE CAN TOMATO SAUCE
	DASH OF WORCESTERSHIRE SAUCE
	PINCH OF OREGANO
1	TEASPOON CHILI POWDER
	RED PEPPER FLAKES
1/4	TEASPOON CUMIN

Brown onions and garlic in oil, then add celery and green pepper. Cook until a little soft. Remove from pan. Add ground meat to oil and brown well. After meat is browned, add salt, pepper, chili powder, cumin, Worcestershire sauce, oregano (easy on this), mushrooms, onions, garlic, celery and green pepper. Sprinkle with red pepper flakes. Add tomatoes and tomato sauce. Allow to cook slowly for one hour until sauce blends.

Assemble by putting a layer of macaroni in casserole; dot with butter, add cheese cubes and then a layer of the sauce. Sprinkle with red pepper flakes. Then another layer of macaroni, butter and cheese cubes, etc., finishing with a layer of sauce.

Top with grated Parmesan or cheddar cheese. Bake in a 350-degree oven for 30 minutes until cheese is melted inside and dish is thoroughly heated. This can be prepared ahead and reheated 30 minutes before serving. Yield: 10 to 12 servings.

Serve with crusty French bread.

IN HER OWN WORDS, WINCHESTER'S DINAH SHORE DESCRIBED THIS DISH BEST: "MY VERSION OF LASAGNA IS ONE OF THOSE DISHES THAT IS MOST USEFUL WHEN PEOPLE UNEXPECTEDLY DROP OVER AND YOU HAVE TO SUBSTITUTE SEVERAL INGREDIENTS TO MAKE IT STRE-EE-ETCH. ON ONE OCCASION I ADDED CHEESE. ON ANOTHER, MORE MACARONI. IT'S AN ECONOMICAL DISH, AND MY USUAL PRACTICE IS TO MAKE TWO AND PUT ONE IN THE FREEZER. THEN WHENEVER GUESTS DROP IN UNEXPECTEDLY, AS THEY SAY IN THE COMMERCIALS, I POP THE FROZEN ONE IN THE OVEN. WHAT'S MORE, TENNESSEE LASAGNA REHEATS WELL, AND IT'S GOOD THE SECOND DAY. REASSEMBLE IT IN A SMALLER CASSEROLE, SPRINKLE MORE CHEESE OVER THE TOP, ADD TOMATO JUICE IF YOU NEED IT, AND REHEAT SLOWLY AND THOROUGHLY. I'VE HARDLY EVER HAD A MORE ACCOMMODATING DISH." HOW PRACTICAL AND PERFECT FOR A TENNESSEE HOSTESS!

Miss Daisy

THE BROWN BOYS MAKE GOOD

Tennessee has had three governors by the name of Brown and all three of them have hailed from Giles County. Aaron Vail Brown, born in Virginia in 1795, was the first of the threesome, serving as a Democrat during the Mexican War. As a young man, Brown had served as Andrew Jackson's private secretary during the Creek War. Afterwards, he became a member of President James Buchanan's cabinet as postmaster-general. The other two Browns were brothers. Neill, a Whig, was born in Giles County in 1810. He served in the Seminole

GILES COUNTY

War and defeated Aaron Brown for the governorship in 1847. His administration was noted for his unsuccessful efforts to establish a public school system across Tennessee. Later, Brown was appointed to the position of minister to Russia, and in 1855, he became speaker of the Tennessee House of Representatives. Brown's younger brother, John, was also born in Giles County. He became a successful lawyer and when the War Between the States approached, he joined and served in the infantry, eventually rising to the rank of major-general. The younger Brown was more successful than his brother in obtaining a state-wide school system. In 1873, legislation passed that permitted individual county school superintendents, as well as for a tax, to pay for public schooling. John Brown served his state for two terms, from 1871 until 1875. When he retired, he went to work for the Texan Pacific Railroad and soon became the company's president. He died in 1889.

Pot Roast Meat Loaf

Loaf

1	POUND GROUND ROUND
2/3	CUP EVAPORATED MILK
1/3	CUP CRACKER CRUMBS
1/4	CUP CHILI SAUCE
2	TEASPOONS WORCESTERSHIRE SAUCE
1	TEASPOON SALT
1/4	TEASPOON BLACK PEPPER

Assemble all ingredients and utensils. In a large bowl combine thoroughly all ingredients. Shape into a loaf in center of baking pan.

Vegetables

3	MEDIUM ONIONS, PEELED
3	MEDIUM POTATOES, PEELED
3	MEDIUM CARROTS, PEELED
1	TABLESPOON DRIED PARSLEY FLAKES OR
1	TEASPOON CHOPPED FRESH PARSLEY
1	TEASPOON SALT
1/4	TEASPOON BLACK PEPPER

Slice onions and potatoes about 1/4 inch thick. Slice carrots lengthwise. Combine parsley, salt and pepper.

Arrange vegetables in layers around meat loaf. Sprinkle each layer with parsley mixture. Bake in a 350-degree oven for 50 to 60 minutes or until vegetables are tender. Uncover and bake 10 minutes more to brown meat. Yield: 6 to 8 servings.

To complete the menu, add your favorite fruit salad from the Salad section and the Quick Spoon Rolls (*see* p. 255).

Per serving: 203 calories; 7.8 g fat; 41 mg cholesterol; 763 mg sodium.

Barbecued Meat Loaf

2	POUNDS GROUND BEEF
1	CUP DRY BREAD CRUMBS OR CRACKER CRUMBS
1	MEDIUM ONION, FINELY CHOPPED
1	EGG, BEATEN
4	TABLESPOONS CATSUP
1/2	CUP WHOLE MILK
1	TEASPOON SALT
1/4	TEASPOON BLACK PEPPER

Assemble all ingredients and utensils. In a large bowl combine all ingredients thoroughly blending. Shape into one large loaf or 4 individual loaves. Prepare sauce and pour over loaves before baking.

Sauce

8	TABLESPOONS VINEGAR
8	TABLESPOONS DARK BROWN SUGAR
4	TABLESPOONS WORCESTERSHIRE SAUCE
1	CUP CATSUP
1/2	CUP CHOPPED ONION

In a saucepan, combine all ingredients and bring to a boil. Lower heat and simmer for 5 minutes. Pour over top of meat loaf. Bake meat loaf in a 350-degree oven for 50 to 60 minutes. Reduce cooking time if preparing small loaves. Yield: 8 to 10 servings.

Per serving: 322 calories; 14 g fat; 82 mg cholesterol; 782 mg sodium.

Serve this Meat Loaf and sauce over Ramsey House Mashed Potatoes (see p. 134). Yum—Real soul food! You will really love the barbecue sauce.

Miss Daisy

A BEAN BY ANY OTHER NAME

The proper name *Bean* is well-known in Tennessee. After all, it was William Bean who is considered to be the state's first resident, locating in present-day Washington County in 1769. But, there was also another Bean from the same general region, and although he is not so well known in Tennessee, he is a legendary figure in the state of Texas. Ellis Peter Bean, no doubt a relative of William's, was born in 1783 in present-day Grainger County. Early in his life, Bean followed an adventurous life, and by the time he was seventeen, he had already floated down the river system to Natchez, where he met Philip Nolan, a self-professed "mus-

GRAINGER COUNTY

tang" hunter. Nolan and others made a career out of traveling to the vast plains of Texas, which then was still under Spanish control, and capturing wild horses to sell back in the United States. In 1800, while on a trip to Texas with Nolan, Bean's party was surrounded by Spanish militamen who attacked and killed several of his companions, including Nolan. Bean was captured and eventually sent to Mexico where he was imprisoned for ten years. Five years later, the former Tennessean fought in the Battle of New Orleans with Jean Lafitte. After the War of 1812, he returned to Mexico, married a native woman, then returned to Tennessee to visit his brother in White County. There, he took a second wife, who divorced him in 1835. Bean eventually moved back to Mexico with his first spouse and lived with her until he died in 1846.

Miss Daisy's
Favorite Roast With Gravy

1	4-POUND BEEF ROAST, RUMP OR SIRLOIN
1	CLOVE GARLIC
1	TEASPOON SALT
1/2	TEASPOON GROUND BLACK PEPPER
3	SLICES BACON, SAUTÉED FOR DRIPPINGS
2	ONIONS, SLICED
2	CARROTS, SLICED
1	STALK CELERY, DICED
1	SPRIG PARSLEY
1	SPRIG THYME
1	BAY LEAF
1	CUP TOMATO PURÉE
2	CUPS RED WINE

A FOOL-PROOF ROAST RECIPE. IF YOU FOLLOW THE INSTRUCTIONS, YOU WILL HAVE A ROAST WHICH TASTES LIKE THE ONE YOUR MOTHER USED TO MAKE. THE ROAST MAKES ITS OWN GRAVY OR SAUCE.

Miss Daisy

Assemble all ingredients and utensils. Rub roast with garlic, salt and pepper. In a large pan sauté bacon. Remove bacon and reserve three tablespoons of drippings. Brown onions in bacon drippings in a large pot or Dutch oven. Remove onions and brown roast on all sides. Add vegetables and brown lightly. Return onions, parsley, thyme, bay leaf, tomato puree and red wine to roast and vegetables in Dutch oven or big pot. Cover and bake in a 350-degree oven for 3 1/2 to 4 hours or until tender. Add small amount of hot water, during baking if needed. Yield: 8 to 10 servings.

Per serving: 333 calories; 15.2 g fat; 99 mg cholesterol; 508 mg sodium.

KING OF THE WILD FRONTIER

Probably no American folk hero is more widely known than Davy Crockett. Made famous by word, song, movie, and television, an entire generation of children—both in the United States and abroad—grew up learning about the legendary Davy Crockett, who, of course, was "born on a mountaintop in Tennessee." Only the life and times of the real, historical David Crockett could be more interesting than his mythical counterpart.

The real Crockett was, indeed, born in Tennessee, although not exactly on a mountaintop, but rather near the confluence of Limestone Creek and the Nolichucky River in Greene County in 1786. Young Crockett, like most boys of his time,

GREENE COUNTY

received a limited education, and when he was old enough, he joined the state militia, later fighting with Andrew Jackson against the Creek Indians in Alabama. After he left Greene County, Crockett moved about the state quite a bit, living at one time or another in Jefferson, Lincoln, Franklin, Lawrence, Carroll, and Gibson Counties. He served in both the Tennessee Legislature and the United States House of Representatives as a Jacksonian Democrat. Later, he broke his ties with Jackson's party and ran for office as a member of the relatively new Whig party. When he lost his election for Congress in 1834, he migrated to Texas. There, at the Alamo in 1836, while "serving as a high private . . . the liberties of our common country," he was killed during the Texas Revolution defending the mission from the Mexican army.

Beef Stroganoff

1	CUP BUTTER, DIVIDED
1 1/2	CUPS FINELY CHOPPED ONIONS
1 1/2	POUNDS FRESH MUSHROOMS, SLICED
3	POUNDS TOP ROUND, SIRLOIN OR TENDERLOIN, CUT INTO SMALL PIECES
1	CUP ALL-PURPOSE FLOUR
3	CUPS BEEF BOUILLON
1	TEASPOON SALT OR MORE TO TASTE
2	TEASPOONS WORCESTERSHIRE SAUCE
1 1/2	CUPS SOUR CREAM
1	CUP HEAVY CREAM

Assemble all ingredients and utensils. In a large saucepan, sauté onions in 1/3 cup of butter until lightly browned. Remove and set aside. In same saucepan, sauté mushrooms in another 1/3 cup of butter. Remove and set aside. Dredge beef in flour and brown in remaining 1/3 cup butter. Add bouillon, salt and onions. Cover and simmer 1 1/2 hours or until beef is tender. Add tomato paste, Worcestershire sauce, sour cream, heavy cream and mushrooms. Heat thoroughly. Serve over noodles or rice. Yield: 10 servings.

Per serving: 601 calories; 43.8 g fat; 182 mg cholesterol; 742 mg sodium.

Try Steamed Artichokes with Tomatoes (see p. 120) along with the Stroganoff; a great complement to the dish.

Miss Daisy

Spiced Corned Beef

4 TO 5	POUNDS CORN BEEF BRISKET
	WATER
	WHOLE CLOVES
1/2	CUP BROWN SUGAR
1/4	CUP CHOPPED FINE BREAD CRUMBS
1/2	TEASPOON DRY MUSTARD
	GRATED PEEL AND JUICE OF 1 ORANGE
	GRATED PEEL AND JUICE OF 1 LEMON
1	CUP APPLE CIDER

Assemble all ingredients and utensils. In a large pot cover meat with cold water, bring to a boil and remove scum. Cover and simmer slowly 2 hours or until tender. Cool in cooking liquid. Place drained corned beef in baking pan; score with fat and stud with cloves. Combine brown sugar, crumbs, mustard and grated peels. Brush meat with crumb mixture. Place in 350-degree oven to brown lightly. Baste frequently with a mixture of the orange and lemon juices and cider. Continue baking 30 minutes or until completely heated. Yield: 8 to 10 servings.

Elegant dish to serve for a dinner party. May be prepared the day before and reheated.

Miss Daisy

Spiced Round

10 TO 12	POUNDS ROUND OF BEEF
1/4	TEASPOON SALT
1/4	TEASPOON PEPPER
2	CUPS BROWN SUGAR
2	CUPS SALT
1	TABLESPOON EACH: GROUND NUTMEG, GROUND GINGER, GROUND ALLSPICE, GROUND CINNAMON AND GROUND BLACK PEPPER
2	TEASPOONS CAYENNE OR RED PEPPER
3	POUNDS BEEF SUET

Assemble all ingredients and utensils. Rub each side of beef with 1/4 teaspoon salt and pepper. Let stand in cool place all night after covering with the 2 cups brown sugar and salt. Combine spices and red pepper. Cover the round of beef with the spices and let stand two weeks, turning each day. Keep in refrigerator. Grind beef suet and combine with juices which have run from the meat. Make gashes or holes through the meat and stuff with the suet. Add additional spices if you like. Tie meat in heavy pudding bag and boil 15 minutes per pound. Slice cold for buffets as an alternative to country ham or turkey.

Yield: This is enough to serve a party of 75 to 100 guests (2 ounces per serving).

Elm Hill Meats

In 1934, Robert Baltz entered the meat packing business when he was a teenager. His father had a farm on Elm Hill Pike in Nashville. Robert bought a sow and raised five pigs finding that "first sausage" experience difficult, but when he met Ed Unger, things

changed. Unger had the knowledge and equipment needed for beginning a sausage operation. In 1936, Ed processed the meat while Robert sold it. Robert "bought out" Ed, and then Robert Baltz, Sr. took out a loan on his farm to help further his son's interests. After World War II the family business included two of Robert's uncles, Will and Louis Baltz, as well. In 1946, Baltz Brothers Meat packing plant was founded. By 1960, a salesman mentioned that some customers had difficulty pronouncing and spelling Baltz, so Robert changed the company's name to Elm Hill Meats.

One Nashville holiday tradition is the Spiced Round. This unusual meat item's secret recipe has been handed down in the city for generations. It was part of the old Maxwell House Hotel Holiday Menu in 1879 and once was listed on Andrew Jackson's Christmas Menu at the Hermitage. Elm Hill Meats makes this delicacy available only during the holiday season.

Standing Rib Roast

1   STANDING RIB ROAST
    GARLIC POWDER, TO TASTE
    GROUND THYME, TO TASTE
    SALT, TO TASTE
    PEPPER, TO TASTE

Assemble all ingredients and utensils. Preheat oven to 500 degrees. Place roast beef fat side up in a shallow roasting pan. Sprinkle with garlic powder, thyme, salt and pepper. Place in oven, uncovered and immediately reduce heat to 350 degrees. Roast 18 to 20 minutes per pound for a medium-rare roast. Yield: The number of servings will depend upon the size of the roast and the number of ounces used for each serving.

To test meat for doneness, insert meat thermometer before roasting in center of thickest part of meat. Be sure not to touch the bone. Rare roast beef temperature, 120 degrees; medium rare, 140 degrees; medium, 145 to 150 degrees; well done, 155 to 165 degrees.

Per serving: 418 calories; 35 g fat; 93 mg cholesterol; 282 mg sodium.

Music City Beef Casserole

1   POUND GROUND ROUND, BROWNED AND DRAINED
4   SMALL BAKING POTATOES, PEELED AND SLICED
1   2-OUNCE CAN SLICED MUSHROOMS, UNDRAINED
1   8 1/2-OUNCE CAN GREEN PEAS, UNDRAINED
3   CARROTS, SLICED
3   STALKS CELERY, SLICED
1/2   CUP CHOPPED ONION
1   TEASPOON SALT
1   10 3/4 OUNCE CAN TOMATO SOUP

Assemble all ingredients and utensils. In a 3-quart greased casserole place all ingredients in layers. Pour the soup over top. Cover and bake in a 350-degree oven for 50 to 60 minutes. Optional: top with 1 cup grated cheddar cheese and brown for the last 10 minutes. Yield: 6 to 8 servings.

Per serving: 247 calories; 8 g fat; 34 mg cholesterol; 929 mg sodium.

WHEN THE COURTS WENT TO THE DOGS

It was with a measure of incredulity that Judge Sam Anderson peered over the makeshift table that served as his bench on that long-ago day in 1848. Judge Anderson was a circuit judge, and on this day he was hearing cases in Grundy County, just one of the towns in the Cumberland Mountains to which he must give his attentions. On this particular morning, the makeshift courtroom was filled to capacity with eight lawyers, forty witnesses, and a dog named "Sharp." Judge Anderson whacked his heavy gavel on the desk and announced that

GRUNDY COUNTY

court was in session. The first case for Judge Anderson and the jury to hear was an appeal to overturn an earlier decision by a local justice of the peace to award Sharp's owner with ten dollars for injuries sustained by Sharp by the other party's hounds. Testimony concerning the integrity of Sharp and the hounds was given for three days and the lawyers' arguments took four more. The hounds' lawyers suggested that since Sharp had been guilty of killing a sheep, he was fair game to anybody. Judge Anderson, however, cautioned the jury members that they should consider the possibility that Sharp might have just been hungry and that he might not be a natural sheep killer! After a full week of court action, the jury quickly returned with a verdict to award Sharp's master with $2.50. That was the good news. The bad news was that the court costs amounted to $320 to be shared by both parties! Both owners eventually went bankrupt over the case.

Miss Daisy's Beef Casserole

2	POUNDS GROUND ROUND
1	CUP DICED CELERY
3/4	CUP CHOPPED ONION
1/4	CUP DICED GREEN PEPPER
1	29-OUNCE CAN TOMATOES, NOT DRAINED
1	16-OUNCE CAN TOMATOES, NOT DRAINED
1	8-OUNCE CAN MUSHROOM PIECES, DRAINED
1	8-OUNCE CAN SLICED WATER CHESTNUTS, DRAINED
1	CUP CUBED AMERICAN PROCESSED CHEESE
1/2	CUP SLICED GREEN OLIVES
1/2	CUP SLICED BLACK OLIVES
1/2	CUP YELLOW CORN NIBLETS, OPTIONAL
1/2	TEASPOON SALT
1/2	TEASPOON BLACK PEPPER
1	6-OUNCE PACKAGE MEDIUM EGG NOODLES, UNCOOKED
2	CUPS SHREDDED CHEDDAR CHEESE

Assemble all ingredients and utensils. In a very large pan or Dutch oven brown beef. Drain any grease! Add celery, onions, green pepper and sauté. Add tomatoes and their juice. Add remaining ingredients except for the cheddar cheese. Simmer 20 minutes, stirring frequently. Pour into a 3-quart casserole dish. Spread cheddar cheese on top. Bake in a 350-degree oven for 30 minutes. Yields: 12 to 15 servings.

Per serving: 319 calories; 17.8 g fat; 69 mg cholesterol; 715 mg sodium.

*T*HIS WAS ONE OF MISS DAISY'S RESTAURANT'S FAVORITE RECIPES. THE CASSEROLE FREEZES WELL—A GREAT POT-LUCK SUPPER DISH. MY FRIEND LINDA FUSON FROM NASHVILLE, TENNESSEE, SHARED THIS RECIPE WITH ME. THE ORIGINAL NAME WAS *YUM YUM GOODIE*. FOR THE BENEFIT OF ALL THE MEN WHO ATE AT MISS DAISY'S RESTAURANT, I CHANGED THE NAME TO SOMETHING MORE GENERIC. AFTER TRYING THOUSANDS OF RECIPES OVER THE YEARS, I STILL CONTEND THIS IS THE BEST BEEF CASSEROLE EVER CONCOCTED!

Miss Daisy

Stuffed Peppers

6	LARGE GREEN PEPPERS, STEMS AND SEEDS REMOVED
1/2	POUND GROUND ROUND
1	CUP COARSE DRY BREAD CRUMBS
1	TABLESPOON CHOPPED ONION
1	TEASPOON SALT
1/4	TEASPOON BLACK PEPPER
1	10 3/4 OUNCE CAN TOMATO SOUP
1/2	SOUP CAN WATER

Assemble all ingredients and utensils. In a large saucepan, cook peppers in boiling water for 5 minutes, drain. Combine remaining ingredients except soup and water. Stuff peppers with meat mixture. Stand upright in a small baking dish. Pour soup and water combined over peppers. Bake in a 350-degree oven covered for 45 minutes. Uncover, bake 15 minutes longer. Yield: 6 servings.

Per serving: 199 calories; 6.7 g fat; 24 mg cholesterol; 940 mg sodium.

A DIFFERENT WAY TO USE A GROUND BEEF RECIPE. PREPARE THIS RECIPE IN THE SUMMER WHEN YOUR GARDEN IS FULL OF GREEN PEPPERS.

Miss Daisy

Sam Davis Home
1871 Beefsteak With Onions

Mrs. Andromedia Moore, a half-sister of Charles Lewis Davis, Sam Davis' father, would take a rump steak and pound it with a rolling pin until it is quite tender; flour and season. Put it into a frying pan of hot lard and fry it. When nicely brown on both sides take it up and dredge with flour. Having ready boiled about 2 dozen onions, strain them in a colander and put them into the frying pan, seasoning with pepper and salt; dredge in a little flour, and add a small lump of butter; place the pan over the fire and stir the onions frequently to prevent their scorching. When they are soft and a little brown, return steak to the pan and heat all together. Place the steak on a large dish, pour the onions and gravy over it and send to the table hot.

Cabbage Rolls

	CABBAGE LEAVES
1/2	POUND GROUND ROUND
1/3	CUP QUICK-COOKING RICE
2	TABLESPOONS MINCED ONION
2	TABLESPOONS PICKLE RELISH, DRAINED
1/2	TEASPOON SALT
1/4	TEASPOON BLACK PEPPER
1/8	TEASPOON CAYENNE PEPPER
1	10 3/4-OUNCE CAN TOMATO SOUP
1	SOUP CAN WATER

Assemble all ingredients and utensils. Cook cabbage leaves in boiling water for 2 minutes, drain. In a bowl, mix ground round, rice, onion, pickle relish and seasonings. Place 2 tablespoons of meat mixture into each leaf. Fold to enclose and fasten with toothpicks. Place in a deep pan. Add remaining soup and water. Cover and simmer 1 hour and 30 minutes. Yield: 6 servings.

Per serving: 132 calories; 4.7 g fat; 24 mg cholesterol; 700 mg sodium.

Sam Davis Home

Sam Davis (1842-1863) was born near Smyrna, Tennessee. In 1863, he was captured near Pulaski with critical Federal intelligence in his possession and was tried and found guilty of spying. Rather than reveal the identity of his associates, Davis bravely faced execution, his last words being, "If I had a thousand lives, I would lose them all before I would betray my friends or the confidence of my informer."

Today, the Sam Davis home has been restored to the way it was when young Sam lived there. Many of the house's furnishings as well as several outbuildings are original.

For years, Mildred Haun told folks she was born in Cocke County, Tennessee. Then, several decades later, she learned that she had actually come into the world at her grandmother's home in Hamblen County. But, regardless of place, Mildred went through life with a character molded and formed from the rigorous life led by her ancestors in Appalachia. As a teenager, she moved to Franklin, Tennessee, to live with an aunt and uncle, and she finished high school there. Later, she commuted to nearby Nashville to attend

**HAMBLEN
COUNTY**

Vanderbilt University, where she was influenced by some of Vanderbilt's Fugitive poets, including John Crowe Ransom and Donald Davidson. Mildred Haun wrote a series of short stories that had as their setting the mountains and valleys of East Tennessee. Part of the appeal of her writing was her ability to capture the language and peculiar dialects of the mountain people. The collection was published in 1940 by Bobbs-Merrill with the title, *The Hawk's Done Gone*. In the introduction to the reprint, issued by Vanderbilt University Press in 1968, Herschel Gower wrote, "No other dialect collection from the South has been as close to the oral tradition or has achieved the same distinctive flavor and natural tonal qualities." In later years, Mildred Haun reviewed books for the *Nashville Tennessean*, served as an editorial assistant for the *Sewanee Review*, and worked as a technical writer. She died in 1966 and is buried in Morristown.

Oven Steak With Potatoes

2	POUNDS ROUND STEAK
1	TEASPOON SALT
1/2	TEASPOON BLACK PEPPER
1/2	CUP ALL-PURPOSE FLOUR
1/4	CUP SHORTENING, MELTED, OR VEGETABLE OIL
1	LARGE ONION, SLICED
5	MEDIUM POTATOES, SLICED 1/2-INCH THICK
1	10 3/4-OUNCE CAN MUSHROOM SOUP
1	SOUP CAN WATER

Assemble all ingredients and utensils. Cut steak into 8 pieces, add salt and pepper. Dredge meat in flour; brown on both sides in shortening in a large skillet. Remove steak from skillet. Sauté onion in same skillet. Place potatoes over onions. Continue browning for 10 minutes, turning frequently. Place meat on top of potatoes. Add soup and water. Cover and cook over medium heat for 35 to 40 minutes. Yield: 6 to 8 servings.

A quick recipe to prepare when you come in from work. Ask your friendly butcher to tenderize your steak.

Per serving: 377 calories; 20.3 g fat; 68 mg cholesterol; 693 mg sodium.

Lemon Veal

2	POUNDS VEAL CUTLETS, TENDERIZED
	SALT, TO TASTE
	PEPPER, TO TASTE
1	CUP BUTTER
	JUICE OF 1 LEMON
	CHOPPED PARSLEY

Assemble all ingredients and utensils. Have veal tenderized by the butcher or pounded with a mallet. Salt and pepper both sides of veal. Heat butter in a large skillet and bring to a boil. Add lemon juice and veal. Saute each side of meat about 3 minutes. Sprinkle with chopped parsley and serve immediately. Yield: 8 servings.

Veal is very elegant and must have Spring Asparagus (*see* p. 120) and tiny new potatoes to complete the dinner plate.

Per serving: 470 calories; 38.2 g fat; 177 mg cholesterol; 441 mg sodium.

Miss Daisy's
Veal With Pecan Sauce

2   POUNDS VEAL CUTLETS, SLICED 1/4 INCH THICK OR
      CUBED
1   TABLESPOON OIL
1/2 CUP WATER
1/2 CUP CHOPPED ONION
1   TEASPOON CHICKEN BOUILLON GRANULES
1   CLOVE GARLIC, MINCED
1   TEASPOON SALT
1/2 TEASPOON THYME
1/2 TEASPOON OREGANO
      PECAN SAUCE
      COOKED RICE

Assemble all ingredients and utensils. In a large skillet, brown veal in oil. Combine remaining ingredients. Simmer, covered 50 to 60 minutes, until meat is tender. Drain. Reserve broth.

Pecan Sauce

2   TABLESPOONS BUTTER
1/4 CUP CHOPPED ONION
1/2 CUP CHOPPED PECANS
4   TABLESPOONS FLOUR
1/2 CUP SOUR CREAM
1 1/2 CUPS LIQUID (RESERVED BROTH PLUS WATER)

In a large saucepan, sauté onion and pecans in butter until onion is browned. Remove from heat. Stir flour into sour cream; stir in liquid. Add to sautéed onion and pecan mixture. Add cooked veal. Return to heat to thicken. Yield: 6 servings.

Serve over cooked rice or pasta.

Special Note: Use tongs to turn foods. A fork pierces the food and delicious juices will escape.

Per serving: 435 calories; 30.9 g fat; 128 mg cholesterol; 574 mg sodium.

CHATTANOOGA'S "FIRST" CITIZEN

Although John Ross was born in Georgia, he moved north into Tennessee as a young man and settled in a bend of the Tennessee River. In 1816 he established Ross's Landing. From this little community that provided a ferry across the river, warehousing facilities for the growing river traffic, and a boat landing, today's city of Chattanooga eventually grew. Ross had earlier participated with Andrew Jackson in the Creek Wars, but for his assistance in defeating the Creeks, he was rewarded a quarter of a century later with removal orders that

HAMILTON COUNTY

had been formulated during Jackson's administration. Ross sued against the Cherokee removal all the way to the U. S. Supreme Court, where Chief Justice John Marshall ruled in his people's favor. Jackson would have none of it, however, issuing his famous reply, "John Marshall has made his decision. Now let him enforce it." As for John Ross, he and his family held out for as long as they could, but finally were forced to leave the Tennessee valley and migrate to present-day Oklahoma during the infamous "Trail of Tears." Ross's efforts for his people continued after his arrival in the new lands. Joining forces with members of the tribe who had emigrated earlier, he helped draft a constitution and was elected principle chief by his grateful countrymen. Ross's leadership during his long years as chief of his united nation was key to the tribe's transition from a southeastern to a mid-western Indian power.

Red Grooms' Family Kusa

Hollow out about twenty yellow squash and wash with salt water and mint leaves. Stuff squash loosely with the following lamb mixture.

1 1/2	POUNDS LAMB
1	CUP RICE (UNCOOKED)
1	TEASPOON SALT
1/2	TEASPOON BLACK PEPPER
	JUICE OF 1 1/2 LEMONS

Cover with tomato sauce diluted with equal amount of water. Put 1 or 2 sliced onions and 1 large green pepper slice over and around squash. Cook slowly 1 1/2 hours.

W ILOMENA AND JERRY GROOMS HAVE BEEN FRIENDS OF THE KING FAMILY FOR GENERATIONS. JERRY ENJOYED COOKING FOR HIS FAMILY AND THIS DELECTABLE DISH OF LAMB WAS HIS FAVORITE TO PREPARE.

RED GROOMS, THEIR SON, AT AN EARLY AGE DEMONSTRATED WITH PEN AND BRUSH ON PAPER HIS PENCHANT FOR AMUSING PEOPLE. PART HISTORY PAINTER, PART GENRE PAINTER, PART PAINTER OF MODERN LIFE, RED GROOMS MAY WELL BE, WITHOUT ANY RESERVATION, THE MOST FAMED ARTIST FROM HIS STATE OF TENNESSEE. RED'S LOVE FOR THIS STATE IS BEING REFLECTED IN HIS SOON-TO-BE CAROUSEL AT RIVER FRONT PARK IN NASHVILLE.

Miss Daisy

Miss Daisy's Mint Stuffed Leg of Lamb

1	8-POUND LEG OF LAMB, BONED
	SALT, TO TASTE
	PEPPER, TO TASTE
2	TABLESPOONS CHOPPED ONION
1/2	CUP CHOPPED CELERY
2	TABLESPOONS BUTTER
1	TEASPOON SALT
2	TABLESPOONS CHOPPED FRESH MINT
2	CUPS BREAD CUBES
1/4	CUP WATER

Assemble all ingredients and utensils. Sprinkle salt and pepper over lamb, inside and out. In a large skillet, sauté onion and celery until lightly browned. Add 1 teaspoon salt and mint. Toss with bread cubes and water. Spoon stuffing into both openings of lamb. Secure with thread. Roast in a 325-degree oven 3 hours or until well done. Yield: 8 servings.

Per serving: 982 calories; 64 g fat; 320 mg cholesterol; 891 mg sodium.

Overton Recipe for Sugar Curing Ham

Trim hams and put a pinch of powdered saltpeter in the back and under the joint in the fleshy side. Sprinkle just a little over the fleshy side and rub in. A little less than half a teaspoon is enough to use in back, joint and fleshy side. Be careful about this as too much would make the meat hard.

Now rub both sides of the hams well with plain salt.

Then spread in fleshy side a mixture made of one half bushel of coarse salt, one quart of molasses and two pounds of brown sugar. Mix thoroughly and put mixture on hams 1/4 inch thick. Pack hams down in a box with holes in the bottom for drainage. Put coarse salt in the bottom of the box first and place hams fleshy side up. Spread coarse salt on top. Mixture enough for 12 hams and 12 shoulders.

If weather is moist, not freezing, hams may be taken out in three to four weeks. But if weather is freezing cold hams should not be taken out for five weeks. If hams are left too long they would be salty. Take hams out of salt box and hang in smokehouse. Smoke with a slow fire (not much fire but a lot of smoke—sawdust or chips of hard maple can be used to smother fire and make smoke) made of sassafrass or hickory chips, until they are a light brown color. After they are smoked enough, submerge—dip in and out for a few seconds in case of insect eggs—each ham in a kettle of boiling water strong with red pepper pods. Dry each ham with a cloth and rub well with a mixture of cornmeal, black pepper and borax. Put each one in a large paper bag. They should be bagged before the first of March before insects are flying. Tie tightly and hang in dry place. When they are hung up it is well to make frequently a little smoke under them to dry.

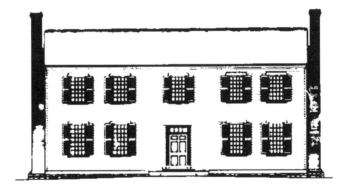

John Overton
Travellers Rest

John Overton (1766—1833) was a former Virginian who moved to Nashville in the late 1780s, and almost immediately struck up a lifelong friendship with Andrew Jackson. He served as Jackson's campaign manager during the unsuccessful 1824 presidential election and again for the victorious 1828 running. Aside from his association with Jackson, John Overton achieved a fame of his own. He served as President George Washington's supervisor of excise and sat on the bench of the predecessor of the Tennessee Supreme Court.

Overton's home, Travellers Rest, was begun in 1799 on 3,600 acres of land located south of Nashville on the road to Franklin. A unique feature of the house, which was originally a rather small, four-room home, was the beaded siding used. Although common on the Eastern seaboard, it was rarely used as far inland as Tennessee.

Apple Cider Pork Chops

1	CUP ALL-PURPOSE FLOUR
1/2	TEASPOON THYME
1/2	TEASPOON SALT
6	3/4-INCH PORK LOIN CHOPS
3/4	CUP EVAPORATED MILK
3	TABLESPOONS BUTTER
3/4	CUP WATER
2	TABLESPOONS LIGHT BROWN SUGAR
2	TEASPOONS CORNSTARCH
1/4	TEASPOON SALT
1/4	TEASPOON GROUND CINNAMON
1/2	CUP APPLE CIDER
1	TABLESPOON FRESH LEMON JUICE
3	TABLESPOONS RAISINS

Assemble all ingredients and utensils. In a bowl or bag, combine flour, thyme and salt. Set aside. Dip chops into 1/2 cup evaporated milk; then cover with flour mixture. In a large skillet, melt butter; sauté chops until lightly browned. Add water; cover. Cook over medium to low heat 1 hour and 30 minutes or until tender.

Remove chops from skillet. Stir brown sugar, cornstarch, salt, and cinnamon into meat drippings. Add cider, lemon juice, remaining 1/4 cup evaporated milk and raisins. Cook, stirring constantly, until thick. Serve sauce over chops. Yield: 6 servings.

Per serving: 525 calories; 35 g fat; 97 mg cholesterol; 404 mg sodium.

YOU CAN'T GO HOME AGAIN

Did somewhere in the distant past Portugese, or perhaps even Phoenician, sailors get blown off their course in the North Atlantic and end up on the eastern shore of the present-day United States? What's more, did these same sailors make their way inland, across the great mountain chain that we call the Appalachians, only to settle in their western foothills in present-day Hancock County, Tennessee? And, if they did, did the wanderers simply cast their fates to the wind and make the most of life in their strange new surroundings when they sadly learned that, No, they could never return to their homelands? Some people have propounded the above scenario when researching and

HANCOCK
COUNTY

writing about the strange "Melungeon" people who live along Newman's Ridge and in the remote valleys of Hancock County, but the truth of the matter is, that the truth might never be known. The Melungeons—dark-complex-ioned people who differ greatly in appearance from the more frequently found fair skinned, Scotch-Irish-descended inhabitants of East Tennessee—have been known about for years. In fact, as early as 1784, John Sevier described a "colony of dark-skinned, reddish-brown complexioned people," living in this part of the recently organized State of Franklin of which Sevier was the first and only governor. Even today, about the only thing known for certain about these people is the fact that they are disappearing rapidly as inter-marriage and outside influences catch up with them.

Oven Barbecued Pork Chops

8   1-INCH THICK LOIN PORK CHOPS
1   TEASPOON OIL
    SALT, TO TASTE
    PEPPER, TO TASTE
8   SLICES LEMON, 1/4 INCH THICK
8   SLICES ONION, 1/4 INCH THICK
1   8-OUNCE CAN TOMATO SAUCE
1/2 CUP DARK BROWN SUGAR

Assemble all ingredients and utensils. Salt and pepper pork chops. In a skillet, sauté pork chops in oil. Transfer to a large, 2-quart, casserole dish. Top with lemon and onion slices. Combine tomato sauce and brown sugar; pour over pork chops. Cover and bake in a 325-degree oven for 60 minutes. Baste occasionally. Remove cover and bake 15 minutes longer, continually basting. Yield: 8 servings.

Per serving: 557 calories; 40 g fat; 108 mg cholesterol; 387 mg sodium.

Fettuccini Carbonara
(Bacon or Ham)

1   POUND BACON OR COUNTRY HAM
1   POUND FETTUCCINI, SLIGHTLY UNDERCOOKED AND
        DRAINED
4   TABLESPOONS BUTTER, SLICED
3   CUPS HEAVY CREAM
1   CUP PARMESAN CHEESE
1/2 TEASPOON BLACK PEPPER
4   EGG YOLKS, BEATEN

Assemble all ingredients and utensils. Cut bacon or country ham into 1-inch pieces and sauté in a large skillet until firm, but not crisp. Pour off all but 3 tablespoons of grease. Add fettuccine and butter to skillet over medium heat. Toss until butter begins to melt. Add about 2 1/2 cups of cream and toss again. When cream begins to bubble, add cheese and stir. Continue tossing until sauce begins to thicken. Add black pepper. In a bowl, have the egg yolks beaten with 1/2 cup cream. Immediately add yolk/cream to pasta mixture. Toss to coat evenly. Remove from heat and serve immediately. Yield: 8 to 10 servings.

Per serving: 591 calories; 43 g fat; 236 mg cholesterol; 430 mg sodium.

When thirteen-year-old John Simpson Chisum moved from his home in Hardeman County to Texas in 1837, there was no way he could have known that before he died at the age of sixty, he would be the owner of the largest ranch and cattle herd in New Mexico Territory. After arriving in Texas, the boy grew to adulthood and became a contractor, being responsible for the construction of the courthouse at Paris, Texas. He served as county court clerk for Lamar County for eight years before he decided to get

HARDEMAN COUNTY

into the cattle business about 1854. A dozen years later, he became one of the first Texas ranchers to move cattle into New Mexico. He liked the new land and settled down on the Pecos River near Fort Sumner. Within a few years, the former Hardeman countian ran nearly one hundred thousand cattle on what may have, at the time, been the largest ranch in the world. In later life, Chisum got caught up in the Lincoln County War that brought Billy the Kid to fame, although his exact role in the affair has never been fully determined. Chisum remained a bachelor all his life. He developed a neck tumor and traveled to Eureka Springs, Arkansas, for treatment where he died in 1884. His estate was estimated to be one-half million dollars, a sum that today would represent probably fifty to one hundred million. Chisum's body was taken back to Paris, Texas, where he was buried and eulogized as "truthful and public spirited."

Country Sausage

For each pound of sausage:

1	pound ground pork shoulder
1	teaspoon salt
1/2	teaspoon ground black pepper
1/4	teaspoon crushed red pepper
1/2	teaspoon dried sage, pulverized
1/4	teaspoon dried rosemary, pulverized
1/4	teaspoon dried thyme, pulverized

*T*HOSE OF YOU WHO MAY BE FORTUNATE ENOUGH TO LIVE ON A FARM AND CURE YOUR HAMS AND GRIND YOUR SAUSAGE, BE SURE TO GIVE SOME TO YOUR CITY FRIENDS.

Miss Daisy

Assemble all ingredients and utensils. Use a sausage grinder to grind pork or have your local butcher prepare for you. Combine pork, salt, peppers and pulverized or crushed herbs. Mix thoroughly. Refrigerate for immediate use or freeze. Yield: 1 pound sausage, 6 to 8 slices.

Per serving: 196 calories; 15 g fat; 62 mg cholesterol; 316 mg sodium.

Tripp Country Hams

As a small family business, Tripp Country Hams started commercial production of "Old Fashioned Smoked Tennessee Country Ham" in 1963.

The Tripp family located the business three blocks from the courthouse in Brownsville, Tennessee. The family still takes pride in the fact that Tripp Country Hams are slow cured with salt, not injected. The hams are smoked over burning hickory wood and not rubbed with liquid smoke. This process has produced several state and national awards: 1989 and 1990 Grand Champion of Mid-South Fair, Country Ham Contest, Memphis, Tennessee; 1990 and 1991 Grand Champion of Tennessee State Fair, Country Ham Contest, Nashville, Tennessee; 1992 Grand Champion of American Association of Meat Processors' American Cured Meat Championships, Orlando, Florida; 1994 Reserve Grand Champion of American Association of Meat Processors' American Cured Meat Championships, Milwaukee, Wisconsin.

The Tripp Country Hams company produces country bacon and packaged slices of country ham ranging from center slice steaks to small boneless slices for "ham and biscuits" in addition to the whole country hams. Customers are provided a pamphlet with product use information. Due to the ham salt content the guide suggests:

It is possible you might have to acquire a taste for country ham, but once you do you will never forget it.

Sausage and Rice Casserole

1	POUND PORK SAUSAGE, HOT
1	MEDIUM GREEN PEPPER, CHOPPED
1	MEDIUM ONION, CHOPPED
1	CUP CHOPPED CELERY
1	CUP WHITE OR HERB UNCOOKED REGULAR RICE
1	10 3/4-OUNCE CAN CREAM OF CHICKEN SOUP
1	10 3/4-OUNCE CAN CREAM OF MUSHROOM SOUP
1 1/2	CUPS GRATED CHEDDAR CHEESE
1/2	CUP CRUSHED CRACKER CRUMBS OR BREAD CRUMBS FOR TOPPING

Assemble all ingredients and utensils. In a large skillet, brown sausage; add green pepper, onion, and celery. Simmer until vegetables are tender. Drain excess grease. Add rice, soups, and cheese. Mix well and pour into a 3-quart casserole. Bake at 350 degrees for 1 hour and 30 minutes. Top with crumbs and bake 10 minutes. Yield: 8 to 10 servings.

One of the best things about this casserole is that it is adaptable for brunch, lunch, or a supper menu.

Per serving: 409 calories; 28 g fat; 52 mg cholesterol; 942 mg sodium.

Wampler Farm Sausage

From the humble beginnings of making sausage in the kitchen of Mr. and Mrs. Riley M. Wampler's farm home to the modern plant located in the Eaton Cross Roads Community of Lenoir City, Tennessee, is a story of growth and development under the American free-enterprise system.

In 1937, Riley M. Wampler organized Wampler's Slaughter House, but it closed some time during World War II. The business reopened when Ted L. Wampler, son of Riley and Edith, graduated from high school in 1947. Ted and Riley each invested $1,100. Ted and his father were soon joined by Harry W. Wampler, nephew of Riley. In 1953 the company became a corporation and in 1981 the name was changed to Wampler's Farm Sausage Company.

The company is one of the most modern, sanitary meat plants in the industry. Wampler's retail sausage is enjoyed throughout the Southeast under the Wampler's name as well as many private label brands. The company's institutional sausage distribution system includes most of the U. S.

Ralph and Joy Emery's Lasagna

1	POUND MILD PORK SAUSAGE
1	TABLESPOON BASIL
1	CLOVE OF GARLIC, MINCED
1/2	TEASPOON SALT
1	16-OUNCE CAN TOMATOES
2	6-OUNCE CANS TOMATO PASTE
3	CUPS COTTAGE CHEESE
2	TABLESPOONS PARSLEY FLAKES
1/4	TEASPOON SALT
1/4	TEASPOON PEPPER
1/2	CUP PARMESAN CHEESE
2	EGGS, BEATEN
10	OUNCES LASAGNA NOODLES, COOKED
1	POUND MOZZARELLA CHEESE, THINLY SLICED

Brown sausage in skillet over medium-low heat, stirring frequently; drain. Add basil, garlic, 1/2 teaspoon salt, tomatoes and tomato paste; mix well. Simmer for 30 minutes, stirring occasionally. Combine cottage cheese, parsley, remaining 1/4 teaspoon salt, pepper, Parmesan cheese and eggs in bowl; mix well. Layer noodles, cottage cheese mixture, mozzarella slices and meat sauce 1/2 at a time in 9x13-inch baking dish. Bake at 375 degrees for 30 minutes. Let stand for 10 minutes; filling will set slightly. Cut into squares. Yield: 12 servings.

I'M NOT SURE WHICH ONE COOKS THIS DISH, BUT I DO KNOW RALPH ENJOYS EATING IT.

Miss Daisy

Scrapple

1	POUND PORK SAUSAGE (BULK)
1	POUND GROUND BEEF
3	CUPS BEEF BROTH (BOUILLON ENVELOPES)
2	TEASPOONS SALT
1/4	TEASPOON PEPPER
1 1/2	TEASPOONS SAGE
	DASH CAYENNE
1	CUP CORNMEAL

Combine pork, beef, and broth in a medium saucepan; bring to a boil. Add seasonings. Gradually sprinkle in cornmeal, stirring constantly; cook 30 minutes over low heat, stirring frequently.

Spoon into a greased pan or dish suitable for forming loaf for slicing; chill until firm. Cut into slices 1/2 inch thick and fry in 1/2-inch hot oil until brown, turning once.

Andrew Jackson's Favorite Pigs' Feet Pickled

Take twelve pigs' feet, scrape and wash them clean, put them into a saucepan with enough hot (not boiling) water to cover them. When partly done, salt them. It requires four to five hours to boil them soft. Pack them in a stone crock, and pour over them spiced vinegar made hot. They will be ready to use in a day or two. If you wish them for breakfast, split them, make a batter of two eggs, a cup of milk, salt, a teaspoonful of butter, with flour enough to make a thick batter; dip each piece in this and fry in hot lard or dip them in beaten egg and flour and fry. Souse is good eaten cold or warm.

Sweet and Sour Pork

1	20-OUNCE CAN PINEAPPLE CHUNKS
2	POUNDS BONELESS PORK, CUT INTO BITE-SIZED PIECES
2	TABLESPOONS PEANUT OIL
2/3	CUP DARK BROWN SUGAR
1/2	CUP VINEGAR
1/2	CUP SOY SAUCE
1/4	CUP CORN STARCH
1/2	CUP CHOPPED GREEN PEPPER
1/2	CUP CHOPPED ONION
1/2	CUP CHOPPED CELERY
	COOKED RICE OR NOODLES

Assemble all ingredients and utensils. Drain pineapple, reserve juice. In a large saucepan or Dutch oven brown pork in oil; drain thoroughly. Combine pineapple juice, brown sugar, vinegar, soy sauce, and cornstarch. Pour over pork. Add green pepper, onion, celery and pineapple chunks. Simmer for 30 minutes or until pork is cooked thoroughly. Serve over hot rice or noodles. Yield: 6 servings.

Try Chicken or Shrimp as substitutions for this recipe.

Per serving: 855 calories; 36.5 g fat; 116 mg cholesterol; 1192 mg sodium.

Odom's Country Sausage

In 1943, Doug and Louise Odom began a one-pig-a-day, meat grinding and mixing business from a converted chicken coop in Madison, Tennessee. Doug Jr. remembers helping his Dad mix and blend the sausage.

Louise sewed cloth bags stamped "Tennessee Pride" for packaging the sausage before Doug and sons Doug Jr. and Richard loaded orders into the back of their Chevy headed for the grocers of Nashville.

The Odom's daughter, Judy, drew a picture of a strolling, pole-toting country boy for her Dad one day at the kitchen table. "People see the farmboy on shirts and stationery and they think of the sausage from Tennessee. I never dreamed what it would become!" marvels Judy.

Tennessee Pride became a sponsor of WSM's Grand Ole Opry in 1956. The "farmboy" remained on a huge backdrop for the Opry stage until 1982 when it came down to be awarded in souvenir portions to donors of the Hank Snow Foundation for Abused Children. Who can imagine a Friday or Saturday night broadcast of Opry music without hearing: "Take H-O-O-ME a package of Tennessee Pride"? For over fifty years, the Odom family has provided sausage for Tennessee and beyond.

Roast Pork With
Currant Mustard Sauce

1	4-POUND BONED, ROLLED AND TIED PORK ROAST
2	CLOVES GARLIC, CRUSHED
2	TEASPOONS SALT
2	TEASPOONS SAGE
1/2	TEASPOON BLACK PEPPER
1/2	TEASPOON NUTMEG
2	MEDIUM YELLOW ONIONS, SLICED
2	MEDIUM CARROTS, SLICED
1	CUP WATER
	WHOLE CLOVES
1	CUP CURRANT JELLY
1	TABLESPOON DRY MUSTARD

*P*ORK AND CURRANTS HAVE AN AFFINITY FOR EACH OTHER. THE FLAVORFUL COMBINATION MAKES THIS DISH DELIGHTFUL. PORK ROASTS ARE EASY TO PREPARE AND WILL SERVE MORE THAN ALLOCATED BY SLICING INTO THINNER PORTIONS.

Miss Daisy

Assemble all ingredients and utensils. Combine garlic, salt, sage, black pepper, and nutmeg. Spread onions and carrots in a shallow roasting pan. Place meat, fat side up, on top of vegetables. Pour water over meat. Roast in a 325-degree oven for 1 hour and 30 minutes. Remove pork from oven. Slash fat in a crisscross pattern and insert whole cloves. Combine jelly and mustard. Spread over roast with cloves and roast 60 more minutes. Yield: 8 to 10 servings.

Per serving: 597 calories; 37 g fat; 162 mg cholesterol; 559 mg sodium.

Rudy's Farm Sausage

The Rudy's Farm Country Sausage recipe goes back to Daniel Rudy, who passed it on to his son, Jacob.

Jacob then passed it to his sons, Frank and Dan Rudy. The Rudy brothers began making sausage in a two-room house in the 1930s, as a part-time business during the winter months. At that time, they sold their products mainly to friends and neighbors. In 1944, Frank and Dan went into business full-time. They were the first in Nashville to use refrigerated trucks to ship their products. They always made a point to make the sausage fresh every morning, using only choice hams, loins

and tenderloins.

The company is now part of the Jimmy Dean Foods Company. Most of the family acreage has been incorporated into the sprawling Opryland USA complex and adjoining attractions.

Pit Barbecue Sauce

1/2	POUND BUTTER
2	CUPS VINEGAR
2	CUPS CATSUP
1/2	CUP WORCESTERSHIRE SAUCE
1	TABLESPOON BROWN SUGAR
1	TABLESPOON ONION JUICE
1	TABLESPOON TABASCO SAUCE
1 1/2	CLOVES GARLIC, CHOPPED FINE
1	TABLESPOON SALT OR MORE
1/2	TEASPOON BLACK PEPPER
1/4	TEASPOON RED PEPPER

Assemble all ingredients and utensils. In a large pot, bring all ingredients to a boil. Then let simmer for about 30 minutes; stirring frequently. Yield: 2 quarts.

Does not have to be refrigerated. Great to use for pork or beef.

Per serving: 75 calories; 6 g fat; 16 mg cholesterol; 497 mg sodium.

Glazed Ribs

2/3	CUP PURE MAPLE SYRUP
1/2	CUP ORANGE JUICE
1/4	CUP MINCED ONION
1	TABLESPOON GRATED ORANGE PEEL
2	TEASPOONS FRESH LEMON JUICE
1	TEASPOON DRY MUSTARD
2	RACKS BABY BACK PORK RIBS, 3 POUNDS
1/2	TEASPOON SALT
1/2	TEASPOON GROUND BLACK PEPPER

Assemble all ingredients and utensils. In a heavy saucepan, combine first 6 ingredients. Cook slowly over medium-low heat for 5 minutes, stirring occasionally. Pour sauce into a large bowl and let cool. Sauce can be refrigerated at this point for 24 hours.

When ready to cook ribs, season rib racks with salt and pepper. Arrange on a large baking sheet. Bake in a 350-degree oven for 30 to 35 minutes. Cool for 15 minutes. Cut racks into individual ribs. Coat ribs with prepared sauce thoroughly. Return ribs to baking pan and bake 15 minutes longer continuously basting with remaining sauce! Yield: 4 servings.

Per serving: 1320 calories; 90 g fat; 316 mg cholesterol; 480 mg sodium.

Barbecued Chicken

| 2 | BROILING CHICKENS CUT IN PIECES OR |
| 6 TO 8 | CHICKEN BREASTS |

Sauce

1	CUP OIL
1	CUP CIDER VINEGAR
1	CUP WATER
1	CUP CATSUP
1/4	CUP WORCESTERSHIRE SAUCE
1/4	CUP CHOPPED ONION
2	TABLESPOONS LEMON JUICE
1	TABLESPOON HONEY
1	CLOVE GARLIC, MASHED
1/2	TEASPOON SALT
1/4	TEASPOON OREGANO

Assemble all ingredients and utensils. Wash and dry chicken. In a bowl combine all ingredients for the sauce. Place chicken in a 13x9x2-inch casserole. Pour sauce over chicken. Cover chicken. Bake in a 350-degree oven for 60 minutes, remove cover and bake an additional 10 minutes. Yield: 6 to 8 servings.

Per serving: 382 calories; 29 g fat; 43 mg cholesterol; 656 mg sodium.

Easy Fried Chicken

Easy Fried Chicken is delicately crisp and browned on the outside, moist and tender within. Take it on a picnic or enjoy this southern dish for lunch or supper.

Miss Daisy

1	CUP ALL-PURPOSE FLOUR
1/8	TEASPOON GARLIC SALT
1/2	TEASPOON BLACK PEPPER
1 1/2	CUPS BUTTERMILK
1	3-POUND BROILER-FRYER, CUT UP
	OIL FOR FRYING

Assemble all ingredients and utensils. In a large bowl, combine flour, salt, and pepper. Pour buttermilk into a deep bowl; dip each piece of chicken in buttermilk and dredge in flour mixture, covering well.

In a large iron skillet pour about 1 inch of oil and heat until hot. Place chicken in hot oil and brown on both sides. Reduce temperature and cook chicken, covered for 15 to 20 minutes. Uncover and cook an additional 5 minutes. Yield: 4 to 6 servings.

Per serving: 349 calories; 22 g fat; 47 mg cholesterol; 148 mg sodium.

Chicken Enchiladas

4	CUPS COOKED AND CHOPPED CHICKEN BREASTS
16	OUNCES SOUR CREAM, DIVIDED
1	10 3/4-OUNCE CAN CREAM OF CHICKEN SOUP
1/4	CUP CHOPPED ONION
8	OUNCES SHREDDED MONTEREY JACK CHEESE
1	SMALL CAN CHOPPED GREEN CHILIES, DRAINED
12	SOFT FLOUR TORTILLAS
1	10 3/4-OUNCE CAN CHEDDAR CHEESE SOUP
1	CUP SALSA, HOT

Assemble all ingredients and utensils. In a bowl, combine chicken, half of sour cream, cream of chicken soup, onion, chilies and cheese. Divide mixture evenly among the 12 tortillas. Roll the tortillas tightly. Place in a 13x9x2-inch baking dish. Pour cheddar cheese over all. Bake in a 350-degree oven for 25 to 30 minutes or until bubbly. Top with remaining sour cream and salsa. Yield: 6 servings of 2 tortillas.

Per serving: 817 calories; 39 g fat; 163 mg cholesterol; 2317 mg sodium.

Baked Chicken Breasts With Wild Rice

3	WHOLE CHICKEN BREASTS, HALVED
3	TABLESPOONS BACON FAT
1/2	CUP CHOPPED ONION
1	SMALL GARLIC CLOVE, MINCED
1	CUP CHICKEN BROTH
1	CUP LIGHT CREAM, HALF AND HALF
1 1/2	TEASPOONS SALT
1	TEASPOON WORCESTERSHIRE SAUCE
1/4	TEASPOON BLACK PEPPER
	WILD RICE, COOKED ABOUT 3 CUPS

Assemble all ingredients and utensils. In a skillet, sauté chicken breasts in bacon fat until golden brown. Combine onion, garlic, broth, cream and seasonings in a saucepan and heat. Place chicken in a 2-quart casserole dish and pour sauce over. Cover and bake 2 hours in a 300-degree oven. Uncover and bake 15 minutes. Serve over cooked wild rice. Yield: 6 servings.

Per serving: 373 calories; 16 g fat; 101 mg cholesterol; 770 mg sodium.

THE BATTLE OF SHILOH

Following Nashville's occupation in February 1862, it became imperative for Southern military forces to halt the Union invasion of Middle and West Tennessee. General Albert Sidney Johnston marched from Nashville to Corinth, Mississippi, and by spring had amassed forty thousand troops there. General Ulysses Grant's army, after its victories at Forts Henry and Donelson, had followed the Tennessee River to Pittsburg Landing in Hardin County. Near Shiloh Church, on April 6, Johnston attacked the large Union force, catching it by surprise. For sev-

HARDIN COUNTY

eral hours, the Confederates had the upper hand, but around noon, at a place called the Hornet's Nest, Union riflemen held the line, temporarily thwarting efforts by the southerners to break through. Grant, in the meantime, had secured the area with a formidable defense line. Confusion reigned. General Johnston was killed and General P. G. T. Beauregard succeeded him. Tables had suddenly turned, and Union soldiers gradually took command of the fighting. The second day at Shiloh proved disastrous for both armies. The Union suffered thirteen thousand killed, wounded, and missing, while Confederate casualties numbered nearly eleven thousand. So many Confederates were wounded that their blood stained the water of a nearby pond as they cupped their hands in its waters, trying to slake their thirst. Called "Bloody Pond" ever since, it is a surviving reminder of the battle that doomed Confederate aspirations in the Western Theater.

Chicken Almond Casserole

1	CUP CHOPPED COOKED CHICKEN
1	CUP CHOPPED CELERY
1/2	CUP LIGHTLY TOASTED, SLIVERED ALMONDS
1/2	CUP MAYONNAISE
1	4-OUNCE CAN SLICED MUSHROOMS, DRAINED
1	2-OUNCE JAR PIMENTO
2	HARD BOILED EGGS, CHOPPED
1	TABLESPOON CHOPPED ONION
1	10 3/4-OUNCE CAN CREAM OF CHICKEN SOUP
1/2	CUP CRACKER CRUMBS

Assemble all ingredients and utensils. In a bowl combine all ingredients except cracker crumbs. Pour into a 2-quart casserole. Sprinkle cracker crumbs on top. Bake in a 350-degree oven for 30 minutes. Yield: 6 to 8 servings.

Per serving: 263 calories; 21 g fat; 94 mg cholesterol; 514 mg sodium.

*N*ICE DISH TO SERVE FOR YOUR BRIDGE LUNCHEON. ACCOMPANY THE CASSEROLE WITH TOMATO ASPIC (*SEE* P. 36) AND APPLESAUCE MUFFINS (*SEE* P. 252).
Miss Daisy

Hot Chicken Salad Cassserole

2	CUPS CUBED COOKED CHICKEN
2	CUPS CHOPPED CELERY
1/2	CUP SLICED TOASTED ALMONDS
1/2	CUP MAYONNAISE
1/2	CUP CHOPPED GREEN PEPPER
1/2	10 3/4-OUNCE CAN CREAM OF CHICKEN SOUP
2	TABLESPOONS GRATED ONION
2	TABLESPOONS CHOPPED PIMENTO
2	TABLESPOONS LEMON JUICE
1/2	TEASPOON SALT
1/2	CUP GRATED MILD CHEDDAR CHEESE
3	CUPS POTATO CHIPS, CRUSHED

Assemble all ingredients and utensils. In a bowl, combine all the ingredients except cheese and potato chips. Spread into a 1 1/2- to 2-quart casserole. Sprinkle chips and cheese on top. Bake in a 350-degree oven for 25 minutes or until heated through. Yield: 8 to 10 servings.

Per serving: 340 calories; 25 g fat; 37 mg cholesterol; 481 mg sodium.

A LUNCHEON TREAT SERVED WITH PINK ARCTIC FREEZE (*SEE* P. 29) AND QUICK SPOON ROLLS (*SEE* P. 255).
Miss Daisy

Alex Haley's "Chicken George" Chicken and Dumplings

Cook a hen until tender. Remove from broth. Add water if needed to make plenty of broth.

Dumplings

2 1/2	CUPS PLAIN FLOUR
1	TEASPOON SALT
1	TEASPOON BAKING POWDER
2	EGGS

Mix together and add enough milk to make a stiff batter. Knead on dough board using plenty of flour. Roll out to the thickness of pie crust. Cut in 1 inch strips and cut each strip in 3 or 4 pieces. Drop into boiling broth and cook slowly until done. May need to add cover to pan but watch carefully. Add chicken and let stand to blend flavors. You can remove the chicken from the bone but in the old days the chicken was cut in pieces but left on the bone.

Miss Daisy's Make-Your-Own Chicken Stock

Roughly chop all bones and scraps, either cooked or raw, or a combination of both and simmer for an hour in lightly salted water to cover in a big pot. Strain, degrease, and refrigerate uncovered until cool; then cover.

Chicken stock is good to have on hand for use in a quick sauce or soups. The stock is perfect for substitutions in low-fat recipes. An expedient method of degreasing the stock is to blast chill in the freezer and remove the collected grease from top of stock. Chicken stock will keep two or three days under refrigeration or it may be frozen for months.

Alex Haley Home

Although he was born in Ithaca, New York, Alex Haley grew up in Tennessee, living from 1921 until 1928 in a house in Henning. During these Tennessee years, young Haley often listened to his grandmother weave tales of his family's past. (Grandma Cynthia's stove is pictured above.) Out of these stories, told on the front porch of his Henning home, came Haley's most durable work, *Roots.* Haley served in the Coast Guard for twenty years, attaining the rank of Chief Journalist, a position created especially for him. Becoming a freelance writer after his retirement, he completed his first book, *Malcolm X,* which soon became a bestseller. Then he began the research that would lead to his greatest achievement, the book, *Roots.* Haley traced his roots all the way back to West Africa of the 1760s and wrote about the people who made up this past in his book. His efforts won him both the Pulitzer Prize and the National Book Award. The television adaptation of his book drew the largest audience in TV history and was watched by more than 130 million people.

Grandmother's Chicken and Dumplings

Aren't dishes from the past the very best memories? I'm sure your own Grandmother had delicious recipes, so you will believe me when I say this one of my Grandmother's is hard to beat.

Miss Daisy

1	WHOLE CHICKEN
2	CUPS ALL-PURPOSE FLOUR
1	TEASPOON SALT
1/2	TEASPOON BLACK PEPPER
1/2	TEASPOON BAKING POWDER
1/3	CUP VEGETABLE SHORTENING
1/2	CUP CHICKEN BROTH
1/2	CUP WHOLE MILK

Assemble all ingredients and utensils. In a big pot or Dutch oven boil chicken until tender; 50 to 60 minutes. Remove cooked chicken and take off bones. Set broth and chicken aside.

In a large bowl, combine dry ingredients; cut in shortening with knives. Add enough broth to make a stiff dough. Roll dough to 1/4 inch thickness on floured surface. Cut into rounds with biscuit cutter or into strips. Return pot of broth to simmering. Drop pastry into broth. Cover and cook for 10 minutes. Add boned chicken and milk. Cover and simmer 10 additional minutes. Remove from heat. Keep warm until ready to serve. Yield: 8 to 10 servings.

Per serving: 346 calories; 16 g fat; 46 mg cholesterol; 432 mg sodium.

TENNESSEE'S FIRST PRINTER

Printing in Tennessee had its origins in Hawkins County on November 5, 1791, when a transplanted Bostonian, laying over in present-day Rogersville en route to Knoxville, started a newspaper. George Roulstone, along with Robert Ferguson, both of whom most recently had been publishing a newspaper in North Carolina, put out the first issue of *The Knoxville Gazette* while hauling a printing press to Knoxville, where they intended going into business. Roulstone had answered the invitation of territorial governor William Blount to come to the newly established town in the absence of any other printer. In 1794,

by an act passed in the territorial legislature, Roulstone became the official printer for the territory. The state's first newspaper, in the meantime, was published every two weeks, continuing its run from Knoxville during the fall of 1792. After Rogersville's early entry into the printing business, no other printer appears to have established himself there until 1814. During that year, a sermon written by Reverend Isaac Anderson and a booklet entitled, *A Moral and Political Discourse on War*, by D. T. Madox, were printed in the small village. Fifteen years later, a series of sermons was published there and collectively called the *Calvinistic Magazine*. Despite its slow return to printing activity, Rogersville is still recognized for the first production of printed material in the state, and Roulstone is oftentimes called the "father" of Tennessee printing.

Macaroni With Chicken,
Tennessee Ham and Truffles

Skin 2 whole chickens and sauté in 6 tablespoons butter over fairly high heat for 10 minutes or until lightly colored on both sides. Reduce heat and continue cooking breasts for about 3 to 4 minutes or until just cooked thru. Add 1/3 cup Madeira wine and cook for a minute. Remove chicken breasts and reserve them and the pan juices.

In heavy saucepan melt 6 tablespoons butter and blend in 6 tablespoons flour. Cook roux for 2 minutes and stir in 4 cups chicken roux broth. Continue to cook until thickened. Add 1 1/2 cups heavy cream, and 1 cup shredded Gruyere cheese and stir until thoroughly blended. Season with salt and pepper to taste. Sprinkle with freshly grated nutmeg. Reserve.

Cut chicken into julienne pieces and combine with 1/2 pound country ham (lightly fried) add 10-15 green olives or 1 black truffle, adding another to top. Reserve.

Cook 1 1/2 pounds of macaroni, al dente, drain. Arrange in 2 rectangular buttered casserole dishes. Layer, combined chicken, ham and olives or truffles over macaroni. Pour cheese/cream mixture over all and sprinkle with Parmesan cheese and paprika. Bake in a 350-degree oven for 30 minutes or until brown and bubbly. Yield: enough for a dinner party.

SIGOURNEY AND JIM, CHEEK DESCENDANTS, GRACIOUSLY SHARED THIS CHEEK FAMILY RECIPE FOR THE BICENTENNIAL COLLECTION. JIM IS THE GREAT-GRANDSON OF JOEL CHEEK. SIGOURNEY AND I HAVE MODERNIZED THE RECIPE INTO TODAY'S LANGUAGE FOR EASIER PREPARATION. MACARONI WAS CERTAINLY IN ELEGANT COMPANY WITH TENNESSEE COUNTRY HAM, CHICKEN, AND TRUFFLES.

Miss Daisy

Maxwell House Coffee

Joel Owsley Cheek, a twenty-year-old traveling salesman for a Nashville wholesale food company, couldn't have realized in 1872 as he journeyed across Tennessee and Kentucky that he would someday develop the country's best-selling coffee. After years of blending "green" coffee beans and selling the result to his customers, Cheek made a deal in 1892 with the management of Nashville's Maxwell House Hotel to serve his coffee in the hostelry's fine restaurant. When President Theodore Roosevelt visited Nashville in 1907 and lodged and ate at the Maxwell House, he supposedly proclaimed that Cheek's unique blend was "good to the last drop," a slogan that is still used by General Foods, the company that bought out Cheek for more than four million dollars in 1928.

Carnton Chicken Croquettes

Boil your fowl well, chop as fine as possible, add salt, pepper, a little mace, ginger, and mustard, or a little chowchow pickle well drained. Add 4 beaten eggs, a little flour, and bread crumbs. Stew all together a few minutes, and when cool make into cone-shaped balls, roll in pulverized cracker crumbs, and fry in hot lard. For the fowl you can substitute any cold meat.

Carnton Mansion

An antebellum mansion and Civil War hospital, Carnton Plantation was built in 1826 by Randal McGavock. On November 30, 1864, Carnton was

witness to one of the largest and most costly battles of the Civil War. The Union forces, entrenched in an arc around the southern edge of Franklin, were repeatedly charged by the some 20,000 soldiers of the Confederate Army of Tennessee. Randal's son Col. John McGavock and his wife, Carrie, then owned Carnton and offered it as a hospital. When the house could hold no more of the hundreds of wounded brought in during the Battle and after, the yard was then used. The bodies of Generals Cleburne, Granbury, Strahl, Gist, and Adams were laid on the back porch.

In 1866, the McGavocks designated two acres at Carnton for the Southern dead killed at Franklin, and the McGavock Confederate Cemetery is the largest private Confederate cemetery in the country holding some 1500 graves.

Chicken Livers Over Toast Points

1	POUND CHICKEN LIVERS
1/2	CUP SELF-RISING FLOUR
1/2	TEASPOON SALT
1/2	TEASPOON BLACK PEPPER
	COOKING OIL
1/3	CUP BUTTER
1	CUP CHOPPED ONION
1/2	CUP SLICED FRESH MUSHROOMS
2	TABLESPOONS SHERRY
	TOAST POINTS OR COOKED RICE

Assemble all ingredients and utensils. Flour chicken livers. Salt and pepper them. In a large skillet sauté a few at a time in oil, about 1/2-inch deep until golden brown.

In a saucepan, heat butter. Cook chopped onion until clear. Add mushrooms and cook 5 to 10 minutes. Add sherry and livers to pan and simmer an additional 5 minutes. Serve over toast points or cooked rice. Yield: 6 servings.

Per serving: 326 calories; 19 g fat; 31 mg cholesterol; 760 mg sodium.

Miss Daisy's Creamed Chicken

1/4	CUP BUTTER
1/4	CUP ALL-PURPOSE FLOUR
2	CUPS WHOLE MILK
1/4	TEASPOON SALT
1/4	TEASPOON PEPPER
1	10 3/4-OUNCE CAN CREAM OF MUSHROOM SOUP
1	TEASPOON WORCESTERSHIRE SAUCE
1	TABLESPOON GRATED ONION
1/4	CUP CHOPPED GREEN PEPPERS
1	2-OUNCE JAR CHOPPED PIMENTOS, DRAINED
2	CUPS COOKED DICED CHICKEN
	TOAST POINTS, CORNBREAD SQUARES OR PASTRY SHELLS

Assemble all ingredients and utensils. In a large saucepan, melt butter. Blend in flour and gradually stir in milk. Stir constantly until thick. Add remaining ingredients. Heat thoroughly. Serve over bread. Yield: 6 to 8 servings.

Per serving: 352 calories; 20 g fat; 62 mg cholesterol; 827 mg sodium.

DURING HOMECOMING '86 I HAD THE ESTEEMED PRIVILEGE OF SPENDING SOME QUALITY TIME WITH ALEX HALEY. I HAVE ENJOYED HIS WORDS AND KINDNESS AS MUCH AS THAT OF ANYONE I HAVE MET. ALEX HALEY WAS A DIABETIC AND HAD TO MAINTAIN A CONTROLLED DIET, BUT WHEN HE VISITED MISS DAISY'S HE WOULD SAVOR THIS DISH. HE SAVED HIS ALLOTTED FOOD EXCHANGES FOR CREAMED CHICKEN OVER CORN-BREAD.

Miss Daisy

ABOARD A MAGIC CARPET

In the preface to one of his many travel books, Haywood County native Richard Halliburton once wrote of his childhood, "Sometimes I pretended I had a magic carpet, and without bothering about tickets and money and farewells, I'd skyrocket away to New York or to Rome, to the Grand Canyon or to China, across deserts and oceans and mountains . . . then suddenly come back home when the school bell rang for recess." Born in Brownsville in 1900,

Halliburton went on to become one of the world's most prolific travelers and travel writers before his tragic death in 1939. Halliburton was educated at Princeton, and wanderlust hit him early. In 1921, he began the world-wide wanderings that made him legendary in his own time. During his eighteen years of travel, the Tennessean ascended the Matterhorn in wintertime, swam the Hellespont, re-traced Ulysses's journey, rode an elephant across the Alps in Hannibal's tracks, and swam across the Panama Canal. Hardly a country of the world was unvisited by Halliburton. True to his spirit of adventure, he died as he had lived. He was aboard a Chinese junk, the *Sea Dragon,* during the spring of 1939, hoping to sail from Hong Kong to San Francisco, when his boat went down twelve hundred miles west of Midway Island. Despite a search by the U. S. Navy of more than 150,000 square miles of the South Pacific, no survivors were ever found. Ironically, in 1945, part of the ship's wreckage washed ashore on a California beach.

Animaland's
Big John Chicken

12	CHICKEN DRUMSTICKS
	OIL FOR BROWNING
1 1/2	CUPS WATER
4	LARGE ONIONS, SLICED LENGTHWISE
1	BUNCH CELERY, SLICED DIAGONALLY
6	GREEN BELL PEPPERS, CUT INTO QUARTERS
8	POTATOES, PEELED, CUT INTO HALVES LENGTHWISE

Brown chicken in a small amount of oil in skillet. Combine with water, onions, celery, green peppers and potatoes in stockpot. Simmer, covered, for 45 minutes or until potatoes are tender, stirring occasionally. Yield: 6 servings.

$\mathcal{M}$ANY THANKS TO DIXIE AND TOM T. FOR GENEROUSLY LETTING US USE SOME OF THEIR CELEBRITY RECIPES FROM *THE ANIMALAND COOKBOOK*. MISS DIXIE AND TOM T. HAVE SHARED THEIR TALENTS AND HOME OVER THE YEARS TO HELP RAISE MONEY FOR A THIRTY-TWO ACRE COMPLEX KNOWN AS ANIMALAND IN NORTHERN WILLIAMSON COUNTY.

Miss Daisy

Double-Cola Company

The Double-Cola Company began in 1927, when Charles D. Little purchased The Seminole Flavor Company in Chattanooga, Tennessee. At the time the company produced two flavor drinks, Good Grape and Seminole Orange, for regional distribution. Little and his partners immediately began developing a cola drink. In 1933, the company perfected the formula and began marketing Double-Cola, unchanged today. When Double-Cola was introduced, all other major colas in the U.S. were being sold in bottles that contained 6 1/2 ounces or less.

Double-Cola debuted in 12-ounce bottles with the theme, "Double Good, Double-Cola." The marketing strategy paid off, and Double-Cola sales grew rapidly during the 1930s.

The Depression drove many small, regional soft drink companies out of business, and sugar shortages during World War II forced more to close. But Double-Cola survived, continued making a quality product, and actually grew during those decades.

Today it is one of the "top ten franchise companies." Double-Cola brands continue to grow at a pace typically greater than the industry as a whole.

Chicken Pot Pie

	PASTRY FOR A 2-CRUST PIE
6	TABLESPOONS FLOUR
6	TABLESPOONS BUTTER
1/2	TEASPOON SALT
1/4	TEASPOON PEPPER
2	CUPS CHICKEN BROTH
2/3	CUP LIGHT CREAM (HALF AND HALF)
1	CUP COOKED MIXED VEGETABLES OR
1	SMALL CAN GREEN PEAS, CORN, CARROTS
2	CUPS COOKED CHOPPED CHICKEN

Assemble all ingredients and utensils. In a saucepan combine butter, flour, salt and pepper. Cook until heated completely. Add chicken broth and cream. Cook slowly until thickened. Add the cup of vegetables and chicken. Pour this into a 9-inch pastry-lined pan, top with pastry. Pinch edges together. Make three or four slits in top pastry for steam to escape. Bake in a 425-degree oven for 35 to 40 minutes. Yield: 6 servings.

Per serving: 587 calories; 39 g fat; 88 mg cholesterol; 1213 mg sodium.

McCord Family Orange Chicken

6	BONELESS CHICKEN BREAST HALVES
1/4	STICK OLEO
2	TABLESPOONS FLOUR
	DASH OF GROUND GINGER
	COOKED RICE
1/8	TEASPOON GROUND CINNAMON
1 1/2	CUPS ORANGE JUICE
1/2	CUP SLIVERED ALMONDS
1/2	CUP SEEDLESS RAISINS

SANDRA HAYNES OF
MCMINNVILLE COOKS THIS WONDER-
FUL ORANGE CHICKEN RECIPE.
GREAT FOR A QUICK AND FLAVORFUL
DINNER.

Miss Daisy

Sprinkle chicken with salt. Brown in oleo. Take chicken out of pan and pour off drippings except for 2 tablespoons. Blend flour and spices into reserved drippings and brown slightly. Add orange juice. Cook over low heat until thick. Then add almonds and raisins and chicken. Cover skillet and cook on low for approximately 30 minutes. Serve over rice. Yield: 6 servings.

Hope Family
Fondue of Chicken

$\mathcal{T}$his recipe was shared with me for the book by my friend Susan Hope Elrod Creagh of Nashville, Tennessee. Thomas Hope was the architect of Ramsey House, ten miles east of Knoxville. Thomas Hope is Susan's grandfather by five generations for whom she was named (SEE Grandmother Hope's Chess Cakes, p. 200).

Miss Daisy

1	CUP MINCED CHICKEN (TURKEY OR VEAL)
1	CUP BREAD CRUMBS
1	CUP OF BOILING MILK
1/2	ONION BOILED IN THE MILK AND STRAINED OUT
1	TABLESPOON BUTTER
1	SLICE, COLD BOILED HAM, MINCED
2	EGGS, BEATEN
1	PINCH EACH: SODA, PEPPER, AND SALT

Soak crumbs in the milk, stir in the butter and beat very light. Let the mixture cool while you mince the meat and beat the eggs. Stir in the meat when the bread and milk are nearly cold, season, lastly adding the eggs. Beat well up. Put it into a well-greased baking dish; set in a brick oven. When the fondue is a light brown puff send at once to the table in the same dish in which it has been baked.

TENNESSEE'S GENTLE GIANT

Extreme obesity was once looked upon with a great deal more curiosity than understanding of the underlying causes for the condition. As late as the 1850s, nineteenth century medicine was still too much in its infancy to assess the mysterious mechanics within the human body that were responsible. In many cases, persons stricken with the malady that caused their bodies to store such excesses of weight could survive only by becoming curiosities themselves. For years, circuses traveled the United States, making one-night stands in practically every nook and cranny throughout the country. And, just as surely as the circus came to town, one could count on paying a nickle

or a dime and viewing the "Fat Man," or perhaps the "Fat Lady."

As far as we know, Mills (sometimes referred to as Miles) Darden was a healthy, normal child when he entered the world in North Carolina in 1798. But, somewhere along the line, he was stricken with an unknown malady causing him to grow beyond the bounds of any human being who ever lived. Whether Mills was already suffering from the condition when he arrived in Henderson County in 1821 is also unknown, but, while there, first as a farmer and later as the congenial owner of a tavern and inn in Lexington, he got bigger and bigger. When Mills died in 1857, he weighed around 1,050 pounds and stood just two inches short of eight feet. It is reported that his coffin required 520 feet of lumber to build and that the box measured eight and one-third feet long.

Hot Chicken Soufflé

8	SLICES OF WHITE BREAD, CUBED
2	CUPS COOKED DICED CHICKEN
1/2	CUP CHOPPED ONION
1/2	CUP CHOPPED CELERY
1/4	CUP CHOPPED PIMENTO
1/2	TEASPOON SALT
1/2	TEASPOON BLACK PEPPER
1/2	CUP MAYONNAISE
2	CUPS MILK
2	EGGS, BEATEN
1	10 3/4-OUNCE CAN CREAM OF CHICKEN SOUP
1/2	CUP SHREDDED SHARP CHEDDAR CHEESE

*G*REAT LUNCHEON DISH. SERVE WITH GRANDMOTHER'S FROZEN FRUIT SALAD(*SEE* P. 28) AND GARDEN FRESH TOMATOES.

Miss Daisy

Assemble all ingredients and utensils. In a 2-quart soufflé dish or casserole dish, layer 4 slices of cubed bread. Combine chicken, onion, celery, pimento, salt, pepper, and mayonnaise; spoon over bread. Layer remaining 4 slices of cubed bread on top of chicken mixture. Combine milk and eggs and pour over all. Cover and chill at least 1 hour. When ready to cook, pour soup over mixture. Bake in a 325-degree oven for 60 minutes. Remove from oven and sprinkle cheese on top immediately. Yield: 6 to 8 servings.

Per serving: 350 calories; 21 g fat; 123 mg cholesterol; 760 mg sodium.

ORGANIZING AN ARMY

In the old days of war, at least before World War I, troops were usually raised locally. The governor would normally issue a call for so many men, each county would respond to the best of its ability with as many recruits as it could afford, and then the men mustered at a common site and elected their own officers. Unlike modern combat units, wherein men and women from all sections of the country are thrown together, the regiments of old were made up of locals who had most likely known each other from birth. A real feeling of camaraderie existed at all times, and when the conflict was over, the unit's members returned home,

heroes in the eyes of the folks they had left behind. No county in Tennessee can demonstrate this "home-recruiting" methodology better than Henry. When it became imminent that Tennessee would secede from the Union, urgent requests went out all over the state for volunteers to fill up several regiments of infantry, cavalry, and artillery. In Henry County, Colonel William E. Travis was selected to raise a cavalry regiment, but when proper weapons could not be furnished for cavalry operations, it was decided to change the regiment to one of infantry. The county newspaper, the *Paris Sentinel,* ran the appeal for volunteers in its columns, and when the men assembled in Paris in May 1861, to fill the ranks of the Fifth Regiment of the Tennessee Infantry, people from miles around came to lend their support.

Tipper Gore's Spiced Roast Chicken

1	3 1/2-POUND CHICKEN
1	TABLESPOON MARGARINE
2/3	CUP MARSALA

Mushroom Stuffing:

2	TABLESPOONS OLIVE OIL
1	ONION, FINELY CHOPPED
1	TEASPOON GARAM MASALA
4	OUNCES BUTTON OR BROWN MUSHROOMS, CHOPPED
1	CUP COARSELY GRATED PARSNIPS
1	CUP COARSELY GRATED CARROTS
1/4	CUP MINCED WALNUTS
2	TEASPOONS CHOPPED FRESH THYME
1	CUP FRESH WHITE BREAD CRUMBS
1	EGG, BEATEN
	SALT AND PEPPER TO TASTE
	THYME AND WATERCRESS SPRIGS FOR GARNISH

To Serve:

Preheat oven to 375 degrees.

Prepare Stuffing: In a large saucepan, heat olive oil; add onion and sauté 2 minutes or until softened. Stir in garam masala and cook 1 minute. Add mushrooms, parsnips and carrots; Cook, stirring 5 minutes. Remove from heat; stir in remaining stuffing ingredients.

Stuff and truss chicken. Place breast down, in a roasting pan; add 1/4 cup water. Roast 45 minutes; turn chicken breast up and dot with margarine. Roast about 45 minutes or until a meat thermometer inserted in thickest part of thigh (not touching bone) registers 185 degrees. Transfer to platter; keep warm.

Pour off and discard fat from roasting pan; add marsala to remaining cooking juices, stirring to scrape up any browned bits. Boil over high heat 1 minute to reduce slightly; adjust seasoning.

Remove skin and carve chicken. Garnish with thyme and watercress sprigs. Serve with stuffing, flavored meat juices and seasonal vegetables.

Makes 4 servings.

CREDIT MUST BE GIVEN TO TIPPER'S MOTHER-IN-LAW PAULINE GORE FOR ACQUIRING TIPPER'S RECIPES FOR INCLUSION IN THIS COOKBOOK. I CHOSE THIS ONE BECAUSE OF THE RECIPE'S VERSATILITY.

Miss Daisy

Minnie Pearl's Chicken Tetrazzini

2	CUPS CHOPPED CELERY
1 1/2	CUPS CHOPPED ONION
3	TABLESPOONS BUTTER OR MARGARINE
2	CUPS CHICKEN BROTH
1	TABLESPOON WORCESTERSHIRE SAUCE
	SALT AND PEPPER
1	10 1/2-OUNCE CAN CONDENSED CREAM OF
	MUSHROOM SOUP
1/2	CUP MILK
1	CUP GRATED SHARP CHEESE
1/2	POUND SPAGHETTI, COOKED AND DRAINED
6	CUPS CHOPPED, COOKED CHICKEN
1/2	CUP SLICED STUFFED OLIVES
1	CUP CHOPPED PECANS

In a saucepan, cook celery and onion in butter until tender. Add chicken broth, Worcestershire sauce, salt, and pepper. Simmer about 15 minutes. Slowly stir in mushroom soup, milk, and cheese. Mix thoroughly. Remove from heat. Add cooked spaghetti, Let stand for 1 hour. Preheat oven to 350 degrees. Grease a 9x13-inch baking dish. Add chicken and olives to spaghetti. Place in prepared dish. Sprinkle with chopped pecans. Bake 20 to 25 minutes or until hot and bubbly. Makes 12 servings.

*M*ISS MINNIE HAS FAVORITE RECIPES SHE ENJOYS SHARING WITH OTHERS, MOSTLY BECAUSE OF THE STORY WHICH ACCOMPANIES THEM. SHE IS ESPECIALLY FOND OF THIS CHICKEN RECIPE BECAUSE IT IS FROM HER HUSBAND'S (HENRY CANNON) AUNT—CYNTHIA FLEMING OF FRANKLIN, TENNESSEE.

Miss Daisy

Ryman Auditorium

In 1881, Thomas Ryman, a well-to-do Nashville riverboat captain who owned a fleet of steamboats that plied the Cumberland River, was converted to Christianity by the famed preacher, Sam Jones. To prove his sincerity to his new-found religion, Ryman started a campaign to collect money for the construction of a grandiose building where visiting preachers like Jones could hold their revivals. The wealthy captain even donated twenty thousand dollars of his own money. Located on present-day Fifth Avenue near Broad Street, the structure was first called the Union Gospel Tabernacle, but the name was changed upon the death of Captain Ryman in 1904 to the Ryman Auditorium. The fine acoustics and spaciousness of the vast auditorium soon made it a favorite of traveling theatrical shows, and such musical legends as Caruso, Paderewski, and Adelina Patti performed there. A few years later, the Ryman became the home of WSM Radio's Grand Ole Opry, and every Saturday night saw the house packed full of country music fans. The Ryman fell into disrepair after the Opry moved to its new building in the Opryland USA theme park, but recently, it has been restored to its original glory by the Gaylord Entertainment people.

Miss Daisy's Turkey Divan

2	10-OUNCE PACKAGES FROZEN BROCCOLI OR
2	BUNCHES FRESH BROCCOLI
2–3	CUPS COOKED TURKEY, DICED OR SLICED

Cook broccoli according to directions on box or cook fresh broccoli just until tender, but still green. Do not let either cook until mushy!

Sauce:

2	10 3/4-OUNCE CANS CREAM OF CHICKEN SOUP
1	CUP MAYONNAISE
1	TEASPOON LEMON JUICE
1/2	TEASPOON CURRY POWDER
1/2	CUP SHREDDED SHARP CHEDDAR CHEESE
1/2	CUP TOASTED BREAD CRUMBS
1	TABLESPOON BUTTER

Assemble all ingredients and utensils. In a flat 2-quart casserole dish, place a layer of cooked broccoli and turkey. In a bowl, combine all sauce ingredients except bread crumbs and butter. Layer one half of sauce over turkey and broccoli. Repeat layers again. Top with bread crumbs and butter. Bake in a 350-degree oven for 25 to 30 minutes. Yield: 6 to 8 servings.

Per serving: 443 calories; 32 g fat; 70 mg cholesterol; 916 mg sodium.

Over and over again this Turkey Divan solves those holiday leftover problems. Now it is popular all year long. Chicken is an excellent substitute for turkey in this casserole. I have enjoyed this dish prepared by many recipes, but this adaptation can't be beaten. Enjoy!

Miss Daisy

DID DE SOTO SLEEP HERE?

From the first settlement of Middle Tennessee by Anglo-Americans in the late 1770s and early 1780s, there has been debate that maybe other people of European descent actually came through the region hundreds of years earlier. The Old Stone Fort at Manchester is one example of this line of thought. There, some folks believe Welshmen built the large complex in the 1100s, while wandering across eastern America from a shipwreck in the Gulf of Mobile. Of course, De Soto, the Spanish explorer, was a known quantity. Everyone knew that he came through parts of Tennessee during his travels of the southeast in the mid-

1500s, but no one knew just where. Local residents were thus surprised when they read in the February 9, 1872, issue of the Columbia *Herald* that "A Spanish grave has been discovered near the junction of Duck and Piney rivers in Hickman County. A stone was found in the grave upon which were inscribed the initials 'B.D.' and the date 1540. There was also an inscription in Latin partly demolished. . . ." After causing considerable excitement among scientific circles across the state, the so-called "Spanish" grave was discovered to be a hoax. A Hickman County resident named Baird fully investigated the matter and found that although remains of an ancient stone fortification did exist in the vicinity, and in fact, a Spanish coin had been found there years prior, there was absolutely no proof that the fort was of Spanish construction.

Blount Mansion
"*Made*" Dish of Crabmeat

1	POUND CRABMEAT
1/2	POUND MUSHROOMS
4	TABLESPOONS FLOUR
5	TABLESPOONS BUTTER, DIVIDED
1	CUP HEAVY CREAM
2	TABLESPOONS BRANDY OR SHERRY
1	TABLESPOON LEMON JUICE
1/2	TEASPOON DRIED MUSTARD
1	SMALL JAR CHOPPED PIMENTOS
1	TABLESPOON CAPERS
3/4	CUP SHARP CHEESE

Check crab for pieces of shell, try not to break. Lightly sauté mushrooms in 1 tablespoon butter. Make a cream sauce with remaining 4 tablespoons butter, flour and cream. Add brandy, lemon juice and mustard. Carefully fold in crab, mushrooms, pimento and capers. Sprinkle cheese over top. Bake 15 to 20 minutes, just until cheese melts.

Company Crab Cakes

1 1/2	POUNDS BACKFIN CRABMEAT
2	EGGS
1	TABLESPOON WORCESTERSHIRE SAUCE
1	TABLESPOON MAYONNAISE
1	TABLESPOON BAKING POWDER
1	TABLESPOON BUTTER, MELTED
2	TEASPOONS CHOPPED FRESH PARSLEY
1	TEASPOON SALT
1/4	TEASPOON TABASCO SAUCE
6	SALTINE CRACKERS CRUMBLED
4	TABLESPOONS BUTTER

Assemble all ingredients and utensils. In a large bowl mix all ingredients, except crackers and 4 tablespoons of butter, with crabmeat. Shape into cakes about 1/2 inch thick. Roll in cracker crumbs. In a heavy skillet melt butter. Fry crab cakes until golden brown and cooked through. Yield: 6 servings.

You may use salmon instead.

Per serving: 249 calories; 14 g fat; 219 mg cholesterol; 1155 mg sodium.

Blount Mansion

Blount Mansion in Knoxville, Tennessee, was the executive residence of William Blount, governor of the Southwest Territory, his wife Mary and five of their children. This gracious frame home was built between 1792 and 1830 and is Knoxville's only registered National Historic Landmark.

Blount was a signer of the United States Constitution; the first and only governor of the Southwest Territory (1790-1796); and was the first U. S. Senator from the state of Tennessee (1796-1798).

The governor's office, located behind Blount Mansion, served as the capitol of the Southwest Territory from 1792-

1796, and was the site where the Tennessee state constitution was drafted.

Blount Mansion became the center of political, social and cultural activity as Knoxville grew, and Governor Blount entertained frequently. Fish from the local rivers was among the variety of food served to these guests, although the Blounts must have missed the crab, shrimp, and oysters of their native North Carolina coast.

Honey Alexander's Crab Victoria

1	POUND FRESH WHITE LUMP CRAB MEAT
1/2	CUP CHOPPED GREEN PEPPER
1	TABLESPOON COARSE GROUND PEPPER
1/2	CUP CHOPPED ONION
3	TABLESPOONS DURKEES DRESSING

Sauté onions and green pepper until glassy. Add crab meat, pepper, and Durkees. Heat through. Yield: 4 to 6 servings.

Fried Oysters

1	PINT OYSTERS
1	CUP PLAIN WHITE CORN MEAL
1/2	TEASPOON SALT
1/2	TEASPOON BLACK PEPPER
1	CUP COOKING OIL

Assemble all ingredients and utensils. In a bowl combine corn meal, salt and pepper. Dredge oysters in cornmeal mixture until thoroughly covered. In a saucepan or large skillet, heat oil and fry until golden brown. Yield: 4 servings.

Per serving: 432 calories; 30 g fat; 60 mg cholesterol; 354 mg sodium.

*W*HEN I ASKED THE FORMER FIRST LADIES FOR SOME OF THEIR FAVORITE RECIPES, HONEY ALEXANDER WAS ON THE PRESIDENTIAL CAMPAIGN TRAIL WITH HER HUSBAND LAMAR. SHE FAXED ME SEVERAL RECIPES HER MOTHER HAD RECENTLY SHARED WITH HER FROM A SPA IN HONEY'S HOMETOWN OF VICTORIA, TEXAS. MRS. ALEXANDER WAS FIRST LADY OF TENNESSEE DURING HER HUSBAND'S TENURE AS HEAD OF OUR STATE (1979–1987).

Miss Daisy

TENNESSEE'S LOST COUNTY

Counties, just like businesses, must have sufficient resources to operate. If they don't, then, just like businesses, they fail to survive and in some cases, go bankrupt. Such is the story of Tennessee's ninety-sixth county, which saw the light of day way back in 1871, but didn't survive as a political entity but forty-eight years. The county was named "James," after the Reverend Jesse J. James, the father of the representative who had guided the county's formation through the State legislature.

Created from parts of the existing Bradley and Hamilton Counties, the county seat was supposed by most folks to be placed at Harrison, which already had a courthouse. Voters pre-

JAMES COUNTY

ferred Ooltewah, however, so all of the official records were moved there, the courthouse at Harrison was demolished, and useable parts of it moved to Ooltewah and used for building a new courthouse. No sooner had James County—called

by most folks simply, "Jim"—begun to function than it ran into financial difficulties. The expense of suddenly having to provide funding for schools, highways, and the like was just too much for the small population of the county. As an official entity, James County lasted nearly half a century before authorities declared bankruptcy. In late 1919, after the legislature had approved abolishing the destitute county, its residents voted that it be merged with its larger neighbor, Hamilton. And so it was, thus becoming the first county in the United States to merge with another county.

Parson's Table Salmon Cashew

SALMON FILLET
WHITE WINE
LEMON JUICE
CLARIFIED BUTTER
CASHEW NUTS
HERBED CREAM CHEESE (GARLIC, SHALLOTS, DILL,
    SALT, AND PEPPER)

Place the salmon in a baking dish with white wine, lemon juice and clarified butter in the bottom. Place herbed cream cheese in a pastry bag and pipe it out on top of the salmon. Then, cover with cashews. Bake in a 350-degree oven for about 15 minutes.

*N*ESTLED WITHIN TENNESSEE'S OLDEST TOWN ON AN INCLINE BEHIND THE WASHINGTON COUNTY COURTHOUSE IS THE PARSON'S TABLE. ONCE THE HOME OF THE FIRST CHRISTIAN CHURCH, THIS BRICK GOTHIC REVIVAL STRUCTURE HAS STOOD IN JONESBOROUGH SINCE THE EARLY 1870S. WHILE UNDER CONSTRUCTION, A CHOLERA EPIDEMIC SWEPT TENNNESSEE. THE CARPENTERS WORKING ON THE CHURCH STOPPED TO BUILD COFFINS FOR THE VICTIMS. THE CHURCH HAS BEEN A TEMPERANCE HALL, LECTURE HALL, WOODWORKING SHOP, AND PRESENTLY, A RESTAURANT.

Miss Daisy

"LITTLE LORD FAUNTLEROY"

Few Tennesseans today realize that one of the world's most prolific and popular writers of juvenile literature lived part of her life in the Volunteer State. Frances Hodgson Burnett was born in 1849 into a middle-class English family. She grew up in Manchester, England, and as a romantic at heart, she was quick to discern the vast differences that existed between the poorer classes of the city and the noble ones. When her family's business failed in 1865, she and her widowed mother sailed for the United States to be near her brother who operated a grocery store in Knoxville, Tennessee. Frances and her mother located in New Market, a small hamlet in

JEFFERSON COUNTY

Jefferson County, and there, the young girl began her long journey as a writer. Her magazine articles were immediately accepted by such prestigious periodicals as *Scribner's,* among others. She married a local physician, Dr. Swan Burnett, received a sizeable advance from a publisher, and traveled with her husband and young son to Paris, before returning to the United States and the publication of her first novel, *That Lass o'Lowrie's.* This was followed by several other books, most of them featuring fictional depictions of her own sons. *Little Lord Fauntleroy* was an immediate success, but she is probably best remembered for *The Secret Garden.* Frances eventually divorced Dr. Burnett, married and divorced a second time, and finally settled down on Long Island, New York, where she died in 1924.

 East Tennessee is famous for its tailors. Probably the best known one was Andrew Johnson who, of course, became president of the United States after Abraham Lincoln's assassination in 1865. But, Johnson County (incidentally, not named for Andrew Johnson, but rather for Thomas Johnson, an early settler in the area) was the home for a noted tailor as well, Roderick Random Butler. Butler was born in 1827 in Virginia, but made his way to Tennessee as a child with his family. When he was thirteen years old, Butler became apprenticed to a tailor,

JOHNSON COUNTY

but after learning the trade, he decided to become a lawyer instead. He eventually settled in Taylorsville, the county seat, but later moved to Mountain City. Upon admission to the Johnson County bar, the tailor turned lawyer began his practice, as well as a long series of appointed and elected public offices. He served as justice of the peace, postmaster, county judge, circuit judge, and member of the Tennessee Legislature before being sent to the United States House of Representatives as a Republican in 1868, where he served until 1875. Butler then served in the Tennessee Legislature again from 1879 until 1887, when he was again elected to the United States Congress, serving one term. During the War Between the States, Butler joined the Union Army and attained the rank of lieutenant-colonel of the 13th Tennessee Cavalry. During his term in the State Legislature, Butler was successful in having the county seat moved from Taylorsville to Mountain City.

Deep Fried Salmon Puffs

1 1/4	CUPS DRAINED CANNED PINK SALMON
1/2	CUP ALL-PURPOSE FLOUR
1/4	TEASPOON SALT
1/4	TEASPOON SODA
1/2	CUP BUTTERMILK
2	EGGS
1	CUP COOKING OIL TO COVER SALMON MIXTURE

Assemble all ingredients and utensils. Flake the salmon and set aside. Combine the dry ingredients in a bowl and stir in buttermilk and eggs. Mix thoroughly. Add flaked salmon. In a heavy skillet or deep saucepan heat cooking oil to almost boiling. Drop salmon mixture by teaspoonfuls into hot oil. Fry until golden brown. Serve immediately. If using a temperature-controlled pan, temperature should be about 375 degrees. Yield: 6 servings.

Per serving: 289 calories; 23 g fat; 109 mg cholesterol; 375 mg sodium.

Party Salmon Steaks

4	1-INCH THICK SALMON STEAKS
2	LEMONS
1 1/2	TEASPOONS SEASONING SALT
8	TABLESPOONS MAYONNAISE
1	TEASPOON NUTMEG
1	CUP SLICED FRESH MUSHROOMS
1/4	CUP PARMESAN CHEESE

Assemble all ingredients and utensils. In a 13x9x2-inch or oblong baking pan, place steaks. Do not let sides of salmon steaks touch. Squeeze juice of 1/2 lemon over each steak and sprinkle with seasoning salt. Spread 2 tablespoons of mayonnaise over each steak. Sprinkle nutmeg over all. Top each steak with mushrooms and Parmesan cheese. Bake in a 400-degree oven for 15 minutes. Yield: 4 servings.

Per serving: 440 calories; 33 g fat; 102 mg cholesterol; 1115 mg sodium.

Broiled Scallops

3/4	CUP LEMON JUICE
2	CLOVES GARLIC, CRUSHED
1	TEASPOON SALT
1/2	TEASPOON GROUND BLACK PEPPER
1/2	CUP VEGETABLE OIL
1/4	CUP CHOPPED FRESH PARSLEY
2	POUNDS SCALLOPS
8	OUNCES FRESH MUSHROOM CAPS, OPTIONAL

Assemble all ingredients and utensils. In a large bowl, mix all ingredients, marinating at least 1 hour. Remove scallops and mushrooms. Place on foil-lined baking pan or broiler pan. Broil 8 to 10 minutes, 4 to 5 inches from heat, turning once. Yield: 4 servings.

Per serving: 469 calories; 29 g fat; 75 mg cholesterol; 902 mg sodium.

Seafood Casserole

2	10 3/4-OUNCE CANS CREAM OF CELERY SOUP
1/2	CUP WATER
1/4	CUP DRY SHERRY
2	3-OUNCE CANS CRABMEAT, RINSED AND DRAINED
2	3-OUNCE CANS LOBSTER, RINSED AND DRAINED
1	POUND FRESH COOKED, PEELED SHRIMP
1 1/2	CUPS SHREDDED CHEDDAR CHEESE
2	TABLESPOONS MINCED PARSLEY
1	CUP BUTTERED BREAD CRUMBS
	TOAST POINTS OR COOKED WHITE RICE

Assemble all ingredients and utensils. In a bowl, combine all ingredients except 3/4 cup of cheese and bread crumbs. Pour into a 13x9x2-inch casserole dish. Top with remaining cheese and bread crumbs. Bake in a 350-degree oven for 30 to 40 minutes or until bubbly. Yield: 4 to 6 servings.

Per serving: 581 calories; 21 g fat; 272 mg cholesterol; 1576 mg sodium.

KID CURRY IN KNOXVILLE

During the latter days of the nineteenth century and the early ones of the twentieth, Harvey Logan, alias "Kid" Curry, was one of America's most wanted criminals. A former member of the infamous "Wild Bunch," headed by Butch Cassidy and the Sundance Kid, Logan continued his criminal activities after the gang split up and each outlaw went his separate way from the hideout in Wyoming. By the fall of 1901, Logan had traveled far beyond Wyoming and found himself in a pool room in far-away Knoxville, Tennessee, where he got

KNOX COUNTY

into a brawl, shot several men, and barely escaped with his life.

The law caught up with Logan near Jefferson City, hauled him back to Knoxville, and held him in the city jail until he could be tried. In late 1902, he was convicted, but immediately filed an appeal. The Tennessee Supreme Court refused to hear the case, and it was determined to send Logan to a federal prison in Ohio. Logan, however, had different ideas. On June 27, 1903, he overwhelmed his guard, stole a couple of pistols, and lit out for the wilderness of the Great Smoky Mountains. Headlines in *The Knoxville Sentinel* screamed out "Bandit Logan Was Last Seen Five Miles From City . . . Riding Leisurely Along a Byroad." But the Kid made good his escape and made it all the way to Colorado looking for Butch Cassidy when another sheriff's posse caught up with him in July 1903, after he robbed a train. Wounded in the ensuing fracas, Logan ended it all with a bullet to his left temple.

GRANDDADDY OF ALL EARTHQUAKES

During the early morning hours of December 16, 1811, people all over the eastern United States felt the earth shake violently. Curious residents in Charleston, South Carolina, ran out of their homes when the tremors set all of the town's church bells to ringing. In Washington, D. C., windows of houses and businesses vibrated violently as the force of the tremor hit that city. And, in Nashville, construction workers on the Public Square left their jobs when the building upon which they worked shook so much that they feared for their lives.

LAKE COUNTY

The common denominator of these rumblings deep within the earth was an earthquake that had just occurred in the wilderness of West Tennessee, specifically, today's Lake County. The tremors continued for the next two months, with two especially violent quakes occurring on January 23 and February 7, 1812. The epi-centers of all three earthquakes lay in the region that forms the common borders of Tennessee, Kentucky, and Missouri. It is impossible today to assess how high on the Richter Scale the tremors registered, but modern-day scientists are unanimous in describing them as the worst ever to hit the North American continent. Reelfoot Lake is a modern-day reminder of the earthquakes of 1811-12. The nearly sixty thousand acre lake was created when the ground of a swamp fell several feet and allowed water from nearby Reelfoot Creek to rush in. Today, Reelfoot Lake serves as a state park and wildlife sanctuary.

Seafood Gumbo

First you make a roux:

1. Method: In an iron skillet, heat equal parts of oil and flour according to the desired thickness of roux. Start with 1/2 cup of oil; heat until HOT! Add 1/2 cup flour. Stir constantly over medium high heat until the color of milk chocolate. Add 1 cup water and continue to stir out lumps. Set aside.

2. Fat free method: In an iron skillet sprayed with Pam, add 1 cup flour, spread evenly. Place in a heated oven 425 degrees, set timer and check in 15 minutes. Stir well and check the color of the flour every 5 minutes, stirring each time until desired color is reached (medium beige). Take the skillet out and place on top of stove (no heat). STAND BACK and pour 2 cups of water into the skillet. Stir with a long-handled wooden spoon to prevent steam burn. Set aside. In a large soup pot, sauté the following in 1/4 cup oil: (Fat Free Method: Sauté ingredients in own juices over medium heat with a tightly covered top).

4	LARGE CHOPPED ONIONS
3	CLOVES GARLIC MASHED
2	LARGE CHOPPED BELL PEPPERS
4	LARGE STALKS CELERY
1	POUND OKRA SLICED
1	TABLESPOON DRIED PARSLEY

Cook until transparent. Add:

1	LARGE CAN TOMATOES

To taste add salt, pepper and red pepper

1	TABLESPOON PAPRIKA
4	CHICKEN BULLION CUBES
3 1/2	QUARTS HOT WATER

Stir and check taste for salt, pepper and red pepper. Cover and Bake in the oven 275 degrees 3-4 hours. Remove from oven and add

3	POUNDS PEELED UNCOOKED SHRIMP
1	CAN OYSTERS (FRESH OPTIONAL)
1	CAN CRAB MEAT (FRESH OPTIONAL)
1	CHICKEN COOKED, CHOPPED AND DEBONED (OPTIONAL)

Heat on lowest temperature only until the shrimp turn pink. Serve in a bowl of rice sprinkled with 1 teaspoon filé. Yield: 6-8 servings.

Submitted by Mary Worley from the Hardee Murfree chapter of the Daughters of the American Revolution.

Grilled Marinated Shrimp

2	POUNDS JUMBO SHRIMP
1/2	CUP VEGETABLE OIL
1/2	CUP SOY SAUCE
3	CLOVES GARLIC, FINELY MINCED
2	TABLESPOONS LEMON JUICE
1	TEASPOON GINGER

Assemble all ingredients and utensils. Peel, devein and wash shrimp. Pat dry. Place in a bowl. In a bowl, combine remaining ingredients and pour over shrimp. Cover and refrigerate at least 3 hours. Skewer shrimp and cook over hot coals for 4 to 5 minutes on each side. Serve immediately while hot. Yield: 6 servings.

Per serving: 256 calories; 20 g fat; 113 mg cholesterol; 1191 mg sodium.

Creole Shrimp

1/4	CUP VEGETABLE OIL
1	CUP DICED ONION
1	CUP DICED CELERY
1/2	CUP DICED GREEN PEPPER
3 1/2	CUPS CANNED CHUNK OR DICED TOMATOES
1	8-OUNCE CAN TOMATO SAUCE
2	BAY LEAVES
1	TABLESPOON SUGAR
1	TABLESPOON CHILI POWDER
2	TEASPOONS SALT
1/8	TEASPOON HOT SAUCE
2	POUNDS CLEANED, DEVEINED, TAILS OFF MEDIUM SHRIMP
1/4	CUP ALL PURPOSE FLOUR
1/4	CUP WATER
3	CUPS COOKED WHITE RICE

Assemble all ingredients and utensils. In a large saucepan, sauté onion, celery and pepper in oil until tender. Add tomatoes, tomato sauce, bay leaves, sugar, salt and chili powder. Mix well. Simmer 30 minutes. Remove bay leaves. Add shrimp. Simmer an additional 30 minutes. In a small bowl, mix flour and water to a paste; add a cup of hot tomato mixture and stir with wire whisk until blended. Add flour mixture to tomato mixture. Cook until creole is thickened; about 5 to 10 minutes. Serve over cooked rice. Yields: 6 servings.

Per serving: 433 calories; 13 g fat; 230 mg cholesterol; 1860 mg sodium.

VICTORY OR MASSACRE?

At 5:30 A.M. on April 12, 1864, fifteen hundred Confederate cavalrymen attacked the Union garrison at Fort Pillow, perched on the bluffs overlooking the Mississippi River in Lauderdale County. Garrisoned by nearly six hundred white and black Union troops, the fort was commanded by Major Lionel F. Booth. Confederate General James R. Chalmers, under orders of General Nathan Bedford Forrest, hit the earthwork fort with everything he had. By noon, with General Forrest now in command, fierce fighting had given the Confederates

LAUDERDALE COUNTY

the upper hand. One of Forrest's men later wrote that "it was perfectly apparent to any man endowed with the smallest amount of common sense that to all intents and purposes the fort was ours." Yet, when Forrest demanded surrender, Union commanders inside stalled, hoping for the arrival of reinforcements from downriver. Confederate cavalrymen then charged the fort again, driving the Union defenders out of its walls and down to the river banks where they were picked off along the way. Forrest and his command were accused of massacring some of the Union soldiers after they had laid down their arms. He denied the charges, but the incident is still debated among historians today. One of those historians wrote, "Perhaps a reasonable conclusion is that much confusion existed during the attack and that there were some unnecessary acts of violence by the Confederates, but that the majority of the casualties were the result of legitimate, though hardly humane, warfare."

Jonesborough Storytelling Festival

In 1973, the town of Jonesborough hosted the first full-fledged storytelling festival in the nation. It was tiny—and there weren't many tellers or listeners—but something happened that weekend that changed the fate of this small Tennessee town and the future of the art form forever. After that first storytelling event, people the world over began to rediscover the simplicity and basic truth of the well-told tale. The festival, growing larger every year, gradually became the spearhead for a national movement—a movement that celebrates the rich history of American storytelling and the talebearers who share their stories.

By 1975, the tellers and the listeners were emerging in unbelievable numbers. Librarians, teachers, people from every walk of life and geographic location were making their way to Jonesborough. Three years after its simple beginning on a hay wagon, the festival, by necessity, moved from rocking chairs into meeting halls, and finally, into large, colorful tents. Still meeting in tents today, there continues to be more and more listeners and an ever-widening array of talent.

The festival, now attracting audiences of more than 8,000 each year, has received numerous honors and international recognition, including its designation in 1984 and 1995 by the American Bus Association as one of the Top 100 Events in North America.

Storytelling Shrimp Gumbo

1	STICK OF BUTTER
3	BELL PEPPERS CHOPPED
4-6	CANS CHOPPED TOMATOES
2	POUNDS FROZEN OKRA
	FILE POWDER
2	TABLESPOONS GARLIC
	YOUR ROUX ★
3	LARGE ONIONS CHOPPED
1/2	PACK CELERY CHOPPED
	WATER TO BOIL
1/8	CUP WORCESTERSHIRE SAUCE
3	TABLESPOONS CREOLE SPICE
4	POUNDS PEELED UNCOOKED SHRIMP

Melt the butter in large stock pot, add the onion and stir for a few minutes and then add the celery and then the bell peppers. Just cook for a couple of minutes, just to get them started. Add the cans of tomatoes and the water, just enough to make the soup watery to add the shrimp and okra, you can always add more later if needed. Add the okra and the shrimp and stir to mix. Add the remaining spices and let it cook for a few minutes on medium high till the shrimp is done. Meanwhile to make your roux (★) in a separate sauce pan, melt one stick of butter and get it hot (not burning) then add 1/2 teaspoon paprika, and 3 to 6 tablespoons of flour. And stir and stir and stir and stir and stir and stir and stir and stir and stir and stir till you cannot stir anymore and stir some more! This will turn a copper penny color, and that is how you tell when it is ready. Pour it directly into the gumbo and stir to mix and set on low heat and cook for 20 to 30 minutes stirring occasionally till ready to eat. Great when served over steamed rice.

This is the recipe we have been using for storytelling since 1982. You may have to refine it to your tastes. As I have reduced our 10 gallon recipe here for you to make at home, you may want more peppers and less onion, etc. This is your choice and you get to play and make this your very own version, as with any recipe you come across. Bon appetite!

P.S. See you at storytelling to give us the comparison.

VEGETABLES

*Nashville is the turnip-greens
and hog-jowl center of the universe.*

Alfred Leland Crabb

$\mathcal{V}$EGETABLES

Scalloped Artichokes

1/2	CUP CHOPPED YELLOW ONION
1/2	CUP CHOPPED GREEN PEPPER
5	TABLESPOONS BUTTER
2	14-OUNCE CANS ARTICHOKE HEARTS, DRAINED
1/8	TEASPOON BASIL
1/8	TEASPOON THYME
1/4	TEASPOON SALT
1/8	TEASPOON TABASCO SAUCE
1	EGG
1	CUP SOUR CREAM
10	SALTINE CRACKERS
	PAPRIKA FOR GARNISH

Assemble all ingredients and utensils. In a saucepan, cook onion and green pepper in the butter until the onion is clear. Add drained artichoke hearts and seasonings, mixing well. Place in a 2-quart casserole dish. In a separate bowl, beat egg slightly and combine with sour cream. Crumble 5 crackers over artichoke mixture. Pour sour cream over artichokes and crumble remaining crackers on top. Bake in a 375-degree oven 20 minutes or until bubbly. Sprinkle with paprika. Yield: 6 to 8 servings.

A complement to the Lemon Veal (*see* p. 74).

Per serving: 180 calories; 15 g fat; 67 mg cholesterol; 384 mg sodium.

A DARING YOUNG MAN WITH A FLYING MACHINE

Thirty-one years before Orville and Wilbur Wright demonstrated to the world at Kitty Hawk, North Carolina, that machines were capable of flying through the air with humans aboard, a man in Lawrence County had already performed the same feat. James Jackson Pennington had assembled a primitive flying machine, which he called the "Aerial Bird," at his home on the Buffalo River near the small town of Henryville. In April 1872, before a crowd of amazed onlookers, Pennington cranked up his contraption and flew! Pennington was quick to patent his revolutionary idea, although it took five years for

LAWRENCE COUNTY

him to officially obtain the protection offered by the patent. His application described his invention as a machine that "consists of a fan of peculiar construction, which takes air from the front of the airship and forces it out at the rear. The object of my invention is to provide apparatus by which the air may be navigated with facility and safety." In 1883, Pennington attended the Columbian Exposition in Louisville and was confronted by two men who, after reviewing Pennington's working model of the Aerial Bird, wanted to buy the patent. Pennington refused, but after he died in 1884, his widow was visited by two men. Years later, when a search of the Patent Office revealed that the plans to Pennington's airship were missing, speculation arose that the two mystery men might have been the Wright brothers.

When Meriwether Lewis left his job as governor of Louisiana Territory in St. Louis during mid-1809, Tennessee was the furthest thing from his mind. Back only three years from his monumental expedition with William Clark to the Pacific Ocean, Lewis was now en route to Washington D. C. to straighten out some territorial fiscal affairs. When he reached Chickasaw Bluffs, the site of today's city of Memphis, he decided to leave the Mississippi River and travel overland to the Natchez Trace, then follow that trail northward to Nashville,

**LEWIS
COUNTY**

thence to Washington. On the evening of October 10, 1809, the travel-weary Lewis approached Grinder's Stand, a small hostelry located on the Trace some sixty miles south of Nashville. As he neared the log building, situated in a small clearing in the otherwise thick forest, he met Mrs. Robert Grinder, the wife of the owner. With Lewis were his servant, Pernia, and a slave belonging to Major James Neelly, the agent for the Chickasaw Nation. Neelly, looking for runaway horses, was to catch up later. Mrs. Grinder offered Lewis and the others accommodations for the night. After dining, the famed explorer retired to his tiny guest room. Some hours later, Mrs. Grinder was awakened by the sound of gunshots, and when she peered through Lewis's door, she found him suffering from two savage wounds. Lewis died shortly afterwards, and to this day, it remains uncertain if he took his own life or was murdered by persons unknown. Lewis County is named in his honor.

Steamed Artichokes With Tomatoes

4	LARGE TOMATOES, PEELED AND CHOPPED OR
2	14-OUNCE CANS ITALIAN PLUM TOMATOES WITH JUICE
1	14-OUNCE CAN ARTICHOKE HEARTS, DRAINED AND CHOPPED
1	MEDIUM YELLOW ONION, CHOPPED COARSELY
1	TEASPOON SALT IF USING FRESH TOMATOES
1/2	TEASPOON GROUND BLACK PEPPER
1/2	TEASPOON DRIED BASIL

Assemble all ingredients and utensils. In a medium saucepan combine all ingredients and simmer until tomatoes are cooked and tender; 45 minutes for fresh tomatoes and 15 minutes for canned tomatoes. Yield: 4 to 6 servings.

This recipe is equally good served cold. Basil enhances the flavor of the artichokes and tomatoes.

Per serving: 63 calories; 0 g fat; 0 mg cholesterol; 359 mg sodium.

Spring Asparagus

Fresh asparagus is wonderful served simply with lemon juice and butter. Preparation is so easy in a steamer, but you can cook equally as well in a deep pot.

	FRESH ASPARAGUS TIED IN BUNDLES, WASHED AND ENDS CUT OFF
	BOILING WATER
1 1/2	TEASPOONS SALT PER QUART OF WATER
	LEMON JUICE
	BUTTER
	HOLLANDAISE OR VEGETABLE SAUCE
	PIMENTO FOR GARNISH

In a large pot fill with water. Let water come to a boil, add salt. Add asparagus and boil rapidly for 15 minutes or until tender. Drain and serve immediately with lemon juice and butter or Hollandaise or your favorite vegetable sauce. Allow at least 4 to 6 pieces per person.

Tastes of springtime in France on a Tennessee dinner table.

Per serving: 56 calories; 4 g fat; 11 mg cholesterol; 310 mg sodium.

Asparagus Casserole

2	16-OUNCE CANS ASPARAGUS TIPS, DRAINED
1	10 3/4-OUNCE CAN CREAM OF MUSHROOM SOUP
1	2-OUNCE JAR PIMENTO CUT IN SMALL PIECES
3	HARD BOILED EGGS, MASHED
1/2	CUP CHOPPED ONION
1	CUP GRATED MEDIUM CHEDDAR CHEESE
2	CUPS CRUSHED POTATO CHIPS
2	TABLESPOONS MELTED BUTTER

Assemble all ingredients and utensils. In a large, 3-quart casserole dish layer 1 can of asparagus, 1/2 can of soup, 1/2 jar of pimento, 1/2 of mashed eggs, 1/4 cup of onion, sprinkle with 1/2 cup cheese and 1 cup potato chips. Repeat layers and pour melted butter over top layer. Bake in a 350-degree oven for 25 minutes. Yield: 8 servings.

Per serving: 229 calories; 17 g fat; 126 mg cholesterol; 928 mg sodium.

Baked Beans

6	SLICES BACON, PARTIALLY COOKED AND CHOPPED
1	16-OUNCE CAN PORK AND BEANS
1	20-OUNCE CAN PORK AND BEANS
1/2	CUP DARK BROWN SUGAR
1/2	CUP CATSUP
1/2	CUP CHOPPED ONION
1/4	CUP CHOPPED GREEN PEPPER
1/2	TEASPOON CHILI POWDER

Assemble all ingredients and utensils. In a skillet, partially fry bacon; drain. Add with other ingredients in a 2-quart baking dish. Bake slowly in a 275-degree oven uncovered for 2 hours or longer. Yield: 6 to 8 servings.

A must with barbecue sandwiches.

Per serving: 252 calories; 5 g fat; 14 mg cholesterol; 849 mg sodium.

Bush Brothers and Company

Bush Brothers and Company's beginnings trace back to the late 1800s when A. J. Bush and his wife, Sarah, opened a general store in the community of Chestnut Hill, Tennessee. Local customers made purchases by barter. Chickens, eggs, butter and other farm products were exchanged for goods. Mr. Bush recognized the need for a cash economy and, in 1904, with the help of the Stokelys of Newport, began a tomato canning plant in Chestnut Hill.

By 1908, the company was known as Bush Brothers and Company. Today, the plant processes a complete line of bean products, fresh vegetables, specialty items, and pet foods. Through the years, Bush Brothers bought other facilities across the Midwest and the South. This includes Southern Peas in Blytheville, Arkansas, Sauerkraut in Shiocton, Wisconsin, and spinach production in Muskogee, Oklahoma. A. J. Bush and Co, Inc. still operates the same store that A. J. and Sarah Bush opened in Chestnut Hill. A restaurant nearby also serves the community.

Black Beans

2	CUPS UNCOOKED BLACK BEANS
2	QUARTS WATER
1/2	POUND SALT PORK OR BACON
1	CUP CHOPPED ONION
4	CLOVES GARLIC, CRUSHED
1	BAY LEAF
2	TEASPOONS DRIED OREGANO
1	TABLESPOON OLIVE OIL

Assemble all ingredients and utensils. Wash and clean black beans. Pour beans into a large pot, then cover with 2 quarts water and soak 3 or 4 hours. Bring to a boil without salting. Turn down heat and allow to simmer until tender. Sauté salt pork or bacon until crisp. Remove fat. In the grease sauté onion and garlic until tender. Add bay leaf and dried oregano; stir well. Transfer beans, salt pork pieces or bacon, sautéed onion, garlic and seasonings to a large pot. Add olive oil. Simmer 30 minutes and serve. Yield: 6 servings.

Beans are enhanced by adding 1/4 cup red wine during the last 30 minutes of cooking.

Per serving: 315 calories; 9 g fat; 9 mg cholesterol; 173 mg sodium.

*T*HE BEST METHOD OF REHEATING VEGETABLES IS IN THE MICROWAVE OR IN THE TOP OF A DOUBLE BOILER.
Miss Daisy

Creole Green Beans

1	CUP DICED ONION
3	TABLESPOONS BACON GREASE
1	NO. 2 CAN STRING BEANS, DRAINED
1/2	CUP CHILI SAUCE
1	TEASPOON SALT
1/2	TEASPOON GROUND BLACK PEPPER

Assemble all ingredients and utensils. In a saucepan combine onion and bacon drippings. Let simmer on very low heat until onions are tender. Add drained beans, chili sauce, salt, and black pepper. Cover and cook about 30 minutes. Yield: 6 servings.

Per serving: 69 calories; 2 g fat; 4 mg cholesterol; 870 mg sodium.

*L*EST WE FORGET—THERE IS NOTHING BETTER THAN FRESH COOKED GREEN BEANS FROM THE GARDEN WITH BOILED NEW POTATOES COOKED ON TOP OF THE BEANS.
Miss Daisy

Green Bean Casserole

2	16-OUNCE CANS FRENCH CUT GREEN BEANS, DRAINED
2	10 3/4-OUNCE CANS CREAM OF MUSHROOM SOUP
1	CUP CHOPPED GREEN PEPPER
1	CUP CHOPPED YELLOW ONION
1	CUP CHOPPED CELERY
1/4	CUP SLIVERED ALMONDS
1/3	CUP DICED PIMENTO
1	CAN FRIED ONION RINGS

Assemble all ingredients and utensils. In a large bowl combine and mix well all ingredients except fried onion rings. Pour into a buttered 2-quart casserole dish. Top with onion rings. Bake in a 350-degree oven for 35 to 40 minutes or until bubbly. Yield: 8 servings.

Per serving: 197 calories; 13 g fat; 2 mg cholesterol; 873 mg sodium.

GREEN BEAN CASSEROLE IS ALWAYS CERTAIN TO MAKE AN APPEARANCE AT CHURCH SUPPERS. I SUPPOSE THIS RECIPE HAS PROBABLY BEEN SERVED IN EVERY TENNESSEE KITCHEN SINCE CANNED SOUPS AND CANNED ONION RINGS WERE MANUFACTURED. WHEN GROCERY SHOPPING FOR FRIED ONION RINGS LOOK FOR THEM ON THE GROCERY SHELF BESIDE GREEN BEANS.

Miss Daisy

Stokely VanCamp

John B. Stokely was a prominent East Tennessean with farms ten miles out of Newport. He died prematurely and left wife Anna Rorex Stokely with eight children. The eldest child, William, was 17 at the time. Hoping to create a market for their vast produce, Anna and her four sons began a partnership called Stokely Brothers and Company. The company's canning operation began in 1898 after the three oldest brothers had graduated from the University of Tennessee in Knoxville.

The Stokely family packed tomatoes by using an old steam engine to heat water! The tomatoes were cooked in huge metal tubs, put into hundreds of tin cans, and distributed in wooden boxes. Stokely Brothers was soon shipping them down the Mississippi River. Other food items were also introduced and new markets entered.

During World War I, Stokely Brothers became a leading supplier of foods to the armed forces. The VanCamp Packing Company of Indianapolis, Indiana, was also a main supplier. In 1933 William B. Stokely, Jr. acquired VanCamp. Stokely VanCamp is now a household word in America, and it has a large export division servicing over 80 markets worldwide. Anna Rorex Stokely would surely be pleased.

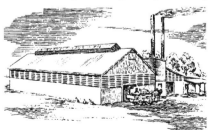

NEWPORT, TENNESSEE SITE OF FIRST
STOKELY BROTHERS PLANT

Red Beans and Rice

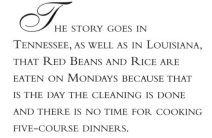

THE STORY GOES IN TENNESSEE, AS WELL AS IN LOUISIANA, THAT RED BEANS AND RICE ARE EATEN ON MONDAYS BECAUSE THAT IS THE DAY THE CLEANING IS DONE AND THERE IS NO TIME FOR COOKING FIVE-COURSE DINNERS.

Miss Daisy

1	POUND RED KIDNEY BEANS, WASHED AND DRAINED
1	POUND CHOPPED HAM
1	HAM BONE
1	CUP CHOPPED CELERY
1	CUP CHOPPED ONION
1/2	CUP CHOPPED GREEN PEPPER
3	CLOVES GARLIC
2	BAY LEAVES
1	TEASPOON OREGANO
1/2	TEASPOON CAYENNE PEPPER
1/2	TEASPOON SALT OR MORE TO TASTE
1	TEASPOON OR MORE TO TASTE OF HOT SAUCE COOKED WHITE RICE, 1/2 CUP PER PERSON

Assemble all ingredients and utensils. Wash, clean and drain kidney beans. Some cooks soak them overnight. In a large pot combine all ingredients and cook about 4 hours after bringing to a boil; then reducing to a simmer. Serve over rice. Yield: 6 servings.

Per serving: 477 calories; 8 g fat; 40 mg cholesterol; 1158 mg sodium.

Beets With Orange Sauce

1/4	CUP FIRMLY PACKED BROWN SUGAR
2	TABLESPOONS ALL-PURPOSE FLOUR
1 1/2	TABLESPOONS BUTTER
3/4	CUP ORANGE JUICE
2	TABLESPOONS GRATED ORANGE PEEL
1/2	TEASPOON SALT
2 1/2	CUPS SLICED, COOKED BEETS, DRAINED

Assemble all ingredients and utensils. In a bowl, combine brown sugar and flour. In a saucepan, melt butter and add brown sugar-flour mixture, stirring until well blended. Add orange juice and peel, stirring until thickened. Add salt and beets. Heat thoroughly. Yield: 4 to 6 servings.

Great dish to serve with Duck Breasts Over Wild Rice (*see* p. 102).

Per serving: 103 calories; 3 g fat; 8 mg cholesterol; 245 mg sodium.

Lima Bean Casserole

1	10 3/4-OUNCE CAN CHEDDAR CHEESE SOUP
1/2	CUP WHOLE MILK
1/2	CUP MAYONNAISE
2	10-OUNCE PACKAGES FROZEN LIMA BEANS COOKED AND DRAINED
3/4	CUP CHOPPED CELERY
1/4	CUP CHOPPED FRESH PARSLEY
2	TABLESPOONS CHOPPED PIMENTO
2	CANS FRIED ONION RINGS

Assemble all ingredients and utensils. In a bowl, combine soup, milk, mayonnaise; add beans, celery, parsley, pimento and 1 can of the onion rings. Pour into a greased 2-quart casserole. Bake in a 350-degree oven for 35 minutes, covered. Then uncover and bake for 10 minutes with the remaining onion rings on top. Yield: 8 servings.

Per serving: 360 calories; 25 g fat; 19 mg cholesterol; 553 mg sodium.

Broccoli Casserole

1	CUP MAYONNAISE
1	10 3/4-OUNCE CAN CREAM OF MUSHROOM SOUP
1	10-OUNCE PACKAGE FROZEN CHOPPED BROCCOLI; THAWED AND DRAINED
1	CUP GRATED SHARP CHEDDAR CHEESE
2	EGGS, BEATEN
2	TABLESPOONS CHOPPED ONION
1	TABLESPOON WORCESTERSHIRE SAUCE
1	TEASPOON SALT OR TO TASTE
1	TEASPOON GROUND BLACK PEPPER OR TO TASTE
1	CUP CRUMBLED RITZ CRACKERS
2	TABLESPOONS MELTED BUTTER

Assemble all ingredients and utensils. In a large bowl, combine all ingredients and pour into a 2-quart buttered casserole. Top with cracker crumbs and pour over butter. Bake in a 325-degree oven for 30 minutes. Yield: 6 to 8 servings.

Per serving: 426 calories; 36 g fat; 108 mg cholesterol; 1325 mg sodium.

KINGS MOUNTAIN MESSENGER

The formation of present-day Lincoln County was still five years into the future when Joseph Greer arrived in the region from East Tennessee in 1804 to claim his land. The giant Greer—he is reported to have stood anywhere from seven feet, two inches to seven feet, six inches tall—had been awarded 2,600 acres for services provided to the United States during the Revolutionary War. He was already working on a large family—eventually to include his wife and eleven children—so he needed a lot of land to clear and farm. But, just

what did a man have to do to be rewarded with 2,600 acres of prime Middle Tennessee land? In Greer's case, it was simple. He served with the Overmountain Men in their decisive defeat of British Major Patrick Ferguson and his loyalist American army at Kings Mountain, South Carolina, in 1780. But, after the battle, the youthful Greer was not finished. When it was decided that someone must make the trip through the wilderness to report the good news to the Continental Congress convening in Philadelphia, Greer cheerfully volunteered. Greer is said to have started out on horseback, but after running into Indians who killed his mount, he completed the 750-mile journey on foot. Arriving at Philadelphia, he barged into the meeting of Congressional leaders, pushed the doorkeeper aside, and proudly announced the victory. George Washington is reported to have said, "With soldiers like him, no wonder the frontiersmen won."

THE PHILADELPHIA AFFAIR

During the late summer and early fall of 1863, East Tennessee was a hotbed of activity for both Union and Confederate armies, each trying its best to maintain a strong presence in this region of largely Union sympathizing residents. Union General Ambrose Burnside, with a newly formed, twenty-thousand-man Army of the Ohio, invaded East Tennessee and occupied Knoxville on August 24, 1863, amid a happy populace. Confederate General Simon Bolivar Buckner, with only around six-thousand troops in the vicinity could do little else than watch the tide of Burnside's army pouring

LOUDON COUNTY

through the mountains. In September, the Confederate army scored a victory at Chickamauga, but its failure to follow up on the Union retreat deprived it of Chattanooga. By October, affairs in East Tennessee remained much the same as before Chickamauga. In nearby Loudon County, however, Confederate forces still had the energy and drive to make one last try at victory. At the small town of Philadelphia, on October 23, 1863, two Confederate cavalry regiments attacked a Union cavalry brigade. In the skirmish that followed, the Confederates captured seven hundred prisoners, six mountain howitzers, fifty supply wagons, ten ambulances, and several horses and mules. Although the "Philadelphia Affair," as the brief, yet decisive skirmish has become known meant little in the larger scope of the East Tennessee campaign, it provided a much-needed respite for the battle-weary Confederates in the region.

Cabbage Soufflé

4	EGGS, BEATEN
3	SLICES BREAD, CRUSTS REMOVED, BUTTERED AND CUT IN SMALL PIECES
2	CUPS WHOLE MILK
1	LARGE HEAD CABBAGE, COOKED AND DRAINED
1	TEASPOON SALT
1/2	TEASPOON BLACK PEPPER
1/2	TEASPOON DILL SEED, OPTIONAL
1 1/2	CUPS GRATED SHARP CHEDDAR CHEESE
1	TEASPOON PAPRIKA

Assemble all ingredients and utensils. Cook cabbage by bringing to a boil in a large pot and simmer over medium heat until tender. Drain. In a large bowl, blend eggs, bread and milk. Fold cabbage into liquid mixture. Add salt and pepper or more to taste, dill seed and 1/2 cup cheese. Pour mixture into a 2-quart casserole dish. Sprinkle with remaining cheese over top. Sprinkle with paprika. Bake in a 275-degree oven for 2 to 2 1/2 hours. Serve immediately! Yield: 6 servings.

Great dish to serve with Spiced Corned Beef (*see* p. 69).

Per serving: 305 calories; 18 g fat; 229 mg cholesterol; 727 mg sodium.

Glazed Carrots

1	MEDIUM BUNCH CARROTS, PEELED
1/2	CUP BUTTER
1/3	CUP FIRMLY PACKED BROWN SUGAR
1	TEASPOON NUTMEG
4	TABLESPOONS FRESH ORANGE JUICE

Assemble all ingredients and utensils. Slice carrots diagonally thin. Steam until tender but firm. In a skillet melt butter, add carrots and heat thoroughly. Add brown sugar, nutmeg, orange juice. Cook and stir until sugar melts and carrots are glazed. Serve immediately! Yield: 6 servings.

Per serving: 218 calories; 16 g fat; 41 mg cholesterol; 185 mg sodium.

Carrot Casserole

2 1/2	POUNDS WHOLE CARROTS
1/2	CUP MAYONNAISE
1	TABLESPOON MINCED ONION
1	TABLESPOON PREPARED HORSERADISH
	SALT AND PEPPER TO TASTE
1/2	CUP SALTINE CRACKERS, FINELY CRUSHED
	PARSLEY, CHOPPED
	PAPRIKA

Cook carrots in boiling salted water until tender. Reserve 1/4 cup cooking liquid. Cut carrots in narrow strips, lengthwise. Arrange in a 9-inch square baking dish and set aside. Combine reserved liquid with mayonnaise, onion, horseradish, salt, and pepper. Refrigerate and add sauce and crumbs just before baking. Pour sauce over the carrots. Sprinkle cracker crumbs over top. Dot with butter or margarine. Sprinkle with parsley and paprika. Bake in a 375-degree oven for 20 minutes. Yield: 8 servings.

Cauliflower/Green Peas Casserole

1	CAULIFLOWER, BROKEN INTO FLOWERETTES
1	16-OUNCE CAN ENGLISH PEAS, DRAINED
2	CUPS WHITE SAUCE
1/2	CUP GRATED SHARP CHEDDAR CHEESE
1	CUP FINELY CRUSHED BREAD CRUMBS
4	TEASPOONS BUTTER, SLICED
1/4	TEASPOON SALT
1/4	TEASPOON PAPRIKA

Assemble all ingredients and utensils. In a large saucepan, cook cauliflower and drain. In a 2-quart casserole place cauliflower, layer with English peas and white sauce combined with cheddar cheese. Top casserole with combination of bread crumbs, butter, salt and paprika. Bake in a 375-degree oven for 30 minutes. Yield: 6 to 8 servings.

White Sauce

4	TABLESPOONS BUTTER
4	TABLESPOONS ALL-PURPOSE FLOUR
2	CUPS WHOLE MILK
1/4	TEASPOON SALT

In a saucepan, melt butter and add flour and blend. Stir over low heat until thick, stirring constantly. Add salt and blend.

Per serving: 227 calories; 13 g fat; 38 mg cholesterol; 519 mg sodium.

James Robertson

When one visits the site of Fort Watauga, considers the view from Cumberland Gap, walks along a riverbank of the Cumberland, or finds the place where so many Chickasaw Treaties were signed, one must remember the Father of Tennessee—James Robertson. That honored title has been bestowed on the man by many throughout the past two centuries; William Blount and Andrew Jackson even called him that.

As an early longhunter, James had ventured into the Tennessee country many times. His wife Charlotte and their (eventual) thirteen children were ambitious to strive for new homes and settlements in the wilderness. It would be Charlotte's quick thinking that saved Fort Nashborough during a major ambush.

Robertson had planned the pilgrimage from Fort Watauga to the Bluffs of the Cumberland and led the overland route himself. Through years of sorrow (losing two sons) and light (seeing Nashville grow), James always had faith in new beginnings and encouraged others to do so. He took part in the new state's Constitutional Convention in 1796 and represented Tennessee and the United States in Indian matters—truly a great Tennessean to remember!

Netherland Inn

The Netherland Inn was a famous stage stop on the Great Stage Road. It was built on the land grant of Kingsport's first permanent settler, Gilbert Christian.

In 1802, it was one of the first lots sold in the newly laid-out town of Christianville. It is recorded that William King of Saltville, Virginia, purchased the lots where he built a fine boat-yard from which to ship his salt.

It was in 1818 that Richard Netherland established this magnificent old building as an inn. The inn then stayed in the Netherland family until 1906, at which time it was sold to H.C. and Nettie Cloud. The Clouds then lived at the inn until 1965.

The present owners, the Netherland Inn Association, purchased the old tavern from Mrs. Leta Cloud Parker in 1966. The Inn and its complex is the only restoration of its kind in the United States.

Margaret Netherland's Corn Pudding

2	CUPS MILK OR THIN CREAM
2	CUPS CORN CUT OFF AND SCRAPED
2	TABLESPOONS MELTED BUTTER
1	TABLESPOON SUGAR
1	TEASPOON SALT
1/4	TEASPOON PEPPER
3	WELL BEATEN EGGS

Mix all and turn into greased baking dish. Bake in moderate oven until set.

Corn Fritters

2	EGGS, SEPARATED
2	CUPS CORN, FRESHLY CUT FROM COB OR
1	12-OUNCE CAN WHOLE KERNEL, DRAINED
1/2	TEASPOON SALT
1/4	TEASPOON BLACK PEPPER
1/8	TEASPOON WORCESTERSHIRE SAUCE
1/4	CUP SIFTED ALL-PURPOSE FLOUR
1/4	TEASPOON BAKING POWDER
1/3	CUP COOKING OIL

Assemble all ingredients and utensils. In a small bowl, beat egg whites until stiff but not dry; set aside. In another bowl, beat egg yolks slightly; add corn, Worcestershire, salt and pepper to yolks, combine thoroughly. Stir in flour and baking powder. Fold in beaten egg whites. In a deep skillet over medium heat; drop tablespoons of corn mixture into 2 to 3 tablespoons of hot oil. Brown about 3 minutes on each side. Remove and keep hot while cooking all mixture. Add remaining oil as needed. Yield: 6 servings.

Helpful Hint: To remove corn silk, dampen a paper towel and brush downward toward the large end of the corn cob. All strands should come off.

Per serving: 148 calories; 9 g fat; 91 mg cholesterol; 225 mg sodium.

Corn Soufflé

1	15-OUNCE CAN CREAM-STYLE CORN
1/2	TEASPOON SALT
1/2	TEASPOON GROUND BLACK PEPPER
1	TEASPOON MINCED ONION
1	TABLESPOON CHOPPED GREEN PEPPER
2	TEASPOONS CHOPPED PIMENTO
2	EGGS
1/2	CUP HEAVY CREAM

Assemble all ingredients and utensils. In a bowl, combine corn, salt, pepper, onion, green pepper and pimento. Beat eggs slightly, add cream and stir into corn mixture. Pour into a greased 2-quart casserole. Bake in a 325-degree oven for 15 minutes; then increase heat to 350 degrees and continue baking another 15 minutes or until firm. Yield: 6 servings.

Per serving: 146 calories; 10 g fat; 119 mg cholesterol; 408 mg sodium.

Baked Eggplant Slices

2	MEDIUM EGGPLANTS, UNPEELED AND CUT INTO 1/2 TO 3/4-INCH CROSSWISE SLICES
6	TABLESPOONS OLIVE OIL
2	TABLESPOONS LEMON JUICE
1/2	TEASPOON OREGANO
1/2	TEASPOON SALT
1/2	TEASPOON GROUND BLACK PEPPER
1/2	CUP GRATED PARMESAN CHEESE

Assemble all ingredients and utensils. In a bowl, combine olive oil, lemon juice, oregano, salt and pepper. In a greased 2-quart casserole dish arrange eggplant slices. Spoon 1/2 of the oil mixture over eggplant and let stand 20 minutes. Turn pieces and repeat the procedure. Sprinkle with the Parmesan cheese. Bake in a 400-degree oven for 20 minutes or until tender. Yield: 6 to 8 servings.

Many vegetables should not be peeled as the vitamins are located in and just under the skin. Use only a stiff brush to scrub them clean.

Per serving: 121 calories; 12 g fat; 4 mg cholesterol; 228 mg sodium.

Sequoyah

Sequoyah (1760-1843) was born in the Cherokee town of Tuskegee near the Little Tennessee River in Monroe County, Tennessee. A man who was a cripple all his life, Sequoyah is said to have never learned to speak or write English. Choosing to live with his mother's people, he never forsook the Indians or his native religion. Noted for the development of the Cherokee alphabet, Sequoyah's invention has been described as "a major event" in the history of the Cherokees, as such an invention would be to any "people who had no system of writing." In earlier times symbolism, such as the waving of eagles' tails at formal conferences, had served, in part, to convey ideas. Belts or strings of beads called *wampum* were similarily used as late as the 1790s. Consisting of eighty-six characters, Sequoyah's alphabet pushed the already highly civilized Cherokees even farther into the white man's world, and by 1828, the *Cherokee Phoenix,* a newspaper written in the native alphabet was published in Georgia. Sequoyah removed himself west of the Mississippi and died in Mexico in 1843.

Uncle Billy's Sausage and Kraut

2	STRIPS BACON
1	MEDIUM ONION, CHOPPED
2	TABLESPOONS BACON DRIPPINGS OR OIL
1	PACKAGE TENNESSEE KRAUT (1 1/2-POUND BAG)
	SPICES SUCH AS FENNEL, DILL
1/2	CUP WINE, BEER OR WATER
1	POUND OF A FAVORITE SAUSAGE

Cut bacon into small pieces and lightly brown in skillet. Save bacon drippings or use oil and lightly brown chopped onion. Transfer to large pot and add kraut. Add any favorite spices. Slowly simmer for 30 minutes. Cut sausages as desired and add to kraut and continue to simmer on low for an additional 15 minutes.

Miss Daisy's Southern Greens

1/2	POUND HAM HOCKS
2	TABLESPOONS COOKING OIL
4	CUPS WATER
1	CUP CHOPPED ONION
1	POUND MUSTARD GREENS, WASHED AND DRAINED
1/2	POUND TURNIP GREENS, WASHED AND DRAINED
1/2	POUND COLLARD GREENS, WASHED AND DRAINED

Assemble all ingredients and utensils. In a large pot, brown ham hocks in oil. Add water and onion, bringing to a boiling point. Add greens and return liquid to boiling again. Reduce heat to a simmer, cover and simmer 2 hours. Drain, remove ham hocks, and cut meat into bite-sized pieces. Add meat to greens. Yield: 6 to 8 servings.

Optional—use all of the same greens for recipe, making sure you use a total of 2 pounds.

Serve with Tennessee cornbread, (*see* page 245), sliced tomatoes, and sliced onion.

Hint: When cooking greens, place a can half full of vinegar near the greens and it will absorb all odor.

Per serving: 176 calories; 11 g fat; 19 mg cholesterol; 93 mg sodium.

Mushrooms Baked in Cream

1/2	CUP BUTTER
1 1/2	TEASPOONS CHOPPED FRESH PARSLEY
1 1/2	TEASPOONS CHOPPED CHIVES
1 1/2	TEASPOONS SHALLOTS
1/4	TEASPOON NUTMEG
1/4	TEASPOON SALT
1/4	TEASPOON BLACK PEPPER
16 TO 20	LARGE MUSHROOM CAPS
1	CUP HEAVY CREAM
	PAPRIKA

Assemble all ingredients and utensils. In a bowl, combine softened butter with parsley, chives, shallots, nutmeg, salt and pepper. Stuff mushroom caps with seasoned butter and set them in a shallow baking dish. Pour 1 cup heavy cream over mushrooms and sprinkle the dish lightly with paprika. Bake in a 450-degree oven for 10 minutes. Yield: 8 servings.

Great with beef or lamb.

Per serving: 217 calories; 23 g fat; 72 mg cholesterol; 197 mg sodium.

Southern Fried Okra

4	CUPS CUT OKRA, 1/4-INCH THICK
1	EGG, BEATEN
1/2	CUP PLAIN CORN MEAL
1/2	TEASPOON SALT OR MORE TO TASTE
1/2	TEASPOON BLACK PEPPER
1/2	CUP VEGETABLE OIL

Assemble all ingredients and utensils. In a shallow bowl beat egg; coat okra thoroughly. In another bowl, mix corn meal with salt and pepper. Dip egg-coated okra in corn meal. In a skillet heat oil to a medium-hot. Fry okra in oil until golden brown, turning once. Serve immediately. Yield: 4 servings.

Must serve fresh garden tomatoes and creamed corn with fried okra. A ritual on so many supper tables.

Per serving: 129 calories; 3 g fat; 68 mg cholesterol; 292 mg sodium.

TENNESSEE'S OWN "RAINMAN"

Several years ago Hollywood produced a best-selling movie entitled, *Rainman,* in which Dustin Hoffman played the leading role. The film, loosely based on the life of a real person, showed, through the excellent acting of Hoffman, how a man who had been previously institutionalized for many years could manipulate and memorize large sets of numbers with no outside assistance. Of course, true to Hollywood standards, the man really comes into his own when he nearly breaks one of the casinos in Las Vegas. Back in the mid-1800s, Tennessee had its

MACON COUNTY

own version of the "Rainman." Merideth Holland was born in Macon County in 1822, when his mother was fifty-six years old. Perhaps his mother's advanced age was the reason for Merideth's supposed retardation. It soon became clear to the parents that something was wrong with their child, and from his early days on, he was treated as mentally deficient. He did, however, have a way with numbers, being able to comprehend, calculate, and solve complex mathematical problems. The showman, P. T. Barnum, soon heard of Merideth, came to Macon County, signed up the young man, and took him on tour. In one spectacular stunt, Merideth was supposedly commanded to figure the flow of water that passed a certain point at the mouth of the mighty Amazon River. He soon delivered his answer, and days later, when mathematicians had performed their calculations, they found the Macon County wonder to be correct!

French Fried Onions

4	LARGE WHITE ONIONS
1	CUP WHOLE MILK
1	CUP ALL-PURPOSE FLOUR
1/2	TEASPOON SALT
2/3	CUP WATER
2	TABLESPOONS SALAD OIL
1	EGG WHITE, BEATEN STIFF
	BACON GREASE OR FAT ABOUT 1/2 CUP

Assemble all ingredients and utensils. Slice onions 1/4-inch thick. Separate and soak in a bowl with milk for 30 minutes. Dip in batter made out of the remaining ingredients. In a heavy skillet add 2 tablespoons of fat or bacon grease, heat until medium hot. Add onion rings slowly, brown and remove from pan. Continue adding onions and grease until all are browned. Yield: 8 servings.

Per serving: 191 calories; 12 g fat; 4 mg cholesterol; 156 mg sodium.

Vidalia Onion Pie

A friend I met thirty years ago from Vidalia, Georgia, gave me this recipe which ignited my taste for Vidalia onions. I use them for my personal cooking when available and in most recipes which call for onions.
Miss Daisy

1	DEEP DISH, 9-INCH, PASTRY SHELL
3	CUPS THINLY SLICED VIDALIA ONIONS OR OTHER SWEET ONIONS
3	TABLESPOONS BUTTER, MELTED
1/2	CUP WHOLE MILK
1 1/2	CUPS SOUR CREAM
1	TEASPOON SALT
2	EGGS, BEATEN
3	TABLESPOONS ALL-PURPOSE FLOUR
4	STRIPS BACON, FRIED AND CRUMBLED

Assemble all ingredients and utensils. Bake pastry shell. In a skillet, cook onions in butter until lightly browned. Spoon into pastry shell. In a bowl, combine milk, sour cream, salt, eggs and flour. Mix well and pour over onion mixture. Garnish with bacon. Bake in a 325-degree oven for 30 minutes or until firm in center. Yield: 6 to 8 servings.

Per serving: 376 calories; 28 g fat; 104 mg cholesterol; 616 mg sodium.

Hot and Spicy Black-Eyed Peas

3	SLICES BACON, COOKED AND CRUMBLED
1	MEDIUM ONION, CHOPPED
1/2	BELL PEPPER, CHOPPED
1	TABLESPOON SOY SAUCE
1	TEASPOON SALT
1	TEASPOON DRY MUSTARD
1	TEASPOON LIQUID SMOKE
1/2	TEASPOON CHILI POWDER
1/2	TEASPOON BLACK PEPPER
1	17-OUNCE CAN BLACK-EYED PEAS
1	16-OUNCE CAN WHOLE TOMATOES, UNDRAINED AND CHOPPED
	FRESH PARSLEY, ABOUT 1 TABLESPOON

Assemble all ingredients and utensils. Cook bacon until crisp. Remove bacon and sauté onions and bell pepper, drain. Crumble and reserve for later. In a saucepan, mix remaining ingredients and heat to boiling, then simmer for 20 minutes. Pour mixture into serving dish; sprinkle with bacon and parsley. Yield: 8 servings.

Per serving: 81 calories; 2 g fat; 2 mg cholesterol; 710 mg sodium.

*L*ETTIE C. CARDY'S (NORMANDY, TENNESSEE) RECIPE IN *A TASTE OF HOMECOMING* IS A DIFFERENT TWIST TO A SOUTHERN FAVORITE—BLACK-EYED PEAS— A MUST FOR NEW YEAR'S DAY—SO YOU WILL HAVE GOOD LUCK FOR THE UPCOMING YEAR. BLACK-EYED PEAS ARE ALSO KNOWN AS COWPEAS. AFRICAN IN ORIGIN, THEY HAVE BEEN A STAPLE IN THE SOUTHERN DIET FOR MORE THAN THREE CENTURIES. IN TEXAS THEY ARE TERMED TEXAS CAVIAR.

Miss Daisy

Pot Luck English Pea Casserole

1	CUP CHOPPED CELERY
1	MEDIUM YELLOW ONION CHOPPED
1/2	CUP CHOPPED GREEN PEPPER
1/4	CUP BUTTER
2	1-POUND CANS ENGLISH OR GREEN PEAS
1	8-OUNCE CAN SLICED WATER CHESTNUTS
1	2-OUNCE JAR DRIED PIMENTO, DRAINED
1	10 3/4-OUNCE CAN CREAM OF MUSHROOM SOUP
1	CUP BUTTERED BREAD CRUMBS

Assemble all ingredients and utensils. In a large skillet, sauté celery, onion and green pepper in butter for 5 minutes. Add peas, water chestnuts, pimento and soup. Pour into a greased 2-quart casserole dish. Cover with buttered bread crumbs. Bake in a 350-degree oven for 30 minutes or until bubbly. Yield: 6 to 8 servings.

Per serving: 240 calories; 12 g fat; 24 mg cholesterol; 721 mg sodium.

*P*OT LUCK CASSEROLES ARE TAKEN TO GATHERINGS SUCH AS CHURCH SUPPERS AND ARE MEANT TO BE SHARED. AN AGE-OLD TERM FOR UNPLANNED "POTS" OF FOOD THAT SOMEHOW COME TOGETHER TO MAKE A FINE MEAL.

Miss Daisy

Ramsey House "Swan Pond"

Ramsey House, originally named "Swan Pond," was built in 1797 by Col. Francis Alexander Ramsey. Col. Ramsey, a Pennsylvanian, employed Thomas Hope, an

English carpenter and joiner, to design his home. Of special interest is the fact that it was the first stone house in the territory.

Visitors touring the picturesque kitchen of Ramsey House are often treated to the spicy odors of delectable foods once served there for the Ramsey family and guests.

Bishop Francis Asbury, in his *Journal,* mentions the hospitality shown him when he visited the Ramsey family in 1800.

Ramsey House "Swan Pond," near Knoxville, Tennessee, is listed on the National Register of Historic Places. The house and grounds are being restored to the period of Col. Ramsey's occupancy by Knoxville Chapter of the Association for the Preservation of Tennessee Antiquities.

Ramsey House Mashed Potatoes

6	POTATOES (COBBLERS)
1/4	CUP BUTTER
1	TEASPOON SALT
1	CUP RICH MILK

Peel and quarter potatoes, steam in salted water until tender. Drain and add butter, salt and milk. Beat with a beater until mixture is free of lumps and smooth. Will whip up to a light creamy mixture. Serve pipin' hot in a hot serving dish. This is a favorite Southern way of serving potatoes.

Au Gratin Potatoes

1	CUP DICED RAW POTATOES
1	TEASPOON SALT
2	TABLESPOONS BUTTER
2	TABLESPOONS ALL-PURPOSE FLOUR
1/2	CUP LIGHT CREAM
1/2	CUP WHOLE MILK
1/2	CUP GRATED SHARP CHEDDAR CHEESE
1/2	TEASPOON BLACK PEPPER
1/2	TEASPOON SALT, OPTIONAL
1/2	CUP PARMESAN CHEESE

Assemble all ingredients and utensils. In a pot, place raw potatoes and salt. Cover with water. Boil until slightly tender. Drain. While potatoes are cooking, make cheese sauce. In a saucepan, combine butter and flour. Heat until butter melts. Add cream, milk, cheese, black pepper and salt. Cook until medium thickness. Pour into a greased 1 1/2-quart casserole. Sprinkle with 1/2 cup Parmesan cheese. Bake in a 400-degree oven for 20 to 30 minutes until cheese is melted. Yield: 4 to 6 servings.

Per serving: 183 calories; 13 g fat; 41 mg cholesterol; 774 mg sodium.

Bacon Stuffed Potatoes

8	LARGE BAKING POTATOES
2	TABLESPOONS OIL
1/4	CUP BUTTER
1	CUP SOUR CREAM
1	EGG
1	TEASPOON SALT
1/4	TEASPOON BLACK PEPPER
8	CRISP COOKED BACON SLICES, CRUMBLED
	PAPRIKA FOR GARNISH
8	TABLESPOONS GRATED CHEDDAR CHEESE FOR TOPPING

Assemble all ingredients and utensils. Scrub potatoes and dry. Rub with oil and bake directly on oven rack at 400 degrees for 1 hour or until tender. Cut an oval section from potato and place in a bowl. Remove any potato peel from scooped potato. Add butter, sour cream, egg, salt and black pepper. Mix thoroughly until well blended. Stir in crisp crumbled bacon. Pile back into the potato shells. Sprinkle with paprika and cheddar cheese. Bake in a 400-degree oven for 8 to 10 minutes. Serve warm. Yield: 8 servings.

Per serving: 438 calories; 22 g fat; 75 mg cholesterol; 510 mg sodium.

Old Fashioned Potato Puffs

3	MEDIUM SIZED RAW POTATOES, PEELED
1	TABLESPOON HEAVY CREAM
1	EGG, BEATEN
1	TABLESPOON ALL-PURPOSE FLOUR
1	TEASPOON SALT
1/2	TEASPOON GROUND BLACK PEPPER
2	TABLESPOONS GRATED ONION, OPTIONAL
	HOT FAT, ABOUT 4 TABLESPOONS

Assemble all ingredients and utensils. Grate potatoes. In a bowl, combine potatoes; add other ingredients. Mix well. Melt fat in a large skillet until hot. Shape mixture into cakes or drop by teaspoonfuls into hot fat. Brown. Turn over. Yield: 6 servings.

For variation: add 3 or 4 pieces of cooked bacon, crumbled.

Per serving: 112 calories; 7 g fat; 49 mg cholesterol; 371 mg sodium.

HOW CASEY JONES GOT HIS NAME

Few are the people in America who haven't heard of Casey Jones. The locomotive engineer, who lived in Jackson for several years was made immortal by the song, *Casey Jones, the Brave Engineer,* which in 1903 was one of the ten top sellers of sheet music in the United States. Casey's death near Vaughan, Mississippi, was even reported in *Life* magazine. When Casey, whose real name was J. L. (John Luther) Jones, moved to a boarding house in Jackson, another engineer who stayed at the place suggested that there were so many

MADISON COUNTY

"Joneses" working for the railroad that J. L. needed a distiguishing name. When J. L. told him that he hailed from Cayce, Kentucky, the other man promptly dubbed him with the name "Cayce," which stuck for the rest of his life. Cayce met his Maker on a cool spring night in April 1900, when he and his fireman, Sim Webb, were driving a train pulled by engine number 382 out of Memphis for the run south into Mississippi. Things went well for several hours, and Old 382 was making record time, almost a mile every fifty seconds. Casey was proud of Old 382 and boasted to Sim that "The old girl's got her high-heeled slippers on tonight!" Shortly afterwards, the train plowed into a stalled train near Vaughan, Mississippi. Jones had called out in time to tell Sim to jump to safety, but Casey stayed on the brake until the crash. When they found his body, he had an iron bolt driven through his neck, with a bale of hay resting on his chest.

Brewster's Smokehouse
Onion Roasted Potatoes

1   ENVELOPE LIPTON OR CAMPBELL'S ONION RECIPE SOUP
     MIX
2   POUNDS POTATOES, CUT INTO QUARTERS
1/3 CUP OLIVE OIL OR VEGETABLE OIL

Preheat oven to 450 degrees (or grill). In large plastic bag or
plastic bowl, add all ingredients. Close bag and shake (or stir
in bowl) until potatoes are evenly coated. Empty potatoes
into shallow baking or roasting pan (best if baked in iron
skillet). Discard bag. Bake or grill in pan, stirring occasionally,
40 minutes or until potatoes are tender and golden
brown.

Homecoming Sweet Potatoes

3   CUPS COOKED SWEET POTATOES, MASHED
3/4 CUP SUGAR
2   EGGS, BEATEN
1   CUP EVAPORATED MILK
1/4 CUP MARGARINE
1   TEASPOON VANILLA

Assemble all ingredients and utensils. Beat all ingredients together and
pour into a greased 2-quart casserole. Cover with topping and bake
in a 375-degree oven for 30 minutes. Yield: 8 servings.

Topping:

1   CUP BROWN SUGAR
1/3 CUP BUTTER, MELTED
1   CUP FLAKED COCONUT
1   CUP PECANS, CHOPPED

Combine ingredients and mix well until crumbly. Sprinkle over
potatoes.

Per serving: 584 calories; 30 g fat; 78 mg cholesterol; 252 mg sodium.

I USED THIS RECIPE IN
A TASTE OF HOMECOMING BECAUSE
SWEET POTATOES IN ANY FORM ARE
FAVORITES OF TENNESSEANS.
SEVERAL TENNESSEANS SUBMITTED
THIS RECIPE FOR THE 1986
HOMECOMING COOKBOOK.
Miss Daisy

Sweet Potatoes in Orange Cups

3	CUPS SWEET POTATOES, COOKED AND MASHED
1	CUP SUGAR
1/2	TEASPOON SALT
2	EGGS
1/4	CUP BUTTER
1/2	CUP WHOLE MILK
1	TEASPOON VANILLA
	ORANGE HALF SHELLS

Assemble all ingredients and utensils. Mix all ingredients together and pour into orange halves which have the pulp removed. Cover with topping.

Topping

1	CUP BROWN SUGAR
1/3	CUP ALL-PURPOSE FLOUR
1	CUP NUTS, CHOPPED
1/4	CUP BUTTER

Mix thoroughly and sprinkle over potato mixture in orange cups. Bake in a 350-degree oven for 35 minutes. Yield: 6 servings.

Per serving: 377 calories; 15 g fat; 68 mg cholesterol; 200 mg sodium.

*M*Y MOTHER-IN-LAW, HAZEL KING, GAVE ME THIS RECIPE. IT HAS BEEN A TRADITION IN THE KING FAMILY FOR MANY YEARS.

GEORGE WASHINGTON CARVER SAID, "AS A FOOD FOR HUMAN CONSUMPTION, THE SWEET POTATO HAS BEEN, AND ALWAYS WILL BE, HELD IN VERY HIGH ESTEEM AND ITS POPU-LARITY WILL INCREASE AS WE LEARN MORE ABOUT ITS MANY POSSIBILITIES" (*BULLETIN NO. 38*, TUSKEGEE INSTITUTE, 1922).

Miss Daisy

THE DESTRUCTION OF NICKAJACK

By the time 1794 rolled around, Indian depredations upon residents of the Cumberland Settlements were at an all time high, and life around Nashville was practically unbearable. During the late summer of that year, despite orders from Territorial Governor William Blount not to, General James Robertson decided to send an expedition to destroy the lower Cherokee towns of Nickajack and Running Water, located in present-day Marion County. Robertson sent messages to all of the stations and communities up and down the Cumberland instructing them to send their best men to Nashville to muster for duty. The expedition, under the command of

MARION COUNTY

Major James Ore, left Nashville on September 7, 1794. Under orders from Robertson to "spare women and children, and to treat all prisoners who may fall into your hands with humanity," Ore and about three hundred men followed a route to Murfreesboro, thence to Manchester, arriving three miles below the confluence of the Sequatchie and Tennessee Rivers on September 12. During the night, the small army crossed the river, and the next morning attacked the town of Nickajack. Running Water, situated four miles away, was also besieged and destroyed. About fifty Cherokees were killed during the two battles, while Ore's men suffered three persons wounded. Governor Blount, shaken by Robertson's disobedience to his orders, mildly chastised his friend in a letter, but he was thankful that peace was finally restored in the Cumberland valley.

Miss Mary Bobo's

Dr. and Mrs. E.Y. Salmon built a Greek Revival frame house in 1867. It was located in Lynchburg near Jack Daniel's new distillery and became known as "The Grand Central Hotel." Many long-term residents stayed there. When the Salmons retired, Jack and Mary Bobo took over. In 1914, "The Bobo Hotel" was a destination for many, yet the reputation of Miss Mary's cooking led the family to change the name to "Miss Mary Bobo's Boarding House." Soon it would be open only for meals. Miss Mary died in 1983 at age 101. She had developed many recipes through the decades of greeting guests. Today, great southern food is still served there.

LYNNE TOLLEY, OWNER OF MISS MARY BOBO'S, PONDERED OVER WHAT TO CONTRIBUTE, BUT FELT JACK DANIEL'S AND SWEET POTATOES HAVE A PERFECT MARRIAGE IN THIS TIPSY SWEET POTATOES RECIPE. LYNNE TOLLEY IS ALSO A PERFECT EXAMPLE OF THE WARMTH AND GRACIOUSNESS OF TENNESSEANS.

Miss Daisy

Miss Mary Bobo's
Tipsy Sweet Potatoes

2 1/2	CUPS COOKED, MASHED, SWEET POTATOES
4	TABLESPOONS BUTTER, SOFTENED
1/2	CUP FIRMLY PACKED LIGHT BROWN SUGAR
	PINCH OF SALT
1/3	CUP JACK DANIEL'S WHISKEY
	PECAN HALVES FOR TOPPING

Preheat oven to 325 degrees. Combine all ingredients except topping. Spoon into a greased, 1-quart casserole. Top with pecans. Bake for 20 to 25 minutes. Makes 6 to 8 servings.

Caution: Everyone will want seconds!

Candied Yams and Apples

6	MEDIUM-SIZE SWEET POTATOES, PEELED
6	SMALL, RED-SKINNED COOKING APPLES
1	CUP BROWN SUGAR
6	TABLESPOONS BUTTER
1/8	TEASPOON EACH: GINGER, NUTMEG AND ALLSPICE
3/4	CUP WATER
1	CUP SHREDDED COCONUT

Assemble all ingredients and utensils. Slice potatoes and apples. In a 2-quart casserole dish, lay slices of potatoes and apples, then layer of 1/2 cup sugar and 3 tablespoons butter. Repeat layers again. Add seasonings and water. Bake in a 350-degree oven for 35 minutes. Sprinkle coconut over top last 5 minutes of baking. Yield: 6 to 8 servings.

Per serving: 386 calories; 13 g fat; 23 mg cholesterol; 135 mg sodium.

Ratatouille

2	POUNDS ZUCCHINI
2	POUNDS EGGPLANT, PEELED
1/3	CUP BUTTER
3	GREEN PEPPERS, THINLY SLICED
2	ONIONS SLICED
3	CLOVES GARLIC
2	POUNDS TOMATOES, PEELED, SEEDED AND SLICED
1/2	TEASPOON EACH: BASIL, THYME, BAY LEAF

Assemble all ingredients and utensils. Cut the zucchini and eggplant into 1/2-inch slices and sauté in butter a few at a time, several minutes on each side. Remove and drain. In the same skillet, stir the green peppers, onions and garlic. Cook for 10 minutes. Remove and discard garlic. Add the tomatoes. In a 2-quart casserole layer eggplant, zucchini and half of tomato mixture. Season with salt, pepper and herbs. Repeat, ending with tomato sauce and seasonings. Cover. Bake in a 350-degree oven for 60 minutes. Yield: 10 to 12 servings.

Per serving: 102 calories; 6 g fat; 15 mg cholesterol; 67 mg sodium.

Spinach Soufflé

1	10-OUNCE PACKAGE FROZEN CHOPPED SPINACH, COOKED AND DRAINED
1	POUND CONTAINER SMALL CURD COTTAGE CHEESE
3	EGGS, BEATEN
4	OUNCES CHEDDAR CHEESE, GRATED
1/4	CUP BUTTER, MELTED
1/2	TEASPOON SALT
1/2	TEASPOON BLACK PEPPER

Assemble all ingredients and utensils. In a bowl, combine all ingredients and pour into a 2 quart casserole. Bake in a 350-degree oven for 45 minutes or until set. Yield: 8 servings.

Per serving: 203 calories; 15 g fat; 141 mg cholesterol; 557 mg sodium.

Company Spinach

2   10-OUNCE PACKAGES FROZEN CHOPPED SPINACH,
    COOKED AND DRAINED ACCORDING TO PACKAGE
    DIRECTIONS
4   GREEN ONIONS, CHOPPED
1   SMALL YELLOW ONION, CHOPPED
3   SLICES BACON, FRIED UNTIL CRISP AND RESERVING
    DRIPPINGS
1   3-OUNCE CAN MUSHROOMS, STEMS AND PIECES,
    DRAINED
1/3 CUP SEASONED BREAD CRUMBS
1/2 TEASPOON SALT
1/2 TEASPOON BLACK PEPPER

Assemble all ingredients and utensils. In a saucepan, sauté the onions in the bacon drippings until soft. Combine drained spinach, onions and remaining ingredients. Pour mixture into a 2-quart casserole. Bake in a 350-degree oven for 20 to 25 minutes. Yield: 6 to 8 servings.

Per serving: 53 calories; 2 g fat; 2 mg cholesterol; 294 mg sodium.

Miss Daisy's Party Squash

1   POUND YELLOW SQUASH, SLICED
1   TEASPOON SUGAR
1/2 CUP MAYONNAISE
1/2 CUP MINCED ONION
1/2 CUP CHOPPED PECANS
1/2 CUP GRATED SHARP CHEDDAR CHEESE
1/4 CUP FINELY CHOPPED GREEN PEPPER
1   EGG, SLIGHTLY BEATEN
1   TEASPOON SALT
1/2 TEASPOON BLACK PEPPER
1/4 CUP CRACKER CRUMBS
4   TABLESPOONS BUTTER, SLICED

*M*ANY FOLKS HAVE TOLD ME THROUGHOUT THE YEARS THAT THIS IS ABSOLUTELY THE BEST SQUASH RECIPE EVER. I REALLY LOVE HOW MY FRIENDS WHO THINK THEY MAY NOT LIKE SQUASH ALWAYS ASK FOR SECONDS WHEN I SERVE THIS DISH. IT IS GREAT REHEATED!

Miss Daisy

Assemble all ingredients and utensils. In a pot cook squash with water to cover. Cook until tender, drain and mash. In a bowl combine squash with other ingredients except bread crumbs and butter. Pour mixture into a 2-quart casserole dish. Top with bread crumbs and butter. Bake in a 350-degree oven for 35 to 40 minutes. Yield: 6 servings.

Per serving: 347 calories; 33 g fat; 87 mg cholesterol; 642 mg sodium.

Betty Dunn's Tomato Pie

1	9-INCH PIE SHELL (FROZEN OR PILLSBURY)
3 OR 4	"HOME GROWN" TOMATOES, PEELED AND THICKLY SLICED
	SALT AND PEPPER TO TASTE
1 TO 2	TABLESPOONS FRESH BASIL, CHOPPED
1 TO 2	TABLESPOONS FRESH CHIVES, CHOPPED
1/2	CUP MAYONNAISE
2	CUPS GRATED CHEDDAR CHEESE, MILD OR SHARP OR 1 CUP OF EACH

Bake pie shell according to the directions. Cool. Place sliced tomatoes between paper towels to absorb some of the moisture. Cover bottom of pie crust with tomato slices. Sprinkle with salt and pepper. Combine mayonnaise, cheese, basil, and chives. Carefully dot this mixture over tomatoes. Bake at 400 degrees for 20 to 30 minutes and share with someone you care about.

BETTY DUNN, WIFE OF GOVERNOR WINFIELD DUNN, SHARED SEVERAL RECIPES FOR THIS BICENTENNIAL COOKBOOK. ACCORDING TO BETTY, THE TOMATO PIE RECIPE IS ONE OF WINFIELD'S FAVORITES. MRS. DUNN WAS FIRST LADY DURING WINFIELD DUNN'S TERM, 1971-1975.

Miss Daisy

THE DARK HORSE PRESIDENT

James K. Polk of Columbia became known as the country's first "dark-horse" president, when he was unanimously nominated on the ninth ballot at the Democratic National Convention in Baltimore during the summer of 1844. Beating out the Democratic Party's perennial favorite, former President Martin Van Buren, at the Convention, Polk went on to win the fall election against the Whig candidate, the formidable Henry Clay of Kentucky. Today, Polk's presidency is not too highly regarded by many historians, yet during his four-year administration, the quiet Tennessean fulfilled every one of the promises that he had made during his campaign. Texas, already in the process of becoming annexed

MAURY COUNTY

to the United States, was admitted, bringing with it a war with Mexico. Successful prosecution of that war by Polk and his able lieutenants won for the U. S. hundreds of thousands of square miles of new territory in the Southwest and California that had previously belonged to Mexico. Polk engineered a final treaty with Great Britain over the Oregon question, bringing with it millions of additional acres of prime northwestern lands. As a result of all these new acquisitions, practically everybody today who lives beyond the Rocky Mountains can thank this man from Tennessee for their homes being part of the United States. Upon his retirement, President Polk returned to Middle Tennessee, but died within just a few months of his arrival. His widow, Sarah, survived him by many years in a home located in Nashville.

Fried Green Tomatoes

3	MEDIUM GREEN TOMATOES
1/2	TEASPOON SALT
1/2	TEASPOON PEPPER
3/4	CUP WHITE CORNMEAL
1/3	CUP BACON DRIPPINGS

Assemble all ingredients and utensils. Slice tomatoes 1/4-inch thick; sprinkle with salt and pepper. In a bowl, pour cornmeal and coat slices of tomato thoroughly with corn meal. In a large skillet heat bacon drippings until hot and add coated slices of tomatoes and brown on both sides over medium heat. Drain. Yield: 4 servings.

Per serving: 192 calories; 11 g fat; 9 mg cholesterol; 279 mg sodium.

June Carter Cash's Vegetable "Stuff"

1	POUND FRESH MUSHROOMS
1	LARGE GREEN BELL PEPPER, SLICED
1/2	CUP OIL
2	MEDIUM GREEN TOMATOES, SLICED 1/4-INCH THICK
2	ZUCCHINI, SLICED 1/4-INCH THICK
1/3	CUP FLOUR
1/8	TEASPOON FRESHLY GROUND PEPPER
1 1/4	TEASPOONS SALT
1	POUND POTATOES, PEELED, THINLY SLICED
1	CUP CHOPPED ONION
1/2	TEASPOON SALT
1/4	CUP BUTTER OR MARGARINE
1	TEASPOON SUGAR
1/2	TEASPOON SALT
1/8	TEASPOON FRESHLY GROUND PEPPER

Rinse mushrooms, pat dry and slice. Sauté green pepper in 1/4 cup oil in large skillet for 2 minutes; remove with slotted spoon. Dredge tomatoes and zucchini in mixture of flour, 1/8 teaspoon pepper and 1 1/4 teaspoons salt. Sauté 2 to 3 slices at a time for 2 minutes on each side or until brown; remove with slotted spoon. Heat remaining 1/4 cup oil in skillet. Add potatoes, onion and 1/2 teaspoon salt. Cook for 10 minutes or until potatoes are tender, stirring frequently. Remove with slotted spoon. Sauté mushrooms in butter in skillet for 5 minutes. Stir in sugar, remaining 1/2 teaspoon salt and 1/8 teaspoon pepper. Add sautéed vegetables; toss gently. Heat to serving temperature. Serve immediately. Yield: 4 servings.

*W*HAT AN AMAZING THING HAPPENS WHEN A FOOD ITEM BECOMES POPULAR BECAUSE OF A MOVIE OR A TELEVISION SERIES. THE FILM *FRIED GREEN TOMATOES* LET THE WHOLE COUNTRY IN ON THIS CLOSELY GUARDED SOUTHERN FOOD FAVORITE.

Miss Daisy

*J*UNE CARTER CASH CAN SURELY MAKE ANYONE FEEL AT HOME—FOR THOSE OF US WHO HAVE BEEN WARMED BY HER SMILE AND HER FAMILY'S TALENT, THIS LADY IS SPECIAL.

Miss Daisy

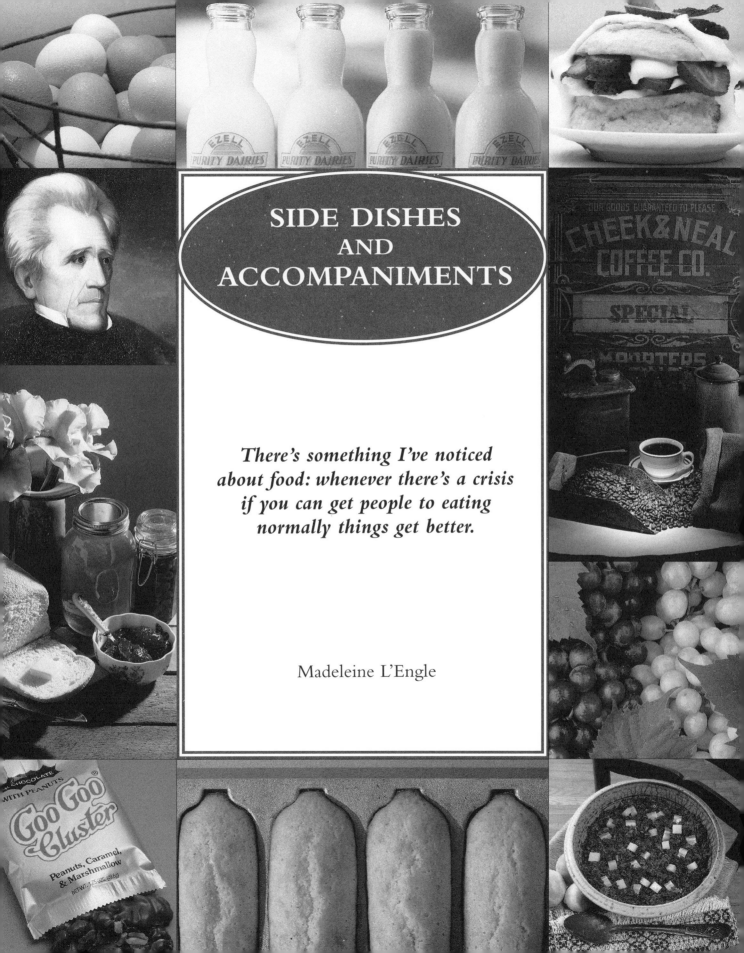

SIDE DISHES
AND
ACCOMPANIMENTS

*There's something I've noticed
about food: whenever there's a crisis
if you can get people to eating
normally things get better.*

Madeleine L'Engle

SIDE DISHES AND ACCOMPANIMENTS

Hot Curried Fruit

1	16-OUNCE CAN SLICED PEACHES
1	16-OUNCE CAN PINEAPPLE CHUNKS
1	16-OUNCE CAN SLICED PEARS
1	16-OUNCE CAN APRICOT HALVES, SLICED
1	CUP BROWN SUGAR
2	TEASPOONS CURRY POWDER
6	TABLESPOONS BUTTER
1/2	CUP SLIVERED ALMONDS
8 TO 10	MARASCHINO CHERRIES, OPTIONAL

Assemble all ingredients and utensils. Drain all fruit and mix together. Place one layer of fruit in a 13x9-inch casserole dish. In a saucepan, combine brown sugar and curry powder; add butter and almonds. Stir until mixture is heated and butter is melted. Pour 1/2 of brown sugar mixture over fruit. Repeat both layers again. Top with cherries, optional. Bake in a 350-degree oven for 60 minutes. Yield: 6 to 8 servings.

This is better when made day before serving and reheated when ready to serve. I serve this for brunch on Christmas Day.

Per serving: 337 calories; 14 g fat; 23 mg cholesterol; 103 mg sodium.

"MIND YOUR MOTHER, SON"

Adding a new amendment to the U. S. Constitution is a two-pronged affair. First, the proposed amendment must be approved by a two-thirds vote of the Congress, then it must be ratified by three-fourths of the states' legislatures. In 1919, when the nineteenth amendment proposing to give women the right to vote was passed in Congress, thirty-six states had to ratify it to make it become law. Women's rights groups all over America frantically tried to convince state legislators to vote for ratification. By early August 1920, thirty-five states, one short of the number required for the amendment's passage, had indeed ratified it in their legislatures.

Attention turned to Tennessee to obtain the necessary last ratification. President Woodrow Wilson urged Governor Albert H. Roberts to call a special session of the legislature just to vote on the proposed amendment. On August 9, the legislature convened. Four days later the senate approved ratification, but the house of representatives appeared to be one vote short. When the role call came a few days later, it passed the house by one vote. The man who changed his vote from "nay" to "yea" was Harry T. Burn of Athens in McMinn County. It was Burn, then, who cast the deciding vote, thus making Tennessee the final state required for ratification. When asked why he changed his vote, Burn read a letter from his mother which pleaded, "Don't forget to be a good boy and . . . put the 'rat' in ratification." He did.

Spoon Bread

1 1/2	CUPS WATER-GROUND CORN MEAL
1	TEASPOON BAKING SODA
1	TEASPOON BAKING POWDER
1	TEASPOON SALT
2	EGGS, BEATEN
3	CUPS BUTTERMILK
2	TABLESPOONS BUTTER
3/4	CUP ALL-PURPOSE MILK

Assemble all ingredients and utensils. In a large bowl, mix cornmeal, baking soda, baking powder and salt. Add beaten eggs and buttermilk; stir well. In a 2-quart casserole dish melt butter. Pour bread mixture into casserole with melted butter. Pour milk over top. Do not stir. Bake in a 450-degree oven for 25 to 30 minutes or until center tests done. Yield: 6 to 8 servings.

Per serving: 180 calories; 7 g fat; 83 mg cholesterol; 567 mg sodium.

The consistency of Spoon Bread is a cross between a pudding and a wet cornbread. It is to be served hot, buttered at the table, and spread with preserves or eaten with the same dishes you would regular cornbread. Wonderful.

Miss Daisy

Cheese Grits Soufflé

1	CUP QUICK COOKING GRITS
3	CUPS BOILING WATER
1/2	CUP BUTTER
3/4	TEASPOON SALT
1/2	TEASPOON BLACK PEPPER
4	EGGS, BEATEN
1	CUP WHOLE MILK
1	CUP GRATED SHARP CHEDDAR CHEESE
	PAPRIKA FOR GARNISH

Assemble all ingredients and utensils. In a large pot, put 1 cup grits in 3 cups boiling water. Cook over medium heat until very thick. Remove from heat and add butter. Stir until melted. Add salt and pepper. Stir eggs into milk, add to grits and mix well. Add grated cheese. Pour into a deep, 3-quart greased casserole and bake in a 350-degree oven uncovered for 40 to 45 minutes. Yield: 6 servings.

Per serving: 315 calories; 27 g fat; 250 mg cholesterol; 696 mg sodium.

The Cheese Factory

"My family has been making cheese for over 40 years," says Chris Huffman, owner of the Cheese Factory at 40 Casey Jones Lane in Jackson. Chris says his family produces quality American cheese through an Old World tradition. They use only 100 percent Grade A milk which is slow cooked and pasteurized. Chris' father, Pat Huffman, was awarded "Best White Cheddar in the Nation" by the American Cheese Society in 1989. The Jackson company's most original cheese is Smoked Barbecue Colby. More than twenty types of cheese are available."

Fried Grits

1   CUP GRITS
4   CUPS BOILING WATER
2   TEASPOONS SALT
1   CUP ALL-PURPOSE FLOUR
1   EGG BEATEN WITH 1 TABLESPOON WATER
      BACON GREASE, ABOUT 1/2 CUP

Assemble ingredients and utensils. In a big pot, bring 4 cups water to a boil; pour grits into pot, add salt. Slowly boil for 10 minutes; stir frequently. While warm fill tall, slender glasses with grits to mold. Chill overnight. When ready to fry, unmold and cut into 1/2 inch thick slices. Dip into flour then into egg mixture. Into a large skillet put enough bacon grease to brown circles of grits. Brown on both sides. Yield: 8 servings.

Serve them with a warm fresh tomato sauce.

Per serving: 140 calories; 8 g fat; 40 mg cholesterol; 609 mg sodium.

Hoppin' John

1   CUP DRIED BLACK-EYED PEAS
1/4   POUND SMOKED BACON OR SALT PORK, CUT INTO
      SMALL PIECES
1   POD RED PEPPER
3   CUPS COOKED WHITE RICE
1   TEASPOON SALT
1   TEASPOON BLACK PEPPER
1/8   TEASPOON CAYENNE PEPPER

Assemble all ingredients and utensils. In a large pot, soak peas overnight in enough water to cover. Cook in same water with bacon and pepper pod until peas are tender, but not overdone. Add cooked rice and mix well. Season with salt, black pepper and cayenne pepper. Place in a covered 2-quart casserole and bake in a 350-degree oven for 15 to 20 minutes until dish is heated. Yield: 8 to 10 servings.

Per serving: 161 calories; 6 g fat; 10 mg cholesterol; 551 mg sodium.

Tennessee Valley Cheese

The Will Jordan family says "cheese" a lot in Morrison, Tennessee. Will Sr. worked for the McMinnville Cheese Corporation for years, and after retiring he and Will Jr. decided to begin their own company: Tennessee Valley Cheese. A friend from the closed Avalon cheese factory, James Martin, was hired to help ready the business for the varied cheeses Tennessee Valley would offer. The company makes Colby, Monterey Jack, Cheddar, American, Mozzarella, Co-Jack, Hot Pepper, and Pizza cheeses. The classic "Three Year Cheese" is a big seller. Will Sr. says that fifty or sixty years ago almost every county seat had a cheese plant. This was before refrigeration trucks were around to transport dairy products far. The Jordans want their company to represent the trend of those old, dedicated cheese factories.

THERE IS A STORY ABOUT A MAN WHO ENJOYED THIS COMBINATION OF PEAS AND RICE SO MUCH THAT WHEN HIS WIFE CALLED HIM TO EAT SHE WOULD YELL OUT, "COME A-HOPPIN', JOHN." SO THE WORD GOT AROUND, AND THE DISH WAS DUBBED *HOPPIN' JOHN.*

Miss Daisy

Like old Davy Crockett, who at one time lived not too far away, Buford Pusser became a legend in his own time. The McNairy County sheriff, before he was killed in 1974, provided material for songs, books, countless magazine articles, and a Hollywood movie. Pusser was a man for all ages but anathema for the operators of scores of beer joints, gambling dens, and houses of prostitution that lined the highways and backroads of McNairy County, Tennessee, and Alcorn County, Mississippi, during the mid- and late-1960s. When

MCNAIRY COUNTY

Pusser was elected sheriff in 1964, he vowed to clean up McNairy County, and over a period of time, he did just that, but not without extreme cost to his family and himself. By the time he was thirty-two years old, Pusser had already been shot eight times, knifed seven times, run over by an automobile, and had killed two men in the line of duty. Then, on August 12, 1967, his wife was gunned down and killed, and he was severely wounded by local thugs intent on putting him out of business for good. But Pusser, a six-foot, six-inch, 250-pound giant of a man, survived his wife's murder. After six operations in which his shot-up jaw was skillfully wired back together by plastic surgeons, he was back on the job, trying to bring law and order to McNairy County as he had promised. Pusser's luck finally ran out on August 21, 1974, when he was killed in a violent automobile accident seven miles west of Selmer.

Wild Rice and Mushroom Dressing

2	CUPS COOKED WILD RICE
2	CUPS COOKED WHITE RICE
3	STRIPS BACON
3/4	CUP CHOPPED ONION
1	BAY LEAF
1/2	TEASPOON THYME
2	TABLESPOONS FINELY MINCED PARSLEY
1	14-OUNCE CAN SLICED MUSHROOMS AND LIQUID
1/2	CUP CHICKEN BROTH
1/2	TEASPOON SALT
1/2	TEASPOON BLACK PEPPER

Assemble all ingredients and utensils. Cook both rices according to package directions. In a skillet, sauté bacon until crisp; remove and crumble. Sauté onion in bacon drippings until soft and clear. Add remaining ingredients using enough chicken broth for a moist dressing. Add salt and pepper. Pour into an 8x8-inch baking pan or 2-quart casserole dish and bake in a 325-degree oven for 30 minutes. Yield: 8 servings.

Great stuffing for turkeys, duck, Cornish hens, and other game birds.

Per serving: 123 calories; 2 g fat; 2 mg cholesterol; 349 mg sodium.

Herbed Rice

1	CUP CHOPPED ONION
3	TABLESPOONS BUTTER, MELTED
1	CUP UNCOOKED RICE
3	CUPS CHICKEN BROTH, FRESH COOKED OR CANNED
1	TEASPOON BASIL
3/4	TEASPOON SAGE
1/4	TEASPOON THYME
1/4	TEASPOON CURRY POWDER

Assemble all ingredients and utensils. In a saucepan, sauté onion in melted butter until clear. Add rice and stir for several minutes. Add broth and seasonings. Bring to a boil, cover and cook over a low heat for 30 minutes or until all the broth is absorbed and rice is cooked. Yield: 6 servings.

Hint: To release the flavor of dried herbs, crush them gently before using.

Per serving: 193 calories; 7 g fat; 16 mg cholesterol; 450 mg sodium.

Miss Daisy's Favorite Dressing
With Chicken or Turkey Giblet Gravy

*D*RESSING SERVED WITH CHICKEN OR TURKEY GIBLET GRAVY IS THE NOSTALGIA DISH OF ALL TIME. IT LINKS US WITH OUR HERITAGE OF THE COLONIES AND THEIR THANKSGIVING.

Miss Daisy

Cornbread

2	CUPS PLAIN CORNMEAL
1/3	CUP ALL-PURPOSE FLOUR
1	TABLESPOON SUGAR
3/4	TEASPOONS BAKING POWDER
1/4	TEASPOON BAKING SODA
1/4	TEASPOON SALT
2	CUPS BUTTERMILK
3	EGGS, BEATEN
1	TABLESPOON BACON DRIP-PINGS, OR VEGETABLE OIL

Assemble all ingredients and utensils. In a large mixing bowl, combine cornmeal, flour, sugar, baking powder, soda and salt. Add buttermilk, eggs and drippings and mix well. In a large skillet place 1 table-spoon oil, heat in very hot oven for 2 to 3 minutes. Remove from oven and lower temperature to 450 degrees. Pour batter into hot skillet. Bake for 20 to 25 minutes for cornbread. Yield: 8 to 10 servings.

Per serving: 175 calories; 4 g fat; 84 mg cholesterol; 173 mg sodium.

For dressing, cool and crumble the above recipe of cornbread. Place into a large bowl along with crumbled white bread. Set aside.

Dressing

6	SLICES WHITE BREAD, CRUMBLED
1	MEDIUM ONION, CHOPPED VERY FINE
1	CUP FINELY CHOPPED CELERY
4	CUPS CHICKEN OR TURKEY BROTH
1	TEASPOON RUBBED SAGE
1	TEASPOON POULTRY SEASONING
1/2	TEASPOON BLACK PEPPER
1/4	TEASPOON SALT
1/4	TEASPOON GARLIC POWDER

In a saucepan, combine onion and celery. Add 3 tablespoons broth. Cook over medium heat until vegetables are tender. Add to bowl with cornbread and white bread mixture. Mix in remaining ingredients. Spoon mixture into a greased 13x9x2-inch baking dish. Bake in a 350-degree oven for 30 to 40 minutes or until dressing is set and browned. Yield: 8 to 10 servings.

Per serving: 226 calories; 5 g fat; 84 mg cholesterol; 630 mg sodium.

Giblet Gravy

	GIBLETS AND NECK FROM 1 TURKEY
1/2	CUP CHOPPED ONIONS
1/4	CUP CHOPPED CELERY
2	HARD COOKED EGGS, CHOPPED
1/2	TEASPOON SALT
1/2	TEASPOON BLACK PEPPER
2	TABLESPOONS CORN STARCH
1/4	CUP WATER

Assemble all ingredients and utensils. In a saucepan, add 3 cups water and giblets and neck from turkey. Bring to a boil; cover and reduce heat to simmer and cook for 1 hour, or until tender. Drain, reserving broth. Discard neck. Chop giblets and return to broth in saucepan. Mix in onion, celery, eggs, salt and pepper. Bring to a boil; reduce heat and simmer, uncovered 40 minutes. Combine corn starch and water in small bowl and then add to broth mixture. Bring entire mixture back to a boil for 1 minute. Pour over dressing or turkey or chicken slices. Yield: about 2 cups.

Per serving: 62 calories; 2 g fat; 144 mg cholesterol; 165 mg sodium.

Ernie Ford's Cornbread and Sausage Holiday Dressing

Hey . . . this is good for making two pans—you might want to double up if you've got a big crew comin' over!

OK, first off, here's what you'll need . . .

ENOUGH CORN MEAL MIX TO MAKE TWO (2) GOOD SIZED
PANS OF CORNBREAD (YELLOW OR WHITE . . . IT'S UP TO
YOU. MAKE SURE IT'S MARTHA WHITE!)
ONE OR TWO PACKAGES OF TURKEY GIBLETS (MAKE SURE
YOU'VE GOT IT ALL . . . NECK, GIZZARDS, LIVER & HEART)
TWO POUNDS OF HOT AND SPICY PORK SAUSAGE (DON'T GET
THE MILD . . . YOU'LL TAKE THE TANG OUT OF IT!)
ONE BUNCH EACH OF CELERY AND GREEN ONIONS
ONE BAY LEAF
POWDERED SAGE
BLACK PEPPER

All right, now, here's what you do . . .

DAY ONE

After you've finished breakfast, pull out a big, deep stew pot and pour just a little water in the bottom.
Unwrap your giblet packages . . . rinse the giblets off, and place them in the pot. (Don't cut anything up-that comes later). Add more water until the giblets are covered.
Get that bay leaf out, and toss it in there.
Measure out close to 1/2 teaspoon of sage, rub it between your hands (did you wash?) and dust it into your pot. Add two healthy pinches of black pepper.
Cover the pot, and put it on the back burner . . . somewhere between simmer and low—no higher!—we're going to let things steep just about all day.
Check the water level every once in a while, making sure the giblets stay covered.
After supper, take the pot off the stove and set it to one side, letting it cool a little on its own. Then, just before you hit the sack, put it in the fridge for the night (keep the lid on!).

DAY TWO (Doesn't your kitchen smell great this morning?!)

In a couple of standard 1-inch deep baking pans, bake your two
pones of cornbread. While they're baking, take your pot of
giblets and broth out of the fridge, and warm things up
just a tad.

Get your best iron skillet out, unwrap your sausage, pinch it off
in chunks, and brown all two pounds of it. Drain the
grease off, and set the sausage to one side.

Take your celery and onions out, and chop them real fine.

Take that pot of giblets off the stove, and . . . whoa! get that
cornbread out of the oven!

While your cornbread's cooling, take all the giblets out of the
pot, get that bay leaf out of there, and set the broth to one
side.

Cut, slice, chop and pull all your giblet meat up (it'll peel right
off that neck bone . . .)

Get out the two BIGGEST mixing bowls you've got. Crumble
both your pones of cornbread up into both bowls.

OK . . . add your browned sausage, your giblet meat and your
chopped greens to your
cornmeal. (Make sure
you've got a good,
balanced mix in each
mixing bowl).

Now, slowly add your broth to
each mixture, one bowl at
a time. Get your hands in
there (did you wash?) and
go for it until you've got a
nice, consistent, moist mix.
Moisture is the key word
. . . you don't want your
dressing to be dry.

Get your baking pans back out
and level off each pan with your dressing mix. If you've
got any broth left over, lightly pour the remainder over the
top of each pan of dressing.

Put both pans in the oven at around 350-375 degrees for about
20 minutes, or until you've got a nice, light brown, moist
sheen on top.

Are you ready? Call everybody to dinner. Say Grace, and watch
your dressing disappear.

—Tennessee Ernie Ford
(Ernie Ford's son Buck shared his dear father's recipe with us.)

(Continued from p. 150)

In 1953, the company hired
an unknown bluegrass group as
spokespersons for Martha
White. Lester Flatt, Earl Scruggs, and
the Foggy Mountain Boys soon
became the Number 1 bluegrass
group in the nation. In 1955
Flatt and Scruggs made their
first appearance for Martha
White on the Grand Ole Opry,
and until 1969 they traveled
millions of miles promoting
their sponsor. Using spokespersons such as Grandpa Jones
and Tennessee Ernie Ford, the
company began using television
and print media to carry its
message.

At the heart of all Martha
White Foods' endeavors lies a
90-year commitment to providing quality, innovative baking
ingredients. In
the early years of
the company,
Martha White
became a pioneer
in the develop-
ment of
self-rising flour
and corn meal
mix with their
introduction of
"Hot Rize." This
unique blend of
leavening ingre-
dients soon
became a Martha
White trademark
and started a
tradition of con-
venience baking products for
the company. In 1963, Martha
White introduced its first line of
family-serving-size packages of
convenience mixes. Today, that
same line includes fruit muffin,
brownie, cornbread, pizza crust,
biscuit, pancake, pound cake,
instant potato, and hush puppy
mixes. Martha White was
aquired by Pillsbury-General
Mills in 1994.

Cheese Soufflé

4	TABLESPOONS BUTTER
4	TABLESPOONS ALL-PURPOSE FLOUR
1/2	TEASPOON SALT
1 1/2	CUPS WHOLE MILK
2	CUPS GRATED SHARP CHEDDAR CHEESE
5	EGGS, SEPARATED
1/4	TEASPOON WHITE PEPPER
1/4	TEASPOON CREAM OF TARTAR
	PAPRIKA

SOME FAMILY TRIVIA—PATRICK KING, MY HIGH SCHOOL SENIOR AT MONTGOMERY BELL ACADEMY IN NASHVILLE, TENNESSEE, PROBABLY ENJOYS COOKING AS MUCH AS MANAGING THE ATHLETIC TEAMS AT M.B.A. PATRICK HAS BASICALLY TAUGHT HIMSELF TO COOK BY WATCHING SOME OF MY FOOD PREPARATIONS. HE WILL TRY ANY RECIPE, NO MATTER HOW COMPLEX. CHEESE SOUFFLÉ IS ONE OF HIS FAVORITE RECIPES. PATRICK MADE THIS DISH THE FIRST TIME AT AGE TEN. WHO KNOWS, MAYBE I HAVE "PIERRE FRANEY" RIGHT IN MY OWN KITCHEN (WRITTEN BY A PREJUDICED MOTHER)?

Miss Daisy

Assemble all ingredients and utensils. In a saucepan, melt butter. Blend in flour, salt and milk stirring constantly. Cook until thick. Stir in cheese and cook until melted. Remove from heat and stir in well beaten egg yolks and white pepper. Add cream of tartar to egg whites and beat until stiff. Gradually fold into cheese mixture. Pour into buttered 2-quart casserole dish. Sprinkle paprika over top. Bake in a 325-degree oven for 55 to 60 minutes. Serve immediately. Yield: 6 servings.

Per serving: 341 calories; 27 g fat; 297 mg cholesterol; 586 mg sodium.

Eggs and Cheese Continental

1	CUP THINLY SLICED ONIONS
1	TABLESPOON BUTTER
9	HARD BOILED EGGS, SLICED
2	CUPS SHREDDED SWISS CHEESE
1	10 3/4-OUNCE CAN CREAM OF MUSHROOM SOUP
3/4	CUP MILK
1/2	TEASPOON SEASONED SALT
1	TEASPOON PREPARED MUSTARD
1/4	TEASPOON EACH: DILL WEED AND PEPPER
6	SLICES CARAWAY RYE BREAD, BUTTERED

YOU WILL ENJOY THE POSITIVE COMMENTS WHEN YOU BAKE THIS DISH FOR YOUR FRIENDS WHO ALWAYS ORDER QUICHE. JANE MILLER LIKES TO SERVE IT WITH HAM AND ROLLS AND A FRUIT COMPOTE.

Miss Daisy

Sauté onion in butter until tender. Spread in 9x13-inch baking dish. Top with slices of eggs; sprinkle with cheese. Beat remaining ingredients except bread with mixer. Pour soup mixture over the cheese and eggs. Cut each bread slice into four triangles; place on top of casserole with points up. Bake 30-40 in 350-degree oven; broil a few minutes. Yield: 6 servings.

Deviled Eggs

12   HARD-COOKED EGGS, PEELED AND CHILLED
1/4   CUP MAYONNAISE OR LESS
1 1/2   TEASPOONS WORCESTERSHIRE SAUCE
1   TEASPOON PREPARED MUSTARD
1/2   TEASPOON SALT
1/2   TEASPOON BLACK PEPPER
1   GREEN ONION, FINELY CHOPPED
2   TABLESPOONS WELL-DRAINED PICKLE RELISH
   PAPRIKA FOR GARNISH

Assemble all ingredients and utensils. Cut eggs in half lengthwise, remove yolks, reserve whites. In a bowl, mash yolks until smooth. Combine mayonnaise, Worcestershire sauce, mustard, salt and pepper and add to yolks. Stir in onion and pickle relish. Spoon mixture into center of egg whites. Sprinkle with paprika. Refrigerate until serving. Yield: 24 eggs.

The story goes that all southern brides must receive a glass deviled egg dish before they begin housekeeping.

Per serving: 59 calories; 5 g fat; 138 mg cholesterol; 109 mg sodium.

Brunch Eggs Florentine

2   10-OUNCE PACKAGES FROZEN CHOPPED SPINACH,
   COOKED ACCORDING TO DIRECTIONS
10   EGGS
1   10 3/4-OUNCE CAN CREAM OF CELERY SOUP
1 1/2   CUPS SHREDDED AMERICAN CHEESE

Assemble all ingredients and utensils. Line the bottom of a 13x9x2-inch baking dish with cooked spinach. Make about 10 indentations in spinach and break an egg into each. In a saucepan, heat soup and 1 cup cheese together. Pour over egg/spinach combination. Sprinkle 1/2 cup cheese on top. Bake in a 350-degree oven for 30 minutes. Yield: 10 servings.

Serve fresh fruit or one of the fruit salads with this delectable dish.

Per serving: 182 calories; 13 g fat; 295 mg cholesterol; 443 mg sodium.

HOME OF "THE RAVEN"

If Sam Houston loved anything as a youth, it was the wild country of Tennessee and the forested haunts of the Cherokee Indians. Once, when he was still a youngster, he ran away from his widowed mother's home to live with his Cherokee friends at the village of the chief, Oo-loo-te-ka, or John Jolly, who lived on an island in the middle of the Tennessee River in present-day Meigs County. Although they knew Sam's tendency to strike out from home for long periods of time, the family eventually became worried and two of Houston's brothers went

MEIGS COUNTY

out to look for him. When they arrived at the Cherokee village on Jolly's Island, they found Sam sprawled out under a tree reading the *Iliad*. Asked when he intended returning home, Houston reportedly replied that he "preferred measuring deer tracks to tape" and "the wild liberty of the Red Men better than the tyranny of his own brothers." Houston stayed with his Indian friends for about a year, during which time he was adopted into the tribe and given the name, "Colonah," or the Raven. Years later, after he had served as president of the Republic of Texas and as governor of the state that followed, Houston, reflecting on his blissful days among the Cherokees, remarked (in third person, as he often did) that he had "seen nearly all in life there is to live for and yet he has been heard to say that when he looks back over the waste . . . there's nothing half so sweet to remember as this sojourn he made among the untutored children of the forest."

LAST DAYS AT THE FIRST FORT

For years, the Cherokees had petitioned their British allies to build a fort in the southern Appalachians to protect them from other Indians in the region. Although the Cherokees were the largest and most feared tribe in the entire South, the eruption of the French and Indian War in 1754 provided British authorities with a reason to give in to the natives' repeated requests. In 1759, the British completed Fort Loudoun, the first English fort to be built west of the Appalachians and located in today's Monroe County, near the confluence of the Tellico

MONROE COUNTY

and Little Tennessee Rivers. By early 1760, affairs between the British and their Cherokee allies had turned sour, certainly in no way helped by the recent British execution of twenty-four Cherokee hostages being held by the governor of South Carolina. In early March, Cherokee braves attacked the wilderness fort, but were repulsed after four days of bitter fighting. The siege of Fort Loudoun began. Throughout spring and summer, the fort's occupants grew weak as their meager food and water supplies ran out. On August 9, British and South Carolina provincial troops lowered the fort's flag and, under terms of the surrender, began the long trek back to Charles Town. On the second day after departure, the Cherokees attacked the British column and killed twenty-four soldiers, the same number as that of the Indian hostages executed by the British earlier. The Cherokees subsequently burned Fort Loudoun to the ground.

Sour Cream and Ham Omelet

6	EGG YOLKS
1	CUP SOUR CREAM
1/2	TEASPOON SALT
6	STIFFLY BEATEN EGG WHITES
1	CUP DICED BAKED HAM
2	TABLESPOONS BUTTER
	PAPRIKA FOR GARNISH

Assemble all ingredients and utensils. In a glass bowl, beat egg yolks until thick and lemon colored; beat in half the sour cream and the salt. Fold in egg whites and ham. Heat butter in a large skillet. Pour in omelet mixture. Cook over low heat until lightly browned on bottom, about 5 minutes. Finish cooking in a 325-degree oven until top is golden, about 10 minutes. Loosen and slide onto warm plate. Cut into pie-shaped slices. Garnish with remaining sour cream. Sprinkle with paprika for garnish. Yield: 4 to 6 servings.

Per serving: 232 calories; 19 g fat; 312 mg cholesterol; 594 mg sodium.

Spinach and Bacon Quiche

1	9-INCH PASTRY SHELL
1	CUP GRATED SWISS CHEESE
1	CUP GRATED MOZZARELLA CHEESE
3	SLICES BACON, COOKED AND CRUMBLED
1/2	CUP COOKED, DRAINED SPINACH
3/4	CUP LIGHT CREAM
2	EGGS, BEATEN
1/4	TEASPOON SALT
1/8	TEASPOON CAYENNE PEPPER
1	TABLESPOON BUTTER, MELTED
1	TABLESPOON GRATED PARMESAN CHEESE

Assemble all ingredients and utensils. In a 9-inch pastry shell, place Swiss cheese, Mozzarella cheese, bacon and spinach. In a mixing bowl, combine cream, eggs, salt and pepper. Mix until well blended. Pour over cheeses, bacon, and spinach. Drizzle with melted butter. Sprinkle with Parmesan cheese. Bake in a 375-degree oven for 35 to 45 minutes. Yield: 6 servings.

This dish is so multifaceted. It can be served from the breakfast hour to the dinner hour. Choose one of our salads to accompany this quiche.

Per serving: 400 calories; 30 g fat; 147 mg cholesterol; 550 mg sodium.

Noodles Supreme

1	5-OUNCE PACKAGE THIN EGG NOODLES, COOKED
4	TABLESPOONS BUTTER
1	CUP SOUR CREAM
1	CUP COTTAGE CHEESE
1/2	CUP CHOPPED ONION
1/2	TEASPOON TABASCO SAUCE
1/2	TEASPOON SALT
1/4	TEASPOON GARLIC POWDER OR LESS
	GRATED PARMESAN TO TASTE

Assemble all ingredients and utensils. In a saucepan, cook noodles in boiling, salted water for 10 minutes. Drain. In a skillet or saucepan melt butter and toss in noodles. Add remaining ingredients except Parmesan until well combined. Pour into a 2-quart casserole dish and bake in a 350-degree oven for 45 minutes. Sprinkle with Parmesan. Yield: 6 servings.

Try substituting noodles for rice or potatoes with some of your favorite entrées.

Per serving: 290 calories; 19 g fat; 67 mg cholesterol; 452 mg sodium.

Mayfield Dairy Farms

In the year 1853, Thomas Brient Mayfield Sr. was born at Live Oak Farm in McMinn County. Traditions began as Thomas bred and sold saddle colts, saddle fillies, mules and jacks, Jersey cows and Berkshire hogs. In the spring and summer, the surplus milk was peddled around Athens, along with some buttermilk and churned butter.

By the early 1900s Thomas Jr. had bought a farm adjoining his father's and started a dairy operation. The original milk plant still stands on the Mayfield farm today. Milk was cooled with spring water. Thomas Jr.'s wife, Goldie Denton Mayfield, made the first cottage cheese ever sold on the milk route.

By 1923, technology had improved and a new plant was built on the corner of Green and Bank Streets in Athens. The name of the company became Mayfield Creamery. The plant produced the first pasteurized milk between Chattanooga and Knoxville.

The family worked hard to keep the business operating through the Depression. After World War II, Thomas Brient Mayfield, III and his brother, C. Scott Mayfield, spirited the company into expansion. By the early 1950s, Mayfield Dairy was the most modern dairy in the southeast.

Mayfield Dairy has been first several times with timely innovation and quality dairy products.

Mayfield was the first dairy in the U. S. to produce milk with a year-round uniform flavor.

Mayfield had the first mechanically refrigerated milk truck fleet in Tennessee.

Mayfield was the first to package milk in a "yellow" plastic bottle, which deflected harmful light rays and protected the milk flavor and nutrients.

Mayfield was the first dairy in the U. S. to market a milk containing acidophilus and bifidum bacterium, to aid digestion.

It is inconceivable today to contemplate what life must have been like to those early pioneers who settled the region that would one day become Tennessee. Amid the dangers of the savage wilderness, the extremes of climate, and the ever-constant inroads by Indians, theirs was a life of continual hardship, trial, and tribulation. A Montgomery County resident confirmed the uncertainty of frontier life when he wrote the following comments in a letter addressed from Clarksville on November 12, 1794. "Yesterday I

MONTGOMERY COUNTY

was a spectator to the most tragical scene ever I saw in my life. The Indians made an attack on Colonel Sevier's station, killed Snyder, his wife, and child, one of Colonel Sevier's children, and another wounded and scalped, which must die. On hearing the guns, four or five of us ran over; we found the poor old Colonel defending his house with his wife. It is impossible to describe this scene to you. . . . This is a stroke we have long expected, and from every intelligence, we hourly expect this place to be assailed by the enemy. Colonel Sevier is now moving. . . . My wife now lies on her bed, so ill that it would be death to move her; thus are we situated. This place will, without doubt, be evacuated in a day or two, unless succor is given by the people from the interior part. Pray ask the influence of Major Tatum, Douglass, and all our friends, with General Robertson, to guard us, or at least help us away."

Angel Hair Pasta With Herb Sauce

1	POUND ANGEL HAIR PASTA, COOKED AND DRAINED
1 1/2	CUPS HEAVY CREAM
4	TABLESPOONS UNSALTED BUTTER
1/2	TEASPOON SALT
1/4	TEASPOON GROUND NUTMEG
1/8	TEASPOON CAYENNE PEPPER
1/4	CUP FRESHLY GRATED PARMESAN CHEESE
1	CUP FINELY CHOPPED MIXED FRESH HERBS: BASIL, MINT, CHIVES, PARSLEY, TARRAGON OR
1/3	CUP IF USING DRIED HERBS

Assemble all ingredients and utensils. In a deep, heavy saucepan, combine cream, butter, salt, nutmeg, and pepper. Simmer 15 minutes or until slightly thickened. Whisk in cheese and herbs, simmer another 5 minutes. Serve over cooked pastsa immediately. Yield: 6 servings.

Refreshing way to use fresh herbs from your garden.

Per serving: 572 calories; 31 g fat; 105 mg cholesterol; 268 mg sodium.

Fettuccine With Pesto Sauce

2	CUPS PACKED FRESH BASIL LEAVES
1/2	CUP OLIVE OIL
3	CLOVES GARLIC
1/2	TEASPOON SALT
1/3	CUP GRATED PARMESAN CHEESE
1/4	CUP NUTS, PINENUTS OR WALNUTS
12	OUNCES FETTUCCINE, COOKED
1/2	CUP BUTTER

Assemble all ingredients and utensils. In a blender or food processer, place basil, oil, garlic, and salt. Process. Add cheese and nuts and mix in. Cook fettuccine, toss with butter, then with Pesto Sauce. Yield: about 2 cups sauce; serves 8 with fettuccine.

Delicious as a side dish for meats.

Per serving: 442 calories; 29 g fat; 34 mg cholesterol; 314 mg sodium.

Vegetable Macaroni

1	8-OUNCE PACKAGE MACARONI, COOKED
1	10 3/4-OUNCE CAN CREAM OF MUSHROOM SOUP
1/4	CUP CHOPPED ONION
1/4	CUP CHOPPED GREEN PEPPER
1/4	CUP CHOPPED PIMENTO
1	CUP MAYONNAISE
1/2	CUP GRATED CHEDDAR CHEESE

Assemble all ingredients and utensils. In a saucepan, heat soup and vegetables. Add mayonnaise and combine with cooked macaroni. Pour into a 1 1/2-quart casserole dish and sprinkle with cheddar cheese. Bake in a 350-degree oven for 20 minutes. Yield: 4 to 6 servings.

Per serving: 500 calories; 36 g fat; 33 mg cholesterol; 689 mg sodium.

Apple Butter

8	CUPS CORED, CHOPPED, UNPEELED COOKING APPLES
1	CUP APPLE CIDER
1	CUP SUGAR
1	TEASPOON GROUND CINNAMON
1/4	TEASPOON GROUND CLOVES

Assemble all ingredients and utensils. Combine apples and cider in a crock pot. Cover and cook on low for 10 to 12 hours. Grind in a food processor. Return puréed mixture to pot and add sugar, cinnamon and cloves. Cover and cook on low for one hour. Pour into hot sterilized jars and seal. Yield: 1 quart.

Delightful heated and served with sausage balls in a chafing dish for brunch.

Per serving: 44 calories; 0 g fat; 0 mg cholesterol; 0 mg sodium.

Loveless Blackberry Preserves

30	POUNDS BLACKBERRIES
15	POUNDS SUGAR

Cook blackberries on medium heat for 1 hour. Stir in sugar. Cook for 2 hours or until blackberries reach desired consistency.

Yield: approximately 1 1/2 to 2 dozen pints.

Loveless Peach Preserves

6	LARGE CANS (1 CASE) OF CALIFORNIA YELLOW CLING PEACHES, PIE SLICED (EACH CAN, 6 POUNDS, 8 OUNCES OF PEACH SLICES PACKED IN WATER)
10	POUNDS SUGAR

Place peaches in large pot. Cook on medium heat for one hour. Add sugar. Cook for 3 hours, or until peaches are caramel colored.

Yield: approximately 2 dozen pints.

Lemon Curd

1	POUND SUGAR
3/4	CUP BUTTER
	GRATED LEMON RIND AND JUICE OF 3 LARGE LEMONS
6	WHOLE EGGS

Assemble all ingredients and utensils. In the top of a double boiler, combine sugar, butter, lemon rind and juice. Stir until butter melts and is dissolved. Beat eggs until creamy colored. Add to first mixture. Stir until this mixture coats a wooden spoon. Remove from double boiler and allow to cool. Will keep weeks stored in refrigerator. Yield: 3 cups.

Great served for breakfast with muffins or toast. Delicious with crumpets and tea. I use it for preparing lemon tarts with 1 cup of whipped cream added to 2 cups of lemon curd.

Per serving: 144 calories; 7 g fat; 84 mg cholesterol; 76 mg sodium.

Strawberry Preserves

1   QUART STRAWBERRIES, HULLED AND WASHED
4   CUPS SUGAR

Assemble all ingredients and utensils. In a large pot stir ingredients together over low heat. When sugar melts, cook on high heat 5 to 10 minutes. Then cook about 8 minutes on medium high. Pour in a pan and refrigerate overnight or 12 hours. Put in sterile jars. Yield: 5 to 6 pints.

Per serving: 34 calories; 0 g fat; 0 mg cholesterol; 0 mg sodium.

*P*ICK YOUR OWN FRESH STRAWBERRIES IN HUMBOLDT OR PORTLAND, TENNESSEE. FRESH BLACKBERRIES ARE GROWN AROUND GALLATIN, TENNESSEE. THE MENNONITES MANUFACTURE FOR RETAIL BLACKBERRY, STRAWBERRY, CHERRY, AND PEACH JAM AND PRESERVES.

Miss Daisy

Blackberry Jam

2   QUARTS FRESH BLACKBERRIES (1/4 OF WHICH ARE UNRIPE)
6   CUPS SUGAR

Assemble all ingredients and utensils. Wash berries and drain. In a saucepan cook berries over moderate heat until juice begins to run and berries are soft. Run through a food mill and processor to obtain juice and pulp. Measure out 4 cups of juice and pulp mixture and place in preserving pot. Bring to a boil. Add sugar and cook over moderate heat until candy thermometer reaches about 220 degrees (about 30 minutes). Pour into jars and seal. Yield: 8 half pints.

Per serving: 82 calories; 0 g fat; 0 mg cholesterol; 0 mg sodium.

Tennessee Chow Chow

*S*ugar Plum Foods, producers of Tennessee Chow Chow Relish, is a family owned and operated business. Production originated in the kitchen of

Doris and Tim Sprecher in 1986. With the help of their children, every jar is dipped, labeled, and boxed by hand. A daily ritual is cutting the fresh vegetables and measuring spices that give this delicious chow chow recipe its unique taste. Tennessee Chow Chow is great on tuna, beans, and hot dogs and gives that special finishing touch to any meal.

Hot Pepper Jelly

2 1/2   CUPS SUGAR
3/4   CUPS APPLE CIDER VINEGAR
1/2   CUP FINELY CHOPPED, SEEDED GREEN PEPPER
1/4   CUP FINELY CHOPPED, SEEDED JALAPEÑO PEPPER
1   3-OUNCE BOTTLE LIQUID FRUIT PECTIN

Assemble all ingredients and utensils. In a large pot, combine sugar and vinegar; bring to a boil. Add peppers and return to a boil. Stir in pectin and boil one minute. Strain liquid through a colander into a large bowl. Pour into hot sterilized jars and seal. Yield: 2 half pints.

Per serving: 83 calories; 0 g fat; 0 mg cholesterol; 21 mg sodium.

Sam Houston

Virginia-born Sam Houston (1793-1863) came to Tennessee in 1807. He began teaching about 1812 at Maryville's now-famous school-house that bears his name. Later, distinguish-ing himself in battle at Horseshoe Bend against the Creek Indians, he came to the attention of his commander, Andrew Jackson, thus paving the way for a lasting friendship between the two men. Houston was elected governor of Tennessee in 1827, but he served for only a short time before resigning the office. His brief marriage to Eliza Allen of Gallatin ended about the same time, and Houston left Nashville to cross the Mississippi and live with his Cherokee friends, who had since been removed to Arkansas.

Moving to Texas, Houston became the commander-in-chief of the Texas army and defeated the Mexican dictator, Santa Anna, at San Jacinto in the spring of 1836. A few months later, he was elected to the presi-dency of the Republic of Texas. After Texas became one of the United States ten years later, the man from Tennessee became the new state's first U. S. senator. He served in that role for thirteen years, then became governor of Texas in 1859.

Sam Houston Apple Relish

14	LARGE APPLES
1	LARGE BUNCH CELERY
6	RED BELL PEPPERS
6	GREEN BELL PEPPERS
12	ONIONS
1	QUART VINEGAR
6	CUPS SUGAR

Put apples and vegetables through a food chopper. Combine with vinegar and sugar and boil about 15 minutes. Can and seal. Yield: 8 to 10 pints.

Mr. Houston's favorite relish recipe handed down from the *Sam Houston Schoolhouse Cookbook.*

Corn Relish

1/2	CUP SUGAR
1/2	TEASPOON EACH: SALT AND CELERY SEED
1/4	TEASPOON MUSTARD SEED
1/4	TEASPOON TABASCO SAUCE
1/2	CUP APPLE CIDER VINEGAR
1	12- TO 14-OUNCE CAN YELLOW CORN NIBLETS OR WHOLE CORN
2	TABLESPOONS CHOPPED GREEN PEPPER
1	TABLESPOON CHOPPED PIMENTO
2	TABLESPOONS FINELY CHOPPED FRESH ONION

Assemble all ingredients and utensils. In a saucepan, heat sugar, salt, celery seed, mustard seed, Tabasco sauce and vinegar. Bring to a boil-ing point. Boil 2 minutes. Remove from heat and stir in remaining ingredients. Cool; cover and chill thoroughly. Refrigerate several days before using. Yield: 2 cups.

Serve this with summer green beans from your garden.

Per serving: 43 calories; 0 g fat; 0 mg cholesterol; 125 mg sodium.

Tennessee Chow Chow

1	QUART GREEN TOMATOES
2	SWEET GREEN PEPPERS
2	SWEET RED PEPPERS
2	LARGE ONIONS
1	SMALL HEAD CABBAGE
1/2	CUP SALT
3	CUPS APPLE CIDER VINEGAR
2 1/2	CUPS BROWN SUGAR
1	TEASPOON DRY MUSTARD
1	TEASPOON TURMERIC
2	TABLESPOONS CELERY SEED

THIS RECIPE GOES BACK MANY YEARS. CHOW CHOW IS A COMPLEMENT TO WHITE BEANS AND JOHNNY CAKES. "CHOW CHOW" MEANS MIXED, AND THE TERM DATES BACK OVER TWO HUNDRED YEARS IN THE SOUTH. IT IS A VEGETABLE RELISH MADE OF CHOPPED VEGETABLES AND MIXED WITH VINEGAR AND SUGAR, SEASONED WITH VARIOUS SPICES, COOKED, AND THEN PUT UP IN JARS.

Miss Daisy

Assemble all ingredients and utensils. Grind all vegetables, add salt and let stand overnight. The next morning, drain liquid off. In a large pot add all other ingredients and bring to a boil. Reduce to a simmer and cook for one hour, stirring occasionally. Put in sterilized jars and store in dark place for three weeks before using. Yield: 7 half pints.

Per serving: 50 calories; 0 g fat; 0 mg cholesterol; 161 mg sodium.

RIGHT COUNTY, WRONG SIZE

Although the Tennessee Constitution of 1870 required all future counties that might be organized in the State to contain at least 275 square miles, when Moore County was created the following year, it was admitted with only half the required acreage, around 130 square miles. The oversight occurred while commissioners were attempting to conform with another section of the law which stated that no boundary line of a newly created county could lie within eleven miles of the courthouse of the old county from which the new entity was being formed. When it was discovered that the proposed line did, indeed, lie closer than eleven miles to the Lincoln County

MOORE COUNTY

Courthouse in Fayetteville, the real estate to be contained in the new county (Moore) was re-shuffled to correct the error, leaving only the diminished size of around 130 square miles. The new county was named in honor of General William Moore, a former resident of Lincoln County and a past member of the Tennessee Legislature. In June, 1873, the village of Lynchburg was chosen to be county seat. Tradition has it that the town's unique name came about by virtue of the presence of a gang of outlaws who operated in the countryside thereabouts. When a vigilante committee of citizens was chosen to enforce the law, they selected a man by the name of "Lynch" to administer public whippings to convicted criminals.

Of national fame is Jack Daniel's Distillery in Lynchburg, the oldest registered distillery in the United States.

Cabbage Pickletts

Four large crisp cabbage, one quart of onions chopped fine, one dozen cucumbers sliced, pack all together with a little salt between layers, let stand overnight, then press it out and add one and a half pounds of brown sugar, two tablespoons of ground mustard, two tablespoons of cinnamon, two tablespoons of celery seed, one tablespoon of mace, two tablespoons of black pepper, two tablespoons of turmeric, one tablespoon of allspice, put this into vinegar enough to cover, then boil five minutes; pack in small jars. This makes an excellent pickle to use in summer and early fall before you have made pickles for winter.

THIS RECIPE COMES FROM MRS. T. S. MCFERRIN OF MURFREESBORO, TENNESSEE. MRS. MCFERRIN IS A MEMBER OF MY D.A.R. CHAPTER AND HAS AN ENORMOUS AMOUNT OF HISTORICAL DATA ABOUT THE STATE OF TENNESSEE. SHE IS SUCH A PLEASURE TO VISIT AND OF COURSE I ALWAYS LEARN SOMETHING.

Miss Daisy

Woodruff-Fontaine House Marinated Onions

12	LARGE WHITE ONIONS SLICED TISSUE THIN
1 1/2	CUPS OF SALAD OIL
1 1/2	CUPS OF LEMON JUICE
1 1/2	CUPS OF VINEGAR
4	TABLESPOONS OF SALT
2	TEASPOONS OF PEPPER

Mix in order given; soak onions 3 hours but not longer than 5 hours.

Woodruff-Fontaine House

The Woodruff-Fontaine House was built in 1870 at 680 Adams Avenue in Memphis. This French-Victorian mansion vies for attention with its twenty rooms. The home was originally built for the Amos Woodruff family. Amos was a wealthy man who had made his fortune as a carriage builder, banker, and railroad owner. The outstanding architects for the mansion were Edward Culliott Jones of Charleston and Mathias Baldwin of New York.

The second family to occupy the house was the family of Noland Fontaine. Noland was a successful cotton factory owner. In later years, the home would become part of the James Lee Art Academy.

Today, the house is listed on the *National Register of Historic Places*. Tours are available through the Memphis Chapter of the Association for the Preservation of Tennessee Antiquities.

Dixie Relish

1	QUART CHOPPED CABBAGE
1	PINT CHOPPED ONIONS
1	PINT RED SWEET PEPPERS
2	TABLESPOONS SALT
1	QUART VINEGAR
3/4	CUP SUGAR

Mix all ingredients and boil 15 minutes. Can in jars and seal.

Refrigerator Pickles

4	QUART JARS OF CUCUMBERS, SLICED THIN
4	CUPS SUGAR
4	CUPS APPLE CIDER VINEGAR
1/2	CUP SALT
1 1/3	TEASPOONS TURMERIC
1 1/2	TEASPOONS CELERY SALT
1 1/2	TEASPOONS DRY MUSTARD

Assemble all ingredients and utensils. Put cucumbers in quart jars. In a sauce pan, heat sugar, vinegar, salt, and spices until sugar is dissolved. Pour over cucumbers to cover. Keep in refrigerator. Yield: 4 quarts, 64 servings.

Per serving: 54 calories; 0 g fat; 0 mg cholesterol; 455 mg sodium.

DEUTCHLAND IN TENNESSEE

It is estimated that between 1830 and 1850, nearly 600,000 Germans immigrated to the United States, searching for new hope and new lands here. As early as 1828, Traugott Bromme, a German traveler, had visited Tennessee and had left especially impressed with the qualities of Morgan County. Soon after his return to Germany, Bromme published a book extolling the virtues of the mineral-rich region, and as a consequence, many German financiers looked to Tennessee for investment opportunities. By 1844, the East Tennessee Colonization Company had been organized and nearly 200,000 acres of land in Morgan,

MORGAN COUNTY

Cumberland, White, Fentress, and Scott Counties purchased. The German economy was at its worst at the time, and when managers of the colonization company scoured the poorer districts of that country for potential settlers, they had no trouble finding many. Fifty Germans arrived first, with prospects of many more. The *Nashville Whig* reported in 1845 that "two or three hundred immigrants are daily expected to arrive," and that "the immigrants are far superior to the general run of that description of persons . . . none but individuals with good character and habits will be permitted to join the colony." The town of Wartburg was soon established and lots sold for ten to thirty dollars each. Crop failure and a decrease in new immigrants finally spelled doom to Morgan County's German colony, but not before it had left its customs and lifestyles on the area.

It was a time when food was scarce and money to buy any was hard to find. It was 1930, and Lonas Swaggerty began to blend a sausage for his family and neighbors in Kodak, Tennessee. Lonas built an ice box on the back of his 1929 Model-T Ford and took his sausage to the Knoxville Market Square. Many neighbors in Sevier County were doing the same thing and the sausages were all called Sevier County Sausage at first. But, since Lonas made and packed his product right on his farm, his was distinctively called Swaggerty's Sausage. The Great Depression passed and customers found Swaggerty's a survivor.

Today, Swaggerty's Sausage is a leading product in East Tennessee. The recipe is the same as it was on the farm back in Kodak. The carefully measured and weighed spices ensure uniform taste and allow Swaggerty's to offer competitive prices. Lonas' descendants now operate the business and call their sausage "a slice of pure country."

Oven Baked Applesauce

12	MEDIUM APPLES (YORK, ROME)
1/2	CUP SUGAR
1/2	TEASPOON CINNAMON
1/4	TEASPOON EACH: SALT, NUTMEG, MACE
1/4	CUP WATER
2	TABLESPOONS BUTTER

Assemble all ingredients and utensils. Peel, core, and cut apples into chunks. Place in a lightly buttered pan. Combine sugar, cinnamon, salt, nutmeg, mace and sprinkle over apples. Add water and dot with butter. Cover and bake in a 300-degree oven for 1 to 1 1/2 hours. Yield: 6 to 8 servings.

A very easy recipe to prepare. A versatile side dish from breakfast to supper.

Per serving: 197 calories; 4 g fat; 8 mg cholesterol; 96 mg sodium.

Homemade Cranberry Sauce

2	POUNDS CRANBERRIES
2	CUPS CHOPPED WALNUTS
3	CUPS SUGAR
2	LEMONS, JUICE OF AND GRATED RIND
2	CUPS ORANGE MARMALADE

Assemble all ingredients and utensils. Wash and drain cranberries. Place in a shallow baking dish and cover with remaining ingredients. Bake in a 350-degree oven, covered for 45 to 50 minutes. Yield: 8 cups, 64 servings.

Per serving: 96 calories; 2 g fat; 0 mg cholesterol; 3 mg sodium.

Jezebel Sauce

1	16-OUNCE JAR PINEAPPLE PRESERVES
1	4-OUNCE JAR HOT MUSTARD
1	16-OUNCE JAR APPLE JELLY
1	6-OUNCE BOTTLE HORSERADISH
1/2	TEASPOON SALT

Assemble all ingredients and utensils. Mix all ingredients in blender. Pour into jars or covered bowl. Will keep refrigerated for months. Yield: 3 cups.

Per serving: 110 calories; 0 g fat; 0 mg cholesterol; 115 mg sodium.

CAKES AND PIES

The pie is an English institution which, planted on American soil, forthwith ran rampant and burst forth into an untold variety of genera and species.

Harriet Beecher Stowe

CAKES AND PIES

Angel Food Cake

1 1/2	CUPS EGG WHITES
1 1/4	TEASPOONS CREAM OF TARTAR
1/4	TEASPOON SALT
1	TEASPOON VANILLA
1 1/2	CUPS SUGAR, DIVIDED
1	CUP ALL-PURPOSE FLOUR

Assemble all ingredients and utensils. In mixing bowl with beater, beat egg whites, cream of tartar, salt and vanilla until mixture holds a peak. Continue beating, adding 1/2 cup sugar a little at a time. Sift together the flour and remaining sugar; then sift again over the egg whites. Fold in. Spoon batter into clean 10-inch angel food cake pan. Bake in a 375-degree oven for 30 minutes. When cake is done, immediately turn pan upside down to prevent cake from falling. Remove from pan when cool. Yield: 12 servings.

Chocolate Angel Food Cake can be prepared using same recipe; substituting 1/4 cup cocoa for 1/4 cup of the flour. A great low-fat and low-cholesterol dessert!

Per serving: 149 calories; .1 g fat; 0 mg cholesterol; 112 mg sodium.

"UNSOLVED MYSTERY"

When Susan Caroline Godsey was seven years old, her family moved from the farm in Gibson County to the tiny village of Woodland Mills, located about twelve miles from Union City in Obion County. Neighbors recalled that when Susan first arrived in Woodland Mills, she appeared perfectly healthy and alert. Yet, within about a year the little girl took seriously ill. For the next two years, Susan suffered from chills and fever, and her frustrated parents were ready to try anything to cure her. A new doctor in the area was called in and treated the girl with what today would be called "quack" remedies. Susan soon developed

OBION COUNTY

severe cramps which she endured for the next three years. When she was about thirteen years old, the child fell into a state of semi-consciousness, wherein she would awaken several times a day, but only for a few minutes at a time. She was seen by physician after physician, including one who traveled all the way from Paris, France, all to no avail. She was treated by the eminent Nashville doctor, Paul Eve, as well as by a battery of physicians in St. Louis. No one could help Susan come out of her coma-like sleep. A Memphis newspaper reported, "Her sleep was more the appearance of death than a peaceful slumber. There was no sign of life." The showman, P. T. Barnum, wanted Susan to travel the circus circuit, but her parents would have no part of it. Finally, at the age of thirty-seven, Susan died peacefully. Her case remains a true "unsolved mystery."

Thelma Harper's Apricot Nectar Cake With Glaze

1	BOX YELLOW CAKE MIX
1/2	CUP OIL
3/4	CUP APRICOT NECTAR
4	EGGS, SEPARATED
1/2	TEASPOON LEMON FLAVORING

Beat egg yolks, add 1/2 teaspoon lemon flavoring. Beat egg whites, fold into cake mixture after adding oil and nectar. Pour into tube pan. Bake at 300 degrees for 50 to 55 minutes. While cake is baking, mix glaze:

2	CUPS POWDERED SUGAR, SIFTED
1 1/2	CUPS LEMON JUICE

When cake is done, spoon glaze on top and sides of cake. Turn oven off and put cake back in oven for about ten minutes. Take out and let stand about 15 minutes.

State Senator Thelma Harper has cooked all her life. She grew up on farms in Wilson and Williamson counties. The daughter of a sharecropper, Thelma told me that her family smoked hams, barbecued goats, canned vegetables, dried fruit for pies, and picked their own fruit for jellies and preserves. She combed her files for the perfect Bicentennial Collection recipe and said, "It is time to Celebrate."

Miss Daisy

Dried Apple Cake

2 1/2	CUPS DRIED APPLES, COOKED AND DRAINED
1	CUP BUTTER
2	CUPS SUGAR
2	TABLESPOONS EACH: CINNAMON AND NUTMEG
1	TEASPOON ALLSPICE
3	TEASPOONS SODA
1	14-OUNCE BOX RAISINS, DUSTED WITH FLOUR
1	CUP PECANS
4	CUPS ALL-PURPOSE FLOUR

Assemble all ingredients and utensils. Cook apples until soft. Drain. Cream butter. Add sugar, spices, and soda, beat well. Add apples while still warm. Add raisins and nuts. Blend in flour. Batter will be stiff. Divide batter into four, 8-inch cake pans which have been lined with wax paper that has been greased and floured. Bake in a 350-degree oven 20 minutes or until cake tests done. Yield: 12-16 servings.

Per serving: 506 calories; 21 g fat; 31 mg cholesterol; 284 mg sodium.

Our family loves this recipe. The cake is delicious with Easy Caramel Icing (see p. 183). This is an old recipe that has been passed through many generations.

Miss Daisy

Fresh Apple Cake

1	CUP COOKING OIL
2	CUPS SUGAR
3	EGGS, WELL BEATEN
2 1/2	CUPS ALL-PURPOSE FLOUR
2	TEASPOONS BAKING POWDER
1	TEASPOON BAKING SODA
1	TEASPOON SALT
1	TEASPOON GROUND CINNAMON
1	TEASPOON GROUND NUTMEG
1	TEASPOON VANILLA
4	CUPS CHOPPED, PEELED, RED DELICIOUS APPLES

Assemble all ingredients and utensils. In large bowl of mixer combine oil and sugar. Beat in eggs. Sift together dry ingredients and add to egg mixture. Gently fold in vanilla and apples. Bake in a 13X9-inch pan which has been greased and floured in a 325-degree oven for 50-55 minutes. Cool and ice cake with Vanilla Cream Cheese Frosting. Yield: 12 servings.

Per serving: 426 calories; 20 g fat; 68 mg cholesterol; 322 mg sodium.

Vanilla Cream Cheese Frosting

1	1-POUND BOX CONFECTIONERS SUGAR
1	8-OUNCE PACKAGE CREAM CHEESE
1/2	CUP MARGARINE OR BUTTER
2	TEASPOONS VANILLA
1	CUP CHOPPED PECANS

Assemble all ingredients and utensils. Have all ingredients at room temperature. In large mixing bowl beat at low speed sugar, cream cheese and margarine or butter until smooth. Add vanilla. Mix well. Stir in pecans.

Recipe will ice one, 13x9-inch pan, two, 9-inch cake pans or a bundt or tube cake pan.

Per serving: 339 calories; 20 g fat; 41 mg cholesterol; 134 mg sodium.

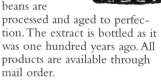

Applesauce Cake

2	STICKS MARGARINE
2	CUPS SIFTED CAKE FLOUR
	(SAVE 1/2 CUP FOR RAISINS AND NUTS)
3	EGGS
1	CUP WHITE SUGAR
1/2	CUP BROWN SUGAR
2/3	BOX RAISINS
1	CUP BLACK WALNUTS (MORE IF DESIRED)
2	CUPS HOT APPLESAUCE MIXED WITH 2 TEASPOONS
	OF SODA
1 1/2	TEASPOONS CINNAMON
1	TEASPOON GROUND CLOVES
1	TEASPOON ALLSPICE

$\mathcal{R}$ECIPE WAS CONTRIBUTED BY DEBBIE SMITH, WIFE OF STEVE SMITH, THE PRESIDENT OF FOOD CITY IN GREENEVILLE, TENNESSEE.

Miss Daisy

Mix cinnamon, cloves, and allspice with flour. Cream sugar, add eggs (one at a time); add applesauce. Add flour and spices. Stir in nuts and raisins. Bake at 350 degrees for 50 minutes in a greased and floured tube pan. Finish with the following glaze:

1/2	CUP BROWN SUGAR
1/2	CUP WHITE SUGAR
6	TABLESPOONS MARGARINE
1/2	CUP MILK
1 1/2	TEASPOONS VANILLA

Combine and cook over medium heat for 5 minutes. Spoon sauce over applesauce cake while hot.

Per serving: 387 calories; 19 g fat; 47 mg cholesterol; 276 mg sodium.

"GO WEST, YOUNG MAN"

The man who may be Overton County's most illustrious citizen left his Tennessee home and heeded Horace Greeley's famous saying years before Greeley ever made the expression a catch-phrase of the day. Josiah Gregg, the son of Harmon Gregg, a wheelwright, and his wife, was born near Eagle Creek in 1806, but left the region when he was about three. As far as is known, he never returned to the forested hills of Overton County. Gregg grew up to be a sickly young man, but well educated for the times, maintaining special interests in mathematics, surveying, and literature. Around 1830, a physician in Missouri

OVERTON COUNTY

advised Gregg to take the next wagon train to Santa Fe. There, in the dry desert air of the Southwest, he might regain his strength. The trip helped, and over the next nine years, the former Tennessean traveled eight times across the southern Great Plains, sometimes spending several months at a time as a trader in New Mexico. Gregg was a keen observer, and he gathered his experiences during travel between Missouri and New Mexico over the Santa Fe Trail into a book he entitled, *Commerce of the Prairies,* published in 1844. The book became extremely popular and quickly established Gregg as the foremost authority on the Santa Fe trade during the 1840s. Gregg fell into anonymity for years after his death in California in 1850, and even today, few people outside those interested in Western history recognize this outstanding Tennessean's name.

Banana Nut Cake

3/4	CUP BUTTER, SOFTENED
2	CUPS SUGAR
3	LARGE EGGS
4	MEDIUM BANANAS
1	TEASPOON BAKING SODA
1/2	CUP PECANS, FINELY CHOPPED
3	CUPS ALL-PURPOSE FLOUR
1/2	TEASPOON SALT
2	TEASPOONS BAKING POWDER
1/2	CUP BUTTERMILK

Assemble all ingredients and utensils. In large bowl of mixer cream butter and sugar well. Add eggs one at a time, beating thoroughly after each addition. Mash bananas and mix in the baking soda. Add to creamed mixture. Add pecans. Sift flour with salt and baking powder. Add to banana mixture, alternating with buttermilk. Beat until smooth. Grease four (8-inch) cake pans and pour batter into them. Bake in a 350-degree oven for 30 minutes. Cool. Frost with Boiled Icing. Yield: 20 servings.

Makes a large moist cake.

Per serving: 258 calories; 10 g fat; 60 mg cholesterol; 204 mg sodium.

Boiled Icing

2	CUPS SUGAR
1/4	CUP LIGHT KARO SYRUP
1/2	CUP BOILING WATER
4	EGG WHITES, STIFFLY BEATEN

Assemble all ingredients and utensils. Mix sugar with Karo syrup; add to the boiling water and stir over medium heat. When the sugar has completely dissolved, remove from heat and cool; then pour very slowly into stiffly beaten egg whites, beating constantly. Continue to beat until icing is stiff enough to spread.

Per serving: 92 calories; 0 g fat; 0 mg cholesterol; 13 mg sodium.

WHEN THE U. S. MAIL CAME BY BOAT

For years during the 1920s and 1930s, John Matthews, the son of a Perry County slave, hauled the United States mail to residents living along the county's shoreline on the Tennessee River. Although there were other rural routes in Tennessee that measured much longer than Matthews' sixty-eight mile course, his was one of only two in the state that was water-borne. Matthews' route and the one that ran across the Mississippi River from Tennessee to Arkansas, were two of only seventeen such water-borne mail routes in the

PERRY COUNTY

entire United States. Aboard the tiny boat, *Virginia B.,* Matthews went about his daily chores of delivering the United States mail to his rural patrons. Matthews worked six days a week and only took Sundays and holidays off from his laborious chores. A local man named A. F. Crockett held the contract for this unique mail service, and his compensation for the operation of the *Virginia B.* and the delivery of the mail was the grand sum of eighteen hundred dollars per year. Crockett furnished the boat, the labor, and the fuel. A newspaper article written in 1940 by soon-to-be U. S. Representative J. Percy Priest revealed that "frequently it takes mail from the county seat [Linden] three days to reach rural route patrons served" from Denson's Landing. Priest explained that the delay came about by the mail being first carried to Nashville, then sent to Johnsonville, then placed on board the *Virginia B.* for local delivery.

FATHER OF THE UNITED NATIONS

When Cordell Hull was growing up in present-day Pickett County, the last thing on his mind was politics, or statesmanship, or public servitude. Hull's primary interests as a youngster were two-fold, the law and the logging business. Born a little over a mile south of Byrdstown in 1871 in a section of the county that was once part of Overton County, young Hull was kept busy as a boy floating logs down the Cumberland River to Nashville and beyond. In fact, his very name, Cordell, was linked to the river. To *cordell* meant to tie a

PICKETT COUNTY

rope to the mast of a flatboat and, by means of walking along the river's bank, to pull it upstream by the rope against the current. Cordelling was hard work, but Cordell Hull lived up to his namesake. Hull saved enough money from his logging business to enter law school at the world-famous Cumberland Univer-sity at Lebanon. After graduating with honors, he sat for the Tennessee bar, passed it, was awarded his attorney's license, and began practice. Soon afterwards, Hull ran for, and was elected to, the Tennessee House of Representatives at the relatively young age of twenty. The Spanish-American War called him away from his civilian duties, but after he returned home, he served as a judge, a U. S. congress-man, a U. S. senator, and finally, as Franklin D. Roosevelt's secretary of state. He served in that position many years and while there, was instrumental in organizing the United Nations, winning a Nobel Peace Prize for his efforts.

Carrot Cake

2	CUPS SIFTED ALL-PURPOSE FLOUR
2	TEASPOONS BAKING POWDER
1 1/2	TEASPOONS SODA
1 1/2	TEASPOONS SALT
2	TEASPOONS CINNAMON
2	CUPS SUGAR
1 1/2	CUPS SALAD OIL
4	EGGS
2	CUPS FINELY GRATED CARROTS
1	8 1/2-OUNCE CAN CRUSHED PINEAPPLE, DRAINED
1/2	CUP CHOPPED PECANS, OPTIONAL
1	3 1/2-OUNCE CAN FLAKED COCONUT
	CREAM CHEESE FROSTING

Assemble ingredients and utensils. In large bowl of mixer sift together flour, baking powder, baking soda, salt and cinnamon. Gradually mix in sugar, oil and eggs; beat well. Add carrots, pine-apple, nuts and coconut; blend thoroughly. Distribute batter evenly among three, 9-inch greased and floured round cake pans. Bake in a 350-degree oven for 35-40 minutes. Cool about 10 minutes in the pans. Turn out on wire racks and cool thoroughly. Fill layers and frost top and sides of cake with Cream Cheese Frosting.
Yield: 15-18 servings.

Per serving: 573 calories; 37 g fat; 88 mg cholesterol; 395 mg sodium.

Cream Cheese Frosting

1	8-OUNCE PACKAGE CREAM CHEESE
1/2	CUP BUTTER, SOFTENED
1	1-POUND BOX CONFECTIONERS SUGAR
1	TABLESPOON VANILLA EXTRACT
1	CUP CHOPPED PECANS, TOASTED

Assemble ingredients and utensils. In large bowl of mixer cream cream cheese and butter. Add sugar gradually; stir in vanilla; beat until light and fluffy. Stir in pecans. Yield: 3 1/2 cups.

Toasting pecans enhances their flavor.

Coconut Cake Supreme

Cake

1	BOX YELLOW CAKE MIX (NOT PUDDING CAKE)
1	TEASPOON LEMON EXTRACT

Assemble all ingredients and utensils. Mix cake according to directions on box, with exception of lemon extract. After layers have cooled, split them in half, making 4 layers.

Filling

1	12-OUNCE PACKAGE FROZEN COCONUT
1	CUP SOUR CREAM
1/2	CUP CRUSHED PINEAPPLE, DRAINED
1	TEASPOON VANILLA EXTRACT

Mix together in a large bowl. Set aside one-half cup of filling to use in frosting. Spread remaining filling between layers. Do not put filling on top layer.

Frosting

1	9-OUNCE CONTAINER WHIPPED TOPPING
1/2	CUP RESERVED FILLING
1	6-OUNCE PACKAGE FROZEN COCONUT, THAWED

Stir filling into whipped topping. Spread over entire cake. Sprinkle on top and sides of cake thawed frozen coconut. Refrigerate. Yield: 15-18 servings.

Cake will last for two weeks in the refrigerator. The flavor is enhanced the longer it sits.

Per serving: 325 calories; 17.4 g fat; 6 mg cholesterol; 260 mg sodium.

NANCY WARD, THE BELOVED WOMAN

In the annals of American history, many Indians appear who came to the rescue of the white settlers in time of strife or need. In Virginia, Pocahontas is remembered for the entreaties she made to her father in order to save John Smith's life. In Massachusetts, a man named Squanto came to the aid of the Pilgrims and assisted them with planting their crops. Lewis and Clark were befriended and partially guided on their twenty-eight month journey to the Pacific Ocean and back by a Shoshoni woman named Sacagawea. And, finally, in Tennessee, there was

Nancy Ward of the Cherokees, whose compassion for the white settlers saved the East Tennessee settlements from annihilation by renegade elements of her own people led by Dragging Canoe. Nancy Ward was born in 1738, the daugher of a British army officer and a Cherokee woman. In adulthood, she reached the highest rank attainable by a female in her mother's tribe. Called "Agi-ga-u-e," or "Beloved Woman," Nancy's powers included a seat in the Council of Chiefs and the final determination in the disposition of prisoners of war. She was a niece of Atta-kullakulla, the civil chief of the Cherokees. Her husband was King-fisher, whose rising popularity was cut short by his premature death. In domestic affairs, Nancy Ward was responsible for the introduction of cattle raising and butter making among the Cherokee women. When she died around 1824, Ward was buried overlooking the Ocoee River, near the town of Benton in Polk County.

Grandmother's Coconut Cake

1/2	CUP VEGETABLE SHORTENING, SOFTENED
1/4	CUP UNSALTED BUTTER, SOFTENED
2	CUPS SUGAR
1 1/2	TEASPOONS VANILLA EXTRACT
1/2	TEASPOON COCONUT EXTRACT
1/2	TEASPOON ALMOND EXTRACT
3	CUPS SIFTED CAKE FLOUR
1	TABLESPOON BAKING POWDER
1/4	TEASPOON SALT
1	CUP WHOLE MILK
6	EGG WHITES
	COCONUT ICING
2	CUPS FLAKED COCONUT, PREFERABLY FRESH

Nowhere else in the world is there a treat as delicious as southern homemade coconut cake. Fortunately my grandmother made sure I learned her best baking secrets.

Miss Daisy

Assemble all ingredients and utensils. In a large bowl, cream shortening and butter, gradually add sugar. Add flavorings. Sift flour, baking powder and salt and add alternately to sugar mixture with the milk, ending with the flour. In small mixing bowl, beat egg whites until stiff peaks form, and fold into batter.

Pour batter into three greased and floured 9-inch cake pans; bake in a 350-degree oven for 20-25 minutes or until a wooden pick inserted in center comes out clean. Cool in pans 10 minutes. Spread plenty of Coconut Icing between layers, then ice entire cake. Sprinkle with remaining coconut pressing into icing. Yield: one 3-layer cake.

Rogersville Milling Company

The Rogersville Milling Company is one of the oldest family operated manufacturing companies in Hawkins County. The Livesay family has been in the milling business since the early 1900s manufacturing flour, corn meal, and animal feeds. The family had operated three water-wheel mills and a diesel engine operated plant before opening an electric plant on the present site in 1939.

At the turn of the century there were as many as 10,000 mills around the country. By 1950, those had dwindled down to about 500, and today less than 50 are still family owned and operated. At the Rogersville factory each product continues to be individually filled, weighed, and hand tied with a string the old fashioned way.

Rogersville Milling Company still grades flour. That means different sizes of silks are used to screen or sift the flour into three different degrees of fineness. Those brand names are Sifted Snow, O-K, and Sweetheart. The brand name of corn meal is E-Z Mix.

(Continued next page)

Coconut Icing

1 1/2	CUPS SUGAR
1/2	TEASPOON CREAM OF TARTAR
1/4	TEASPOON SALT
1/2	CUP HOT WATER
5	EGG WHITES
3/4	TEASPOON COCONUT EXTRACT
1/2	TEASPOON VANILLA EXTRACT

Assemble all ingredients and utensils. In a heavy saucepan, combine sugar, cream of tartar, salt and hot water. Cook over medium heat, stirring constantly, until sugar is dissolved and mixture becomes clear. Cook without stirring, until syrup mixture reaches the soft-ball stage (238-240 degrees) on a candy thermometer.

In a large bowl, beat egg whites until soft peaks form; continue to beat, slowly adding syrup mixture. Add coconut and vanilla extracts. Continue beating until stiff peaks form and frosting is thick enough to spread. Yield: Icing for three, 9-inch layers (about 3 cups).

Per serving: 380 calories; 12.8 g fat; 10 mg cholesterol; 220 mg sodium.

THE FOLLOWING TECHNIQUES WILL ALLOW YOU TO TEST YOUR CAKE TO SEE IF IT IS DONE: LAYER CAKES AND CUPCAKES, TOUCH THE CAKE LIGHTLY IN THE CENTER WITH YOUR FINGERTIPS. IT SHOULD SPRING BACK. THE SIDES ALSO WILL BEGIN TO PULL AWAY FROM PAN. FOR POUND CAKES, INSERT A SKEWER IN THE CENTER OF CAKE. IT WILL COME OUT CLEAN WHEN THE CAKE IS DONE.

Miss Daisy

(Continued from p. 174)
During the 1980s, a professional baker from Maryland used the Sifted Snow flour to win International Bakeoffs three different times. The same baker used the flour in baking President Reagan's Inaugural Cake.

One only has to enter the mill to step back into a nearly forgotten era of our history. Farmers raised wheat and corn which they brought to area mills. When these products

were milled, the farmer took part of the flour or corn meal to meet the needs of his family and sold the rest. That was when flour and meal were real staples at home and many people would stack 25-pound bags to the ceiling. The leftover part of wheat, not used in flour, is reground, and is used to make animal feeds. Farmers were used to "coming to the mill" to buy both flour and feed. Many old mills gave up flour production years ago, but have turned old mills into feed and seed stores. The Rogersville Milling Company is one of the few that still manufactures flour, meal, and feeds and sells lines of commercial feeds ranging from cat to cow feed, pig to parrot feeds. Visitors and tourists can still visit the mill, watch flour being made, and make purchases to take home. Rogersville Milling Company is truly a Tennessee treasure.

Turner Dairies

Tennessee is blessed with several dedicated families committed to excellence in dairy products. One such West Tennessee family is the Turners.

Turner Dairies started in Covington, Tennessee, around 1920 as a small dairy farm. The four Turner sons helped to milk the cows each morning and evening, and then delivered the milk from door to door in the small town of Covington.

P. A. Turner, the youngest brother, graduated from the University of Tennessee in 1939 with a degree in dairying and a dream of starting a full scale milk plant in Covington. On his birthday, January 22, 1946, the first bottle of pasteurized milk was processed at the new dairy plant in Covington.

Turner Milk Products were distributed from U. S. Army surplus ambulances until enough money was saved to buy refrigerated trucks. The business grew to use many of those trucks and now sends them to parts of six states with "Turner Quality" dairy products. Customers are served from one of three plants or twelve distribution locations.

Today, Turner Dairies employs about six hundred people on a full-time basis and has sales of about $100 million. P. A. Turner's dream certainly came true.

Simply Chocolate Cake

1	4-OUNCE PACKAGE PLUS 2 SQUARES GERMAN'S SWEET CHOCOLATE
1 1/2	1-OUNCE SQUARES UNSWEETENED CHOCOLATE
1/2	CUP BOILING WATER
1	CUP BUTTER, SOFTENED
2	CUPS SUGAR
4	EGGS, SEPARATED AND BEATEN
2 1/2	CUPS ALL-PURPOSE FLOUR
1/2	TEASPOON SALT
1	TEASPOON BAKING SODA
3/4	CUP BUTTERMILK
2	TEASPOONS VANILLA
	ICING
	GLAZE OR FROSTING

Assemble all ingredients and utensils. In a double boiler, melt chocolate over hot water. Add boiling water and blend well. Cream butter and sugar in large mixing bowl. Add melted chocolate and beaten egg yolks. Blend. Sift together flour, salt and soda. Add to chocolate mixture alternately with buttermilk and vanilla. Fold in stiffly beaten egg whites. distribute batter evenly into three, 9-inch cake pans which have been greased, floured and lined with foil or wax paper. Bake in a 350-degree oven for 25 minutes. Cool. Remove layers from pans. Ice between layers with Divinity Icing then pour Chocolate Glaze over top of cake. Yield: 8 to 10 servings.

Per serving: 737 calories; 31 g fat; 161 mg cholesterol; 462 mg sodium.

Divinity Icing

3   EGG WHITES
3/4   CUP SUGAR
1/3   CUP LIGHT KARO SYRUP
1/4   TEASPOON CREAM OF TARTAR

Place ingredients into top of a double boiler. Cook, beating constantly for 8-10 minutes or until mixture is of spreading consistency. Ice between the cake layers.

Chocolate Glaze

1   1-OUNCE SQUARE UNSWEETENED CHOCOLATE
1   TEASPOON BUTTER
2   TABLESPOONS BOILING WATER
3/4 TO 1   CUP CONFECTIONERS SUGAR

Melt chocolate and butter in top of a double boiler. Add the boiling water and sugar and beat until smooth to make a thin glaze. Pour over top of cake.

The delicious taste is worth all the effort in preparation.

Fruit Cake

Twelve eggs beaten separately, one pound sugar, one pound flour, one pound butter, two pounds raisins, one pound currants, one-half pound cherries, one-half pound pineapple, one pound English walnuts shelled, one-half pound figs, one-half glass jelly, one pound citron, one-half pound shelled almonds, one-half pound pecans, one teacup buttermilk, with one teaspoon soda dissolved in it, one teacup jam, one teacup sherry wine, one tablespoon cloves, two tablespoons cinnamon, two nutmegs grated. Soak raisins over night in brandy, flour fruit with extra flour, two squares of bitter chocolate and one cup sugar melted in saucepan. After baking and while hot pour whiskey over the cake.

From the recipe files of Mrs. J. B. Murfree, Jr., wife of the gentleman for whom the Col. Hardy Murfree Chapter of the D.A.R. of Murfreesboro, Tennessee, was named.

NOW YOU SEE IT, NOW YOU DON'T

Most folks who resided in the region where Overton, Jackson, and White Counties met were happy in 1842 when they heard that the state legislature had passed an act establishing a new county that encompassed the area in which they lived. A new county was a definite advantage to the farmers and other settlers since, among other things, it meant that a county seat would be selected for the new entity which would be more centrally located than any of the towns they traded with now. However, two men—Patrick Pool, the chairman of the

PUTNAM COUNTY

Overton County Court, and William Goodbar, his Jackson County counterpart—objected to a new county being created out of lands previously part of their counties and took the new legislation to task by suing the State to rescind its action. In March, 1845, the case was tried in chancery court in Livingston, and since no response had been issued by the new Putnam County officials, it was ruled that Putnam County be officially abolished and the records sent to Gainesboro. The ruling was appealed by residents of the new county, and it eventually ended up being reviewed by the Tennessee Supreme Court. In its 1848 session, the high court ruled that, since chancery courts had no authority or jurisdiction over what the Tennessee legislature passed, the establishment of Putnam County was legal after all. Accordingly, on February 11, 1854, Putnam County was re-established with much the same boundaries as the original one.

Tennessee Fruit Cake

Miss Roberta, who died in July 1995, sent the letter below with her recipe. She was the last surviving member of the Robert R. Church Family of Memphis, Tennessee. Mr. Robert R. Church, Sr., founded the Solvent Savings Bank and established Church's Auditorium and Church Park on Beale Street in Memphis. Thanks to Kate Gooch and Perre Magness of Memphis who have been so helpful in acquiring recipes for the Bicentennial Collection.

Miss Daisy

Roberta Church
99 N. Main Street, No. 10001 Tower Apts.
Memphis, Tennessee 38103

Here is the recipe I promised
Years ago fruit cake was considered a popular and delicious delicacy and was not ridiculed as it sometimes is today.
As a child I recall ladies visiting each others homes making "pop" calls during the holidays. Each lady had her own special fruit cake recipe which was served to the visitors along with a glass of mild wine and other kinds of cakes. Unfortunately, delightful customs such as this have disappeared. In my opinion, my aunt's recipe has a delicious blend of flavors and I remember when she sliced the cake it would not crumble and the various fruit and nuts looked pretty in the slice.
All good wishes,
Sincerely,

Roberta Church

1	CUP BUTTER
1	CUP SUGAR
1 1/2	CUPS FLOUR
6	EGGS
1/2	CUP MOLASSES
1/4	CUP BRANDY
1/2	CUP WINE
	FRESH NUTMEG GRATED
1 1/2	TEASPOON CINNAMON
1 1/2	TEASPOON ALLSPICE
1	TEASPOON BAKING POWDER
1	TEASPOON VANILLA EXTRACT
1/2	TEASPOON LEMON EXTRACT
1/4	TEASPOON MACE
1/4	CUP ORANGE MARMALADE
1 1/4	CUPS SEEDED RAISINS
1 1/2	CUPS SEEDLESS RAISINS
1	CUP CURRANTS
1	CUP DATES, CHOPPED
1	CUP FIGS, CHOPPED
3/4	CUP CANDIED PINEAPPLE, CHOPPED
3/4	CUP CANDIED CHERRIES, CHOPPED-SAVE SOME FOR DECORATION ON TOP
1/2	CUP ENGLISH WALNUTS, CHOPPED
1	CUP ALMONDS, CHOPPED
1	CUP BLACK WALNUTS, CHOPPED
1	CUP PECANS, CHOPPED-SAVE SOME WHOLE HALVES FOR DECORATION
	CANDIED PEEL OF ONE ORANGE CHOPPED
	CANDIED PEEL OF ONE LEMON CHOPPED

Cream butter, add sugar, molasses, egg yolks, beaten until light, fruit, flour sifted with spices and baking powder, nuts. Add brandy, wine and egg whites beaten until stiff. If batter is too stiff to stir with spoon wash hands and complete mixing by hand. Cut a circle or square according to shape of pan from a brown paper bag and place in bottom of pan. Line pans with greased wax paper. Place batter in pan and decorate top with pecan halves and candied cherries. Preheat oven to 250 degrees and bake 3-4 hours. Makes 2-3 cakes according to size of pan. Enjoy!

Bulla's Fudge Cake

- 2 CUPS SUGAR
- 2 STICKS BUTTER
- 4 SQUARES UNSWEETENED BAKING CHOCOLATE
- 4 EGGS
- 2 CUPS, LESS 2 TABLESPOONS FLOUR
- 1 CUP CHOPPED PECANS
- 2 TEASPOONS VANILLA

Cream together sugar and butter, pour melted chocolate over this and mix well. Add eggs one at a time. Slowly add the flour. Then add the pecans and vanilla. Pour into two 8-inch square, ungreased pans and bake in a 325-degree oven for about 25 minutes. Do not over cook. Frost with Minute Fudge Frosting while cake is still warm.

Bulla's Minute Fudge Frosting

- 2 CUPS SUGAR
- 2/3 CUP MILK
- 1/4 TEASPOON SALT
- 2 SQUARES UNSWEETENED BAKING CHOCOLATE
- 1/2 CUP SHORTENING, OR BUTTER
- 2 TEASPOONS VANILLA

Combine the above ingredients, except vanilla, in a medium-size saucepan and bring slowly to a boil over low heat, stirring constantly until the sugar is dissolved and the chocolate is melted. Boil hard for 3 minutes, with no stirring. Remove from heat and cool until bubbling stops. Then add the vanilla and beat until frosting is thick enough to spread. If it gets too hard, add a little cream, a few drops at a time, until it is a desirable consistency to spread.

Spread on Fudge Cake while it is still warm from the oven.

ADDIE KIRKLAND HAMRIC, KNOWN LOVINGLY AS "BULLA" BY HER GRANDCHILDREN AND GENERATIONS OF BABIES SHE TENDED IN HER CHURCH'S NURSERY, WAS BORN APRIL 23, 1898. SHE LOVED TAKING CARE OF BABIES AND SHE LOVED BAKING HER FUDGE CAKE TO SHARE WITH LOVED ONES. THE RECIPE, HAVING BEEN PASSED DOWN THROUGH SEVERAL GENERATIONS, IS TREASURED BY ALL HER FAMILY. HER DAUGHTER, MARY JEAN (MRS. BILL) CROOK, AND HER GRANDSON, STEVEN E. CROOK, PROUDLY SHARE THIS RECIPE WITH US.

Miss Daisy

*J*EAN FAIRCLOTH
MCARTHUR (MRS. DOUGLAS
MCARTHUR, JR.) IS A MEMBER OF
THE HARDY MURFREE CHAPTER
D.A.R. OF MURFREESBORO,
TENNESSEE. SHE PRESENTLY LIVES
IN NEW YORK CITY AT THE
WALDORF ASTORIA HOTEL. SHE
HAS SHARED THIS RECIPE WITH THE
HOTEL DINING ROOM.

Miss Daisy

Jean Faircloth McArthur's Waldorf Astoria Fudge Cake

Melt 2 squares of baking chocolate in top of double boiler with 1/4 cup of butter. When melted remove and add 1 cup of granulated sugar. Mix well and then add 2 unbeaten eggs. After all this is well mixed add 1/2 cup flour (unsifted) with a good pinch of salt. Blend and then add 1/2 cup of chopped nuts, either broken pecans or walnuts. Add 2 teaspoons of vanilla. Mix well and pour into a wax-paper lined pan (an ice cube tray is best for thick pieces). Spread evenly and bake at 300 degrees for about 35 minutes. Turn out on sugared board, remove wax paper, cool and then cut in squares and dust with powdered sugar.

The Best Fudge Cake

1	CUP BUTTER
4	1-OUNCE SQUARES UNSWEETENED CHOCOLATE
4	EGGS, BEATEN
2	CUPS SUGAR
2	TABLESPOONS WHOLE MILK
1/4	TEASPOON SALT
1	CUP SIFTED ALL-PURPOSE FLOUR
1	CUP CHOPPED PECANS OR WALNUTS
	ICING

Assemble all ingredients and utensils. In a saucepan, melt butter and chocolate together. Cool. In a large mixing bowl, combine eggs, sugar, milk and salt; add flour and nuts. Mix well. Add chocolate and butter mixture. Pour batter into a well greased and floured 10x15-inch pan. Bake in a 350-degree oven for 25 to 30 minutes. Do not overbake! Cake should be moist.

Icing

1	TABLESPOON BUTTER, MELTED
2	TABLESPOONS COCOA
1	CUP CONFECTIONERS SUGAR
1	EGG WHITE

In a mixing bowl, beat together all ingredients. Ice cake immediately while hot. Yield: 16 to 20 servings.

Per serving: 291 calories; 17.7 g fat; 81 mg cholesterol; 144 mg sodium.

Italian Cream Cake

1/2   CUP BUTTER, SOFTENED
1/2   CUP VEGETABLE SHORTENING
2   CUPS SUGAR
5   EGGS, SEPARATED
2   CUPS SIFTED ALL-PURPOSE FLOUR
1   TEASPOON SODA
1   CUP BUTTERMILK
1   TEASPOON VANILLA
1   3 1/2-OUNCE CAN COCONUT
1   CUP CHOPPED PECANS
    CREAM CHEESE FROSTING, *SEE* P. 172

Assemble all ingredients and utensils. In large bowl of mixer, cream butter and shortening; gradually add sugar, beating until light and fluffy. Add egg yolks, one at a time, beating well after each addition. Combine flour and soda, add to creamed mixture alternately with buttermilk. Stir in vanilla, coconut and pecans. Beat egg whites until they form peaks. Fold into batter. Pour batter into three, 9-inch greased and floured cake pans. Bake in a 350 degree oven for 30-35 minutes or until layers test done. Cool. Frost with Cream Cheese Frosting (*see* p. 172). Yield: 15-18 servings.

Per serving: 509 calories; 31.2 g fat; 118 mg cholesterol; 224 mg sodium.

*A*N OLD FAMILY RECIPE FOUND IN MANY TENNESSEANS' HOMES. BLUE RIBBON WINNER IN A STATE FAIR MANY YEARS AGO, RECIPES SUCH AS THIS ONE HAVE BEEN SERVED TO PRESIDENTS, GUESTS AT DINNER PARTIES, AND AS A FAVORITE LATE-NIGHT SNACK WITH A GLASS OF MILK.

Miss Daisy

"MONKEY SEE, MONKEY DO"

During mid-July 1925, scores of radio and newspaper correspondents from all over the United States and Europe descended upon the Rhea County Courthouse in tiny Dayton, Tennessee. They were there to witness what became one of the most dramatic—and at times, comical—court battles in the history of American jurisprudence. Before the twelve-day-long trial was over, Dayton had assumed a carnival atmosphere as reporters and commentators clamored to be the one to scoop the latest-breaking developments. The affair at Dayton had begun months earlier, when the Tennessee legislature passed a law forbidding the teaching of evolution in the state's public schools. John

RHEA COUNTY

Scopes, a local high school teacher, decided to test the law and openly discussed the theory of evolution before his students. Scopes was arrested and quickly indicted by the Rhea County Grand Jury. The Scopes trial provided the perfect opportunity for leading advocates of the conservative and liberal movements in the United States to debate. William Jennings Bryan, a three-time, unsuccessful presidential candidate and former secretary of state in President Woodrow Wilson's cabinet, was summoned to help the prosecution. The equally famous criminal lawyer, Clarence Darrow, was rounded up by the defense. For days, in no-holds-barred action, Bryan and Darrow went at each other tooth and nail. The trial ended with Scopes being fined $100, a conviction later overturned. Bryan died a week later, some say of a broken heart.

For the first forty-seven years of statehood—before Nashville was named the State's permanent capital in 1843—many towns and villages scattered all over much of the State were considered candidates for the post. Among them were McMinnville, Carthage, Clarksville, Lebanon, Sparta, Woodbury, Shelbyville, Chattanooga, Jackson, Smithville, Paris, Savannah, Manchester, and Charlotte, among others. Only four towns actually served as capital: Knoxville, Kingston, Murfreesboro, and Nashville. Of these, circumstances surrounding the naming of Kingston

ROANE COUNTY

were the most bizarre. Knoxville was the capital from 1796 until 1802, when the site was to be reconsidered. That year came and passed, with no effort made to move the location of state government from Knoxville. Three years later, a treaty was negotiated between the U. S. government and the Cherokee Indians for the cession of certain lands in East Tennessee, a portion of which was to be used for "public purposes and not for individual advantages." As history soon proved, the purported use of the land for "public purposes" was simply a ruse to flim-flam the Cherokees into relinquishing some very valuable land. Out of a feeling of obligation to the terms of the treaty, the Legislature did meet for one day at Kingston, a village located in the newly acquired territory. The session, held on September 21, 1807, was completed in less than two hours, when legislators packed up and returned to Knoxville where they met for the next five years!

Blackberry Jam Cake

1	CUP BUTTER, SOFTENED
2	CUPS SUGAR
6	EGGS
1	CUP BUTTERMILK
1	TEASPOON BAKING SODA
3	CUPS SIFTED ALL-PURPOSE FLOUR
1	TABLESPOON GROUND CINNAMON
1	TABLESPOON GROUND ALLSPICE
1	TABLESPOON GROUND CLOVES
2	CUPS SEEDLESS BLACKBERRY JAM

Assemble all ingredients and utensils. In a large bowl cream butter and sugar. Beat in eggs, one at a time; then add buttermilk in which soda has been dissolved. Stir in dry ingredients and mix in jam. Grease and flour three, 9-inch cake pans. Distribute batter evenly in the pans. Bake in a 325-degree oven for 25-30 minutes or until cake tests done. Cool and remove from pans. Frost each layer and entire cake generously with Confectioners' Sugar Icing. Yield: 16-20 servings.

Cake is equally delicious with Easy Caramel Icing (*see* facing page). This cake freezes well.

Per serving: 340 calories; 11 g fat; 107 mg cholesterol; 174 mg sodium.

Confectioners' Sugar Icing

3/4	CUP BUTTER, SOFTENED
6	CUPS CONFECTIONERS SUGAR
3	EGG YOLKS
1 1/2	TEASPOONS VANILLA
6	TABLESPOONS HEAVY CREAM

Assemble all ingredients and utensils. In a medium mixing bowl, cream together butter and sugar. Beat in egg yolks, then vanilla and cream until icing is smooth. Yield: Icing for three, 9-inch layer cake, about 3 1/2 cups.

Per serving: 225 calories; 9 g fat; 66 mg cholesterol; 74 mg sodium.

Strawberry Jam Cake

2	CUPS FLOUR
1	CUP LIGHT BROWN SUGAR
1	TEASPOON CINNAMON
1/2	TEASPOON CLOVES
1/4	TEASPOON SALT
1	CUP BUTTER, SOFTENED
3	EGGS, BEATEN
1	TEASPOON SODA
1/2	CUP BUTTERMILK
1 1/2	CUPS STRAWBERRY JAM
1/2	CUP CHOPPED PECANS

Assemble ingredients and utensils. Sift dry ingredients in a large bowl. Gradually cream in butter and add eggs. Mix well. Dissolve soda in buttermilk and mix into creamed mixture. Continue beating for 3 minutes. Add jam and pecans, mix well. Grease and flour a 9x13-inch pan. Pour batter into pan and bake in a 350-degree oven for 55-60 minutes. Cool. Ice with Easy Caramel Icing. Yield: 24 servings.

An easy cake to take to your favorite luncheon.

Easy Caramel Icing

1/2	CUP BUTTER
1/4	CUP MILK
1	CUP LIGHT BROWN SUGAR
2	CUPS SIFTED CONFECTIONERS SUGAR

Assemble ingredients and utensils. In a large saucepan, melt butter and brown, but do not burn. Bring to a full boil for 2 minutes stirring constantly. Add milk, bring to a full boil again. Cool just to lukewarm, and then add sugar, mix well, and pour over cool cake. Yield: about 2 cups.

Per serving: 320 calories; 14 g fat; 66 mg cholesterol; 197 mg sodium.

TENNESSEE'S TOBACCO WARS

During the early part of the twentieth century, Robertson County farmers, as well as those from neighboring counties, found themselves in a dilemma. The price of tobacco, the staple crop of this part of Middle Tennessee, had dropped dramatically, and at one time brought as little as two or three cents per pound. An acre would yield between one thousand and twelve hundred pounds of tobacco, meaning that the farmer realized on the average only about twenty-eight dollars per acre. But, the cost to the farmer of maintain-

ROBERTSON COUNTY

ing the same acre was forty-two dollars. Obviously, something had to be done about the situation. In 1904, local Tennessee, Virginia, and Kentucky farmers organized the Planter's Protective Association, an outfit designed to bring the power of numbers to the negotiating table between farmers and the tobacco buyers. One of the large buyers, the American Tobacco Company, tried to destroy the influence of the Planter's Protective Association by paying non-member farmers in the region, collectively called the "Hill Billies," higher prices for their tobacco. Affairs reached serious proportions in 1906 when several Association members who called themselves the "Possum Hunters" took the law into their own hands and began burning warehouses and tobacco barns in the region. In 1907, while possum hunters were torching the barns of L. W. Lawrence and G. W. Fletcher, one of the raiders was killed, and the violence ceased soon afterwards.

David Crockett

David Crockett (1786–1836) was a true native Volunteer. He was born near the present-day town of Rogersville, Tennessee. Crockett's early education was limited and he joined the army at a young age, fighting with Andrew Jackson's command against the Creek Indians in Alabama. He eventually had a falling out with Jackson and opposed his fellow Tennessean's iron-like grip which "Old Hickory" held over the country. Crockett later moved about Tennessee and lived at one time or another in Jefferson, Lincoln, Franklin, Lawrence, Carroll, and Gibson Counties.

Crockett served in the U. S. House of Representatives for several terms, but when he was defeated in the 1834 elections, he moved on to Texas where he lost his life in defense of the Alamo. A "no-nonsense" politician, Crockett lived by his own words, "Be always sure you're right—then go ahead."

David Crockett was one of the few persons in history who truly became a legend in his own lifetime.

Crockett Tavern Museum's Alamo Lemon Jelly Cake

3	CUPS SIFTED ALL-PURPOSE FLOUR
3	TEASPOONS BAKING POWDER
1/4	TEASPOON SALT
3/4	CUP BUTTER OR SHORTENING
2	CUPS SUGAR
6	EGGS
1/2	TEASPOON LEMON EXTRACT
1 1/2	CUPS MILK

Grease and flour three 8-inch cake pans.

Sift flour, baking powder and salt together several times. Work fat in a mixing bowl until soft, then add the sugar gradually and continue working the mixture until it feels smooth and creamy. Separate egg yolks from whites, beating the yolks one at a time into the creamed mixture. Beat hard after each addition. Stir lemon extract into the milk and mix the liquid alternately with dry ingredients into the creamed sugar mixture. Beat egg whites until they hold a point and mix gently or fold into the batter until all patches of egg white are blended in.

Pour into cake pans and bake 35 minutes or until cakes pull away from the sides of the pans. Remove from pans, and when layers are cool spread a thin coating of lemon filling between layers and over the top.

Filling

2	EGGS
1	CUP SUGAR
1	TABLESPOON BUTTER
	GRATED RIND OF 1 LEMON
	JUICE OF 2 LEMONS (1/4 CUP)

Beat eggs slightly in a saucepan. Stir in sugar, butter, lemon rind and juice and cook over a low heat, stirring constantly until filling is thick enough to coat a spoon. Takes about 10 to 15 minutes. Cool.

Mississippi Mud Cake

1 1/2	CUPS ALL-PURPOSE FLOUR
1	CUP CHOPPED PECANS OR WALNUTS
1	3 1/2-OUNCE CAN COCONUT
1	CUP BUTTER OR MARGARINE, MELTED
2	CUPS SUGAR
4	EGGS
1/2	CUP COCOA
1/8	TEASPOON SALT
1	7-OUNCE JAR MARSHMALLOW CREME
	TOPPING

Assemble all ingredients and utensils. In a bowl, mix flour, nuts and coconut and set aside. Combine butter, sugar, eggs, cocoa and salt in large bowl of mixer; add flour mixture and mix well. Pour into greased and floured 13x9-inch pan and bake in a 350-degree oven for 30 to 35 minutes. Remove from oven and immediately spread with marshmallow creme and cool. Combine all topping ingredients. Spread over cooled cake. Yield: 12 to 15 servings.

Topping

1	BOX CONFECTIONERS SUGAR
1/3	CUP COCOA
1/4	TEASPOON VANILLA
1/2	CUP BUTTER, MELTED
1/3	CUP EVAPORATED MILK

Combine all topping ingredients in a large bowl. Spread over cooled cake.

This cake recipe has as many versions as there are states. Some recipes use marshmallows instead of creme. This recipe is very easy. Can be prepared in advance and refrigerated until ready to serve. Wonderful!

Per serving: 526 calories; 28.4 g fat; 124 mg cholesterol; 244 mg sodium.

"I HOPE YOU ENJOYED THE PLAY, MR. CRADDOCK"

For as long as she could remember, Mary Noilles Murfree had wanted to write about the sturdy, rural people of Tennessee, like those who lived in the Cumberland Mountains whom she visited every summer from her home in Murfreesboro. Educated at the Nashville Female Academy, young Mary prepared herself carefully for a writing career, but she forgot one very important element: this was the 1880s, and she was a woman wanting to pursue what was primarily a male-dominated career in America. Well,

RUTHERFORD COUNTY

Mary decided to change all that. She solved the problem with a simple solution. She submitted her stories to the big eastern publishing houses using the pseudonym of a man, Charles Egbert Craddock. Publishers were delighted to have discovered this wonderful new talent, and one by one, her books were published for a national audience, who believed that Charles Craddock was, indeed, a man. Mary even fooled her own publishers, and she often received correspondence from them addressed to "Mr. M. N. Murfree." Once, on a trip to Boston to visit with her chief editor, Thomas Bailey Aldrich, she revealed her true identity to him, and the delighted Aldrich joined in the fun. At a play, Aldrich soon boasted to the famed actor, Edwin Booth, that his best-selling writer was present for the performance. "There's no man in your box," exclaimed Booth. The wily Aldrich replied, "Oh, Craddock is the fellow with the red flower in her hat!"

THE INDEPENDENT STATE OF SCOTT

Folks in predominantly pro-Union Scott County were not very happy when Tennessee voters in a statewide referendum held on June 8, 1861, decided by a margin of two to one to secede from the United States. But, after Governor Isham Harris had successfully urged the state legislature to endorse the secession move the previous April, that's exactly what happened, much to the chagrin of many small East Tennessee farm owners, most of whom did not own slaves. Scott Countians were particularly dismayed since its population was practically 100 percent pro-Union.

SCOTT COUNTY

Later figures showed that out of 560 men of fighting age who lived in the county, 541 served in the Union army and only the remaining nineteen fought for the Confederacy. In order to combat this travesty of justice shared by most Scott Countians, the county court met in special session soon after the statewide referendum and unanimously passed a resolution calling for the secession of Scott County from Tennessee! The proper documents declaring the "Independent State of Scott" were prepared and sent by messenger to the Secretary of State in Nashville, who refused them and instead, called out troops to march on Huntsville. Later, during World War I, county court members of Scott County independently declared war on the German nation, and so far, has never made peace. Not until the 1980s did Scott County apply to become part of Tennessee again, at which time tongue-in-cheek legislators all voted for readmission.

Chocolate Pound Cake

1	CUP BUTTER, SOFTENED
1/2	CUP SHORTENING
3	CUPS SUGAR
5	EGGS, BEATEN
3	CUPS CAKE FLOUR
1/2	TEASPOON BAKING POWDER
1/2	TEASPOON SALT
5	TABLESPOONS COCOA
1	CUP WHOLE MILK
1	TABLESPOON VANILLA

Assemble all ingredients and utensils. In large bowl of mixer cream butter, shortening and sugar until fluffy. Add eggs. Mix well. Sift dry ingredients. Add to butter mixture, alternately with milk and vanilla. Grease and flour a 10 inch tube pan or Bundt cake pan; pour in batter. Bake in a 300-degree oven for 1 1/2 to 2 hours. Cool before removing from pan. Yield: 12-15 servings.

Cake freezes well.

Per serving: 449 calories; 22 g fat; 127 mg cholesterol; 240 mg sodium.

Cream Cheese Pound Cake

3	CUPS SUGAR
1 1/2	CUPS BUTTER, SOFTENED
1	8-OUNCE PACKAGE CREAM CHEESE, SOFTENED
6	EGGS
3	CUPS CAKE FLOUR
1	TEASPOON VANILLA EXTRACT
1	TEASPOON BUTTER FLAVORED EXTRACT

Assemble all ingredients and utensils. In large bowl of mixer cream sugar, butter and cream cheese until fluffy. Add eggs, one at a time, beating well after each addition. Stir in flavorings. Add flour, one cup at a time and beat well. Pour batter into a greased and floured 10-inch tube pan or bundt cake pan. Place in cold oven. Turn oven to 275 degrees and bake for 1 3/4 to 2 hours or until cake tests done. Yield: 12-15 servings.

Excellent served with raspberry purée or your favorite fudge sauce.

Per serving: 486 calories; 26 g fat; 176 mg cholesterol; 260 mg sodium.

Armour's Hotel
Molasses Cake With Sauce

1/4	POUND BUTTER
1/2	CUP SUGAR
1	CUP MOLASSES
1	TEASPOON CINNAMON
1	TEASPOON GINGER
1	TEASPOON CLOVES
2	TEASPOONS SODA
2 1/2	CUPS FLOUR
2	EGGS, BEATEN

Cream butter and sugar together, add molasses and spices. Dissolve soda in one cup boiling water, stir into creamed mixture. Fold in flour and add eggs. Bake 30 minutes in two round cake pans at 350 degrees.

Sauce

1/2	CUP BUTTER
1	CUP SUGAR
1/2	CUP PET MILK
1/4	TEASPOON EACH: CINNAMON, GINGER, AND CLOVES

Mix butter, sugar, milk and boil slowly for 10 minutes. Stir often. Stir in spices. Pour over cake hot and serve.

Armour's Red Boiling Springs Hotel

The Red Boiling Springs, popular in an era before modern medicine, attracted thousands of people each summer to take the "waters," bowl, swim, participate in the fox hound races, or simply to meet new friends. The "waters" were used to perform miracles for maladies such as iron-poor blood, kidney diseases, and acid indigestion. At its peak, the resort grew from rustic cabins in the 1800s to eight hotels and more than a dozen boarding houses.

Today, Red Boiling Springs has three remaining hotels including the Armour's Hotel which was the first brick hotel structure.

The healing waters continue to flow offering a variety of five kinds of mineral water due to the unique rock formation in this Highland Rim area. Wells are found throughout the town under gazebos for drinking the water and mineral baths are available at Armour's Hotel.

Wilma Rudolph's Sour Cream Pound Cake

No Tennessee Bicentennial Collection of recipes would be complete without something from Clarksville's Olympic Gold Medal winner Wilma Rudolph. Wilma's recipe, shared with us by her family, turns out best when mixed in the order listed.

Miss Daisy

2	STICKS OF BUTTER
3	CUPS OF SUGAR
1/4	TEASPOON OF BAKING SODA
1/2	PINT (8 OUNCES) OF SOUR CREAM
1	TABLESPOON OF LEMON EXTRACT
2	TABLESPOONS OF VANILLA
3	CUPS FLOUR
6	EGGS, WELL BEATEN

Bake 1 1/2 hours in a 350-degree oven.

Miss Daisy's Five Flavor Pound Cake With Glaze

My grandmother helped me prepare this cake when I was about eight-to-ten years of age. The original recipe was made only with vanilla extract and no glaze. My senior year of college in Recipe Development class I added the other flavors and the glaze. I served this cake opening day of Miss Daisy's Tea Room in Franklin, Tennessee, twenty years ago and the cake has been a treasured favorite.

Miss Daisy

1	CUP BUTTER, SOFTENED
1/2	CUP VEGETABLE SHORTENING
3	CUPS SUGAR
5	EGGS, WELL BEATEN
3	CUPS ALL-PURPOSE FLOUR
1/2	TEASPOON BAKING POWDER
1	CUP WHOLE MILK
1	TEASPOON EACH: COCONUT, BUTTER, LEMON, RUM AND VANILLA EXTRACTS

Assemble all ingredients and utensils. In large bowl, cream butter, shortening and sugar until light and fluffy. Add eggs. Combine flour and baking powder. Add to cream mixture alternately with milk. Stir in flavorings. Spoon batter into a greased 10-inch tube pan. Bake in a 325-degree oven for 1 1/2 hours or until cake tests done. Add glaze or cool in pan about 10 minutes before turning out.

Glaze

1	CUP SUGAR
1/2	CUP WATER
1	TEASPOON EACH: COCONUT, BUTTER, LEMON, RUM, AND VANILLA EXTRACTS

In a saucepan, combine all ingredients and gently bring to a boil. Pour over cake in pan. Let cake sit in pan until cool. Yield: 14 to 16 slices.

Per serving: 412 calories; 18 g fat; 106 mg cholesterol; 140 mg sodium.

Rutledge Family Lafayette Cake

Bake a plain poundcake, about an inch and a half thick; slice it across, so as to make three large, flat cakes; put in between layers of sweetmeat (mincemeat). It is better if the sweetmeat is strongly flavored.

The Rutledge family spoke only French on Fridays so the children were able to enjoy the gala conversation when General Lafayette visited Nashville.

Pineapple Upside Down Cake

1/2	CUP BUTTER, MELTED
1	CUP BROWN SUGAR
1	SMALL CAN SLICED PINEAPPLE, DRAINED, SAVE JUICE
10	MARASCHINO CHERRIES, STEMS REMOVED
3	EGGS, BEATEN
1	CUP SUGAR
1	CUP SIFTED ALL-PURPOSE FLOUR
1	TEASPOON BAKING POWDER
1/4	TEASPOON SALT
5	TABLESPOONS PINEAPPLE JUICE

Assemble ingredients and utensils. In a heavy iron (preferably) skillet blend melted butter and brown sugar. Arrange pineapple slices and cherries in skillet. In large bowl of mixer combine remaining ingredients and pour over pineapple mixture in skillet. Bake in a 350 degree oven for 35 to 40 minutes. Cool in skillet and turn upside down onto your favorite plate. Yield: 8 to 10 servings.

Recipe has been around for years. Quick dessert! Wonderful warm with whipped cream.

Per serving: 306 calories; 11 g fat; 107 mg cholesterol; 208 mg sodium.

Middleton/ Rutledge Family

Henry Rutledge was the official escort/interpreter for Lafayette's entourage during the French general's visit to Nashville in 1825. As a young man Rutledge had traveled to France with his uncle Charles Cotesworth Pinckney as part of the official staff.

Septima Sexta Middleton and Henry Middleton Rutledge (children of Arthur Middleton and Edward Rutledge, South Carolina signers of the U.S. Declaration of Independence) married in 1799.

Henry Rutledge traveled to Tennessee in 1807, where he surveyed and registered in his name over 73,000 acres of land and built a magnificent country home on the Elk River in Franklin County. In 1816 he brought his wife and five children, twenty wagons of belongings, and fifty slaves to Tennessee. By 1820 the family had built Rose Hill, a fine town house and twenty-acre estate in the much-desired area near the University of Nashville. Henry Rutledge became a member of the Davidson County bar and a well-respected citizen of his adopted state of Tennessee.

PIGS OR 'POSSUMS

Even today, folks in Sequatchie County still argue over the real meaning of the name of their county. Organized in December 1857, from three civil districts of Hamilton County that originally belonged to neighboring Bledsoe and Marion Counties, Sequatchie was named for the Sequatchie Valley, after a motion to call the new entity "Herndon" failed. Most people assumed that the Sequatchie Valley and its namesake river were named in honor of an early Cherokee chief named "Sequachee," but beyond that, no one really knew how the county got its

name. One theory held that "Sequachee" meant "hog trough," and was used in reference to the long, narrow shape of the valley through which the beautiful Sequatchie River runs. John Haywood, Tennessee's first historian, on the other hand maintained that one variation of the word, in the Cherokee language, meant "hog" and another variation referred to "opossum." John P. Brown, author of a definitive history of the Cherokees, maintained that the Cherokee spelling of the word, Sequatchie, was "sikna' utset' tsi," and translated to "opossum he grins." Finally, another historian of the Cherokees, James Mooney, suggested that the word comes from the name of a Cherokee town on the French Broad River. Today, many authorities—based on the assumption that the word was in use before De Soto introduced the first hogs to the region in the mid-1500s and therefore could not refer to hogs, which were unknown prior to then—agree with Brown.

Prune Cake With Buttermilk Topping

3	EGGS
1 1/2	CUPS SUGAR
1	CUP VEGETABLE OIL
1	TEASPOON SODA
2	CUPS ALL-PURPOSE FLOUR
1	TEASPOON NUTMEG
1	TEASPOON CINNAMON
1	TEASPOON ALLSPICE
1/2	TEASPOON SALT
1	CUP BUTTERMILK
1	CUP MASHED COOKED PRUNES
1	CUP PECANS, CHOPPED
1	TEASPOON VANILLA EXTRACT
	HOT TOPPING

Assemble all ingredients and utensils. In large bowl of mixer, beat eggs until light in color. Add sugar, beat well. Add oil. Sift together dry ingredients. Add alternately with buttermilk. Add prunes, nuts, and vanilla. Pour batter in a greased, floured 9-inch tube pan or bundt pan. Bake in a 375-degree oven for 60 minutes. Remove cake from pan while warm, punch holes in top of cake with toothpick. Pour hot topping over cake. Yield: 10 to 12 servings.

Topping

1	CUP SUGAR
1/2	CUP BUTTERMILK
1/2	TEASPOON SODA
1	TABLESPOON LIGHT CORN SYRUP
1/4	CUP BUTTER
2	TEASPOONS VANILLA

In a saucepan, combine ingredients and simmer for 30 minutes. Yield: about 1 1/2 cups.

Cake doesn't taste much like prunes. It is a very moist, dense cake with the flavor of spices and delightful aftertaste of chocolate. Serve cake with Old-Fashioned Boiled Custard (*see* p. 228).

Per serving: 607 calories; 36 g fat; 80 mg cholesterol; 283 mg sodium.

Civil War Raisin Cake

1	CUP BUTTER, SOFTENED
2	CUPS SUGAR
2	CUPS BUTTERMILK
2 2/3	CUP ALL-PURPOSE FLOUR OR
3	CUPS CAKE FLOUR
1	TEASPOON ALLSPICE
1	TEASPOON CINNAMON
1	TEASPOON BAKING SODA DISSOLVED IN 1 TABLESPOON WATER
1/2	POUND BOX RAISINS
	FROSTING

Assemble all ingredients and utensils. In large bowl, cream butter and sugar until smooth, add buttermilk and beat together. Sift flour and mix with spices. Add flour mix to the creamed butter, sugar and milk mixture, small amounts at a time, beating well. Add soda mixed with water and the raisins and beat well. Pour into three well greased and floured 8-inch cake pans. Bake in a 350 degree oven for about 20 minutes or until cake tests done. Cool in pans about 10 to 15 minutes. Remove. Spread frosting between layers and on top of cake.

Frosting

2	CUPS SUGAR
1	CUP WHOLE MILK
2	TABLESPOONS BUTTER
1	TEASPOON VANILLA

In a saucepan, cook sugar and milk together until mixture reaches the soft boil stage, add butter. Remove from heat, add vanilla and beat until thickens, spread on cake. Yield: 12-14 servings.

This cake is prepared without eggs. The recipe was given to me from a friend who's family used this cake recipe. Dates may also be substituted for the raisins.

Per serving: 511 calories; 16g fat; 43mg cholesterol; 260 mg sodium.

GONE TO TEXAS

Of the tens of thousands of Texans who visit Gatlinburg every year, it is doubtful that few ever notice the historical marker located on the Parkway that denotes the birthplace of John Henninger Reagan. Born in October 1818, near the center of the present-day town, Reagan was educated locally before moving to Texas when he was about twenty years old. Reagan, of necessity, became an Indian fighter and later followed a career of surveyor, studied and practiced the law, was elected judge in Henderson County, Texas, and finally was

SEVIER COUNTY

elected to the U. S. House of Representatives, where he was serving when the War Between the States broke out. Reagan was quickly elected to the Confederate Congress, and, in 1861, accepted the cabinet position of postmaster general of the Confederacy. He was a devoted friend of President Jefferson Davis, and when Davis was taken prisoner by Union authorities after the War, Reagan went to prison with him. When he was paroled, he went home to Texas to attempt to persuade his neighbors to acknowledge civil rights for black residents. His ideas were not well accepted. Later, after the pain of Reconstruction had subsided, Reagan was again elected to the U. S. Congress, serving from 1875 till 1887, when he became a U. S. senator. While in the senate, he masterminded the formation of the Interstate Commerce Commission, before taking control of the Texas Railroad Commission in 1891. He died in 1905.

Old Fashioned
Strawberry Shortcake

2	TABLESPOONS SALAD OIL
7	TABLESPOONS WHOLE MILK
3/4 TO 1	CUP SELF-RISING FLOUR
2-3	CUPS FRESH STRAWBERRIES
	SUGAR
1/2	CUP WATER
	WHIPPED CREAM

Assemble ingredients and utensils. In a large bowl combine oil and milk. Add enough flour for consistency of biscuit dough. Roll 1 tablespoon of dough paper thin. Repeat to make 7-8 crusts. Place crusts on biscuit or cookie sheet. Bake in a 450 degree oven until golden brown about 10 minutes. Clean and mash berries. Sweeten to taste; add water. When ready to serve, alternately stack crusts and berries. Top with whipped cream. Yield: 7-8 servings.

Fresh strawberries from Portland and Humboldt, Tennessee, make for some delicious shortcake.

Per serving: 204 calories; 10 g fat; 22 mg cholesterol; 167 mg sodium.

FATHER OF THE BLUES

If it had not been for W. C. Handy's tenacity as a boy, the world would never have known and appreciated his outstanding musical talent. According to Handy, one of his earliest childhood experiences with a musical instrument came when he had saved his money for month upon month and purchased his own guitar. Carefully carrying the instrument home and proudly displaying it to his parents, he was shocked that they wanted no part of it. Unfit to be in a Christian home, they told the young boy and forced him to exchange his prized guitar for a dictionary. Other children might have been dismayed at this rude awakening, but Handy took

SHELBY COUNTY

it in stride and pursued his musical career anyway, giving Tennessee and America one of their all-time great artists. W. C. Handy was born in Florence, Alabama in 1873, son of recently freed slaves. After traveling with a minstrel show, Handy settled in Memphis, where he and his band played ditties for political candidates. There, he wrote *Memphis Blues,* originally called *Mr. Crump,* after "Boss" Crump, a Memphis political magnate. In 1914, Handy wrote *St. Louis Blues,* destined to be one of the outstanding pieces of jazz in all history. *Beale Street Blues* came a little later, followed by *John Henry Blues.* Handy was also a writer. Before he died in 1958, he had penned an anthology of Negro authors and composers, as well as a collection of Negro spirituals. For his work in traditional black music, Handy is called the "father of the blues."

Red Velvet Cake

1/2	CUP BUTTER, SOFTENED
1/2	CUP SHORTENING
2	CUPS SUGAR
4	EGGS
2 1/2	CUPS ALL-PURPOSE FLOUR
1	TEASPOON SODA
1/2	TEASPOON SALT
4	TABLESPOONS COCOA
1	CUP BUTTERMILK
1	TEASPOON VANILLA
3	TABLESPOONS RED FOOD COLORING
	FROSTING FOR CAKE

Assemble all ingredients and utensils. In large bowl of mixer cream butter, shortening and sugar. Add eggs one at a time. Combine flour, soda, salt and cocoa, gradually add to butter mixture; alternating with buttermilk. Add vanilla and food coloring. Blend well. Distribute batter evenly among three 9-inch greased and floured cake pans. Bake in a 350-degree oven for 25 to 30 minutes. Cool and frost. Yield: 15-18 servings.

Perfect cake for Valentine's Day. Also, your favorite cream cheese frosting (*see* pp. 169 and 172) may be used for this cake.

Per serving: 270 calories; 13 g fat; 75 mg cholesterol; 187 mg sodium.

Red Velvet Frosting

1	16-OUNCE BOX CONFECTIONERS' SUGAR
1	CUP BUTTER, SOFTENED
1	TEASPOON VANILLA EXTRACT
4	TABLESPOONS HEAVY CREAM
1/2	CUP SHREDDED COCONUT
	RED FOOD COLORING

In large bowl of mixer, blend confectioners' sugar, butter, vanilla and cream until smooth and fluffy. Additional cream may be needed for the perfect consistency. Frost between layers, and assemble. Tint coconut with red food coloring and sprinkle over top.

Per serving: 212 calories; 12 g fat; 32 mg cholesterol; 112 mg sodium.

TENNESSEE'S "LOST" GOVERNOR

When Don Sundquist recently stepped into the governor's office, history books tell us that he was the forty-seventh man to take over the helm of Tennessee's highest office. What most history books fail to recall, however, is that actually, there was a forty-eighth governor of Tennessee. You never hear about this mystery man because, although he was elected to office, he never was inaugurated. Robert Looney Caruthers, a Republican lawyer, was born in Smith County in 1800, the year after the county was organized out of lands that were once part of

SMITH COUNTY

Sumner County. Caruthers served in the Tennessee House of Representatives from 1835 until 1837. He was a founder of Cumberland University at Lebanon, as well as an organizer of its world-renowned law school in 1847. He served in the U. S. House of Representatives from 1841 until 1843, and later, sat on the Tennessee Supreme Court for several years. When Governor Isham G. Harris' term was due to be up in 1863, Robert Caruthers ran for the office in the fall of 1862 and won the election. But, President Abraham Lincoln appointed former governor, Andrew Johnson, to the office of military governor of the state, so Caruthers was refused his legally won position. Although he was unable to serve actively in the War Between the States, Caruthers did perform duty in the Confederate Secret Service. After the War, Caruthers returned to Lebanon where he continued to teach at Cumberland. He died there in 1882.

The Hermitage

Andrew Jackson (1767-1845) arrived in Nashville in 1788 to be the attorney-general for the western district of North Carolina. He soon met Rachel Donelson Robards (1767-1828), the daughter of Nashville's co-founder, John Donelson. Although married at the time, Rachel soon obtained a divorce and she and Andrew were married. The later revelation that her divorce was not legal caused Rachel tremendous pain throughout her life as political wags continuously kept the issue alive. Her grief overpowered her health during the slanderous political campaign mounted against her husband during the 1828 presidential elections. Rachel soon died and never even saw Andrew off to the White House. In the meantime, the Jacksons had built the Hermitage, a magnificent home located a few miles east of Nashville. The house gradually evolved through several versions—from simple Federal style house to elegant antebellum plantation, until it became the home that can still be seen today. After Jackson, himself, died in 1845, his son sold the home to the State of Tennessee which chartered the Ladies' Hermitage Association in 1889. They have restored it to its present splendor.

Andrew Jackson's Hickory Nut or Walnut Cake

Two cups of fine white sugar creamed with half a cup of butter, three eggs, two thirds of a cup of sweet milk, three cups of sifted flour, one heaping teaspoonful (level) of powdered mace, a coffee cup of hickory nuts or walnut meats chopped a little. Fill the cake pans with a layer of the cake, then a layer of raisins upon that, then strew over these a handful of nuts, and so on until the pan is two-thirds full. Line the tins with well-buttered paper and bake in a steady, but not quick, oven. This is most excellent.

"Our federal union. It must be preserved."
—*favorite saying of Andrew Jackson.*

THE FALL OF MIDDLE TENNESSEE

On the sixth of February 1862, Confederate General Lloyd Tilghman surrendered Fort Henry, located on the Tennessee River in Stewart County, to Union forces under the command of Admiral A. H. Foote. The surrender greatly jeopardized the safety of Fort Henry's sister installation, Fort Donelson, situated nearby on the Cumberland River, and left a gaping hole in the northern defenses of Nashville, several miles to the south. Immediately after Fort Henry's surrender, General Albert Sidney Johnston began increasing the strength of Fort Donelson, until by

STEWART COUNTY

February 13, around 15,000 Confederate soldiers manned its walls. Two days later, however, when he discovered that the fort was surrounded by Union forces, Johnston ordered his men to break out. The next day the sad task of surrender fell upon General Simon Bolivar Buckner, who had been left behind by the retreating Confederate command, and he ruefully turned the garrison over to General Ulysses S. Grant. However, a dashing young cavalry officer, Colonel Nathan Bedford Forrest, did escape the surrender and headed for Nashville. A defender of Fort Donelson later described the savage fighting and later surrender. He wrote, "Pandemonium itself would hardly have been more appalling." Nashvillians, in the meantime, now fearful of the imminent Union invasion of their city, destroyed several bridges that spanned the Cumberland River and sent what few Confederate troops as remained in the city to the south.

Vanilla, Butter, and Nut Cake

2 STICKS PARKAY MARGARINE
2 CUPS SUGAR
3 CUPS PLAIN FLOUR (SIFT BEFORE MEASURING)
1 CUP BUTTERMILK WITH 1 TEASPOON SODA
1 TEASPOON SALT
3 EGGS SEPARATED-BEAT WHITES UNTIL STIFF
3 TEASPOONS EACH: SUPERIOR VANILLA, BUTTER AND NUT FLAVORING

Heat oven to 350 degrees. Grease bundt or 10-inch tube pan and dust with flour. Have ingredients at room temperature. Cream margarine and sugar thoroughly, mix soda and stir in buttermilk until foamy, adding alternately with the flour to above mixing after each addition. Add the Superior flavoring and egg yolks one at a time mixing after each. Gently fold into the stiffly beaten egg whites. Put in prepared pan and bake at 350 degrees one hour or until done.

Vanilla, Butter, and Nut Frosting

1 8-OUNCE PACKAGE CREAM CHEESE
1 BOX CONFECTIONERS SUGAR
1/2 STICK PARKAY MARGARINE
1 LEVEL TABLESPOON EACH: SUPERIOR VANILLA, BUTTER AND NUT FLAVORING
1 CUP PECANS (CHOPPED AND TOASTED IN A LITTLE MARGARINE)

Raves at the table!

This recipe comes from the C. E. Sparkman family. The Sparkmans have been in Bone Cave, Tennessee, since the early 1800s.

Catherine Ellington's
Rich White Cake

Grease and flour two, 9-inch layer pans. Cream together until fluffy:

1	CUP SOFT SHORTENING
2	CUPS SUGAR

Sift together:

3	CUPS SIFTED CAKE FLOUR
4	TEASPOONS BAKING POWDER
1	TEASPOON SALT

Stir in alternately with:

1 1/3	CUPS MILK
2	TEASPOONS FLAVORING

Fold in:

6	EGG WHITES, STIFFLY BEATEN

Pour into prepared pans. Bake until cake tests done. Cool. Finish with Divinity frosting and fresh coconut.

CATHERINE ELLINGTON RESEARCHED HER FILES FOR RECIPES SHE AND GOVERNOR BUFORD ELLINGTON ENJOYED TOGETHER. THIS RICH WHITE CAKE (OR COCONUT CAKE IF YOU ADD THE COCONUT) WAS HER HUSBAND'S FAVORITE. MRS. ELLINGTON SENT THE RECIPE ON THE ACTUAL EXECUTIVE RESIDENCE STATIONERY SHE USED WHILE SHE WAS FIRST LADY DURING GOVERNOR ELLINGTON'S TERMS AS GOVERNOR, 1959-1963, 1967-1971.

Miss Daisy

TRIAL RUN AT STATEHOOD

In one sense, the history of Tennessee as a political entity goes back six years further than its official entry into the Union as a state on June 1, 1796. Six years earlier, following the precedent established when the Northwest Territory was organized in 1787, the federal government likewise established the Southwest Territory, to include that part of North Carolina that eventually became Tennessee. With the hefty, official name of Territory of the United States South of the River Ohio, the new entity went into business on May 26, 1790, upon President George Washington's signing into law the earlier Congressional act that provided for

SULLIVAN COUNTY

the territory. The Southwest Territory was formed in the first place because of a number of reasons, North Carolina's inability to provide services and defense against the Indians to the backwoodsmen of the region was among the most impor-tant. When North Carolina authori-ties offered the region lying between the crest of the Appalachian Moun-tains in the east all the way to the Mississippi River in the west to the federal government, the cession was accepted and the territory was formed. The first order of the day was the establishment of a capital. The newly appointed governor, William Blount, traveled to William Cobb's residence, "Rocky Mount,"—in pre-sent-day Sullivan County, but then in Washington County—and estab-lished his capital there, where it stayed until 1792 when it was moved to Knoxville.

Sour Cream Apple Pie

3/4	CUP SUGAR
1/3	CUP ALL-PURPOSE FLOUR
1	TEASPOON CINNAMON
1/4	TEASPOON NUTMEG
1/4	CUP BUTTER
6	TART APPLES, CORED, PEELED AND SLICED
1	9-INCH UNBAKED PASTRY SHELL, *SEE* P. 205
1/2	CUP SOUR CREAM

Assemble all ingredients and utensils. Combine in a bowl sugar, flour, cinnamon, nutmeg and butter until crumbly. Arrange apples in pastry shell. Sprinkle crumbly mixture over the apples. Spoon the sour cream over the top. Bake in a 400-degree oven for 30 minutes, then reduce heat to 350 degrees and bake an additional 20 minutes. Yield: 8 servings.

Per serving: 341 calories; 17 g fat; 22 mg cholesterol; 204 mg sodium.

SEE P. 205

Mrs. Jean Cotton from Spring Hill, Tennessee, introduced this special apple pie recipe of hers to the guests of Miss Daisy's Tea Room some twenty-one years ago. Jean was a wonderful cook who worked at the restaurant for about ten years. I will always be appreciative of Jean and her friend Maggie Wiggins who, in my lineup of "the best cooks," will continue to win the Blue Ribbons any time they prepare a dish!

Miss Daisy

Banana Cream Pie

1/2	CUP SUGAR
6	TABLESPOONS ALL-PURPOSE FLOUR
1/8	TEASPOON SALT
2 1/2	CUPS WHOLE MILK
1	EGG, BEATEN
2	TABLESPOONS BUTTER
1	TEASPOON VANILLA
3	MEDIUM BANANAS, DIVIDED
1	9-INCH PIE CRUST, BAKED, *SEE* P. 205
1	CUP HEAVY CREAM, WHIPPED AND SWEETENED WITH 1 TABLESPOON SUGAR
1/2	CUP TOASTED COCONUT

Assemble all ingredients and utensils. In top of double boiler, mix sugar, flour and salt. Gradually stir in milk and cook over boiling water until thickened, stirring constantly. Cover and cook for 10 minutes. In a separate bowl, add 1/4 cup of milk mixture to beaten egg; return to double boiler and cook another 2 minutes, stirring constantly. Remove from heat; add butter and vanilla. Cool. Slice 2 bananas into the baked pie shell. Pour custard over bananas and chill several hours. When ready to serve, cover pie with cream, and sprinkle with toasted coconut. Arrange remaining banana slices around edge of pie. Yield: 8 servings.

Per serving: 442 calories; 27 g fat; 94 mg cholesterol; 274 mg sodium.

South Fulton, Tennessee, and its twin city of Fulton, Kentucky, host their International Banana Festival annually to promote friendship between banana-producing countries and the United States.

Miss Daisy

Margaret Hughes'
Buttermilk Coconut Pie

1/4   CUP BUTTER OR MARGARINE
1   CUP SUGAR
2   TABLESPOONS ALL-PURPOSE FLOUR
   DASH OF SALT
4   EGGS, BEATEN LIGHTLY
1   CUP BUTTERMILK
2   TEASPOONS VANILLA EXTRACT
1   CUP GRATED COCONUT

Melt butter or margarine. Remove from heat and stir in sugar, flour, and salt. Add the beaten eggs, vanilla, and buttermilk and stir until well blended. Stir in coconut. Pour into unbaked pie shell. Bake in 350-degree oven approximately 45 minutes, or until set and lightly browned.

Pie will puff up as it bakes, then sink some as it cools. Can be served at room temperature or chilled. Serve topped with a dollop of whipped cream sprinkled with coconut. Refrigerate any leftovers.

Buttermilk Pie

1/2   CUP BUTTER, SOFTENED
1 1/2   CUPS SUGAR
3   TABLESPOONS ALL-PURPOSE FLOUR
3   EGGS, WELL BEATEN
1   CUP BUTTERMILK
1   TEASPOON FRESH LEMON JUICE
1   TEASPOON VANILLA
1/8   TEASPOON SALT
1   UNBAKED 9-INCH PIE CRUST, *SEE* P. 205

Assemble all ingredients and utensils. In large mixing bowl, cream butter and sugar until smooth. Blend in remaining ingredients. Pour filling into pie crust and bake in a 350-degree oven for 50 to 60 minutes or until center is set and top is golden brown. Yield: 6 to 8 servings.

Delicious warm or cold. Fresh whipped cream sprinkled with nutmeg is a tasty garnish for this many-years-old recipe.

Per serving: 411 calories; 21 g fat; 135 mg cholesterol; 346 mg sodium.

Historic Rugby

For we are about to open a town here—in other words to create a new centre of human life . . . in this strangely beautiful solitude."

These words were spoken by Thomas Hughes, the founder of Rugby, at opening ceremonies in 1880. High atop the Cumberland Plateau, this

English colony came to be due to Hughes' distinct decision to move to the United States. He wished to provide a class-free community. Younger sons of the English gentry were interested in such a village.

The town flourished to a population of 450 by 1884. Some seventy buildings, many with high-peaked roofs, gabled windows, and decorative mill-work dotted the city paths. The social center was the Tabard Inn.

Thomas Hughes' mother, Margaret, gave up an interesting social life in England. When she came to Rugby, she made sure culture continued. She offered several recipes to young brides.

Today, with seventeen original buildings standing, Historic Rugby is registered on the National Register of Historic Places. The Hughes Public Library still holds over 7,000 volumes of Victorian literature. The Harrow Road Cafe is open for meals which visitors rave about.

Grandmother Hope's Chess Cakes

YOLKS OF 12 EGGS
2   CUPS SUGAR
1/2   CUP OF PURE CREAM
1/2   POUND BUTTER
1/2   CUP CORN MEAL

Mix and pour into crust below and bake.

1 1/2   CUPS FLOUR
1/2   TEASPOON SALT
1   TEASPOON BAKING POWDER
5   TABLESPOONS LARD
4   TABLESPOONS COLD WATER

MRS. CECIL ELROD HAS THIS TO SAY ABOUT THIS RECIPE SHE CONTRIBUTED: "HANDLE AS LITTLE AS POSSIBLE WHILE MIXING. THIS MAKES CRUST FOR TWO PIES. ONE-HUNDRED-FIFTY-YEAR-OLD RECIPE HANDED DOWN FROM ELIZABETH LARGE HOPE, WIFE OF ARCHITECT THOMAS WHO WAS BROUGHT FROM ENGLAND IN 1757 TO BUILD HOUSES—MY GREAT-GREAT-GREAT-GREAT-GRANDPARENTS."

Miss Daisy

Chess Pie

3   EGGS
2   CUPS SUGAR
1   HEAPING TABLESPOON CORN MEAL
1   LEVEL TABLESPOON FLOUR
1/2   STICK BUTTER, MELTED
1   CUP RICH MILK
1   TEASPOON VANILLA
1   LARGE PIE SHELL OR 16 TART SHELLS

THIS CHESS PIE WAS SERVED AT THE SAM DAVIS HOME IN 1941 BY MRS. WALTER H. KING OF MURFREESBORO, TENNESSEE, CHARTER MEMBER OF THE SAM DAVIS ASSOCIATION. PRESENT WERE GOVERNOR GORDON BROWNING AND ACTOR ANDY DEVINE. SARAH, AS SHE IS KNOWN, WAS PRESIDENT OF THE NATIONAL D.A.R. DURING THE ANNIVERSARY OF THE SIGNING OF THE TREATY OF PARIS AND VERSAILLES, AND SHE TOOK A CONTINGENCY WITH HER TO FRANCE IN 1983 TO CELEBRATE THE SIGNING.

Miss Daisy

Beat eggs well with mixer and add sugar, corn meal, flour mixed with melted butter, milk, and vanilla. Pour immediately into a large pie shell or into tart shells. Bake at 325 degrees (300 degrees for tart shells) for about an hour. A slow oven is very important. Yield: 8 or more servings.

Per serving: 416 calories; 28 g fat; 155 mg cholesterol; 387 mg sodium.

Adelicia Acklen's Chess Pie

2   CUPS SUGAR
1/2 CUP BUTTER, MELTED
4   EGGS
1   SMALL JAR APPLE JELLY
1   TEASPOON VANILLA OR NUTMEG
2   TEASPOONS (HEAPING) CORN MEAL

Cream butter and sugar. Put in one bowl and beat. Preheat oven to medium (350 degrees), lower temperature to 300 degrees. Bake about 20 minutes. Makes 14 small pies (tarts).

This recipe from Jeanette Acklen Noel, Nashville, Tennessee, is printed in its original form of ingredients. The directions have been altered to reflect today's cooking methods. Jeanette is Adelicia Acklen's fourth-generation granddaughter.

Belmont

During her lifetime, Adelicia Hayes Franklin Acklen Cheatham (1813—1887) was considered to be one of the wealthiest women in America. Her first husband, Isaac Franklin, was a planter from Gallatin, who also maintained several plantations in Louisiana. Upon Franklin's death, Adelicia married Joseph Acklen, a descendant of the family that founded Huntsville, Alabama. Her third husband was Dr. William Cheatham, a Nashville physician. It was during Adelicia's marriage to Joseph Acklen during the 1840s and 1850s that the mansion known as Belmont was built. The 170-acre estate extended all the way from Hillsboro Road to Eighth Avenue, and Belmont, the center-piece, provided an outstanding example of Italian and Greek design. After Adelicia's death, the old homeplace became a college, called Belmont, then an exclusive girl's school, called Ward-Belmont, and finally, in 1951, a co-educational Baptist college, again called Belmont (now Belmont University). Fortunately, through all of the transition, the original Belmont mansion has retained most of its original majesty and beauty.

Dinner-on-the-Grounds Pie

6	EGGS, SEPARATED
2	3 1/2-OUNCE CANS SHREDDED COCONUT OR
3	CUPS FRESHLY GRATED COCONUT
2	CUPS BUTTER
2 1/2	CUPS SUGAR
3/4	CUP WHOLE MILK
1	TABLESPOON ALL-PURPOSE FLOUR
2	TEASPOONS VANILLA
2	9-INCH UNBAKED PIE CRUSTS, *SEE* P. 205

*N*AME WAS DERIVED FROM THE SOCIALS HELD ON THE GROUNDS OF CHURCHES MANY YEARS AGO. IT IS KNOWN TODAY AS FRENCH COCONUT PIE. THE NAME IS UP TO YOU; IT IS IDEAL FOR ANY DINNER TABLE.

Miss Daisy

Assemble all ingredients and utensils. Beat egg yolks in a separate bowl and set aside. Melt butter in a saucepan. Combine butter, sugar, milk, flour, vanilla with beaten egg yolks. Add coconut. Beat egg whites until stiff. Fold into pie mixture. Pour into pie shells. Bake in a 350-degree oven for about 45 to 50 minutes or until set and golden brown. Yield: 2 pies, 6 to 8 servings each.

Per serving: 739 calories; 51 g fat; 222 mg cholesterol; 543 mg sodium.

HOME ON THE RANGE

The American bison, commonly called the "buffalo," is usually associated with the endless grasslands of the Great Plains, that vast region of America lying between the Mississippi River and the Rocky Mountains. Conservative estimates place as many as sixty million buffalo in North America when the continent was first spied by European explorers. By 1880, however, the animal was practically extinct, his demise brought about by greedy hunters who wanted noth-ing but the tongue, relished by gourmet diners back East, and the hide. When the first longhunters reached the Cumberland River valley, they found the animal to be

SUMNER COUNTY

quite common. One hunter wrote in 1769 that the land surrounding Bledsoe's Lick in present-day Sumner County "was principally Covered with Buffelows [sic] in every direction—not hundreds but thousands." But, Man's destruction of his environment had already begun, and soon, the bison, along with other large mammal species, had vanished from Middle Tennessee. One year after the long-hunter above had witnessed the large herds at Bledsoe's Lick, he commented that "One could walk for several hundred yards around the Lick and in the Lick on Buffelow Skuls and bones, and the whole flat around the Lick was bleached with Buffelow bones, and they found out the Cause of the Canes growing up so suddenly . . . which was in Consequence of so many Buffelows being killed."

Southern Egg Custard Pie

4	EGGS
1	CUP SUGAR
1/4	TEASPOON SALT
1	TEASPOON VANILLA
3	CUPS MILK
1	UNBAKED 9-INCH PIE SHELL
2	TABLESPOONS BUTTER, SLICED THIN

Assemble all ingredients and utensils. In a large bowl, beat eggs lightly. Blend in sugar, salt, vanilla and milk. Pour custard into pastry shell and dot with butter. Bake in a 425-degree oven for 10 minutes; reduce heat to 325 degrees and bake until filling is set, about 35 minutes. Yield: 6 to 8 servings.

Per serving: 330 calories; 16 g fat; 157 mg cholesterol; 313 mg sodium.

Two-hundred years ago when this recipe was created, eggs, milk, and butter were always available! During those years the pie shells were made from scratch (see p. 205).

Miss Daisy

Chocolate Pie

Mix one tablespoon of flour and one-half cup sugar, put this into two beaten egg yolks, then three tablespoons of chocolate, then one cup milk and a little butter. Put in double boiler and cook until thick. Cool this and put into pastry that has been cooked. Use whites of eggs for meringue.

Mrs. Lester Dann is the grandmother of Murfreesboro's Rhea Seddan, the first female astronaut. Mrs. Dann has served this Chocolate Pie to many friends and family but never knew that number would include a granddaughter who later became nationally known.

Miss Daisy

ONE BEAN TOO MANY

The love affair that many Tennesseans had for Texas existed for years before Texas won its independence from Mexico in 1836. During the 1820s and 1830s, hundreds of the state's residents pulled up stakes, sold the family farm, and hightailed it to the vast lands beyond the Mississippi. One such family was that of Robert Holmes Dunham of Tipton County. Texas existed as an independent republic for about ten years. In 1842, when soldiers from Mexico attacked San Antonio, a small Texan army was formed to drive out the foreigners. The main army stopped short of crossing the border at the Rio Grande, but several Texans separated

TIPTON COUNTY

from the rest and entered Mexico anyway. At the small town of Mier, this vastly outnumbered group battled for seventeen hours before finally surrendering. One of those captured was Robert Dunham. When the Mexican general, Santa Anna, ordered that ten percent of the 176 Texan captives be executed, lots were drawn among the men by selecting a single bean from an earthern pot held by a Mexican officer. In the pot were 176 beans, 159 of them white and 17 black. Whoever drew a black bean was to be executed immediately. When it came Dunham's turn to draw, he opened his hand to reveal a black bean. It is said that when he realized his choice, he said, "I am prepared to die and would to God I had the chance to do the same thing over again." After writing a letter to his mother, the young former Tennessean was taken out and shot along with the sixteen others.

Coconut Cream Meringue Pie

2/3   CUP SUGAR
5   TABLESPOONS ALL-PURPOSE FLOUR
1/4   TEASPOON SALT
2   CUPS WHOLE MILK
3   EGG YOLKS, SLIGHTLY BEATEN
2/3   CUP SHREDDED COCONUT
1   TEASPOON VANILLA EXTRACT
1   BAKED, COOLED 9-INCH PIE SHELL, *SEE* P. 205
    MERINGUE

Assemble all ingredients and utensils. Combine sugar, flour and salt in a large saucepan. Stir in milk gradually. Bring to boil, stirring constantly. Cook over low heat until thick. Remove 1/4 cup of the mixture and combine with slightly beaten egg yolks, stir and return to hot mixture in saucepan. Cook for another 2 minutes, stirring constantly. Add coconut and vanilla. Pour into baked pie shell.

Meringue

3   EGG WHITES
1/4   CUP SUGAR
1/3   CUP SHREDDED COCONUT

Beat whites until stiff. Fold in sugar and coconut. Spread on pie. Bake pie in a 325-degree oven for 15 to 20 minutes or until meringue is lightly browned. Yield: 6 servings.

Per serving: 459 calories; 21 g fat; 147 mg cholesterol; 382 mg sodium.

*G*RAHAM CRACKER PIE CRUST (*SEE* RECIPE BELOW) IS A TASTY SUBSTITUTE FOR A TRADITIONAL CRUST. ALSO, FOR A REFRIGERATED PIE OMIT THE MERINGUE TOPPING AND ADD SOME SWEETENED WHIPPED CREAM.

Miss Daisy

Graham Cracker Pie Crust

1   CUP GRAHAM CRACKERS
1/2   CUP MELTED BUTTER
1/4   CUP CONFECTIONERS' SUGAR, OPTIONAL
1   TABLESPOON LIGHT CREAM

Assemble all ingredients and utensils. Roll 15 graham crackers fine or use packaged crumbs. For a sweeter crust, stir in sugar. Add gradually to melted butter, mixing thoroughly. Stir in cream or milk. Press over bottom and sides of a 9-inch pie pan. Bake in a 325-degree oven for 10 minutes. Chill before filling.

Chocolate Meringue Pie

3	EGGS, SEPARATED
1	CUP SUGAR
3	TABLESPOONS ALL-PURPOSE FLOUR
4	TABLESPOONS COCOA
1/8	TEASPOON SALT
2	CUPS WHOLE MILK
1	TABLESPOON BUTTER
1	TEASPOON VANILLA EXTRACT
1	9-INCH PASTRY SHELL, BELOW MERINGUE

Assemble all ingredients and utensils. In a heavy saucepan combine egg yolks, sugar, flour, cocoa and salt. Gradually add milk. Cook over low heat, stirring occasionally until thick, add butter and vanilla. Pour into 9-inch pastry shell. Top with Meringue and bake in a 350-degree oven for 10 to 12 minutes. Yield: 6 servings.

Meringue

3	EGG WHITES
1/4	TEASPOON CREAM OF TARTAR
1/8	TEASPOON SALT
4	TABLESPOONS SUGAR

Beat egg whites in large bowl of mixer until stiff. Gently fold in cream of tartar, salt and sugar. Cover pie filling.

Per serving: 438 calories; 18 g fat; 153 mg cholesterol; 375 mg sodium.

*J*OHN EGERTON SAYS IT BEST IN HIS *SOUTHERN FOOD*, "TODAY, IT MAY BE TRUER THAN EVER THAT THE PREPARATION OF FINE PIES, COOKIES, CAKES, AND THE LIKE REQUIRES A GOOD BIT OF EXPERIENCE, IF NOT SPECIAL SKILLS, AND CERTAINLY TAKES MORE TIME AND EFFORT THAN MOST PEOPLE ARE WILLING TO DEVOTE TO THE TASK. NEVERTHELESS, THERE IS SUCH PLEASURE AND SATISFACTION TO BE DERIVED FROM PREPARING A TIME-HONORED DELICACY IN THE TRADITIONAL WAY."

Miss Daisy

Never-Fail Pie Crust

1	CUP ALL-PURPOSE FLOUR
1/2	TEASPOON SALT
1/3	CUP VEGETABLE SHORTENING
3	TABLESPOONS COLD WATER

Assemble all ingredients and utensils. In a bowl, combine flour and salt. With fork, work in shortening until mixture resembles coarse meal. Sprinkle water over flour mixture until completely moistened. Form into a ball. Roll dough out on a floured board or surface. Place in a 9-inch pie pan.

Baked Pie Shell

Prick pastry with a fork. Bake in a 375-degree oven for 5 minutes. Reduce heat to 350 degrees and bake 15 to 20 minutes longer.

Unbaked Pie Shell

Keep frozen until ready to use.

Sevier Family
150-Year-Old Lemon Pie

1/2	CUP BUTTER
2	CUPS SUGAR
3	SODA CRACKERS, ROLLED FINELY AND SIFTED
2	LEMONS, JUICE AND RIND
6	WHOLE EGGS, WELL BEATEN
2	UNBAKED PIE SHELLS

Cream butter and sugar thoroughly. Add sifted cracker crumbs. Add lemon juice and rind. Blend well, until smooth. Add well-beaten eggs and blend well. Pour into unbaked pie shells and bake in 375-degree oven from 35 to 40 minutes. Makes 2 small pies.

Deep Dish Lemon Pie

1 1/2	CUPS SUGAR
1/3	CUP CORNSTARCH
1/4	TEASPOON SALT
1 1/2	CUPS COLD WATER
3	LARGE LEMONS, JUICE
5	EGG YOLKS, BEATEN
2	TABLESPOONS BUTTER
3	TEASPOONS GRATED LEMON RIND
1	9-INCH DEEP-DISH PASTRY SHELL, PRE-BAKED, *SEE* P. 205

Assemble ingredients and utensils. In a saucepan, mix sugar, cornstarch and salt. Add water and juice from lemons and cook over medium heat until mix is very warm, stirring constantly. Remove 1 cup of warm mixture and add to beaten egg yolks. Add all together and cook until thick. Add butter and stir in lemon rind. Pour mixture into pre-baked shell. Cover with meringue and bake in a 350-degree oven for 12 to 15 minutes or until brown. Yield: 8 servings.

Meringue

5	EGG WHITES
1/4	TEASPOON CREAM OF TARTAR
1/2	CUP SUGAR
1	TEASPOON VANILLA

Combine ingredients in a small mixing bowl and beat until stiff.

Per serving: 400 calories; 14 g fat; 178 mg cholesterol; 277 mg sodium.

Pecan Fudge Pie

1/2	CUP BUTTER
4	1-OUNCE SQUARES UNSWEETENED CHOCOLATE
4	EGGS, LIGHTLY BEATEN
3	TABLESPOONS LIGHT CORN SYRUP
1 1/2	CUPS SUGAR
1/4	TEASPOON SALT
1	TEASPOON VANILLA EXTRACT
1	CUP CHOPPED PECANS
1	9-INCH PASTRY SHELL, *SEE* P. 205

Assemble all ingredients and utensils. In top of double boiler or in a saucepan over low heat, melt butter and chocolate. Combine in a bowl beaten eggs, syrup, sugar, salt, vanilla and pecans. Mix well. Add chocolate mixture and mix thoroughly. Pour filling into the pie shell. Bake in a 350-degree oven for 30 to 35 minutes until filling is set, but soft inside. Yield: 6 to 8 servings.

Sinfully rich with vanilla ice cream or sweetened whipped cream.

Per serving: 550 calories; 36 g fat; 31 mg cholesterol; 353 mg sodium.

Holiday Mincemeat Pie

1	EGG WHITE, BEATEN UNTIL FROTHY
2	CUPS MINCEMEAT FROM A JAR
3	CUPS GRANNY SMITH APPLES, PEELED AND THINLY SLICED
1/2	CUP HONEY
1/4	CUP BUTTER, SOFTENED
1/4	CUP SUGAR
1/2	CUP ALL-PURPOSE FLOUR
1	9-INCH DEEP DISH PIE CRUST, UNBAKED, *SEE* P. 205

Assemble all ingredients and utensils. Brush bottom and sides of pie crust with beaten egg white. Bake in a 350 degree oven for 3 minutes. Cool. Layer mincemeat over bottom of cooled crust. Combine apples and honey and pour over mincemeat. In a small bowl mix until fine butter, sugar and flour. Sprinkle over apples. Bake in a 400-degree oven and bake for 30 minutes until topping is golden brown. Yield: 6 to 8 servings.

The apples are a special tasty addition to this one-hundred-year-old Mincemeat Pie.

Per serving: 448 calories; 14 g fat; 16 mg cholesterol; 376 mg sodium.

White Lily Foods Company

In the 1850s, the Knoxville City Mills became the reliable source for quality flour during a time when hot biscuits became the three-meal-a-day staple for a great number of southern families. In 1883, five Knoxville businessmen incorporated a new company which operated the old Knoxville City Mills facility. The men built a larger mill at the present Depot Street location in 1885. It was here that the wheat flour was ground to an increasingly finer particle size. This was the beginning of White Lily Flour. Only pure 100 percent soft red winter wheat with a low percentage of protein is used to make it. Since White Lily's granulation is finer, it is less dense than most national brands. A cup of White Lily weighs less than a cup of other brands. White Lily produces all-purpose, self-rising, unbleached self-rising and bread flours. The production of corn meal and buttermilk biscuit mixes is also a hallmark of the company. Unlike other corn meal producers, White Lily retains the wheat grain. This unique fact yields the distinctive flavor that sets it apart from its competition.

Peanut Butter Meringue Pie

1	CUP CONFECTIONERS' SUGAR
1/2	CUP CREAMY PEANUT BUTTER
1	BAKED 9-INCH PASTRY SHELL
2/3	CUP SUGAR
2	CUPS WHOLE MILK, SCALDED
2	TABLESPOONS BUTTER
1/4	TEASPOON VANILLA EXTRACT
1/4	CUP CORN STARCH
1/4	TEASPOON SALT
3	EGG YOLKS, BEATEN
3	EGG WHITES

Assemble all ingredients and utensils. Combine confectioners' sugar and peanut butter; mix with a fork until mixture resembles corn meal. Spread half the mixture in baked pastry shell; set remaining mixture aside. In a saucepan, combine remaining ingredients except egg whites and cook until thickened, stirring constantly. Spoon filling over peanut butter layer in pastry shell. Beat egg whites until stiff; spread over filling. sprinkle remaining peanut butter mixture over meringue. Bake in a 325-degree oven for 20 minutes, until meringue is firm and browned. Cool before serving. Yield: 6 to 8 servings.

Per serving: 436 calories; 23 g fat; 118 mg cholesterol; 363 mg sodium.

Southern Pecan Pie

1/2	CUP SUGAR
1/4	CUP BUTTER, SOFTENED
3	EGGS, SLIGHTLY BEATEN
1 1/2	CUPS PECANS
1/8	TEASPOON SALT
1	TEASPOON VANILLA EXTRACT
1	CUP LIGHT CORN SYRUP
1	9-INCH PASTRY SHELL

Assemble all ingredients and utensils. In large bowl of mixer cream butter and sugar. Add eggs, pecans, salt, vanilla and corn syrup. Mix well. Pour into unbaked pie shell. Bake in a 350-degree oven for 50 to 60 minutes. Yield: 6 servings.

Growing up in Georgia with pecan trees on our farm, pecan pie was always on our dinner table. This recipe is very easy and very good.

Per serving: 652 calories; 39 g fat; 157 mg cholesterol; 346 mg sodium.

Holiday Sweet Potato Pie

2 CUPS COOKED, MASHED SWEET POTATOES OR
1 16-OUNCE CAN SWEET POTATOES, DRAINED, MASHED, AND SIEVED
1/2 CUP FIRMLY PACKED BROWN SUGAR
1/2 TEASPOON SALT
1/2 TEASPOON GROUND CINNAMON
1/2 TEASPOON GROUND NUTMEG
1/4 TEASPOON GROUND ALLSPICE
1 CUP LIGHT CREAM
3 EGGS, BEATEN
1 UNBAKED 9-INCH PIE SHELL, *SEE* P. 205

Assemble all ingredients and utensils. In a large bowl, combine sweet potatoes, brown sugar, salt and spices. Combine cream and eggs; add to sweet potato mixture, blending until smooth. Pour filling into pie shell and bake in a 425-degree oven for 15 minutes. Reduce heat to 325 degrees and bake an additional 35 to 40 minutes until filling is set. Yield: 6 to 8 servings.

Serve with a garnish of sweetened whipped cream.

Per serving: 292 calories; 13 g fat; 114 mg cholesterol; 347 mg sodium.

Raisin Pie

1 CUP RAISINS, DARK
2 CUPS WATER
1 1/2 CUPS SUGAR
4 TABLESPOONS ALL-PURPOSE FLOUR
1/4 TEASPOON SALT
3 TABLESPOONS LEMON JUICE
2 TABLESPOONS GRATED LEMON RIND
1 EGG, WELL BEATEN
2 8-INCH PASTRY SHELLS

Assemble all ingredients and utensils. Wash raisins and soak in cold water for three hours. Drain. Combine raisins, water, sugar, flour, salt, lemon juice, rind and egg. In a heavy saucepan or double boiler cook ingredients for 15 minutes, stirring occasionally. Cool. Pour into pastry shell. Cover with remaining shell which has been cut into narrow strips. Bake in a 450-degree oven for 10 minutes. Reduce heat to 350 degrees and bake for an additional 30 minutes. Yield: 6 servings.

Per serving: 299 calories; 11 g fat; 23 mg cholesterol; 236 mg sodium.

*V*ERY OLD RECIPE. KNOWN ALSO AS "FUNERAL PIE" BECAUSE IT WAS A QUICK-AND-EASY PIE TO PREPARE WITH INGREDIENTS ALWAYS ON HAND.

Miss Daisy

Green Tomato Pie

3	CUPS SLICED GREEN TOMATOES, COMPLETELY DRAINED
2	TABLESPOONS FRESHLY SQUEEZED LEMON JUICE
3	TABLESPOONS GRATED LEMON RIND
1 1/3	CUPS SUGAR
3	TABLESPOONS ALL-PURPOSE FLOUR
1/4	TEASPOON SALT
1/2	TEASPOON CINNAMON
3	TABLESPOONS BUTTER
2	9-INCH UNBAKED PIE CRUSTS, *SEE* P. 205

THIS SOUTHERN RECIPE HAS BEEN TRACED BACK EIGHT GENERATIONS.

Miss Daisy

Assemble all ingredients and utensils. Combine tomatoes with ingredients except pie crusts and butter. Pour batter into 1 of the pie crusts. Dot with butter. Cover with top crust; cut several vents in crust and bake in a 400-degree oven for 35 to 40 minutes or until golden brown. Yield: 6 to 8 servings.

Per serving: 425 calories; 20 g fat; 12 mg cholesterol; 398 mg sodium.

Transparent Pie

2	CUPS SUGAR
1/2	CUP BUTTER
2	TABLESPOONS CAKE FLOUR
1/4	TEASPOON SALT
6	EGGS
1 1/2	CUPS BOILING WATER
	VANILLA FLAVORING
2	UNBAKED (9-INCH) PIE CRUSTS

CALLED BY SOME A VANILLA MERINGUE PIE, THIS PARTICULAR RECIPE WAS DATED 1892.

Miss Daisy

Sift flour, sugar, and salt. Beat egg yolks with sugar until light; add butter (room temperature). Beat well and add boiling water and flavoring. Pour into two 9-inch unbaked pie crusts or fifteen 3-inch unbaked tart shells. Bake 8 minutes in 375- to 400-degree oven; reduce heat and bake at 325 for 15 minutes. Let cool slightly and cover with meringue.

Meringue:

6	EGG WHITES
8	TABLESPOONS SUGAR

Beat whites until stiff and add sugar gradually. Beat until meringue will make a peak when beater is lifted. Cover pies, making sure that meringue completely covers pies. Bake in 350-degree oven for 10 minutes. Yield: two, 9-inch pies or fifteen 3-inch tarts.

Southern Fried Pies

Dough

2 1/2	CUPS ALL-PURPOSE FLOUR
1	TABLESPOON BAKING POWDER
1	TABLESPOON SUGAR
1	TEASPOON SALT
1/3	CUP SHORTENING
1	EGG, BEATEN
1	6 1/2-OUNCE CAN EVAPORATED MILK

Assemble all ingredients and utensils. Sift dry ingredients together in a large bowl. Cut in shortening with pastry cutter or two knives. Mix egg with milk and add to dry mixture to make a stiff dough. Chill for at least 24 hours. Roll out to 1/8 inch thickness and cut into 3- or 4-inch circles. Place two tablespoons of the fruit off center of each circle. Fold over and press edges together with a fork and prick on both sides with fork to vent. Fry in medium hot oil until golden brown. Drain. Yield: about 24 pies.

Filling

1	CUP DRIED FRUIT (APPLE, PEACHES, APRICOT, FIGS, PRUNES) PER RECIPE
2	CUPS WATER
	SUGAR TO TASTE
	SPICES TO TASTE: CINNAMON, NUTMEG, CLOVES, ALLSPICE

Combine dried fruit with water in a saucepan. Bring to a boil, reduce heat. Cover and simmer for 30 minutes or until fruit is tender and water is absorbed. Combine fruit with sugar and spices to taste. Mix well. Each dough circle needs about 2 tablespoons of fruit mixture.

Per serving: 117 calories; 4 g fat; 14 mg cholesterol; 155 mg sodium.

FRIED FRUIT PIES HAVE MANY NAMES: HALF MOON, FRIED PIES, AND SO ON. BUT WHATEVER THEY ARE CALLED THEY ARE MOUTHWATERING AND FINGER-LICKING GOOD. THEY TAKE PRACTICE TO PERFECT. I REMEMBER USING TWO OR THREE DIFFERENT SIZED SAUCERS AS MY OUTLINE ON THE PASTRY DOUGH TO SECURE JUST THE EXACT SIZE TO HOLD THE TWO TABLESPOONS OF DRIED COOKED PEACHES IN THE CENTER. THEN THE FUN PART BEGAN WHEN I FOLDED ONE HALF OF THE PASTRY OVER THE OTHER AND HAD TO USE SOME REAL DESIGN CREATIVITY IN SEALING THE EDGES. YUM!

Miss Daisy

John Donelson

John Donelson, a surveyor by profession, came to the Tennessee country when it was still part of North Carolina. He brought his family from Virginia where he had served in the State House of Burgesses before independence was achieved for the United States. He moved to the Watauga Settlements in the 1770s, and in 1779, he and James Robertson led parties to settle the Middle Cumberland River area. John led the flatboat expedition of women, children and household goods on a long, perilous journey that covered over a thousand miles on the Holston, Tennessee, and Cumberland Rivers. The men who came with John aptly maneuvered the currents, ice, and Indians encountered along with him. They reached the Robertson party's fort at the Bluffs on the Cumberland on April 24, 1780.

John's daughter, Rachel, came on the journey and would one day be known as Mrs. Andrew Jackson.

Strawberry Cream Pie

4	CUPS FRESH STRAWBERRIES, STEMS REMOVED
3	TABLESPOONS CORNSTARCH
1	CUP SUGAR
2	TABLESPOONS LEMON JUICE
1/8	TEASPOON SALT
1	9-INCH BAKED PASTRY SHELL OR
1	GRAHAM CRACKER CRUST SHELL
	WHIPPED CREAM

Assemble all ingredients and utensils. Wash and drain berries. In a bowl crush or mash half or 2 cups of berries. In a saucepan combine crushed berries, cornstarch, sugar, lemon juice and salt. Cook over medium heat until mixture is thickened and clear. Cool. Slice the remaining 2 cups of berries and add to the cooked berry mixture. Pour into pie shell and chill. Top with whipped cream. Yield: 6 servings.

An old favorite still being enjoyed today.

Per serving: 339 calories; 12 g fat; 5 mg cholesterol; 240 mg sodium.

Southern Heavenly Pie

15	GRAHAM CRACKERS
1/2	STICK MARGARINE, MELTED
1/2	CUP BUTTER
3/4	CUP SUGAR
1	EGG
1/2	CUP CRUSHED PINEAPPLE, DRAINED
1/2	PINT WHIPPING CREAM
1/2	CUP CHOPPED NUTS (PECANS OR WALNUTS)

Crush crackers and add 1/2 stick melted margarine. Press into pie pan. Cream 1/2 cup butter with sugar. Add beaten egg, nuts, and pineapple. Fold in whipped cream and pour into crust. Chill for 3 or more hours. Does not freeze well.

Per serving: 339 calories; 12 g fat; 5 mg cholesterol; 240 mg sodium.

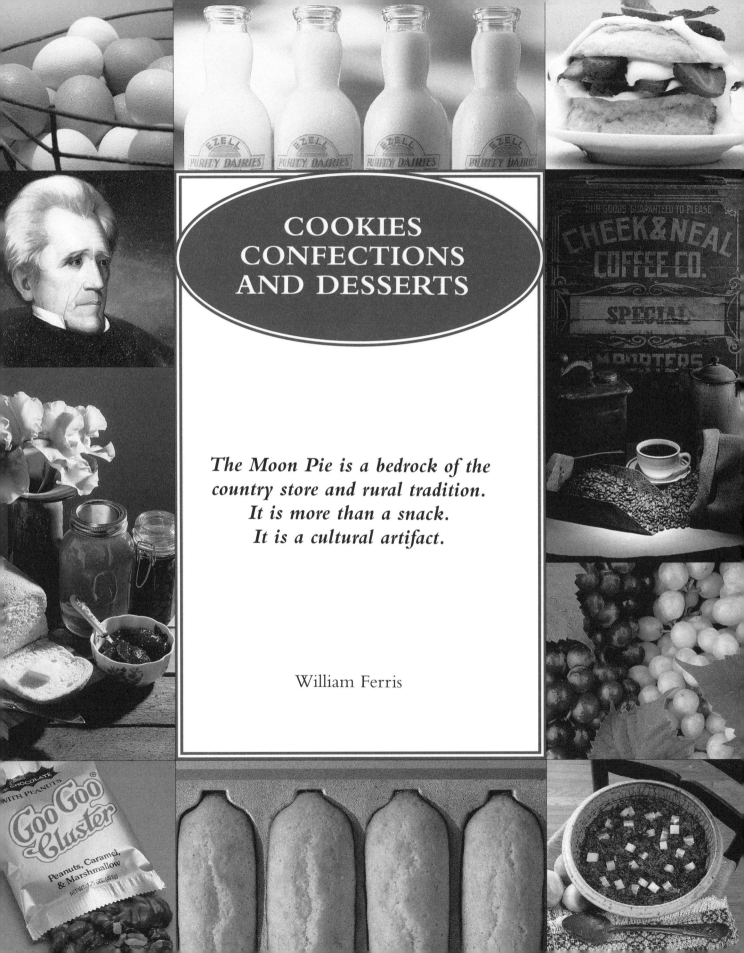

COOKIES CONFECTIONS AND DESSERTS

The Moon Pie is a bedrock of the country store and rural tradition. It is more than a snack. It is a cultural artifact.

William Ferris

COOKIES, CONFECTIONS, AND DESSERTS

Iced Butter Cookies

Cookies

1/2	POUND BUTTER, SOFTENED
1	CUP ALL-PURPOSE FLOUR
3/4	CUP CORN STARCH, SIFTED
1/3	CUP CONFECTIONERS' SUGAR, SIFTED

Assemble all ingredients and utensils. In large bowl of mixer; mix all ingredients well. Batter will be stiff. Drop by teaspoonfuls onto greased baking sheet. Bake in a 350-degree oven for 10 to 12 minutes.

Icing

3	OUNCES CREAM CHEESE, SOFTENED
1 1/2	CUPS CONFECTIONERS' SUGAR, SIFTED
1	TEASPOON VANILLA EXTRACT

Mix cream cheese and sugar; add vanilla. Frost tops of cookies while still warm. Yield: 36 cookies.

Very light but rich cookies.

Per serving: 94 calories; 6 g fat; 16 mg cholesterol; 59 mg sodium.

A CONSTITUTIONAL COUNTY

Most of the ninety-five counties of Tennessee were established by acts of the state legislature, either North Carolina's, for the early counties, or Tennessee's, for the later ones. A few of the entities, however, were created during the Constitutional Convention of 1870, among them Trousdale, thus putting these counties in the unique position of being part of the State Constitution. Trousdale County came about when George Seay, who represented Sumner, Smith, and Macon Counties in the 1870 convention, proposed that a new entity be created from existing lands in the three represented counties. Since Trousdale County's

TROUSDALE COUNTY

establishment is embodied in the Constitution, it cannot be consolidated with another county or abolished or undergo any type of border change without the approval of a constitutional convention, which is a rare occurence in Tennessee. The county took its name from former Governor William Trousdale, sometimes called the "warhorse of Sumner County," who was an active participant in the Creek Wars, the War of 1812, and the Mexican War. After his tenure as governor was up in 1851, Trousdale served in the post of U. S. Minister to Brazil in President Franklin Pierce's administration. Today, Trousdale County is the smallest county in Tennessee from a land area standpoint with only 116 square miles, but it is the fourth least populated, being superseded by Moore, Pickett, and Van Buren Counties.

Christie Cookies

L ife can be sweet" so the saying goes, and life for a former Vanderbilt football player has led to "sweet success." Christie Hauck began his pursuit for the "perfect cookie" in 1985. He wanted to duplicate a recipe that a neighbor in Atlanta had baked for him during his childhood. After experimenting for two years, he finally created the Christie Cookie. It was his idea from the beginning to pro-

duce an "elegant, gourmet cookie that would truly be unique."

Christie chose the finest ingredients: french chocolate, real butter, pure vanilla, white chocolate and macadamia nuts from Hawaii. Each cookie recipe attracted repeat customers as he opened his first retail store on Church Street in downtown Nashville. Soon, a second store was added at Third National Financial Center. Today, there are five retail stores with expansion of a wholesale division.

The Christie Cookie Company sells frozen, unbaked dough to universities and institutions. The mail order division provides cookies to corporate and individual clients both nationally and internationally. The corporate division provides custom design logo tins for companies to use as client gifts.

Ninety employees successfully help make Christie Hauck's mission for the "perfect cookie" a reality.

Crescent Cookies

1/2	POUND BUTTER, SOFTENED
1/2	CUP CONFECTIONERS' SUGAR
2	CUPS ALL-PURPOSE FLOUR
1/2	CUPS PECANS, FINELY CHOPPED
2	TEASPOONS VANILLA EXTRACT
1/8	TEASPOON SALT

Assemble all ingredients and utensils. In large bowl of mixer, cream butter and sugar, gradually mix in flour. Add remaining ingredients and mix well. Pinch off small piece, teaspoon size. Roll and shape as desired. Place on lightly greased cookie sheet and bake in a slow oven, 300-325 degrees until lightly browned. Cool and roll in additional confectioners' sugar. Yield: about 5 dozen cookies.

Serve for a wedding or an afternoon tea. Store covered.

Per serving: 57 calories; 4 g fat; 8 mg cholesterol; 36 mg sodium.

Fruitcake Cookies

1/2	CUP BUTTER
1	CUP BROWN SUGAR
4	EGGS
2 1/2	CUPS ALL-PURPOSE FLOUR
1/2	POUND CANDIED CHERRIES
1/2	POUND CANDIED PINEAPPLE
1 1/2	POUNDS (6 CUPS) CHOPPED NUTS
2 1/4	CUPS WHITE RAISINS
3	TABLESPOONS WHOLE MILK
2	TEASPOONS SODA
1	TEASPOON GROUND CLOVES
1	TEASPOON GROUND NUTMEG
1	TEASPOON GROUND CINNAMON
2	TABLESPOONS ORANGE JUICE

Assemble all ingredients and utensils. In large bowl of mixer cream butter and sugar; add eggs, one at a time. Use 1/2 cup of flour to sprinkle over fruit. Then combine all ingredients. Drop by teaspoonfuls on a greased cookie sheet. Bake in a 250-degree oven for about 30 to 35 minutes. Yield: about 72 cookies.

Great for holiday gifts. Delightful served with Boiled Custard.

Per serving: 134 calories; 8 g fat; 4 mg cholesterol; 41 mg sodium.

Hortense Cooper's Oatmeal Cookies

In large bowl, mix together:

1	CUP BROWN SUGAR (FIRMLY PACKED)
1/2	CUP VEGETABLE OIL

Then add:

1	CUP FLOUR (OR 3/4 CUP FLOUR AND 1/4 CUP WHEAT GERM)
1/2	TEASPOON SALT
1/2	TEASPOON SODA
1	TEASPOON CINNAMON
1	EGG, UNBEATEN
2	TABLESPOONS SWEET MILK

Mix together, then add:

1 1/2	CUPS ROLLED OATS
1/2	CUP RAISINS AND PERHAPS NUTS

Shape dough into small balls or drop from spoon onto greased (PAM works well) cookie sheet; flatten. Bake at about 325 to 350 degrees. Do not overbake. Recipe can be doubled. Yield: 50-60 cookies.

HORTENSE COOPER SENT ME HER FAVORITE RECIPE OF OATMEAL COOKIES. I UNDERSTAND THAT HER SON JIM THINKS THEY ARE THE MOST DELICIOUS COOKIES EVER! MRS. COOPER WAS MARRIED TO PRENTICE COOPER WHO WAS GOVERNOR OF TENNESSEE FROM 1939-1945.

Miss Daisy

Shelly West's Oatmeal Crispies

1	CUP SHORTENING
1	CUP BROWN SUGAR
1	CUP GRANULATED SUGAR
2	WELL-BEATEN EGGS
1	TEASPOON VANILLA
1 1/2	CUPS FLOUR
1	TEASPOON SODA
1	TEASPOON SALT
3	CUPS QUICK-COOKING OATMEAL

Cream shortening and sugar. Add eggs, vanilla. Beat well. Add sifted dry ingredients and oats. Mix well. Shape in rolls, wrap in waxed paper, chill. Bake on ungreased cookie sheet at 350 degrees for 10-13 minutes. Yield: 5 dozen.

SHELLY SENT ME THIS RECIPE WHEN SHE SHARED HER MOTHER DOTTIE'S VERY SPECIAL PEANUT SOUP WITH THE BICENTENNIAL COLLECTION.

Miss Daisy

Lookout Moon Pies

Chattanooga Bakery was founded in 1902. The company had a mill in Knoxville as well as Chattanooga. It was the general manager of the Knoxville mill who went into the "Appalachia" area to sell some of the bakery's cookies and crackers in 1917. His report back to the Chattanooga manager went something like this:

They don't want anything we sell. What they want is something big, round, filled with marshmallow, and covered in chocolate, and it needs to be as big as the moon!

The Chattanooga Bakery had something similar to this desired product already, but without coating. When the bakery added the chocolate, the Moon Pie was born!

A worker could go to a country store, pick up an RC Cola (10 ounces) for a nickel, and a Moon Pie, the biggest snack there, also for a nickel and have the "working man's lunch"!

Old Fashioned Molasses Cookies

1/2	CUP BUTTER, SOFTENED
1/3	CUP BROWN SUGAR
1	EGG
1/2	CUP MOLASSES
1/4	CUP WHOLE MILK
2	CUPS ALL-PURPOSE FLOUR
1	TEASPOON SODA
1/2	TEASPOON SALT
1/2	TEASPOON GINGER
1/2	TEASPOON CINNAMON

Assemble all ingredients and utensils. In a large bowl of the mixer combine softened butter and sugar and cream. Add egg, molasses and milk. Sift the dry ingredients and mix well into creamed mixture. Place teaspoonfuls of the stiff dough on the cookie sheet, leaving space for spreading during baking. Bake in a 375-degree oven for 10 to 12 minutes. Yield: about 48 cookies.

A very old recipe which came from my father's side of the family. I have reformulated the ingredients to conform with today's cooking procedures.

Per serving: 50 calories; 2 g fat; 11 mg cholesterol; 63 mg sodium.

Peanut Butter Cookies

1/2	CUP CREAMY PEANUT BUTTER
1/2	CUP SHORTENING
1/2	CUP SUGAR
1/2	CUP BROWN SUGAR, PACKED
1	EGG
1/2	TEASPOON VANILLA EXTRACT
1 1/2	CUPS ALL-PURPOSE FLOUR, SIFTED
1/2	TEASPOON SALT
2	TEASPOONS BAKING POWDER

Assemble all ingredients and utensils. In large bowl of mixer cream peanut butter and shortening. Add sugars and beat until light and fluffy. Add egg, vanilla and remaining dry ingredients. Mix until smooth. Form tablespoons of dough into balls. Place 2 inches apart on ungreased cookie sheet. Press crosswise with fork. Bake in a 350 degree oven for 12 to 15 minutes. Yield: 36 cookies.

Perfect cookie for children to learn to bake. They enjoy putting their thumbprint into cookie or using fork to create the design.

Per serving: 88 calories; 5 g fat; 8 mg cholesterol; 69 mg sodium.

Lemon Tea Cookies

1	CUP SHORTENING
1/2	CUP BROWN SUGAR
1/2	CUP SUGAR
1	EGG, WELL BEATEN
2	TABLESPOONS LEMON JUICE
1	TABLESPOON GRATED LEMON RIND
2	CUPS SIFTED ALL-PURPOSE FLOUR
1/4	TEASPOON BAKING SODA
1/2	TEASPOON SALT
1/2	CUP FINELY CHOPPED PECANS

Assemble all ingredients and utensils. In large bowl of mixer, cream the shortening and sugars gradually. Add the egg, lemon juice and rind, mix well. Add the sifted flour, baking powder, salt and pecans. Mix thoroughly. Form into a roll about 2 inches in diameter. Wrap in waxed paper and chill. Slice into 1/4-inch slices and bake on cookie sheets. Bake in a 400-degree oven for 8 to 10 minutes. Yield: about 48 to 50 cookies.

Delightful for a tea, wedding reception or to enjoy by the "handful."

Per serving: 86 calories; 5.7 g fat; 6 mg cholesterol; 28 mg sodium.

Pecan Sandies

1	CUP BUTTER, SOFTENED
1/3	CUP SUGAR
2	TEASPOONS VANILLA EXTRACT
2	CUPS ALL-PURPOSE FLOUR
1 1/4	CUPS CHOPPED PECANS
1/3	CUP CONFECTIONERS SUGAR

Assemble all ingredients and utensils. In large bowl of mixer cream butter and sugar until light. Add vanilla and water; mix well. Stir in flour and pecans. Shape into 1-inch balls. Place on ungreased cookie sheet. Bake in a 325-degree oven for 15 to 20 minutes. Remove to a wire rack and cool. Sprinkle confectioners sugar over cookies until thoroughly coated. Yield: 36 cookies.

A recipe handed down for many years.

Per serving: 107 calories; 7.7 g fat; 14 mg cholesterol; 52 mg sodium.

Little Debbie Cakes

In 1933, O.D. and Ruth King McKee began selling cakes in the Chattanooga area. O. D. always had a gift for innovation and automation. He developed recipes and invented the soft Oatmeal Creme Pie. The McKees named their snack cake line after a granddaughter, Debbie.

Little Debbie is now America's leading snack cake based on volume. There are 65 varieties available. In 1960, McKee Foods became the first to package twelve individual cakes in a "family" pack. The Little Debbie line is sold in 49 states and advertised on national television.

The McKee sons, Ellsworth and Jack, grew up in the business and eventually became company officers. Several third-generation family members have made careers with the Collegedale, Tennessee, company as well. Today, McKee Foods has approximately 2,700 full-time employees in three states.

Lucille McWherter's
Vanilla Wafer Orange Balls

3/4	CUP POWDERED SUGAR
1	POUND VANILLA WAFERS, CRUSHED
1	STICK MELTED BUTTER
1	CUP CHOPPED NUTS
1	6-OUNCE CAN FROZEN ORANGE JUICE
1	CAN FLAKED COCONUT

Mix all ingredients except coconut. Shape into balls, then chill. Roll in coconut.

*M*RS. MCWHERTER HAS BEEN THE ONLY MOTHER OF A GOVERNOR IN THE LAST ONE-HUNDRED YEARS TO BE THE STATE'S FIRST LADY. HER SON, NED RAY MCWHERTER (WHO SERVED FROM 1987-1995) SENT ME SEVERAL OF HIS MOTHER'S FAVORITE RECIPES.

Miss Daisy

Adelene Cannon Maney's Tea Cakes

4	EGGS SEPARATED
3	CUPS SUGAR
1	CUP MILK
1	PINT MELTED LARD
4	TEASPOONS BAKING POWDER
2	TEASPOONS VANILLA

Add just enough flour to handle, the less flour the better. Drop from spoon on pan and bake.

*D*ATED 1857, THIS TEA CAKE RECIPE WAS USED BY RACHEL ADELENE CANNON MANEY. SHE WAS DAUGHTER OF TENNESSEE GOVERNOR NEWTON CANNON WHO SERVED FROM 1835-1839.

Miss Daisy

YES, VIRGINIA, THEY DID HANG THE ELEPHANT

*N*o doubt, in prehistoric times, the woolly ancestors of today's modern elephant roamed the wilderness of present-day Unicoi County. And, no doubt, circus elephants have played to Erwin's residents many times. But, it is to one special elephant that Erwin and Unicoi County owe their fame. That animal's name was Mary, and on a distant day in 1916, she provided the story that has forevermore become linked with this East Tennessee community. Mary was a circus elephant, and like all animals who perform under duress, she had her good days and her bad days. One day, while Mary's circus was performing in Kingsport, her temper got the best of her and she

UNICOI COUNTY

trampled one of her handlers to death. The circus owner was frantic. What if Mary were to go on the rampage again? What was he to do? The circus owner finally decided that Mary must be put to death, rather than risk another tragedy. But how? Someone said that the Clinchfield Railroad had a big crane at Erwin, and since no one had a rifle big enough to shoot and kill Mary, it was suggested that the poor pachyderm be transported there and hanged from the giant crane which was parked on the side of the tracks in downtown Erwin. After hours of pulling and pushing and chaining and re-chaining Mary, the crane finally hoisted her into the air and left her suspended for several minutes, until she was dead. Then, workers dug a huge hole right there on the spot and lowered Mary's limp body to its final destination, where it still lies buried today.

Blondies

2/3	CUP BUTTER
1	16-OUNCE BOX LIGHT BROWN SUGAR
3	EGGS
2 3/4	CUPS CAKE FLOUR
1/2	TEASPOON SALT
2 1/2	TEASPOONS BAKING POWDER
1	CUP CHOPPED PECANS
1	6-OUNCE PACKAGE CHOCOLATE CHIPS

Assemble all ingredients and utensils. In a large saucepan, melt butter. Remove from heat, stir in brown sugar. Let mixture cool. Add eggs to mixture one at a time, beating well. Sift flour, salt, and baking powder together. Add flour mixture to sugar mixture and combine. Stir in nuts and chocolate chips. Pour into greased 13x9x2-inch pan and bake in a 325-degree oven for 25 to 30 minutes. Cool and cut into squares. Yield: 16 servings.

Per serving: 348 calories; 17.6 g fat; 73 mg cholesterol; 225 mg sodium.

Purity Dairies

Miles Ezell, Sr., started Purity Dairies in 1926 on a farm, with a rented herd of cows, delivering milk from a rented truck. From this humble beginning has emerged the only remaining full-service dairy in Middle Tennessee today. During the Depression,

the growth of Ezell's Dairy was painfully slow; the real struggle being just to remain in business. Most of his 250 competitors were not so fortunate. By 1945, when Ezell moved into the small but modern milk plant he had built on Murfreesboro Road, all but about 15 were out of business. In the next few years Ezell, now joined by sons Miles, Jr., and Bill, bought out many of the remaining companies. Purity Dairies, as it was now called, was on the way to becoming the major player in the milk and ice cream market. Mr. Ezell was always particular about the quality of his dairy products. This trait led his company to be a leader in the adoption of many practices which were to later be copied by his competitors. Innovations which kept Purity in the forefront were refrigerated tanks on all dairy farms, vacuum pasteurization (which kept the "onion" flavor out of milk), non-wax milk cartons and the yellow plastic jug. In the 1960s Purity entered the mass media advertising market and scored a number of hits with the Cow and Kangaroo, Sergeant Glory, Orange-in-the-Face orange juice commercials, the nationally recognized Ernest and Vern series, and a host of others.

Frosted Brownies

Brownies

1/2	POUND BUTTER, MELTED
4	TABLESPOONS COCOA
1	CUP WATER
2	CUPS ALL-PURPOSE FLOUR
2	CUPS SUGAR
1	TEASPOON BAKING SODA
1/2	TEASPOON SALT
1/2	CUP BUTTERMILK
2	EGGS, BEATEN
1	TEASPOON VANILLA EXTRACT

Assemble all ingredients and utensils. In a saucepan, add cocoa and water to melted butter. Bring to a boil. Sift together flour, sugar, soda and salt. Add to boiling cocoa mixture alternately with a mixture of buttermilk, eggs, and vanilla. Stir until blended. Pour batter into greased 13x9-inch pan. Bake in a 350-degree oven for 15 to 20 minutes.

Frosting

1/4	POUND BUTTER, MELTED
4	TABLESPOONS COCOA
6	TABLESPOONS BUTTERMILK
1	BOX CONFECTIONERS' SUGAR
1	TEASPOON VANILLA EXTRACT
1	CUP CHOPPED PECANS OR WALNUTS

In a saucepan, combine melted butter, cocoa and buttermilk. Bring to a boil. Add sugar and vanilla, stirring until smooth. Pour over warm brownies; sprinkle with chopped nuts. Yield: 36 small squares.

Per serving: 334 calories; 18.6 g fat; 54 mg cholesterol; 285 mg sodium.

Chess Cake Squares

1   CUP BUTTER
1   1-POUND BOX LIGHT BROWN SUGAR
1/2   CUP WHITE SUGAR
4   EGGS, BEATEN
2   CUPS SIFTED ALL-PURPOSE FLOUR
1   TEASPOON BAKING POWDER
1   CUP CHOPPED PECANS
1   TEASPOON VANILLA
      CONFECTIONERS' SUGAR FOR TOPPING

Assemble all ingredients and utensils. In a saucepan, heat butter and both sugars. Add remaining ingredients except confectioners' sugar. Pour batter into a greased and floured 13x9x2-inch pan. Bake in a 300-degree oven for 45 minutes. Cool for 10 minutes. Dust with confectioners' sugar. Cut in squares. Yield: 24 squares.

The squares are wonderful served slightly warm with vanilla ice cream.

Per serving: 217 calories; 11.7 g fat; 66 mg cholesterol; 108 mg sodium.

Hello Dollies

1/2   CUP MELTED BUTTER
1 3/4 CUPS GRAHAM CRACKER CRUMBS
1   14-OUNCE CAN SWEETENED CONDENSED MILK
1   CUP CHOCOLATE CHIPS
1   CUP BUTTERSCOTCH CHIPS
1   CUP CHOPPED PECANS
1   CUP FLAKED COCONUT
1 1/2 TEASPOONS SHORTENING
1   CUP SEMISWEET CHOCOLATE CHIPS

Assemble all ingredients and utensils. In a bowl, combine butter and graham cracker crumbs. Mix well. Put into a 13x9x2-inch baking pan. Pour condensed milk over crumb layer. Cover with chocolate chips, butterscotch chips, pecans and coconut. Press firmly into pan. Bake in a 350-degree oven for 30 minutes. Cool. Combine shortening and semisweet chocolate chips in saucepan. Cook until smooth stirring constantly. Drizzle over baked squares. Yield: about 36 squares.

Per serving: 210 calories; 12.8 g fat; 12 mg cholesterol; 87 mg sodium.

RIGHT MAN, WRONG HALL OF FAME

All that Roy Acuff ever wanted to do as a youth was to play baseball. Growing up in the 1920s in Union County near Maynardsville, Acuff, although he was already beginning to appreciate music, had one primary goal in mind and that was to pitch professional baseball. He was good enough. His high school yearbook proclaimed that "having played football, baseball, and basketball, he has won for himself twelve letters, a very enviable record." And, in 1929, when scouts for the New York Yankees spotted him playing in Knoxville, they

UNION COUNTY

invited him to try out during the following year's spring training. But fate had other plans for Roy Acuff. Later in 1929, while in Florida, he suffered severe sunburn. Soon afterwards, when he attempted to play a game of baseball, he fell out from exhaustion in the second inning. Diagnosed with a case of sunstroke, Acuff was told by the doctor that he would be confined to bed for a year and that his ambitions to become a baseball player were obviously over. While in the hospital and afterwards when he returned home, Acuff started listening to WSM's Grand Ole Opry on the radio and became infatuated with the style of music played on the program. He could play that same sound, he thought. In 1938, Acuff saw his second dream come true, the first of a long series of appearances on the Grand Ole Opry, where for the next half century and more, he became a legend in his own time and, quite literally, the "king" of country music.

Luscious Lemon Bars

Pastry

2	CUPS ALL-PURPOSE FLOUR
1/2	CUP CONFECTIONERS' SUGAR
1	CUP SOFTENED BUTTER

Assemble all ingredients and utensils. In a bowl combine flour and sugar. Cut in butter, mixture is similar to a pie crust. Pat into a 13x9x2-inch pan also forming dough around sides of pan. Bake in a 350-degree oven for 20 minutes.

Filling

4	EGGS, BEATEN
2	CUPS SUGAR
4	TABLESPOONS ALL PURPOSE FLOUR
1/2	TEASPOON BAKING POWDER
4	TABLESPOONS LEMON JUICE
	GRATED RIND OF 1 LEMON
	CONFECTIONERS' SUGAR FOR TOPPING

In large bowl of mixer, mix ingredients and pour over hot crust. Bake in a 350-degree oven for 25 minutes. Cool slightly. Dust with confectioners' sugar. Cut into bars or squares. Yield: 32 servings of 1-inch squares.

Excellent made ahead of time.

Per serving: 153 calories; 6.5 g fat; 50 mg cholesterol; 73 mg sodium.

Oatmeal Macaroons

4	CUPS QUICK-COOKING OATMEAL
2	CUPS LIGHT BROWN SUGAR
1	CUP SALAD OIL
2	EGGS, BEATEN
1/2	TEASPOON SALT
1	TEASPOON ALMOND FLAVORING

Assemble all ingredients and utensils. In a bowl, mix oatmeal, sugar and oil. Let sit overnight. When ready to bake, add eggs, salt and almond flavoring to oatmeal mixture. Drop by teaspoonfuls onto greased cookie sheet. Bake in a 375-degree oven for 12 to 15 minutes. Remove when browned. Yield: 72 cookies.

Per serving: 52 calories; 3.3 g fat; 8 mg cholesterol; 18 mg sodium.

Brock Candy Company

Brock Candy Company of Chattanooga was founded by William Emerson Brock. Mr. "W. E.", as most of his associates called him, bought Trigg Candy Company and began candy manufacturing in 1909. His

salesmen began to call on retail stores with penny candies and bulk products packed in wooden pails. None of the products were individually wrapped at the time.

Throughout decades of America's growth, Brock Candy Company withstood the sugar rations during wars, overcame national economic ups and downs, and shared Mr. W. E. Brock with the United States Senate! In 1973, Paul (Pat) K. Brock was elected president of the company, thus carrying on family traditions.

Today, the company remains innovative and is known as the first American company to produce gelatin-based gummy candies (at its acquired Winona, Minnesota facility)!

Pecan Tassies

Pastry

1	3-OUNCE PACKAGE CREAM CHEESE, SOFTENED
1/2	CUP BUTTER, SOFTENED
1	CUP ALL-PURPOSE FLOUR

Assemble all ingredients and utensils. In large bowl of mixer combine softened cream cheese and butter. Mix in flour. Chill for 1 hour. Shape into 24, 1-inch balls and put in ungreased miniature muffin tins. Press dough into cups.

Filling

1	EGG, BEATEN
1	CUP LIGHT BROWN SUGAR
1	TABLESPOON BUTTER, SOFTENED
1	TEASPOON VANILLA EXTRACT
3/4	CUP CHOPPED PECANS

In large mixing bowl, combine filling and mix well. Fill centers of pastry shells. Bake in a 325-degree oven for 25 to 30 minutes. Cool slightly; but then you should remove from muffin tins while still warm. Yield: 24 tiny pecan pies.

An old favorite which will always be a family tradition.

Per serving: 115 calories; 7.9 g fat; 15 mg cholesterol; 58 mg sodium.

AN ARTIST IN THE WILDERNESS

In his time, Gilbert Gaul was one of America's most prominent artists. Born in New Jersey in 1855, Gaul was fascinated with the War Between the States, which he just barely missed serving in himself. His art recorded the agonies of the great conflict in a way that can never be forgotten. In a series of oil paintings, Gaul captured for all time the sadness of a young boy departing for battle in *Leaving Home,* a mother's joy upon receiving word from her son in *Tidings,* and the faithfulness of a horse to his stricken master in *Faithful to the End.* The anticipation of battle can almost be felt in *Waiting for Dawn,* and the odor of gun-

powder smelled in *Holding the Line at All Hazards.* When still a young man, Gilbert Gaul inherited several thousand acres of primitive farm and timber land in Van Buren County near Fall Creek Falls. Moving there in 1881, he took possession of his property and lived for a while in a small cabin situated in the vast forests of the region. It was an extremely good year for the twenty-six-year-old Gaul, because in addition to acquiring his East Tennessee acreage, he was advised that his painting, *Holding the Line at All Hazards,* had won a gold medal from the American Art Association. Gaul maintained his holdings in Van Buren County for several years before moving to Nashville in 1905, where he opened an art studio and became well-known to the city's culturally elite. He returned to New York in 1910 and died there in 1919.

Strawberry Tassies

1	CUP BUTTER, SOFTENED
1	8-OUNCE PACKAGE CREAM CHEESE, SOFTENED
2	CUPS SIFTED ALL-PURPOSE FLOUR
	STRAWBERRY JAM
	CHOPPED PECANS

Assemble all ingredients and utensils. In large bowl of mixer combine butter and cream cheese. Gradually add flour and mix well. Chill 1 hour. Pinch off pieces of dough about the size of a nickel and place in miniature muffin tins, molding into shells. Add small amount of jam to each shell and top with pecans. Bake in a 375-degree oven for 15 to 20 minutes or until shells are light brown in color. Remove and cool. Yield: about 70-75 cookies.

These cookies freeze well. A favorite for an afternoon tea or wedding reception.

Per serving: 69 calories; 4.3 g fat; 10 mg cholesterol; 35 mg sodium.

Quick and Easy Fudge

2	TABLESPOONS BUTTER
2/3	CUP EVAPORATED MILK
1 2/3	CUPS SUGAR
1/2	TEASPOON SALT
2	CUPS MINIATURE MARSHMALLOWS
1 1/2	CUPS SEMI-SWEET CHOCOLATE CHIPS
1	TEASPOON VANILLA EXTRACT
1/2	CUP CHOPPED WALNUTS, PECANS, OR CASHEWS

Assemble all ingredients and utensils. In a large saucepan over medium heat bring to a boil butter, milk, sugar, and salt. Cook 4 to 5 minutes stirring constantly. (Start timing when mixture starts to bubble around edges of pan.) Remove from heat. Stir in marshmallows, chocolate, vanilla and nuts. Stir vigorously for 1 minute, until marshmallows melt and blend. Pour batter into a greased 8x8-inch pan. Cool. Cut in squares. Yield: about 2 pounds.

Per serving: 46 calories; 2 g fat; 1 mg cholesterol; 19 mg sodium.

Holiday Candy

3	CUPS SUGAR
1	CUP LIGHT CORN SYRUP
1 1/2	CUPS HEAVY CREAM

Assemble all ingredients and utensils. In a saucepan, combine ingredients to a soft ball stage (238 degrees on candy thermometer). Beat immediately until thick and gooey.

Add the following:

1/2 POUND EACH: BRAZIL NUTS
                    WALNUTS
                    PECANS
                    CANDIED CHERRIES
                    CANDIED PINEAPPLE

Pack in buttered 13x9x2-inch baking dish and let set in refrigerator 24 hours. Keep in a cool place. Yield: about 5 pounds of candy. Slice or cut into small squares.

Great for gifts packed in a decorative tin. Recipe is from my mother-in-law's collection of old recipes.

Per serving: 290 calories; 16.1 g fat; 14 mg cholesterol; 11 mg sodium.

Pecan Pralines

2	CUPS SUGAR
1	TEASPOON SODA
1	CUP BUTTERMILK
3	TABLESPOONS BUTTER
2	CUPS PECANS

Assemble ingredients and utensils. In a large saucepan bring to a boil: sugar, soda, and buttermilk. Then add butter. Cook until soft ball stage. Remove from heat and beat until thick. Immediately add pecans. Drop by tablespoonfuls on waxed paper. Yield: about 36 pralines.

Sinfully delicious!

Per serving: 94 calories; 5.1 g fat; 3 mg cholesterol; 40 mg sodium.

Dolly Parton's
"Islands in the Stream"

3	EGGS, SEPARATED
2/3	CUP SUGAR
2	HEAPING TEASPOONS FLOUR
1	QUART MILK
1	TEASPOON VANILLA
	NUTMEG, OPTIONAL

Cream egg yolks with sugar and whip until smooth, add flour and mix well. Scald the milk, and when hot enough, add the cream mixture. Stir constantly 20 to 25 minutes until it thickens, remove from heat and add vanilla.

Boil some water. Whip egg whites and add to water until hardened. Remove with spatula and put on top of the cream mixture. Sprinkle with nutmeg. Chill.

FOLKS WHO KNOW DOLLY WELL ALL KNOW THAT SHE LOVES THIS DESSERT. OF COURSE KENNY ROGERS WOULD LIKE IT TOO SINCE IT IS NAMED FOR THEIR POPULAR DUET.
Miss Daisy

Old Fashioned Boiled Custard

1/2	GALLON MILK
9	EGGS
1 1/2	CUPS SUGAR
1/8	TEASPOONS SALT
2	TABLESPOONS CORN STARCH
4	TEASPOONS VANILLA EXTRACT

GARNISH WITH A DOLLOP OF SWEETENED CREAM AND A SPLASH OF NUTMEG. OLD RECEIPT FROM MY MOTHER-IN-LAW'S COLLECTION.
Miss Daisy

Assemble all ingredients and utensils. In top of a double boiler heat milk. In a large bowl beat eggs; add sugar, salt and cornstarch. Mix well. Pour a small amount of the hot mixture, 1/4 cup, over the egg mixture. Stir well. Combine with remaining milk and cook until thick. Flavor with vanilla and refrigerate until thoroughly chilled. Yield: 10 to 12 servings.

Per serving: 260 calories; 9.6 g fat; 228 mg cholesterol; 155 mg sodium.

Old Fashioned Gingerbread

2	EGGS, BEATEN
3/4	CUP BROWN SUGAR
3/4	CUP MOLASSES
3/4	CUP VEGETABLE OIL
2 1/2	CUPS ALL-PURPOSE FLOUR
2	TEASPOONS BAKING SODA
1/2	TEASPOON BAKING POWDER
2	TEASPOONS GINGER
1 1/2	TEASPOONS CINNAMON
1/2	TEASPOON CLOVES
1/2	TEASPOON NUTMEG
1	CUP BOILING WATER
	LEMON SAUCE, BELOW
	SWEETENED WHIPPED CREAM

Assemble all ingredients and utensils. In large bowl of mixer combine eggs, sugar, molasses and oil thoroughly. Sift dry ingredients and add to egg mixture beating well. Stir in boiling water. Pour into a greased 13x9-inch pan. Bake in a 350-degree oven for 25 minutes or until cake tests done. Yield: 16 servings.

Serve warm with Lemon Sauce or whipped cream. Wonderful.

Per serving: 357 calories; 18 g fat; 84 mg cholesterol; 196 mg sodium.

Lemon Sauce

8	TABLESPOONS BUTTER, SOFTENED
2	CUPS CONFECTIONERS' SUGAR
2	EGGS BEATEN
3	TABLESPOONS FRESHLY SQUEEZED LEMON JUICE
2	TEASPOONS GRATED LEMON RIND

Assemble all ingredients and utensils. In the top of a double boiler combine butter and sugar. Place over boiling water and stir until smooth. Stir 1/4 cup of hot mixture into beaten eggs. Return to mixture in double boiler. Cook until thickened. Add lemon juice and rind. Yield: 16 servings placed on top of gingerbread or another favorite cake or ice cream. Sauce refrigerates well and can be reheated when ready to use.

Sally Lane's Candy Farm

During the 1950s, Sally Lane Jones was widely known in West Tennessee for her delightful fruit cakes. She had been making extra Christmas money selling the cakes as ordered. In May of 1958, Sally and her husband, Jack Jones, officially began Sally Lane's Candy Farm in Paris, Tennessee. They developed several products, then sold the company to Mr. and Mrs. Ken Hanna in 1973.

The Hanna family continued the traditions of Sally Lane's for nine years before selling the business to Jean and Jerry Peterson in October of 1982. The Petersons have extended the line of confections to include a variety of hand-dipped chocolates, pecan logs, peanut brittle, pecan divinity, pralines, and sugar-free candies. The pink and green peppermints are the specialty of the shop. And, they still make "Miss Sally's" fruit cakes without citron or peels.

Sally Lane's Candy Farm is located just thirteen miles west of Kentucky Lake. Tourists from around the world stop by, and mail orders come from all over the United States.

Favorite Strawberry Dessert

2   CUPS WATER
1   CUP SUGAR
1   6-OUNCE PACKAGE STRAWBERRY GELATIN
1   TABLESPOON LEMON JUICE
1   QUART FRESH STRAWBERRIES, SLICED
1   CUP HEAVY CREAM, WHIPPED
1   16-OUNCE OR LARGE ANGEL FOOD CAKE,
     TORN IN PIECES
     WHIPPED CREAM FOR TOPPING AND WHOLE
     STRAWBERRIES

Assemble all ingredients and utensils. In a saucepan bring water and sugar to a boil. Stir in gelatin and lemon juice. Let stand until partially set. Fold in strawberries and 1 cup whipped cream. Fold in cake pieces. Pour into a 2-quart dish. When ready to serve top with whipped cream and a fresh strawberry. Yield: 24 squares.

Friends from Humboldt, Tennessee, gave this recipe.

Per serving: 194 calories; 5.6 g fat; 19 mg cholesterol; 75 mg sodium.

Standard Candy Company

In 1912, in a copper kettle at the Standard Candy Company at Clark and First Avenue in Nashville, the world's first-ever combination candy bar was invented! A round mound of caramel, marshmallow, fresh roasted peanuts, and pure milk chocolate were combined into a renegade circular shape. For a time, it was impossible to ask for the new candy by name since no one could decide what to call the delicious thick clusters of candy!

The story of how the candy came to be named is varied. Some people say it was named Goo Goo because it is the first thing a baby says. But Howell Campbell, Jr., whose father invented the Goo Goo Cluster, says Mr. Campbell, Sr. rode the streetcar everyday and talked the matter over with fellow passengers. He maintains that the name Goo Goo was suggested to Mr. Campbell one morning by a lady schoolteacher.

At first, Goo Goos were hand-dipped and sold without wrappers under glass at drugstore candy counters. Later, with the dawn of hand-wrapping, four ladies would swaddle the Goo Goos in tin foil . . . a look nearly duplicated today by the shiny silver labels with the Goo Goo logo in red letters.

Another old fashioned item that Standard Candy Company manufactures is King Leo, "the pure stick candy that roars with flavor." It comes in four flavors: peppermint, clove, lemon, and vanilla.

Chocolate Cheesecake

Crust

1	8 1/2-OUNCE BOX THIN CHOCOLATE WAFERS, CRUSHED
3/4	CUP BUTTER, MELTED
1/4	TEASPOON CINNAMON

Assemble ingredients and utensils. In a large bowl combine crushed wafers with butter and cinnamon. Press into bottom and sides of a 9-inch spring form pan. Chill.

Filling

1	12-OUNCE PACKAGE SEMISWEET CHOCOLATE MORSELS
2	POUNDS CREAM CHEESE, SOFTENED
2	CUPS SUGAR
4	EGGS, ROOM TEMPERATURE
3	TEASPOON COCOA
2	TEASPOONS VANILLA
2	CUPS SOUR CREAM

Assemble ingredients and utensils. Melt chocolate in top of double-boiler over warm water. In large bowl of mixer, beat softened cheese until fluffy and smooth. Gradually beat in sugar, then eggs, one at a time. Add melted chocolate, cocoa and vanilla. Stir in sour cream and pour into chilled crust. Bake in a 350-degree oven for 60 to 70 minutes until knife comes out clean when tested for doneness. Cool at room temperature and then refrigerate several hours before serving. Yield: 18-20 servings.

Beautiful and delicious for a dinner party. Can be made several days ahead of party. A vanilla, raspberry, or lemon sauce is delightful served with this cheesecake.

Per serving: 502 calories; 36.2 g fat; 134 mg cholesterol; 321 mg sodium.

Casey Jones Village

In Jackson, Tennessee, the life of legendary folk-hero Casey Jones inspired the creation of a museum and village around the

home in which he was living at the time of his death.

J. L. (John Luther) Jones was the real name of the celebrated railroad man immortalized in 1903 by the song *Casey Jones, the Brave Engineer* (*see* Madison County, p. 135). At Brooks Shaw's Old Country Store over 15,000 items of southern country antiques are displayed. There is an 1890s ice cream parlor and outside is the 100-ton Baldwin engine No. 382 similar to the one on which Casey Jones rode on April 30, 1900.

Miss Daisy's
Tennessee Cheesecake

Crust

1 1/3	CUPS GRAHAM CRACKER CRUMBS
3	TABLESPOONS BUTTER, SOFTENED
2	TABLESPOONS SUGAR

Assemble all ingredients and utensils. Mix together crumbs, butter and sugar. Press mixture firmly and evenly in bottom of ungreased 9-inch springform pan. Bake in a 350-degree oven for 10 minutes. Cool.

Filling

5	8-OUNCE PACKAGES CREAM CHEESE, SOFTENED
1 3/4	CUPS SUGAR
3	TABLESPOONS ALL-PURPOSE FLOUR
1/4	TEASPOON SALT
5	EGGS
2	EGG YOLKS
1	TEASPOON VANILLA EXTRACT
1/4	CUP HEAVY CREAM

Assemble all ingredients and utensils. In large bowl of mixer, beat cream cheese, sugar, flour, salt and 2 eggs until smooth. Continue beating, adding remaining 3 eggs and the egg yolks, one at a time until blended. Stir in vanilla and heavy cream.

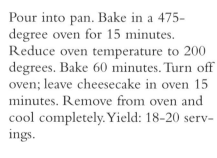

Pour into pan. Bake in a 475-degree oven for 15 minutes. Reduce oven temperature to 200 degrees. Bake 60 minutes. Turn off oven; leave cheesecake in oven 15 minutes. Remove from oven and cool completely. Yield: 18-20 servings.

This delicious cheesecake is very versatile to serve as is or with your favorite sauce. Will keep up to 14 days covered in the refrigerator.

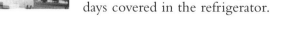

Per serving: 345 calories; 24.9 g fat; 166 mg cholesterol; 267 mg sodium.

Tennessee Blackberry Cobbler

4	CUP FRESH BLACKBERRIES OR
24	OUNCES FROZEN BLACKBERRIES, THAWED AND DRAINED
1 1/2	CUPS SUGAR
3	TABLESPOONS ALL-PURPOSE FLOUR
1	TABLESPOON FRESH LEMON JUICE
3	TABLESPOONS BUTTER

Assemble all ingredients and utensils. Fruit mixture: toss berries, sugar and flour, place in an ungreased 9-inch baking dish. Sprinkle berries with lemon juice and dot with butter, set aside.

2	CUPS ALL-PURPOSE FLOUR
1/4	TEASPOON SALT
1	TABLESPOON BAKING POWDER
1	CUP HEAVY CREAM, WHIPPED
1	TABLESPOON SUGAR

Assemble all ingredients and utensils. In a large bowl mix flour, salt and baking powder. Gently fold cream into flour mixture. Place dough on floured board and knead for 1 minute. Roll dough to 1/2 inch thickness. Cut into lattice strips or place the entire sheet of dough on cobbler. Sprinkle with sugar. Bake in a 400-degree oven for 10 to 12 minutes then reduce heat to 325 degrees and bake another 20 minutes or until golden brown. Yield: 8 servings.

Per serving: 475 calories; 15.9 g fat; 52 mg cholesterol; 282 mg sodium.

Easy Peach Cobbler

3/4	CUP ALL-PURPOSE FLOUR
1	CUP SUGAR
2	TEASPOONS BAKING POWDER
1/8	TEASPOON SALT
3/4	CUP MILK
6	TABLESPOONS BUTTER
2	CUPS SLICED, FRESH PEACHES (FRUIT/BERRIES)
1	CUP SUGAR

Assemble all ingredients and utensils. Combine in a bowl, flour, sugar, baking powder, milk and salt. In a 2-quart baking dish, melt butter. Pour batter over melted butter. Toss peaches with 1 cup sugar and pour over batter. Do not stir. Bake in a 350 degree oven for 60 minutes or until brown and bubbly. Yield: 6 servings.

Per serving: 459 calories; 12.7 g fat; 35 mg cholesterol; 292 mg sodium.

EYEWITNESS TO THE TRAIL OF TEARS

It is difficult to imagine the misery and suffering that the Cherokee people of Tennessee and Georgia experienced in the fall of 1838, when they began the long trek to present-day Oklahoma. The Cherokees had been native to the region for hundreds of years, and at one time were the masters of an even larger area that included, in addition to Tennessee and Georgia, parts of North and South Carolina, Virginia, and Kentucky. Now, as wards of the federal government, they were being forced off their traditional lands so that greedy white men could claim

WARREN COUNTY

the gold that had recently been discovered there. The removal of the Cherokees and other eastern tribes had been plotted during President Andrew Jackson's administration, but now Martin Van Buren was president, and his feelings toward Indians were the same as his mentor. Accordingly, as the cool winds of autumn began to stir among the forested slopes of Southern Appalachia, the U. S. Army rounded up thousands of Cherokee men, women, and children and started them on the long journey west. Ten thousand Cherokees passed through Warren County during the "Trail of Tears" episode. Accompanying them were five thousand horses, 646 wagons, and hundreds of cattle and oxen. The Indians pitched makeshift camps at several locations, including Martin's Ford, one near Shellsford, and another on the old Shelbyville Road. It is said that for years afterwards, one could see mounds of rocks marking the graves of those who died along the way.

Martha Ingram's Chocolate Mousse

4	SQUARES UNSWEETENED CHOCOLATE
1	CARTON OF UNSALTED BUTTER
1	TEASPOON VANILLA EXTRACT
3/4	CUP CONFECTIONERS' SUGAR
6	EGG YOLKS
6	EGG WHITES
1/3	CUP MILK
3	DOZEN LADYFINGERS

Melt chocolate in double boiler. Cream butter and sugar. Add egg yolks and milk. Place all in double boiler and cook until thick. Cool.

Put egg whites in large mixing bowl. Add salt and beat until stiff. Add 3/4 cup confectioners' sugar. Fold the chocolate mixture into the egg whites. Add vanilla.

Split the ladyfingers (about 3 dozen) and line the spring pan on bottom and sides. Pour in half of the mixture, add more ladyfingers and the rest of mixture, and cover top with ladyfingers. Place in icebox overnight. Remove from pan to plate and cover with lightly whipped cream. You may sprinkle with grated chocolate or chopped nuts.

Pass and allow guests to serve themselves.

*W*HEN I SPOKE WITH MARTHA ABOUT THE BICENTENNIAL COOKBOOK SHE TOLD ME THAT THE RECIPE SHE SENT FOR CHOCOLATE MOUSSE WAS A SPECIALTY OF HER MOTHER'S. MARTHA INGRAM IS CHAIRWOMAN OF THE BOARD FOR INGRAM INDUSTRIES AND ALSO CHAIRS THE TENNESSEE 200 BICENTENNIAL CELEBRATION.

Miss Daisy

Chocolate Mousse

4	OUNCES UNSWEETENED CHOCOLATE
8	EGGS, SEPARATED
1	CUP CONFECTIONERS' SUGAR, SIFTED
1 1/2	OUNCES BOURBON
3/4	CUP HEAVY CREAM, WHIPPED
1	TABLESPOON SUGAR

Assemble all ingredients and utensils. In a heavy saucepan, melt chocolate. In a bowl, beat yolks, adding confectioners' sugar gradually, until yolks are pale yellow. Slowly mix yolks into chocolate over low heat until very smooth. Add bourbon. Beat egg whites until almost stiff. Fold whites into chocolate mixture until no whites show. Pour into desired individual dishes or oiled mold. Cover. Refrigerate overnight. When ready to serve combine whipped cream and sugar and garnish Mousse. Yield: 8 servings.

Per serving: 290 calories; 19.4 g fat; 304 mg cholesterol; 78 mg sodium.

You may substitute one tablespoon vanilla extract for the bourbon. I especially like to prepare this recipe for dinner parties because it is made the day before—a really delicious time saver.

Miss Daisy

Old Recipe Banana Pudding

1 1/2   CUPS SUGAR
1/4   CUP ALL-PURPOSE FLOUR
1/2   TEASPOON SALT
4   CUPS WHOLE MILK
6   EGG YOLKS, BEATEN
1   TABLESPOON VANILLA EXTRACT
1   16-OUNCE PACKAGE VANILLA WAFERS
4   BANANAS, SLICED
6   EGG WHITES
1/2   CUP SUGAR

Assemble all ingredients and utensils. In top of double boiler, combine 1 1/2 cups sugar, flour, and salt. Stir in milk. Cook over boiling water until thickened, stirring constantly. Remove from heat. Stir a small amount of hot mixture, 1/4 cup, into egg yolks. Return egg yolk mixture to hot mixture in double boiler. Cook over boiling water, stirring constantly for about 5 minutes. Remove from heat. Stir in vanilla.

Layer wafers, bananas, and custard alternately in a 2-quart baking dish. Beat egg whites until stiff and peaks form. Beat in 1/2 cup sugar. Spread over top of pudding. Bake in a 350-degree oven for 8 to 10 minutes or until lightly browned. Yield: 10 to 12 servings.

Per serving: 439 calories; 12.1 g fat; 163 mg cholesterol; 259 mg sodium.

Grandma Buddy's Date Nut Pudding

Cut fine one pound of dates. Add 2 teaspoons baking soda and one cup boiling water. Let stand while you mix the following:

Cream 1 tablespoon butter with 1 cup sugar. Add 1 beaten egg. Combine 1 1/4 cups flour and 1 teaspoon baking powder; combine all ingredients. Add 1/2 teaspoon vanilla and 1 cup chopped nuts. Bake slowly 25 minutes. Serve with whipped cream.

Warrenton Old English Plum Puddings

The Warrenton story begins in the late 1600s, when the Warrens, a family of Virginia settlers, began to recreate a cherished recipe that they had brought to the New World from England. This recipe was handed down from generation to generation, and came to a Nashville belle named Nancy Warren deLuca.

Every year during the holidays, Nancy prepared her recipe of traditional plum pudding to send to all of her friends. In 1936, Nancy began to sell her puddings to support herself and her two young children. She also began making a prized buttery Holiday Cake.

In 1956, Nancy sold the business and personally instructed the new owners in the preparation of the products. Today, Warrenton Ltd. provides detail and personal service to customers through custom orders.

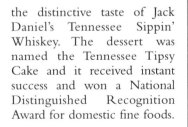
Bread Pudding

4	LARGE HOMEMADE BISCUITS, CRUMBLED
1	EGG, BEATEN
1	CUP APPLESAUCE
1/4	CUP SHREDDED COCONUT
1	CUP MILK
1	CUP BROWN SUGAR
1/4	CUP FINELY CHOPPED PECANS
1	TEASPOON VANILLA EXTRACT

Assemble all ingredients and utensils. In a large bowl mix all ingredients and pour into a 1 1/2-quart buttered casserole. Bake in a 350-degree oven for 50 to 60 minutes. Top with Whiskey Sauce below (optional). Yield: 6 to 8 servings.

Whiskey Sauce

1 1/2	CUPS SUGAR
1	5.33-OUNCE CAN EVAPORATED MILK
4	TABLESPOONS MARGARINE
1	EGG, BEATEN
3	TABLESPOONS WHISKEY

In top of double boiler, combine all ingredients, except whiskey. Place over boiling water and cook, stirring well until thick. Keep warm until serving time or make ahead and keep refrigerated. Just before serving while warm, add whiskey. Yield: 1 1/2 cups.

Per serving: 511 calories; 17.5 g fat; 79 mg cholesterol; 225 mg sodium.

Pepper Patch
Tennessee Tipsy Sauce

1	CUP CONFECTIONERS' SUGAR
4	TABLESPOONS REAL BUTTER
3-4	TABLESPOONS JACK DANIEL'S BLACK LABEL WHISKEY

Soften butter to room temperature, add sugar, beat well. Add Jack Daniel's to taste and refrigerate 2 hours before serving. Yield: approximately 1 1/2 cups.

Coconut Topped
Sweet Potato Pudding

3	CUPS GRATED RAW SWEET POTATOES
1/2	CUP BUTTER
1 1/2	CUPS WHOLE MILK
3	EGGS
1 1/2	CUPS SUGAR
1/2	TEASPOON EACH: GROUND CINNAMON, NUTMEG, CLOVES AND ALLSPICE
1	TEASPOON VANILLA EXTRACT
1	TEASPOON SALT

Topping

1/2	CUP SHREDDED COCONUT
1/4	CUP CHOPPED PECANS

Assemble all ingredients and utensils. In a large bowl mix all ingredients except topping. Place in a 2-quart baking dish. Bake, covered in a 350-degree oven for 45 minutes. Remove cover and add topping. Continue baking uncovered for 15 minutes. Serve warm. Yield: 8 to 10 servings.

A very old fashioned recipe which is popular all over the South.

Per serving: 347 calories; 17.6 g fat; 112 mg cholesterol; 364 mg sodium.

THE BRITISH COLONISTS WHO CAME TO AMERICA BROUGHT WITH THEM A LOVE OF PUDDINGS. SOME WERE BAKED IN A CRUST, OTHERS WITHOUT A CRUST. THE BASIC INGREDIENTS WERE MILK, EGGS, SUGAR, SPICES, AND THE FRUIT OR VEGETABLE OF THEIR CHOICE. NO MATTER HOW MANY TIMES PUDDING WAS OR IS SERVED FOR DESSERT IT REMAINS A FAVORITE.

Miss Daisy

Southern Rice Pudding

2	CUPS MILK
1/2	CUP UNCOOKED WHITE RICE
1/4	TEASPOON SALT
3	EGG YOLKS
3	TABLESPOONS SUGAR
3/4	CUP HEAVY CREAM
1	CUP RAISINS OR CHOPPED DATES

Assemble all ingredients and utensils. In top of double boiler, bring milk to a boil; stir in rice and salt. Continue cooking over hot water until milk is absorbed, about 30 minutes. Beat egg yolks with sugar and cream. Combine with rice mixture. Add raisins or dates. Pour into a 2-quart casserole. Bake in a 350-degree oven until top is brown about 15 minutes. Yield: 6 to 8 servings.

A dessert staple for many years.

Per serving: 259 calories; 12.6 g fat; 141 mg cholesterol; 111 mg sodium.

DURING THE WAR BETWEEN THE STATES, ACCORDING TO SOME RUTLEDGE FAMILY DESCENDANTS, A RECIPE FOR "POOR MAN'S" RICE PUDDING WAS USED. A QUART OF MILK WAS SWEETENED TO TASTE, POURED IN A DISH WITH A SMALL TEACUP OF RICE AND A SPOONFUL OF BUTTER AND BAKED FOR ONE HOUR.

Miss Daisy

Woodford Pudding

3   TABLESPOONS BUTTER, SOFTENED
1   CUP SUGAR
3   EGGS, BEATEN
3/4   CUP ALL-PURPOSE FLOUR
1   CUP BLACKBERRY JAM
1   TEASPOON BAKING SODA
3   TABLESPOONS BUTTERMILK
1/2   TEASPOON EACH: GROUND CLOVES, GROUND ALLSPICE
1/2   CUP RAISINS
1/2   CUP CHOPPED PECANS
      CARAMEL SAUCE OR WHIPPED CREAM, OPTIONAL

Assemble all ingredients and utensils. In large bowl of mixer cream butter and sugar. Stir in eggs. Mix in flour, jam and soda-buttermilk mixture. Fold in raisins and pecans. Pour batter into a greased 13x9x2-inch pan. Bake in a 350-degree oven for 30 minutes or until done. Serve warm topped with caramel sauce or whipped cream. Yield: 8 servings.

A favorite Tennessee dessert for many years, handed down from our friends in Kentucky.

Per serving: 390 calories; 11 g fat; 114 mg cholesterol; 185 mg sodium.

Mrs. Cordell Hull's Charlotte Rousse

MRS. CORDELL HULL IS FAMOUS FOR HER QUOTE, "FOOD IS AN AMBASSADOR OF GOOD WILL. IT IS A LINK BETWEEN OUR PAST AND THE PRESENT."

Miss Daisy

1/2   ENVELOPE OF GELATIN
2   PINTS OF CREAM
6   EGG WHITES

Dissolve gelatin in cold water. Let it stand until it swells. Beat egg whites stiff. Whip cream. Sweeten and flavor to taste. Fold whipped cream in egg whites. Add dissolved gelatin and stir in thoroughly. Place in icebox until ready to use. Serve with Lady Fingers.

James K. Polk
Memorial Association
Charlotte Rousse

Take an ounce of isinglass, quite fine, dissolve it in a coffee cup of water, and let it simmer slowly until it is reduced to less than a quarter. Next take a stick of vanilla and put it in a cup and a half of milk, sweeten it to your taste, and let it boil slowly fifteen minutes. Then take the yolks of four eggs, beat them a little, and when the milk is so cooled that it will not cook the eggs, stir them carefully in. Put the milk again over the fire, and the eggs; keep stirring until thick, (it must on no account boil), then put it through a sieve. Put the isinglass through too, but keep them separate. Cover the bottom and sides of your mould with finger biscuits, neatly fitted into each other, and set the mould in a pail of ice. Beat a pint of cream, and mix all together, milk, isinglass, and cream, and pour it into the mould; cover the mould and lay ice over it, and leave it in the ice three hours. The cream should be beaten just before you are ready to put it into the ice.

—from *The Improved Housewife, or Book of Receipts, by a Married Lady* published in 1847, found in Mrs. Polk's library with her name inscribed inside the front cover.

*"I would bring the government
back to what it was
intended to be—a plain
economical government."*
—saying of James K. Polk in 1830.

James K. Polk

James K. Polk (1795—1849), Tennessee's second resident to be elected president of the United States, moved to Columbia from North Carolina when he was a boy. Receiving his elementary education in Murfreesboro, Polk later pursued a law degree before returning to Columbia to open his practice. He was virtually unknown outside Tennessee and Washington, D. C., when he was nominated for the presidency in 1844. Elected as the nation's first "dark-horse" candidate, President Polk achieved the unique distinction among American chief executives of fulfilling all of his campaign promises, in addition to adding more than one million square miles of territory to the continental United States.

Pauline Gore's Flan

Beat together:

4	EGG YOLKS
4	EGGS
1	CUP SUGAR

Heat:

2	CUPS WHIPPING CREAM
2	CUPS MILK

Pour hot liquid over eggs and sugar. Vanilla to taste. Caramelize about 3/4 cup sugar and pour into casserole, then pour other ingredients. Cook at 350 degrees about 45 minutes, until desired thickness.

*M*RS. GORE IS WIFE OF SENATOR ALBERT GORE, SR. AND MOTHER OF THE VICE PRESIDENT OF THE UNITED STATES, ALBERT GORE, JR. I UNDERSTAND SHE IS A MARVELOUS COOK. THIS FLAN RECIPE IS DELIGHTFUL.

Miss Daisy

Chilled Lime Soufflé

1	ENVELOPE PLAIN GELATIN
1/4	CUP COLD WATER
4	EGG YOLKS, LIGHTLY BEATEN
1	CUP SUGAR
1/2	CUP LIME JUICE
1/2	TEASPOON SALT
1	TABLESPOON GRATED LIME RIND
6	EGG WHITES
1	CUP HEAVY CREAM, WHIPPED
	TOASTED COCONUT FLAKES

*Y*OU WILL BE VERY HAPPY WITH THE WONDERFUL COMPLIMENTS YOU RECEIVE WHEN YOU SERVE THIS DISH. THE SAME RECIPE IS GREAT USING LEMONS.

Miss Daisy

Assemble all ingredients and utensils. Sprinkle gelatin over cold water in a small bowl, to soften. In top of double boiler, mix egg yolks with 1/2 cup sugar, lime juice and salt. Cook over simmering water, stirring constantly with whisk, until slightly thickened. Remove from heat. Add gelatin and lime rind, stirring until gelatin is completely dissolved. Cool. Beat egg whites until they hold a soft shape; beat in remaining sugar a tablespoon at a time until mixture is stiff. Fold in lime mixture and whipped cream. Pour into a 1 1/2-quart oiled soufflé dish, which has a foil collar around it extending above rim. Chill until set. To serve, remove collar and springform pan. Top with toasted coconut flakes. Yield: 6 servings.

Per serving: 362 calories; 20.4 g fat; 236 mg cholesterol; 266 mg sodium.

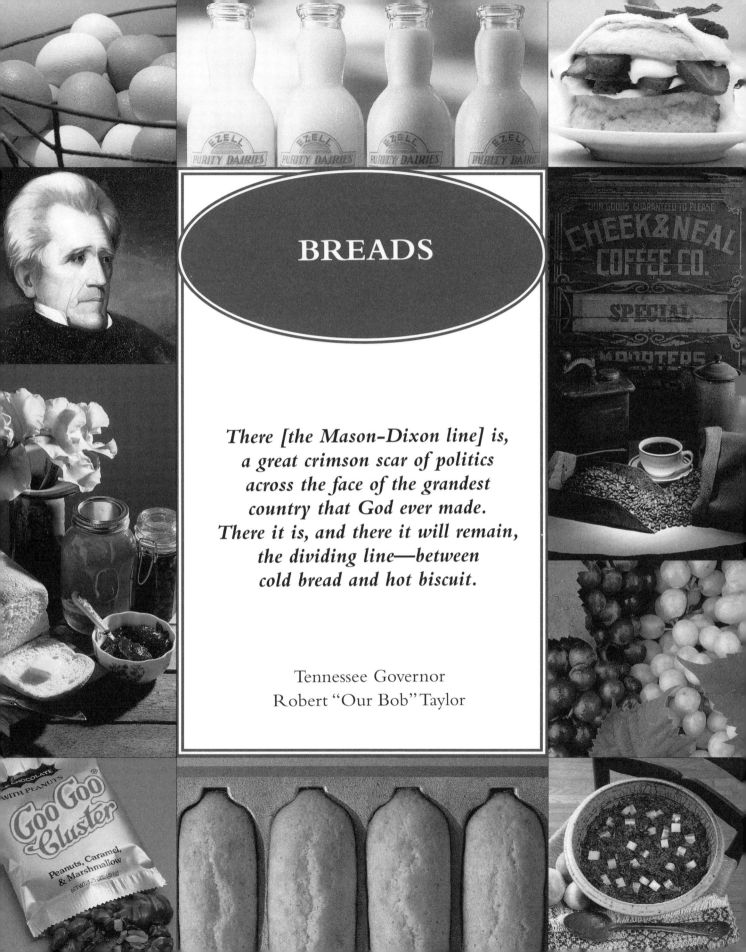

BREADS

*There [the Mason–Dixon line] is,
a great crimson scar of politics
across the face of the grandest
country that God ever made.
There it is, and there it will remain,
the dividing line—between
cold bread and hot biscuit.*

Tennessee Governor
Robert "Our Bob" Taylor

BREADS

Angel Biscuits

5	CUPS ALL-PURPOSE FLOUR
4	TABLESPOONS SUGAR
1	TABLESPOON BAKING POWDER
1	TEASPOON SALT
1	TEASPOON BAKING SODA
3/4	CUP BUTTER
1	ENVELOPE DRY YEAST
3	TABLESPOONS WARM WATER
2	CUPS BUTTERMILK
1/8	CUP MELTED BUTTER

Assemble all ingredients and utensils. In a deep bowl, sift dry ingredients together; cut in butter with fork or pastry blender until mixture is crumbly. Dissolve yeast in water. Stir yeast and buttermilk into flour mixture. Roll out onto a floured board about 1/2-inch thickness. Cut with biscuit cutter. Brush with melted butter. Place on a baking sheet and bake in a 400-degree oven 10 to 12 minutes or until brown. Yield: 24 to 36 biscuits depending on size of your biscuit cutter.

These biscuits melt in your mouth.

Per serving: 109 calories; 5 g fat; 13 mg cholesterol; 178 mg sodium.

DANIEL BOONE'S BEAR

Along with Davy Crockett and Kit Carson, there is probably no more legendary figure in American history than Daniel Boone. Born in Pennsylvania in 1734, Boone migrated to North Carolina, where he became involved with Judge Richard Henderson, a land speculator and developer of Transylvania, a settlement colony located in present-day Tennessee and Kentucky. In fact, it was Boone who, shortly after Henderson acquired the land, blazed a trail for Henderson through Cumberland Gap in 1775, anticipating the large movement of settlers along the Wilderness Road to Kentucky to settle the Transylvania lands. But Boone was already familiar with much of the

WASHINGTON COUNTY

trans-Appalachian wilderness long before his work carried him to Kentucky. As early as 1760, the frontiersman was exploring the remote recesses of Tennessee. There, in present-day Washington County, he left a calling card that was visible for many years afterwards. The twenty-six year old Boone had only recently left his home in Yadkin County, North Carolina, on an exploring trip, when some Indians caught up with him about six miles north of today's Johnson City. He hid under a small waterfall until he was sure that the Indians had given up the search and that it was safe to continue his journey. On the same trip, and in the same neighborhood, he carved in the trunk of a tree that "D. Boon Cilled a bar on tree in year 1760." The giant beech tree stood until about 1920 when it was destroyed by a storm.

Beaten Biscuits

3	CUPS SIFTED ALL-PURPOSE FLOUR
1/2	TEASPOON SUGAR
1/2	TEASPOON SALT
3	TABLESPOONS COLD BUTTER
3	TABLESPOONS COLD LARD OR VEGETABLE SHORTENING
1/2	CUP COLD MILK
1/2	CUP COLD WATER

Assemble all ingredients and utensils. Sift flour, sugar and salt into a bowl. Add butter and lard; blend with pastry blender or forks until mixture looks like coarse corn meal. Add milk and water, tossing mixture with a fork. Knead 15 minutes; then beat with rolling pin or mallet for 20 minutes, or until blistered. Roll dough 1/2-inch thick or less. Cut with small floured biscuit cutter. Prick tops 3 times with a fork. Place on baking pan. Bake in a 325-degree oven for 25 to 30 minutes. Biscuits will be a very light brown. Serve cold. Yield: about 34 to 36 biscuits

Per serving: 55 calories; 2 g fat; 4 mg cholesterol; 41 mg sodium.

*S*ERVE FOR THE HOLIDAYS WITH COUNTRY HAM. A TRULY SOUTHERN DELICACY! THESE NEED TO BE SERVED WITH THE TRAVELLERS REST/OVERTON HAM RECIPES (*SEE* P. 77).

Miss Daisy

Buttermilk Biscuits

1	CUP ALL-PURPOSE FLOUR
2	TEASPOONS BAKING POWDER
1/4	TEASPOON SALT
1/4	TEASPOON SODA
2 1/2	TABLESPOONS VEGETABLE SHORTENING OR BUTTER
1/2	CUP BUTTERMILK

Assemble all ingredients and utensils. In a deep bowl, sift dry ingredients; cut in shortening. Add buttermilk all at once and stir into a ball of dough. Knead lightly. Roll out onto a floured board into 1/2-inch thickness. Cut with a biscuit cutter. Place on a baking sheet and bake in a 450-degree oven for 10 to 12 minutes. Yield: 12 biscuits.

Per serving: 63 calories; 3 g fat; 0 mg cholesterol; 131 mg sodium.

*T*HESE BISCUITS HAVE UNIVERSAL APPEAL. THEY ARE LIGHT, MOIST, AND FLAKY. THE BUTTERMILK ENHANCES THE FLAVOR OF THE RECIPE. BISCUITS ARE DONE WHEN GOLDEN BROWN AND SPRINGY TO THE TOUCH. TRY THEM WITH PRESERVES OR JAM (*SEE* PP. 158-159). DELICIOUS.

Miss Daisy

Cracklin' Corn Bread

1 1/2   CUPS PLAIN CORN MEAL
3/4   CUP ALL-PURPOSE FLOUR
1/2   TEASPOON SODA
1/4   TEASPOON SALT
1   CUP BUTTERMILK
1   CUP CRACKLINS, CHOPPED

Assemble all ingredients and utensils. In a bowl, sift together corn meal, flour, soda and salt. Add buttermilk and cracklins; stir well. Pour into a greased 9x9x2-inch pan or 9-inch skillet which has been greased and heated. Bake in a 400-degree oven for 30 minutes.

Tennessee Corn Bread

2   EGGS
2   CUPS BUTTERMILK
1   TEASPOON BAKING SODA
2   CUPS WHITE PLAIN CORN MEAL
1   TEASPOON SALT
1   TEASPOON SUGAR

Assemble all ingredients and utensils. Preheat oven to 450 degrees. Generously grease a 9x9x2-inch pan or 8-inch iron skillet. Heat in oven while mixing batter. In a bowl beat eggs and add buttermilk. In a separate bowl combine remaining ingredients and mix well. Add egg-buttermilk mixture. Beat with rotary beater or vigorously by hand until smooth. Bake in a 450-degree oven for 20 to 25 minutes. Serve hot! Yield: 8 or 9 servings.

Per serving: 153 calories; 2 g fat; 63 mg cholesterol; 401 mg sodium.

Corn Light Bread

2   CUPS PLAIN CORN MEAL
3/4   CUPS SUGAR
1/2   CUP FLOUR
1/4   TEASPOON SODA
1   TEASPOON SALT
2   CUPS BUTTERMILK
3   TABLESPOONS SHORTENING, MELTED

Assemble all ingredients and utensils. In a bowl, mix dry ingredients with buttermilk and shortening. Pour into a greased loaf pan. Bake in a 350 degree oven for 45 minutes or until done. Turn out on a rack and cool. Yield: 1 loaf, 8 to 12 servings.

Per serving: 194 calories; 4 g fat; 1 mg cholesterol; 238 mg sodium.

THE "BADDEST" OF THE BAD MEN

Today, the name Robert Clay Allison doesn't mean much to folks in Wayne County. There was a time, however, whether local citizens wanted to admit it or not, that Clay, who became one of the country's most notorious outlaws, was the county's most noted product. Born in 1841, Allison served with Nathan Bedford Forrest during the War Between the States and probably saw duty as a spy. Captured by Union forces during the Battle of Shiloh, Clay soon escaped and eventually migrated to Texas, where he worked for the famed cattleman, Charles

WAYNE COUNTY

Goodnight. Clay reportedly killed his first man in Wayne County while he was on medical leave from the Confederate army. Allison spied a Union officer snooping around his mother's farm and promptly shot him. After migrating to Texas, and then to New Mexico, he spearheaded an effort to hang an incarcerated murderer named Kennedy. Allison demonstrated his maniacal temperament when he cut off Kennedy's head and sported it in a local saloon. In 1874, he shot and killed a man at Clifton House, New Mexico, over a horse race. And, in 1875, he was involved in a second lynching after which he gleefully dragged the body of the victim about the countryside. Clay, after a brief life as badman and outlaw, returned to Texas where he settled down on a ranch near the small town of Pecos. There, at the age of forty-six, while driving a wagon from town where he had just purchased supplies for his ranch, he fell and fractured his skull, dying shortly afterwards.

Andrew Johnson

Andrew Johnson (1808—1875), fell heir to the office of the presidency of the United States upon Abraham Lincoln's assassination in April 1865. Born in North Carolina, Johnson emigrated to Greeneville, Tennessee, and opened a tailor shop in that town. He soon was elected mayor of Greeneville. Later, he became a state legislator, U. S. congressman, governor of Tennessee, U. S. senator, and vice-president.

President Andrew Johnson did not move into the White House until three weeks after President Lincoln's death. In August of 1865, his invalid wife Eliza and their children, Martha, Mary, Robert, and Andrew, Jr. came to reside with him at 1600 Pennsylvania Avenue. Another son, Charles, had died during the Civil War.

When daughter Martha looked after her father's meals, she instructed the White House cooks to make one of his favorite foods—buckwheat cakes—in the manner which she made them for him. In later years, the family recipe was given to a great-granddaughter, Martha Willingham.

Andrew Johnson's Favorite Buckwheat Cakes

In the evening mix:

1	QUART OF BUCKWHEAT FLOUR
4	TABLESPOONS OF YEAST
1	TEASPOON OF SALT
1	HANDFUL OF INDIAN MEAL
2	TABLESPOONS OF MOLASSES (NOT SYRUP)
	WARM WATER, ENOUGH TO MAKE A THIN BATTER

Beat very well and sit to rise in a warm place. If the batter is the least bit sour in the morning, stir in a very little soda, dissolved in hot water. Mix in an earthen crock and leave some in the bottom each morning, a cupful or so, to serve as a sponge for the next night, instead of getting fresh yeast. In cold weather this plan can be sucessfully pursued for a week or ten days, without setting a new supply. Of course, you must add the usual quantity of flour etc., every night, and beat well. Do not make your cakes too small. Buckwheats should be of generous size.

"We are swinging 'round the circle."
—Saying of Andrew Johnson on the Presidential Reconstruction Tour, August 1866.

Dear Mr. Lawing,

This is a copy of the recipe I sent Miss Ervin. In my letter to her I added the fact that I had lived with my grandmother, Martha Johnson Patterson, in the Johnson home until I was fourteen—that I had seen the recipe mixed by the cook in the basement kitchen.... Also, that this was the only recipe I could state positively that she had said was a favorite of her father's, and that she had taught the White House cooks to make it her way for him. I doubt this is of any value to you, and if not, tear it up.

Cordially,

Martha L. Willingham

Falls Mill
Harvest Bread

2	PACKAGES DRY YEAST
1 2/3	CUPS WARM SKIM MILK (105 TO 115 DEGREES)
3 1/3	CUPS BREAD FLOUR, DIVIDED
1 1/2	CUPS RYE FLOUR
1 1/2	CUPS WHOLE WHEAT FLOUR
1	CUP STONE-GROUND CORN MEAL
3/4	CUP MASHED COOKED PUMPKIN
1/3	CUP MOLASSES
2	TABLESPOONS MARGARINE, MELTED
1 1/2	TEASPOONS SALT
	VEGETABLE COOKING SPRAY

Dissolve yeast in warm milk in a large bowl; let stand 5 minutes. Add 2 2/3 cups bread flour and next 7 ingredients, stirring until a soft dough forms.

Turn dough out onto a well-floured surface; knead until smooth and elastic (about 15 minutes). Add enough of remaining bread flour to prevent dough from sticking to hands. Place in a large bowl coated with cooking spray, turning to coat top. Cover and let rise in a warm place (85 degrees), free from drafts, 1 hour or until doubled in bulk.

Punch dough down, and divide in half; roll one portion of dough into a 15x7-inch rectangle. Roll up dough, starting at short side, pressing firmly to eliminate air pockets; pinch ends to seal. Place loaf, seam side down, in an 8 1/2 x 4 1/2 x 3-inch loaf pan coated with cooking spray. Repeat procedure with remaining dough.

Cover and let rise in a warm place (85 degrees), free from drafts 40 minutes or until doubled in bulk. Bake at 375 degrees for 35 minutes or until loaves sound hollow when tapped. Remove bread from pans; cool on wire racks. Yield: 2 loaves, 16 (1/2-inch) slices each (serving size: 1 slice).

Falls Mill

Ten miles west of Winchester, nestled in a lush green cove along the banks of Factory Creek stands Belvidere's Falls Mill and Country Store. The site was built as a cotton and woolen factory in 1873. It was then converted to a cotton gin before becoming a woodworking shop. Today it is a grist mill producing stone-ground corn meal, grits, and flour. Listed on the National Register of Historic Places, Falls Mill provides visitors a look at water-powered milling. Visitors may view a slide show on the history of the mill, then take a self-guided tour of the building and scenic grounds.

Owners John and Jane Lovett produce several products at the mill. These include some limited amounts of Wheat Bran, Rye Flour, Buckwheat Flour, Rice Flour, and Bird Food (which is cracked corn and wheat). John and Jane are proud to supply their stone-ground flour, meal and grits to the Peabody Hotel in Memphis, The Inn at Blackberry Farm in Walland, Granny Fishes House in Shelbyville, and the Adams Edgeworth Inn in Monteagle. Other restaurants and hotels in South Carolina and Florida include Falls Mill products as well. The Lovetts are pleased to have visitors tour the country store at Falls Mill. In addition to the company's food products, hand-crafted items and books are available through mail order if a visit is not possible.

Hush Puppies

2	CUPS PLAIN CORN MEAL
1	TEASPOON SALT
1/2	TEASPOON BLACK PEPPER
1/2	CUP FINELY CHOPPED ONION
	HOT WATER
	HOT OIL

Assemble all ingredients and utensils. In a bowl, combine cornmeal, salt, pepper, and onion. Add enough hot water to make a stiff dough. Shape into round small pones. Fry in deep hot oil in a heavy pot until done; about 5 to 7 minutes. Yield: about 20 hush puppies.

Serve with Pan Fried Catfish (*see* p. 107) or the delicious Southern Greens (*see* p. 130).

Per serving: 94 calories; 6 g fat; 0 mg cholesterol; 107 mg sodium.

Hush puppies have one of those legacies much like Brunswick Stew: every state wants to lay claim on the recipe. People from coast to coast contend their recipe is the best. My advice is to just enjoy them and don't worry about the recipe's origin.

Miss Daisy

Sally Lunn Bread

1	CUP SCALDED MILK (BRING MILK ALMOST TO A BOILING POINT)
1/2	CUP MELTED BUTTER
2	EGGS
2	TEASPOONS SALT
3	TABLESPOONS SUGAR
4	CUPS SIFTED ALL-PURPOSE FLOUR
1	PACKAGE (ENVELOPE) YEAST DISSOLVED IN 1/2 CUP WARM WATER
1/4	CUP BUTTER, MELTED

Assemble all ingredients and utensils. In a saucepan, heat scalded milk and butter together. In a large bowl, beat eggs and add milk, butter, salt and sugar. When cooled to lukewarm, add dissolved yeast. Beat in flour until smooth, using mixer. Cover and set to rise in a warm place until doubled. Punch down and put in a large greased loaf pan or a bundt pan. Pour melted butter over top. Bake in a 350-degree oven for 45 to 60 minutes. Yield: 10 to 12 servings.

Per serving: 280 calories; 14 g fat; 79 mg cholesterol; 495 mg sodium.

Sally Lunn bread is named after a young English woman who sold this warm yeasty egg bread in the streets of eighteenth-century England's most fashionable spa. Her name became a household word in the American colonies. The recipe migrated from Virginia down to Tennessee. Great with Brunswick Stew (*see* p. 57).

Miss Daisy

Salt Rising Bread

Yeast

4	SMALL IRISH POTATOES (SHRED)
3	TABLESPOONS SUGAR
4	TABLESPOONS CORN MEAL
1	TEASPOON SALT
1	QUART BOILING WATER POURED OVER THE ABOVE

Mix well. Cover and keep in warm place over night.

Sponge

Strain yeast and add:

1	CUP MEAL
2	CUPS WARM WATER OR MILK
1/4	TEASPOON SODA
	FLOUR ENOUGH TO MAKE STIFF BATTER

Mix well, place in bowl and set in pan of fairly hot water. Cover. This sponge should rise in an hour. Keep water 1 inch above where sponge comes to in its container.

Dough

After sponge has risen, add:

1	CUP CRISCO
2	TEASPOONS SALT
1	TABLESPOON SUGAR

Add enough flour to make bread consistency. Knead well, but do not let it get chilled. Make into loaves and put into well greased pans. Let rise until double its size. Bake in a medium oven for an hour.

Doreen Lewis of Erwin, Tennessee, said this was her grandmother's recipe. There's no temperature given as all baking was done on a wood stove.

A TREE GROWS
IN WEAKLEY

Normally, when big trees are thought of, the species that comes to mind is the one containing the giant sequoia and redwood trees of California. These massive plants are capable of growing to more than three hundred feet tall and living for a thousand years or more. Tennessee has or has had some giant trees of its own, however, including the world's largest pecan tree, located in Natchez Trace State Park, and the world's largest dogwood, found in Williamson County. And, down in Weakley County, there once existed another

WEAKLEY
COUNTY

forest giant, that, unfortunately, is no longer with us. It was a bald cypress tree that in its prime may have grown to over three hundred feet tall. The tree, located near the town of Sharon, grew in the dense swamps along the middle fork of the Obion River, before it was partially destroyed by lightning in 1976. In 1946, when a core sample of its trunk was taken, the cypress was estimated to be 1350 years old which would mean that it started growing about the same time as the Dark Ages dominated Europe and not too long after the fall of the Roman Empire. The giant was nearly fifty-six feet in circumference at breast height (considering that a man's average arm spread is about six feet, this means that it would take ten men holding hands to stretch around the tree's base), and its diameter was estimated to be almost eighteen feet. W. Eli Tillman, who owned the property upon which the tree stood, donated the site to the State in 1965.

Banana Nut Bread

1	CUP SUGAR
1/2	CUP BUTTER
3	RIPE MEDIUM BANANAS, MASHED
2	EGGS
4	TABLESPOONS BUTTERMILK
1	TEASPOON SODA
2	CUPS ALL-PURPOSE FLOUR
1/8	TEASPOON SALT
1/2	CUP CHOPPED WALNUTS OR PECANS

Assemble all ingredients and utensils. In large bowl of mixer, cream sugar and butter. Add bananas and mix well. Add eggs and continue mixing. Add soda that has been dissolved in buttermilk. Next add flour and salt gradually. Fold in nuts. Pour mixture into 1 large or 2 small greased and floured loaf pans in a 350-degree oven for 60 minutes. Yield: 1 large or 2 small loaves.

Per serving: 152 calories; 7 g fat; 36 mg cholesterol; 102 mg sodium.

Farm Pumpkin Bread

1	CUP WATER
1	CUP VEGETABLE OIL
1	POUND CAN PUMPKIN OR PUMPKIN PIE FILLING
3	CUPS SUGAR
3	EGGS
1	CUP BLACK WALNUTS, CHOPPED
1 1/2	CUPS DATES, CHOPPED
3 1/2	CUPS SELF-RISING FLOUR
1	TEASPOON EACH: SALT, GINGER AND NUTMEG
1/2	TEASPOON BAKING POWDER
1/2	TEASPOON CLOVES
2	TEASPOONS CINNAMON
2	TEASPOONS SODA

Assemble all ingredients and utensils. In a large mixing bowl combine first seven ingredients. Sift together remaining ingredients. Mix well with pumpkin mixture. Pour into 2 large greased loaf pans. Bake in a 325-degree oven for 1 and 1/2 hours. Yield: 2 large loaves.

Per serving: 271 calories; 11 g fat; 29 mg cholesterol; 305 mg sodium.

Strawberry Bread

3	CUPS FLOUR
1	TEASPOON SODA
1	TEASPOON SALT
1	TEASPOON CINNAMON
2	CUPS SUGAR
4	EGGS, BEATEN
2	CUPS THAWED, SLICED FROZEN STRAWBERRIES
1 1/2	CUPS VEGETABLE OIL
1 1/4	CUPS BROKEN PECANS

Preheat oven to 325 degrees. Sift dry ingredients together. Combine eggs, strawberries, and oil and add to sifted ingredients. Add pecans. Pour into 2 well-greased 9x5x3-inch loaf pans. Bake for about 1 hour or until bread tests done. Cool in pan for 5 minutes, then cool on wire rack. Yield: 14-16 slices per loaf.

Per serving: 438 calories; 28 g fat; 69 mg cholesterol; 203 mg sodium.

Zucchini Bread

3	EGGS, BEATEN
1	CUP VEGETABLE OIL
1 1/2	CUPS SUGAR
2	CUPS ZUCCHINI, GRATED AND WELL DRAINED
2	TEASPOONS VANILLA
2	CUPS SIFTED ALL-PURPOSE FLOUR
1/2	TEASPOON BAKING POWDER
1 1/2	TEASPOONS BAKING SODA
1/2	TEASPOON SALT
1	TABLESPOON CINNAMON
1	CUP CHOPPED PECANS
1	CUP RAISINS

Assemble all ingredients and utensils. In a large bowl, combine beaten eggs, oil, sugar, zucchini and vanilla. Sift flour, baking powder, soda, salt and cinnamon into egg mixture. Stir in pecans and raisins. Pour batter into 2 well-greased loaf pans. Bake in a 375-degree oven for 60 minutes. Yield: 2 loaves, 24-30 slices.

Per serving: 233 calories; 13 g fat; 34mg cholesterol; 198 mg sodium.

THE ANTI-DUELING JUDGE

For many years in Europe, dueling was considered an acceptable way for gentlemen to solve disputes. Naturally, the custom had vast numbers of followers in the United States as well. Men of note—all highly regarded in their professions—often resorted to dueling as a normal means of resolving differences. Aaron Burr, Alexander Hamilton, Andrew Jackson, and other prominent Americans are among their number. In 1801 Tennessee became the first state to enact an anti-dueling law. However, the custom continued to be widely practiced, the law being

WHITE COUNTY

circumvented by the participants going elsewhere (usually Kentucky) to hold their duels. Judge John Catron practiced law in White County. Although largely forgotten today, Catron was widely known in his time as the man who put a real stop to dueling in Tennessee. Catron was born in Virginia in 1786, but had migrated to Tennessee as a young man. In 1824, he was appointed to the Tennessee Supreme Court of Errors and Appeals (today's Supreme Court), and in 1829, he heard a dueling case before his court. "We are told that this is only a kind of honorable homicide!" declared Judge Catron. "The law knows that it is wicked and willful murder." Thus, with the stroke of a pen, dueling finally became a crime in Tennessee. One of Andrew Jackson's last acts as president of the United States was to appoint John Catron to the U. S. Supreme Court. The White Countian served in the position until he died in 1865. He is buried in Nashville's Mount Olivet Cemetery.

Applesauce Muffins

1/2	POUND BUTTER, SOFTENED
2	CUPS SUGAR
2	EGGS
4	CUPS ALL-PURPOSE FLOUR
1	TABLESPOON CINNAMON
2	TEASPOONS ALLSPICE
2	TEASPOONS GROUND CLOVES
2	TEASPOONS BAKING SODA
2	CUPS APPLESAUCE
1	CUP CHOPPED PECANS
1	CUP RAISINS

Assemble all ingredients and utensils. In large bowl of mixer cream butter and sugar. Add eggs and mix well. Sift all dry ingredients together. Add to creamed mixture alternately with applesauce. Add pecans and raisins. Fill muffin tins 2/3 full and bake in a 400-degree oven for 12 to 15 minutes. Yield: 48 medium-size muffins.

Batter will keep covered in refrigerator for 4 weeks.

Per serving: 138 calories; 6 g fat; 22 mg cholesterol; 78 mg sodium.

---

*M*UFFINS ARE POPULAR FOR SURE. I HAVE SAVED AN ARTICLE FROM THE FORUM PAGE OF THE *NASHVILLE BANNER* (FRIDAY, AUGUST 19, 1983) WRITTEN BY JOANNE GORDON, OKLAHOMA COLUMNIST FOR THE *TULSA WORLD*. SHE WROTE, "GETTING BACK TO TENNESSEE FOOD, I MUST MENTION MISS DAISY'S TEAROOM . . . REPLETE WITH SOUTHERN COOKING AT ITS BEST. . . . I MUST WRITE AND ASK FOR THE RECIPE FOR THOSE MUFFINS." NOW YOU KNOW WHY I LIKE THE ARTICLE SO MUCH.

Miss Daisy

Blueberry Muffins

3	CUPS ALL-PURPOSE FLOUR
1	TABLESPOON BAKING POWDER
1/2	TEASPOON BAKING SODA
3/4	CUP SUGAR
1 1/2	TEASPOONS SALT
2	CUPS BLUEBERRIES (FRESH, WASHED AND DRAINED)
2	EGGS, BEATEN
3/4	CUP WHOLE MILK
1/2	CUP BUTTER, MELTED
1	TABLESPOON GRATED ORANGE PEEL
1/2	CUP ORANGE JUICE
2	TABLESPOONS LEMON JUICE

Assemble all ingredients and utensils. In large bowl of mixer, sift flour, baking powder, soda, sugar and salt. Add blueberries gently until coated. Combine liquid ingredients starting with the eggs. Stir into bowl of dry ingredients. Mix well. Pour batter into greased muffin tins. Bake in a 350 degree oven for about 20 to 25 minutes. Yield: 24 to 30 muffins.

---

*P*REPARE MUFFINS AND BAG THEM AND FREEZE FOR LATER USE. TAKE A FEW DIRECTLY FROM THE FREEZER AND ARRANGE IN A CIRCLE ON A PAPER TOWEL IN THE MICRO-WAVE. HEAT A FEW SECONDS. THEY WILL SEEM AS THOUGH THEY HAVE JUST BEEN FRESHLY BAKED.

Miss Daisy

Miss Daisy's
Tea Room Bran Muffins

1	CUP WATER
2	CUPS BRAN BUDS
1 1/2	CUPS SUGAR
1/2	CUP VEGETABLE SHORTENING
2	EGGS, BEATEN
2	CUPS BUTTERMILK
1	CUP ALL BRAN
2 1/2	TEASPOONS SODA, DISSOLVED IN BUTTERMILK
2 1/2	CUPS ALL-PURPOSE FLOUR
2	CUPS RAISINS
1	CUP CHOPPED PECANS

Assemble all ingredients and utensils. In a bowl, pour water over Bran Buds. Let set for 1 hour. In large bowl of mixer, cream sugar and shortening. Add eggs. Add Bran Buds, buttermilk and All Bran. Mix dry ingredients and add to Bran mixture. Fold in raisins and pecans. Pour into medium-size muffin tins. Bake in a 375-degree oven for 20 to 25 minutes. Yield: about 3 dozen muffins.

Batter will keep tightly covered for up to 4 weeks.

Per serving: 160 calories; 6 g fat; 16 mg cholesterol; 125 mg sodium.

Rock Castle

Rock Castle, located on the shores of Old Hickory Lake in Hendersonville, was the home of General Daniel Smith (1748-1818). Smith, originally from Virginia, moved to the Cumberland settlements in 1783 after seeing service in both Lord Dunmore's War and the Revolution. He became secretary of state for the Southwest Territory (today's Tennessee) in 1790, and several years later was responsible for the production of the first map of the new state. Using stone masons from Lexington, Kentucky, Smith started construction on Rock Castle in around 1784, but the house required seven years to build due to the fierce Indian resistance in the area. After Andrew Jackson resigned his seat in the U. S. Senate in 1798, Smith was appointed to fill the unexpired term.

Daniel Smith was quite a farmer. When the French naturalist, F. A. Michaux, visited him in 1801, he described the general's holdings as "a beautiful plantation cultivated in Indian wheat and cotton; he has also a neat distillery for peach brandy which he sells at five shillings per gallon."

Sweet Potato Muffins

4	OUNCES BUTTER, SOFTENED
1	CUP SUGAR
1 1/2	CUPS COOKED, MASHED SWEET POTATOES
2	EGGS
2 1/2	CUPS ALL-PURPOSE FLOUR
1 1/2	TABLESPOONS BAKING POWDER
1	TEASPOON SALT
1	TEASPOON NUTMEG
1/2	TEASPOON CINNAMON
1 1/2	CUPS WHOLE MILK
1/2	CUP FINELY CHOPPED PECANS
1 1/2	TEASPOONS LEMON EXTRACT

Topping

1/2	CUP SUGAR
1	TABLESPOON CINNAMON

Assemble all ingredients and utensils. In large bowl of mixer, cream butter and sugar until light and fluffy. Stir in sweet potatoes. Add eggs, one at a time, stirring well. Sift together flour, baking powder, salt, nutmeg and cinnamon. Alternately add milk and dry ingredients to the sweet potato mixture stirring well after each addition. Gently stir in pecans and lemon extract. Fill medium-sized greased muffin tins about 2/3 full. Mix topping ingredients together; sprinkle evenly over muffins. Bake in a 400-degree oven for 20 to 25 minutes. Yield: 24 to 30 muffins.

Per serving: 289 calories; 11 g fat; 56 mg cholesterol; 359 mg sodium.

HOME IS WHERE THE HEART IS

Frances Courtney loved George Grummond, and that's all there was to it. And, that love transcended all of the blazing cannon fire and all of the tragic deaths that had recently marked the bloody Battle of Franklin, in which so many Confederate and Union soldiers had died. Frances, a young girl of the Old South, had been a northern sympathizer, and although she was a rare breed in her hometown of Franklin, she was admired by her neighbors as she nursed men on both sides during the terrible conflict. Now that the War was over, she and her new husband, Lieutenant Grummond, a Union officer she had met during her care-giving, could start a

new life. The open plains of Dakota Territory (in today's state of Wyoming) were a far cry from the warm climes of Williamson County, Tennessee. It was December 1866, and frigid cold when young Lieutenant Grummond rode out of the gates of Fort Phil Kearny on his first major assignment. He was chasing Sioux and Cheyenne Indians who had been giving trouble in the area for some time. His brash commander, Captain William Fetterman, had been ordered not to pursue the Indians beyond a certain point, but when the captain sent his men, including Grummond, ahead anyway, his entire command was ambushed and every man slaughtered. Frances claimed George's body and escorted it back to Franklin, sometimes in forty-below-zero weather. She buried her husband in the town's Rest Haven Cemetery, where his remains are today.

Sunday Dinner Rolls

1	CUP BOILING WATER
2	TABLESPOONS VEGETABLE SHORTENING
2	ENVELOPES DRY YEAST
1/2	CUP LUKEWARM WATER
1	CUP SUGAR
4	CUPS SELF-RISING FLOUR
1	CUP COLD WATER
4	CUPS SELF-RISING FLOUR
1/4	CUP MELTED BUTTER

Assemble all ingredients and utensils. Pour water over shortening in a bowl. Set aside to cool. In a large deep bowl, dissolve yeast in warm water; add sugar. Add 4 cups of flour. Beat thoroughly. Add cold water; mix thoroughly. Add remaining flour. Knead until dough forms a ball. Cover and let rise in warm place until doubled in size, about an hour. Roll out on floured surface and cut in rolls. Dip tops in melted butter. Place close together on 13x9-inch baking sheets. Let rise again, about 30 to 45 minutes. Bake in a preheated 425-degree oven for 10 to 12 minutes. Yield: 40 to 48 rolls depending on your size and shape of rolls.

Per serving: 98 calories; 2 g fat; 3 mg cholesterol; 217 mg sodium.

Quick Spoon Rolls

1	PACKAGE DRY YEAST
2	TABLESPOONS WARM WATER (110 DEGREES)
2	CUPS WARM WATER (110 DEGREES)
3/4	CUP VEGETABLE OIL
4	CUPS SELF-RISING FLOUR
1/4	CUP SUGAR
1	EGG, BEATEN

Assemble all ingredients and utensils. In a small bowl, dissolve yeast in 2 tablespoons warm water. In large bowl of mixer alternately combine remaining liquid and dry ingredients. Add beaten egg and dissolved yeast and water mixture. Spoon rolls into greased muffin tins. Bake in a 400-degree oven for 15 to 20 minutes. Yield: 24 rolls.

The batter will keep in refrigerator for several days. Bake as you need them.

Per serving: 140 calories; 7 g fat; 11 mg cholesterol; 210 mg sodium.

TENNESSEE'S LUTHER BURBANK

William Haskell Neal was a simple man. He was elected to no high office, nor was he a hero in any war. He was just a plain Wilson County farmer who spent his entire life within a fifty-mile radius of Lebanon. What he achieved in life, though, was far from simple when it came to the Nation's agricultural economy. Neal's experiments with corn and the development of a strain which provided multiple ears to the stalk—over the previous variety which bore only one ear—enabled corn producers the world over to multiply their yield many fold. His

WILSON COUNTY

contribution was the result of thirteen years of laborious study and work. Because of his contributions to agronomy, Neal has often been compared to the great Luther Burbank. Both men pioneered in experimentation with plants in order to make them more productive for mankind. Both succeeded. Upon Neal's death in 1934, he was eulogized as the provider of much added income to the farmer's pockets. "Without his great achievement in plant breeding . . . Mr. Neal would have been a man of outstanding importance to his country," read one editorial. Continuing, it reported that, "With that achievement, he became benefactor to his country, and to mankind. Neal's Paymaster Corn never made its originator a rich man, but it has added to the wealth of millions of American farmers." In 1937, for his outstanding contribution to the people and welfare of his state and country, William Neal became the first inductee to the Tennessee Agricultural Hall of Fame.

Divine Pop Overs

2   EGGS
1/2   TEASPOON SALT
1   CUP ALL-PURPOSE FLOUR
1   CUP WHOLE MILK
3   TABLESPOONS BUTTER, DIVIDED

Assemble all ingredients and utensils. In a deep bowl combine and mix well eggs, salt, flour, and milk. Pour mixture into 9 or 12 cold greased muffin tins. Fill about 2/3 full. Add 1 teaspoon of butter to the top of mixture. Place in cold oven. Set oven to 450 degrees. Bake about 30 to 35 minutes. Serve hot! Yield: 9 to 12 Pop Overs.

Per serving: 86 calories; 5 g fat; 56 mg cholesterol; 140 mg sodium.

*P*OP OVERS ARE FUN TO EAT BECAUSE YOU CAN FILL THEM WITH A VARIETY OF MEATS AND SAUCES. DELIGHTFUL WITH MISS DAISY'S CREAMED CHICKEN (*SEE* P. 93). USE THEM AS A DESSERT SERVED WITH FRESHLY MADE PRESERVES, APPLE BUTTER, OR YOUR FAVORITE JAM OR JELLY (*SEE* ACCOMPANIMENTS PP. 157–164).

Miss Daisy

Raisin Scones

2   CUPS SIFTED ALL-PURPOSE FLOUR
1   TABLESPOON BAKING POWDER
1   TABLESPOON SUGAR
1/2   TEASPOON SALT
1/2   CUP FINELY CUT RAISINS
1/4   CUP BUTTER, SOFTENED OR VEGETABLE SHORTENING,
        OR LARD
2   EGGS
1/3   CUP WHOLE MILK

Assemble all ingredients and utensils. Sift together flour, baking powder, salt and sugar into mixing bowl. Add cut up raisins. Cut in butter or shortening until mixture resembles coarse meal. Make a hollow in center. Beat eggs slightly; combine with milk and stir into center of dry mixture. Avoid overmixing. You just want mixture to be moistened. Turn mixture onto floured board and knead lightly 5 or 6 times. Roll to 1/2 inch thickness and cut with a 2-inch biscuit cutter. Bake in a 400-degree oven for about 15 minutes or until brown. Yield: 18 scones.

Per serving: 97 calories; 4 g fat; 38 mg cholesterol; 167 mg sodium.

*S*ERVE HOT FOR BREAKFAST OR FOR TEA TIME WITH LEMON CURD (*SEE* P. 158). CURRANTS MAKE A DELIGHTFUL SUBSTITUTE FOR RAISINS. THESE SCONES MELT IN YOUR MOUTH.

Miss Daisy

Buttermilk Pancakes

3	CUPS ALL-PURPOSE FLOUR, SIFTED
2 1/2	TEASPOONS BAKING POWDER
1/2	TEASPOON SODA
1	TEASPOON SALT
3	TABLESPOONS SUGAR
3	EGGS WELL BEATEN
3	CUPS BUTTERMILK
1/2	CUP BUTTER, MELTED

Assemble all ingredients and utensils. In a bowl, measure sifted flour, baking powder, soda, salt and sugar. Sift again. Combine eggs and buttermilk; add to flour mixture. Add melted butter and stir until all flour is moistened. Bake on hot greased griddle, turning once. Serve immediately with maple syrup and butter.

Per serving: 229 calories; 10 g fat; 91 mg cholesterol; 445 mg sodium.

Waffled French Toast

1/2	CUP WHOLE MILK
4	EGGS
2	TABLESPOONS BUTTER, MELTED
1	TABLESPOON SUGAR
1/2	TEASPOON SALT
8	SLICES BREAD

Assemble all ingredients and utensils. In a deep bowl, mix ingredients except bread. Dip bread slices, one at a time; let drain. Preheat the waffle iron. Bake slices in the oiled waffle iron 2 or 3 minutes, or until brown. Yield: 8 servings.

Per serving: 147 calories; 7 g fat; 148 mg cholesterol; 331 mg sodium.

American Bread Company

In modest quarters at 711 Church Street, Nashville, Tennessee, Charles K. Evers opened the American Bread Company on August 15, 1889.

By 1899, American Bread had grown to include ten retail stores. The company was incorporated under the original name and moved to what later became the Vendome Building at 629 Church Street. By 1908, the company's horse-drawn delivery wagons bearing the name Tip Top Bread were a familiar sight on Nashville streets. In 1924, American Bread switched to the Holsum label. In the 1930s the company became known as The Holsum Bakery. As part of its contribution to the war effort in the 1940s, Holsum supplied bread to the army troops at Tullahoma's Camp Forrest. In 1951, a new facility on Murfreesboro Road was the largest and most modern bakery in the area and the South's first million-dollar baking facility. By 1953, the Sunbeam label was used exclusively.

By 1980, the company was producing 250,000 pounds of baked goods a day. With their purchase of the Swan Baking Company of Knoxville in 1989, they became one of the region's largest bakeries.

Granny Wolff's Moravian Sugar Cake

1	CUP MASHED POTATOES
1	CUP POTATO WATER (THE WATER YOU BOILED THE POTATOES IN)
1	CUP CRISCO
3/4	CUP SUGAR
	ABOUT 1 TEASPOON SALT
7-9	CUPS FLOUR
2	TEASPOONS SUGAR
3	PACKAGES YEAST
2	HANDS OF TAP WATER (ABOUT 1 CUP)
6	ROUND PIZZA PANS
1	STICK OF BUTTER
	WHITE SUGAR
2	BOXES LIGHT BROWN SUGAR
	CINNAMON
1	8–OUNCE CAN EVAPORATED MILK

Nashville's Kat Manier, who sent this recipe for the Bicentennial Collection notes: "If you are going to freeze the sugar cake you might want it lightly brown. When you take it out of the oven sprinkle evaporated milk over the top. It is best eaten straight out of the oven with a cup of coffee. This is served at the Moravian Love Feast and is a family tradition we enjoy."

Miss Daisy

Cook potatoes, drain, and save the water. Mash the potatoes. In small bowl mix 2 hands of warm water with the yeast and 2 teaspoons sugar and let sit while you start the dough. In large mixing bowl cream Crisco, sugar and salt and then add the mashed potatoes and the potato water. Add your flour one cup at a time. I usually add 3 cups and then the yeast when it's ready. Then continue to add flour till it takes all it will take. Knead the dough till smooth, when you pat it, it will sound hollow. Grease bowl and put dough seam down, cover with damp cloth and let rise till double in size (about 2 hours).

Grease pizza pans. Punch dough down and then pinch it into 6 equal size balls. Pat the dough out on the pizza pans, be careful not to tear or stretch the dough. Use the balls of your fingers and work from the center out till the pan is covered. Cover with a damp cloth and let rise till fluffy, about 1 hour.

Take one pan at a time and poke holes about one inch apart all over the dough, letting air out of the bubbles. (Try not to go all the way through to the pan when punching holes. If you do, it will make it messy to eat.) Put a little dab of butter in each hole. Sprinkle white sugar very lightly all over the cake. Sprinkle a third of a box of light brown sugar on top of the white sugar. Sprinkle cinnamon over top of cake. Put in 375-degree oven for about 15 to 20 minutes, or until brown. Check the underneath side to be sure it is brown, too.

Martha Sundquist's
Swedish Cardamom Coffee Bread

2	PACKAGES ACTIVE DRY YEAST
9	CUPS (ABOUT) ALL-PURPOSE FLOUR, DIVIDED
1/2	CUP SUGAR
2	TEASPOONS GROUND CARDAMOM
	PINCH SALT
2 1/2	CUPS MILK
1/2	CUP (1 STICK) MARGARINE OR BUTTER
2	EGGS, SLIGHTLY BEATEN

Glaze:

1	EGG YOLK MIXED WITH 1 TEASPOON WATER
4	TABLESPOONS SUGAR
1	TEASPOON GROUND CINNAMON

Combine yeast, 1 cup of the flour, sugar, cardamom and salt in bowl of electric mixer fitted with dough hook or large mixing bowl. Combine milk and margarine (or butter) in saucepan and heat until margarine melts. Cool to lukewarm. Pour milk mixture into yeast mixture and beat to combine. Stir in eggs. Add remaining flour slowly to make a soft but workable dough. Let stand covered about 10 minutes. Turn out onto a floured board and knead. Dough should be kneaded 5-10 minutes or until it doesn't stick to your hands. Cover and let rise in a warm place for 1 hour.

Punch down dough and divide into 4 pieces. Divide each of the 4 pieces into 3 equal parts—about 5 ounces each if you want to weigh them on the kitchen scale. Roll each part between your hands to make a 12-inch strip. Braid strips together pinching ends under. Transfer braided loaves to a lightly greased baking sheet. You can fit two loaves on each sheet. Repeat with remaining strips.

Brush tops of loaves with beaten egg yolk. Sprinkle generously with sugar and cinnamon mixed together. Let rise, uncovered, for about 45 minutes to 1 hour or until loaves double but don't begin to split their braids.

Bake at 350 degrees for 15-20 minutes or until browned and baked through. Let cool before slicing. These freeze well. Makes 4 large braided loaves.

TENNESSEE'S FIRST LADIES ARE SPECIAL! WHEN MY PUBLISHERS AND I VISITED THE TENNESSEE EXECUTIVE RESIDENCE TO DISCUSS WITH MARTHA SUNDQUIST OUR PLANS FOR THIS BICENTENNIAL COLLECTION, SHE RESPONDED WITH ENTHUSIASM FOR OUR PROJECT. SHE PROMISED TO CONTRIBUTE A RECIPE AND ALSO TO WRITE THE FOREWORD FOR *MISS DAISY CELEBRATES TENNESSEE*. HER PARTICIPATION HIGHLIGHTS THE INCLUSION OF HERITAGE RECIPES, PAST TO PRESENT, USED THROUGHOUT THIS VOLUME. GOVERNOR DON SUNDQUIST WAS INAUGURATED IN JANUARY 1995.

Miss Daisy

$\mathscr{A}$CKNOWLEDGMENTS

The authors wish to thank their families first of all: Daisy King—my husband Wayne, our sons Kevin and Patrick, and of course Wayne's parents Hazel and Herman King; Jim Crutchfield—my wife Regena; and Winette Sparkman—my parents Robert and Edwina Sparkman for always encouraging me and my two dreams that came true—my sons, Brent and Trey Brundige. Also, the authors wish to thank the staff at Providence House Publishers for all their encouragement, creativity, and dedication to excellence: Andrew B. Miller, Mary Bray Wheeler, Joanne Jaworski, Charles W. Deweese, Trinda Cole, Judy Coursey, Charles H. Flood, Holly Jones, and Frances Jones.

The authors gratefully acknowledge the cooperation and permissions from the following sources whose recipes, illustrations, corporate histories, and biographical information served as reference material or are reprinted in this work: April Almond—*The Ramsey House*; Claudette Austin—*Malone & Hyde/Fleming Companies*; *Baptist Hospital*; Sue Barnes; Danny Barnwell, Melinda Ingram, and Debbie Underwood—*Piggly Wiggly*; Wes Ball—*Tennessee Grocer's Association*; Shepard Bentley, McCabe family—*Loveless Cafe*; Helen Black, Neola Sutton, and Dr. James Anderson—*Ames Plantation*; Joy Bland—Martha Jackson; Bobbie—*Tennessee Historic Commission*; Pat Boren—*Memphis Museum System/Pink Palace Museum*; Carolyn Brackett—*Tennessee 200 Inc.*; Deltina Braden; Jack P. Bradley and Charles Bradley—*Bradley Candy Manufacturing Co., Inc.*; Ronald Brewster Family—*Brewster's Smokehouse, Inc.*; Jim Broderson—*Robert Orr/Sysco*; Patsy Brown—*Sam Davis Home*; *Brueck Advertising Design*; Teenie Hooker Buchtel; Sam Campbell IV and Beverly—*Chattanooga Bakery*; Linda Carmen—*Martha White Foods, Inc.*; Sandra Chaffin; Jim and Sigourney Cheek III; Mr. Will T. Cheek; Stephanie Chivers; Elaine R. Clark—*Andrew Johnson National Historic Site*; Risa Cline—*Clearidge, Inc.*; Mackenzie Colt—*Colt's Bolts*; Jim Cooper; Mary L. Cowan—*Gov. John Sevier Memorial Association*; Mary Creagh; Susan Creagh; Karen Crocker and Mary Shaffer—*Belle Meade Plantation;* David Crockett Descendants; Bobbie Cronin; Bill and May Jean Crook; Steven Crook—*Steven's Fun Fresh Food Stores*; Amy R. Cross; Dan Crowe—*Odom's Tennessee Pride Sausage*; Beth Cunningham—*Travellers Rest*; Connie Davenport—*Rock Castle*; Frank Delaney—*Kelly Foods, Inc.*; Taylor Delaney and Lloyd Stevens—*JFG Coffee Company*; Diane—*Seessel's*; Charlotte Donahey; Don Dortch—*Tennessee Mountain Pure*; Bettina B. Drury and Marketing Staff—*The Maxwell House*; Anita Durham—*Mike Rose Foods*; John and Anne Egerton; March Egerton; Betty Elrod; Jane Erwin, Ruth Garren, Donna Herrel, and Evalin Disbro—*McKee Foods Corporation*; Linda Evers—*Sunbeam*; Miles Ezell, Jr.—*Purity Dairies, Inc.*; Jim Farrell; Glenn Ferguson, Jr.—Congressman Bob Clement's office; Alma Ford; Buck Ford; John W. Ford, Jr. and Carolyn Tomko—*City of Jonesborough*; Sam Foster and Ashley Caldwell—*H.G. Hill's*; Carl Frost—*Carl's All Purpose Seasoning*; Kenneth Funger—*Mrs. Grissom's Salads*; John Fuqua—*Alegro Marinade*; Judi Gardner—*Homestead Hills*; Barbara Gibson—*Carnton Plantation*; Giles County Chamber of Commerce; Kate Gooch—*Leadership Memphis*; Sheri Gramer—*Yarrow Acres*; Robert Grimes—*Lay Packing*; Wilomena Grooms; Cherrie Hall—*Association for the Preservation of Tennessee Antiquities*; Tom T. and Dixie Hall—*Animaland*; Mary Glenn Hearne—*Public Library of Nashville and Davidson County/Ben West Library;* Pam Herron;

Judson S. Hill—*Food City*; Bob W. Hitch—*Crockett Creek Beef Jerky Co.*; Chris Huffman—*The Cheese Factory of Tennessee*; Janet Jeffers—*Goodson Brothers Coffee*; Andrew Johnson; Debbie J. Johnson and Christy Sills—*Elvis Presley Enterprises, Inc.*; Marlene Jones—*Sam Houston Schoolhouse*; Sue Jones—*Clifty Farm;* Will Jordan—*Tennessee Valley Cheese Co.*; Charles Kimbro and Betty—*American Tea & Coffee Co.*; Sarah King; John Kosik—*Moon Pie*; Lil Krauth, Diane Krauth, and Floydaline Cole Limbaugh—*Franklin County Chamber of Commerce and Library*; Nick LaGrande, Jim Bowman, and Peggy—*Red Foods/BILO*; Sheldon Livesay—*Rogersville Milling Co.*; Anne Locke—Administrative Assistant to Tennessee's First Lady Martha Sundquist; Lorena and Belinda—*Tennessee Department of Tourism*; The Lovett Family—*Falls Mill*; Mike MacDonald and Jimmy Spradley—*Standard Candy Co., Inc.*; Mrs. T. S. McFerrin; Trena McGammon—*Swaggerty's Country Sausage*; Melinda McMasters—*Chattanooga Coca-Cola Bottling Co.*; Perre Magness—*Memphis Commercial Appeal*; David Mauk—*Mauk's Jonesborough Pharmacy*; Renee S. Mayer—*Bush Bros. & Co.*; Scotty Mayfield, Donna, and Lisa—*Mayfield Dairy Farms, Inc.*; Frank Mayo—*Mayo Sausage*; Mindy Merrell—*Dye Van Mol & Lawrence*; Alice C. Merritt—*Tennessee Association of Craft Artists*; Bill Miller—*Uncle Billy's Sauerkraut*; Lloyd Montgomery—*White Lily Foods, Inc.*; Karen Morris; R. C. Morris—*Big John's Bar B-Q*; *National Park Service*; Jeff Noland; June Nottingham and Paige Brown—*Netherland Inn*; Beth Odle; Sue O'Donnell and Jenny—*Christie Cookie Co.*; Martha Dixon Olive; Genella Olker—*Tennessee State Library and Archives*; Phyllis Ervin Orman; Crain and Peggy Patterson—*Dutch Maid Bakery, Inc.*; Betty Pearson—*American Tea & Coffee Co., Inc.*; Jean Peterson—*Sally Lane's Candy Farm*; Dan Pomeroy and Lois Riggins—*Tennessee State Museum*; Danny Potter—*Elm Hill Meats Inc./Baltz Bros.*; Madeline Pritchett—Assistant to Governor Ned McWherter; Frances Rainey and Jeff Walters—*James K. Polk Home*; Charlene Rudolph; Schwalb Creative Communications, Inc.; John and Angie Sevier; Barbara Simmons—*Walking Horse Celebration Museum*; Tara Sims—*Warrenton Plum Pudding, Ltd.*; Anne W. Smith—*Sassafras Herbs, Inc.*; Dorothy Smith—*Pepper Patch, Inc.*; Maggie R. Smith—*Tennessee Department of Agriculture*; Winston Smith—*Varallo's Famous Foods*; Karl M. Sooder—*Double Cola Co.*; Bobby Sparkman; Barbara Stagg—*Historic Rugby*; Pam Stockton—*Country Fresh Food & Confections, Inc.*; *Tennessee Department of Tourist Development*; *Tennessee Genealogy Association*; *Tennessee Pork Producers Association*; *Texas Historic Commission*; Brenda Thomas—*Armour's Red Boiling Springs Hotel*; Tracy Thurmond—*Carter House*; Lynne Tolley—*Miss Mary Bobo's*; Charlie Tripp—*Tripp Country Ham, Inc.*; Carol Troutt; Jackie Tucker; Steve Turner—*Turner Dairies*; United States Department of the Interior—*Andrew Johnson Historic Site*; Lenore Vanderkooi; Burton Verner; Peggy Vessels—*Brown Forman Beverage Company*; Brad Vietti, Kim, and Mary—*Vietti Foods Co.*; Gary Volpe—*Southern Taffy Co.*; Linda Waggoner—*Milky Way Farm*; Patty Waldrop—*Brock Candy*; Harry Wampler, John Ed Wampler, and Ted Wampler, Jr.—*Elm Hill Meats, Inc./Wampler's Farm Sausage*; Shelly West; Peggy Whitted; Thelma Winbush and Fred Montgomery—*Alex Haley House*; Patricia Woods, Jeanette Rudy, Pam Greene, Carol Hardee, Jim Horton, Kelly, and Rhonda—*Rudy's Farm*; George Wright—*Walking Horse Hotel*; Nick Wyman—*University of Tennessee Library/Stokely VanCamp*; Billie Young.

INDEX
PEOPLE, PLACES, AND PRODUCTS

INDEX

ℛECIPES

About the Authors

DAISY KING, known to most Tennesseans as "Miss Daisy," is a well-established author whose five cookbooks have combined sales of over 1.3 million copies. Her experiences as an author, restauranteur, and home economist give her great expertise in selecting, testing, and preparing this valuable recipe collection.

JAMES A. CRUTCHFIELD, author of twenty-one books, has served as president of the Williamson County Historical Society and as a director of the Tennessee Historical Society. He is the recipient of numerous national writing awards.

WINETTE SPARKMAN, a Metro-Nashville school teacher for more than twelve years, is Heritage Education Consultant for Middle Tennessee Schools and education coordinator for Historic Nashville, Inc.